MOVIES *of the* FORTIES

MOVIES of the FORTIES

EDITED BY ANN LLOYD
CONSULTANT EDITOR
DAVID ROBINSON

ORBIS · LONDON

Acknowledgments

Many of the illustrations come from stills issued to publicize films made or distributed by the following companies: ABC Circle Films, Allied Artists, The Archers, Barbican Films, Carlo Ponti Productions, COI, Columbia, Crown Film Unit, Dino de Laurentiis, Eagle Lion, Ealing Films, L'Ecran Française, EMI, Gainsborough Pictures, GPO Film Unit, Howard Hawks Productions, Howard Hughes, Janus Films, London Films, Lucas Film, Lux Films, MGM, Monogram, Mosfilm, National Film Board of Canada, Nero Film, Palladium, Paramount, Pathé-Cinema, Andre Paulvé, Rank Films, Republic, RKO, Samuel Goldwyn, Selznick International, Shintoho, Shochiku, Thames Television, Tobis, 20th Century-Fox, Two Cities, UFA, United Artists, Universal, UPA, Vittorio de Sica, © Walt Disney Productions, Warner Brothers.
Although every effort is being made to trace the present copyright holders, we apologize in advance for any unintentional omission or neglect and will be pleased to insert the appropriate acknowledgment to companies or individuals in any subsequent edition of this publication.

Arts Council, Atmosphère, Bison Archives, Kingsley Canham, Cinema Bookshop, Československý, Filmexport, Downton Advertising, Greg Edwards Archive, Joel Finler Collection, Dennis Gifford, Ronald Grant Archive, Imperial War Museum, Japanese Film Library Council, Kobal Collection, Museum of Modern Art, National Film Archive, Popperfoto, Leevers-Rich, David Robinson Collection, Samuelson Film Services, Saturday Evening Post, United States Brewers Association, Vinten Limited, Graham Webb, Bob Willoughby, Wisconsin Center, For Film and Theatre Research.

© 1982 Orbis Publishing Limited, London
First published in hardcovers by Orbis Publishing Limited, London 1982
Reprinted 1984, 1985
First published in paperback 1984
Reprinted 1985

Printed in Italy by Eurograph S.p.A., Milano

ISBN: 0-85613-454-6 (hardback)
ISBN: 0-85613-661-1 (paperback)

Abbreviations used in text

add: additional; **adv:** advertising; **anim:** animation; **art dir:** art direction; **ass:** assistant; **assoc:** associate; **chor:** choreography; **col:** colour process; **comm:** commentary; **cont:** continuity; **co-ord:** co-ordination; **cost:** costume; **dec:** decoration; **des:** design; **dial:** dialogue; **dial dir:** dialogue direction; **dir:** direction; **doc:** documentary; **ed:** film editing; **eng:** engineer; **ep:** episode; **exec:** executive; **loc:** location; **lyr:** lyrics; **man:** management; **mus:** music; **narr:** narration; **photo:** photography; **prod:** production; **prod co:** production company; **prod sup:** production supervision; **rec:** recording; **rel:** released; **r/t:** running time; **sc:** scenario/screenplay/script; **sd:** sound; **sp eff:** special effects; **sup:** supervision; **sync:** synchronization; **sys:** system. Standard abbreviations for countries are used. Most are self-evident but note: A = Austria; AUS = Australia; GER = Germany and West Germany after 1945; E.GER = East Germany.

Editor
Ann Lloyd
Consultant Editor
David Robinson
Editorial Director
Brian Innes

Deputy Editor
Martyn Auty
Chief Sub Editor
Maggie Lenox
Senior Sub Editors
Alastair Dougall, Graham Fuller
Editorial Assistant
Lindsey Lowe

Research Consultant
Arnold Desser
Picture Researchers
Dave Kent, Sue Scott-Moncrieff
Research
Kingsley Canham, Paul Taylor, Sally Hibbin

Designers
Ray Kirkpatrick, Richard Burgess

CONTENTS

INTRODUCTION

Few periods in the history of mankind have had effects so far-reaching as the Forties. The world that went to war at the start of the decade was vastly different from the world that emerged at the end of it. Two halves of the globe were by the Fifties in permanent confrontation, each dominated by a new and monolithic great power. The British Empire was in voluntary dissolution. A Third World was a reality.

The cinema witnessed this changing world, recorded it, and underwent its own transformations. When World War II began, the role of the film as the world's great popular entertainment was unchallenged. Practically everywhere that films were shown during the war years saw a great boom in audiences and revenues: in America, Britain and many countries across the world, the start of the second half of the decade represented an all-time peak of economic prosperity for the movies. Yet by the close of the decade, the cinema practically everywhere was already embarked on that process of decline that was to accelerate in the subsequent years.

The war created new needs and showed new possibilities for the cinema. In Britain the school of realist film-makers, nurtured through the Thirties by the energetic Glaswegian polemicist John Grierson, found its purpose and fulfilment in making films of propaganda and record for the war effort. Some of its directors and much of its influence passed to feature-film making. Many of the best wartime films, such as Pat Jackson's *Western Approaches* and Carol Reed's *The Way Ahead* owe their attraction above all to a new neo-documentary quality. Understandably, alongside this urge to face up to reality in a cinema that until then had been determinedly escapist, there was a yearning for the heroic and nostalgic past – satisfied admirably by films like Olivier's *Henry V* and Powell and Pressburger's *The Life and Death of Colonel Blimp*.

The other embattled European coun-tries adapted to war circumstances in different ways. The German cinema, more directly under state control and commanding a vast audience enlarged by conquest, fulfilled its propaganda tasks by the production of films exalting German history, strength and achievement, alongside escapist pictures. In France, the pressures of occupation censorship drove film-makers in a different direction. The still memorable films of the war-time years – *Les Visiteurs du Soir*, *Les Enfants du Paradis*, *Les Dames du Bois de Boulogne*, *L'Eternel Retour* – were all expressions of what might be styled 'poetic romanticism' as distinguished from the 'poetic fatalism' of the preceding decade.

In Italy the Forties saw a remarkable renaissance and the flowering of the neo-realist cinema, beginning with Blasetti's *Uomini sul Fondo* and Visconti's *Ossessione* and culminating in works like De Sica's *Shoeshine*, *Bicycle Thieves* and *Umberto D.*, Rossellini's *Open City* and *Paisà* and Visconti's *La Terra Trema*.

In America, the war produced less radical effects upon film production. The established genres adapted easily: gangster characters became German spies and war made for lively action pictures. Technical development and artistic sophistication were nevertheless marked in the period. The Forties saw rapid advances – often responding to war needs – in camera technology, film stocks, colour, and sound recording. Technical developments were further stimulated towards the end of the decade when Hollywood saw that the theatrical film could only win the race with television by entering new areas where the smaller screen could not readily follow.

The artistic conquests of the period included the development of a sophisticated style of film musical which finally emancipated itself from the stage, exemplified by the MGM masterworks like *Meet Me in St Louis* and *On the Town*. The economies forced on Hollywood in the difficult late Forties resulted, not unprofitably, in a realist tendency parallel to, and perhaps in part influenced by, what was happening in Europe. Hollywood film-makers began to take their cameras out of the studios and into the city streets.

New directors made their influence felt. Orson Welles in his first two films proved perhaps the most innovatory new director since D.W. Griffith. Elia Kazan, coming from the modern American theatre, helped to introduce new styles and standards of acting. Others who left their mark on the decade were Jules Dassin, Nicholas Ray, John Huston, Fred Zinnemann, Joseph Losey, Joseph L. Mankiewicz, Robert Rossen, Edward Dmytryk and Billy Wilder. The stars of 1940 included Ingrid Bergman, Humphrey Bogart, Betty Grable, Rita Hayworth, Carmen Miranda, Bob Hope, Bing Crosby, Dorothy Lamour and Pinocchio. By 1950, Marlon Brando and Marilyn Monroe signalled a new age.

When the process of decline first hit Hollywood, it was often attributed, simply and naively, to competition from television. In fact, the reasons were more complex, having to do with the changed social patterns of a post-war population. Hollywood had incidental troubles too. Labour problems, strikes and overseas trade wars took their toll. Anti-trust laws broke up the old production-exhibition organizations on which Hollywood's security and prosperity depended. Still worse were the effects – the demoralization and depletion of talent – wrought by McCarthy's witch hunts.

European cinema felt the reverberations and suffered their own problems. Italy and France – with a less monolithic cinema organization and bright new talents like Claude Autant-Lara, Jacques Becker, Jacques Tati, Jean Cocteau and Robert Bresson to earn post-war prestige and income – for the moment escaped the worst of the storm. England felt the effects more sharply, perhaps, since the decline followed immediately upon one of the most brilliant periods in the history of her cinema. During the immediate post-war years, directors like Asquith, Lean, Reed, Powell and Pressburger and the group of Ealing directors were at their peak, and the prestige of British cinema stood at its highest.

The major revolution of these years followed upon the new political division of the world. The new socialist societies of Eastern Europe embarked with high optimism on a new era of film-making. Industries were revived in old, pre-war production centres like Poland, Hungary and East Germany; new ones were established in countries like Albania, Bulgaria, Czechoslovakia and Yugoslavia which before the war had had no regular cinema production of their own.

The tasks of building the new society seemed at first stimulating and thrilling, but the euphoria was short-lived. In the Soviet Union the Stalinist years and Cold War attitudes had brought the cinema practically to extinction. Even when films were made, they were generally revised, recut or banned altogether. Eisenstein died in 1948 having seen the suppression of Part II of his uncompleted historical epic *Ivan the Terrible*. The dead hand of 'socialist realism' was soon similarly felt in all the cinemas of the Soviet bloc. By 1950 the cinemas of socialist Europe had embarked on their most sterile period.

The changes of the decade are reflected in the films with which it began and ended. The films of 1940 included *Citizen Kane*, *Dr Ehrlich's Magic Bullet*, *The Great Dictator*, *Fantasia*, *The Grapes of Wrath*, *Rebecca*, *Philadelphia Story*, *The Thief of Bagdad*. In 1950 the notable titles were *The Asphalt Jungle*, *The Men*, *Wagonmaster*; from France, *Les Enfants Terribles*, *Orphée*, *La Ronde*; from Italy, Fellini's *Luci del Varieta* and Antonioni's *Cronaca di un Amore*; from Japan, *Rashomon*; from Mexico, Buñuel's *Los Olvidados*. The essays that follow tell the story of what went between.

David Robinson

Europe at war

When war broke out in 1939 the cinema was mobilized to provide vital footage from the front and morale-boosting propaganda for the home screens

When Archduke Ferdinand was assassinated at Sarajevo in June 1914, precipitating World War I, the movie industry was still in its infancy. Many pioneers were just getting into their stride, exploring the power of the medium and its potential hold over audiences. When Hitler invaded Poland in September 1939, precipitating World War II, a huge, profitable, world-wide industry had long been established with massive resources of equipment, manpower and 'star power'.

European governments had an unparalleled weapon at their command in the film medium. It was vastly popular with the public, it could easily disseminate war information, instruction and, if necessary, lies, through documentaries, newsreels or (most persuasively of all) in dramatic features. The cinema even served a valuable purpose by providing a few hours of escapist fun before audiences stepped out into their beleaguered, blitzed cities. There was no better way of keeping a controlling hand on national morale.

In a way the industry had long been preparing for war, though the bosses – their eyes glued to production schedules and box-office receipts – might not have realized it. Ever since Hitler took control in 1933, studios throughout Europe and America had absorbed directors, producers, cameramen, writers, composers, actors and actresses, all escaping from the threat of persecution under Nazi Germany's anti-Semitic laws.

Hitler himself had partly designed the 1934 Nuremberg rally as a cinema spectacle (duly filmed as *Triumph of the Will*). In place of Hollywood's all-talking, all-singing, all-dancing musicals, here was the Nazi equivalent – all-shouting, all-stomping, all-saluting. For Hitler knew that potent images and the emotional fury of his speeches had far more power to persuade than any rational argument.

The world watched Hitler's activities with unease and incomprehension. He had risen to power by marshalling nationalistic feelings of discontent with the 1918 defeat and the harsh terms of the Versailles treaty. He had rearmed the country and proclaimed the notion of *lebensraum* – the right of the German nation to have enough living space. And by the end of the Thirties Hitler was taking his first steps in this search for extra accommodation by

attacks, annexations and alliances.

Austria was invaded in March 1938. Sudetenland (on Czechoslovakia's borders) in October. Further east, Hitler formed an opportunistic non-aggression pact with Stalin. In the West, Britain's Prime Minister, Neville Chamberlain, naively joined the French in a policy of appeasement and met the Führer at Berchtesgaden and Munich in September 1938. On his return he waved at the newsreel cameramen a bit of paper which promised 'peace in our time'. Unfortunately it guaranteed nothing of the kind. Czechoslovakia fell to Hitler in March; with the invasion of Poland one year later, Britain and France entered the battle and the world war was on.

Britain's television service, only three years old and serving a tiny minority, was promptly shut down. Film-studio space was requisitioned for storing ammunition, greatcoats and all the paraphernalia of war. But the industry continued. Indeed, the experience of working with limited resources under pressure concentrated the minds of many film-makers. And the involvement of the entire country in the war effort – all classes, both sexes – made many old cinema genres and attitudes inadequate. No longer could studios rely upon laboured farces or thrillers featuring stereotypes of the elegant rich or the rude poor.

The transformation, however, did not occur overnight. Alexander Korda's *The Lion Has Wings* (dir. Michael Powell, Brian Desmond Hurst, Adrian Brunel), a hopeful salute to the fighting power of the RAF, was rushed into release in the autumn of 1939. The film was a mixture of newsreel footage, and mocked-up battles but was over-burdened by a quaintly genteel, fictional sub-plot.

Yet slowly the industry buckled to. The Ministry

Top: Douglass Montgomery (left) as an American fighter-pilot teams up with RAF aces David Tomlinson (centre) and Trevor Howard (right) in Anthony Asquith's Battle of Britain film The Way to the Stars. *Above: in Cavalcanti's* Went the Day Well? *a sleepy English village is invaded and occupied by Germans disguised as Royal Engineers, but eventually the British Army and the Home Guard come to the rescue. Left: the San Demetrio was a merchant ship carrying a precious cargo of oil from the USA to besieged Britain. Crippled by enemy fire, the ship limped home to port, a testament to the quiet heroism of the times*

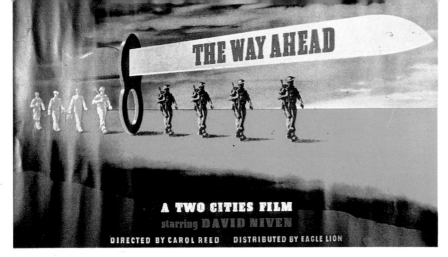

together to produce *The True Glory* (1945), a film charting Europe's liberation.

But the greatest changes in British cinema occurred in feature films. Previously the feature industry had been inhibited by American competition, and the presence of so many foreign moguls and visiting directors hardly promoted indigenous product. But with the war, the visitors returned home and rising talent, previously confined to scriptwriting or editing, eagerly moved into the director's chair – David Lean, Charles Frend, Frank Launder, Sidney Gilliat were among them.

All at once there were dramatic subjects to make feature films about: life at RAF and army bases in *The Way Ahead* (1944) and *The Way to the Stars* (1945); war service on the high seas in *In Which We Serve* (1942) and *San Demetrio, London* (1943); and in the munitions factories – *Millions Like Us* (1943). Here was an area where the Americans could not compete. The tone of the films – humorous, quietly heroic – was also unique.

British films found an audience and a popularity they had never enjoyed before. As the war went on escapist entertainment increased in volume and popularity. Traditional tosh was given a topical inflection in *Dangerous Moonlight* (1941), where a Polish concert pianist joined the RAF and played Richard Addinsell's popular 'Warsaw' Concerto.

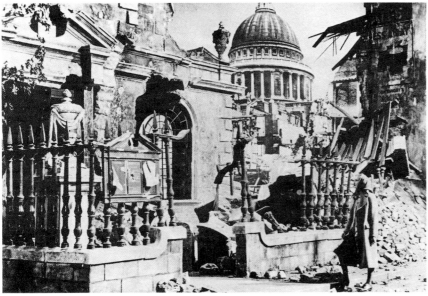

As the bombs fell on her cities, Britain's cinemas kept open a vital channel of information about the war

---

Gainsborough studios produced period melodramas like *The Man in Grey* (1943), with ladies and gentlemen behaving amorally, dressed in wigs, masks and riding boots. On a far higher artistic level were the films of Michael Powell and his Hungarian collaborator Emeric Pressburger, who viewed the war through a complex maze of satire and fantasy in bold creations like *The Life and Death of Colonel Blimp* (1943), a film that was loathed by Churchill for its caricature of the army's upper crust. The same team also produced *A Canterbury Tale* (1944). And no world war, however devastating, could halt Gabriel Pascal's determination to film Shaw's *Caesar and Cleopatra* (1945), which began shooting at Denham six days after D-Day, despite the threat of flying bombs and the difficulties of securing nubile young ladies and white peacocks to flit by in the backgrounds.

While British cinema stumbled uncertainly into war production, Germany began with its propaganda machine in top working condition. Ever since Hitler secured control in 1933, his propaganda minister Josef Goebbels had organized the industry to fit Nazi requirements. Jews were banned immediately; a film censor office was established in 1934; film criticism (and all arts criticism) was abolished in 1936, thereafter newspapers could print only facts, not opinions. The independent studios, including the mighty Ufa, were absorbed by the government during 1937. By 1939 many of Germany's best film talents had emigrated; those that remained were regarded as part of the country's fighting forces.

Goebbels sensed how powerful a weapon film could be, but he had known for a long time that audiences resented hard-core propaganda in fictional, dramatic formats. Instead propaganda was channelled into newsreels, compiled or doctored from material shot at the fighting fronts and decked out with animated maps full of pulsating arrows that indicated German advances.

Top: David Niven had trained at Sandhurst in the Thirties and saw active service during the war before returning to films. This one, scripted by Eric Ambler and Peter Ustinov, was a great success and was used at Sandhurst as a training film. Above: The Bells Go Down *featured the work of the Auxiliary Fire Service during London's Blitz. Below:* The Gentle Sex *(1943), showing women's role in the war, was directed by Leslie Howard*

of Information, after many changes of personnel and unfortunate gestures like the slogan '*Your* Courage, *Your* Cheerfulness, *Your* Resolution, will Bring *Us* Victory' (hardly the best way to bind a nation together), established a solid system of film distribution, sending out to cinemas short films on war topics every week. In addition, travelling projectionists showed films in those parts of the country where there were no proper cinemas.

Style and subject in these shorts varied tremendously. Most artistically polished were the poetic essays of Humphrey Jennings, who found in the war an ideal way of expressing his strong feelings for Britain's cultural heritage. Richard Massingham found a similar niche providing crisp, comic illustrations of wartime regulations, such as bathing in only five inches of water.

At the other end of the scale there were filmed lectures given by Ministry men seated behind desks and blinking nervously. These films were so embarrassing that cinema managers occasionally showed them with the curtains tactfully drawn. But it is clear that some of this huge output had considerable effect – particularly abroad, where America was uninvolved in the fighting until Japan attacked Pearl Harbor in December 1941.

Jennings' *London Can Take It* (devised for showing in Allied countries in 1940) filled out its Blitz images with a commentary by the American journalist Quentin Reynolds, full of praise for London's 'unconquerable spirit and courage'. Later, there was much direct film cooperation between the Allies, as each arm of the services prepared photographed accounts of their operations. In the war's last stages Carol Reed and the American Garson Kanin came

The newsreels were eventually lengthened to as much as forty minutes, and there are reports that cinema doors were carefully secured so that there was no possibility of escape. Special productions were concocted to lower the morale of countries about to be occupied: *Feuertaufe* (1940, Baptism of Fire), a film that glorified the Luftwaffe's conquest of Poland, was shown at the German Embassy in Oslo four days before the invasion of Norway in April 1940. The most notorious production of all, however was *Der Ewige Jude* (1940, The Eternal Jew), an illustrated lecture by Dr Fritz Hippler designed to fan the flames of anti-Semitism to inferno proportions.

Once the newsreels were over, audiences could settle down to suffer bombastic, shoddy epics glorifying various sections of the armed forces, or Veit Harlan's viciously anti-Semitic *Jud Süss* (1940, Jew Süss) – a key exhibit in the post-war trials. Other films aimed at influencing the all-important German youth included *Kadetten* (1941, Cadets) which told the story of young Prussians fighting in 1760 during the Seven Years' War. History, in fact, proved a boon for German film-makers who wanted to please their Nazi overlords without being rabidly propagandistic. German history was, after all, well-stocked with belligerently nationalistic heroes. Films about Frederick the Great of Prussia had long formed a separate genre and the actor Otto Gebühr did little else but play him.

Colonial activities in Africa proved a fruitful source of anti-British propaganda. *Ohm Krüger* (1941, Uncle Kruger), though one of the more impressive productions, offered a wickedly coarse caricature of Queen Victoria and blithely credited the British with inventing concentration camps.

Other films slanted the same way included *Titanic* (1943), where the ship hit the iceberg as a result of the sins of Jewish–English plutocracy, and two films by Goebbels' brother-in-law Max Kimmich, portraying British brutalities in Ireland: *Der Fuchs von Glenarvon* (1940, The Fox of Glenarvon) and *Mein Leben für Irland* (1941, My Life for Ireland).

Many other films were simply escapist entertainment with the odd twinge of propaganda. Goebbels spent much money developing Agfacolor so that German audiences would not lose out on colour films while the rest of the world was enjoying the early Technicolor movies.

In celebration of Ufa's twenty-fifth anniversary, Goebbels planned the highly elaborate fantasy film *Munchhausen* (1943) and studied Disney's feature cartoons and Korda's *The Thief of Bagdad* (1940), and almost produced something comparable. But his monumental undertaking was *Kolberg*, begun in 1943 and completed towards the end of 1944. Geared to the declining course of the war, the film shrewdly portrayed the citizens of Kolberg, besieged during the Napoleonic wars and heroically holding out against amazing odds. By the time the film was ready for release in early 1945, it had no value as propaganda for Germany was close to defeat.

Italy, Germany's ally in Europe, went about its film-making as it went about its fighting, with little of the manic fervour displayed by Goebbels. Most of the country's fascist tub-thumping had been performed in the late Thirties, when mammoth spectacles like *Scipione l'Africano* (1937) were mounted to reflect Italy's new image as an imperial, conquering power. Mussolini had ensured that the film industry was well equipped for the task. The vast Cinecittà film studios were built outside Rome and a film school (Centro Sperimentale di Cinematografia) was established. Mussolini's own son Vittorio pursued an active interest in the medium, securing his name on film credits and on the mast-head of a cinema magazine.

Many directors in the war avoided overt propaganda by retreating to unassuming romantic comedies and tales of provincial life. Some talents did manage to cut through the dross. Alessandro Blasetti's *Quattro Passi fra le Nuvole* (1942, Four Steps in the Clouds) focused sharply on the torments of daily life and had a script co-written by Cesare Zavattini, who was later associated with the director Vittorio De Sica and the neo-realist movement. In the same year, Visconti's *Ossessione* (1942, Obsession), a story of adultery and murder, exploded onto the screen with a kind of brute force unseen before in the Italian cinema.

Equally distinctive, though now largely forgotten, were the films of Francesco De Robertis. He was head of the Naval Ministry's film department and made features imbued with the spirit, and often the footage, of documentary, with non-professional players and location shooting.

La Nave Bianca (1941, The White Ship), for instance, began as a straight documentary about the brave work of a hospital ship. When the authorities wanted to boost the Italian entries at the 1941 Venice Film Festival, De Robertis obligingly built in a love story. Despite such compromises, his films had great impact, and his assistant, Roberto Rossellini (nominally the director of *La Nave Bianca*), followed this style in his own wartime films, *Un Pilota Ritorna* (1942, A Pilot Returns) and *L'Uomo della Croce* (1943, The Man of the Cross).

Looking back on the wartime period from the safe distance of 1960, De Sica observed that 'the war was a decisive experience for all of us. Each of us felt the wild urge to sweep away all the worn-out plots of the Italian cinema and to set up our cameras in the midst of real life.' With the studios under allied bombardment, there was also little alternative.

When Italy surrendered to the Allies and declared war on Germany, it only produced more turmoil, with facilities, equipment and talent scattered throughout the country. De Robertis went north, obstinately loyal to Mussolini who was now installed as puppet-head of the short-lived Salò

Top and above: two examples of the virulent anti-Semitic propaganda shown on German screens during the war; Veit Harlan's Jew Süss *was adapted from a novel while* Der Ewige Jude *purported to be a documentary. Left: the disastrous sinking of the* Titanic *was blamed on the Jews and the English. During the filming, the director Herbert Selpin complained about the interference of several Nazi naval advisers. He was arrested and later found murdered in his prison cell. Below: Ginette Leclerc in Clouzot's* Le Corbeau *made by the German-backed Continental studio in Paris*

REGIE: HERBERT SELPIN

SYBILLE SCHMITZ · HANS NIELSEN
KIRSTEN HEIBERG · E.F. FÜRBRINGER
KARL SCHÖNBÖCK · OTTO WERNICKE
CHARLOTTE THIELE · THEODOR LOOS
SEPP RIST · FRANZ SCHAFHEITLIN

OHM KRÜGER

Top: Feuertaufe *celebrated the role of the German air force in the conquest of Poland, offering heroic images of the 'master race' on the attack. Above:* Ohm Krüger *dealt a blow at the British, charging them with great brutality in the course of their imperialist adventures in Africa. Right:* Les Visiteurs du Soir *proved that the French cinema was able to continue its great tradition despite the restrictions imposed upon it by the German army of Occupation*

Republic. Rossellini went south and helped establish the cinema branch of the Committee of National Liberation.

A few weeks before the Allies entered Rome in June 1944, his film *Roma, Città Aperta* (1945, *Rome, Open City*) went into production. It was a harsh, moving tale of a Resistance leader's betrayal. But the Italian cinema had already encountered its own kind of liberation.

The Soviet Union's path through the war was just as checkered as Italy's. After several years of mounting tension on its western borders with the dismembered parts of the old Austro–Hungarian Empire, Stalin concluded the non-aggression pact with Hitler in 1939. Feature films described the occupation of Poland, the invasion of Finland; items with anti-German leanings such as *Professor Mamlock* and *Alexander Nevsky* (both 1938) swiftly returned to the vaults. But they soon emerged after June 22, 1941, when Germany's shock invasion brought the pact to an end. Film studios were now uprooted from Moscow to safer surroundings. Various Soviet policies were modified and the customary anti-religious bias was abandoned. Suddenly the much-despised Tsarist generals received homage from the cinema for their part in the Napoleonic wars and other conflicts. There were also new forms of presenting films in the Soviet Union during the war. From August 1941 so-called 'Fighting Film Albums' appeared in cinemas every month; these were a mixture of short films that included miniature dramas, satiric japes and war-effort propaganda. Cameramen at the front maintained a constant stream of filmed dispatches which were edited into powerful documentaries. Alexander Dovzhenko supervised and wrote a moving

---

From 1940 French cinema was made to toe the Nazi line. When Hitler laid siege to Russia, the cinema became a weapon of resistance

---

commentary for *The Fight for Our Soviet Ukraine* (1943) that reflected his feelings for his homeland.

Soviet features tended to follow the usual propaganda pattern, spotlighting German atrocities or the heroic activities of the partisans. But as in other countries pure entertainment was never neglected, indeed its quantity increased as the war continued. One of the most popular films of 1944 was a musical entitled *At 6 pm After the War*.

The celebrated Soviet director Sergei Eisenstein spent most of the war engaged on *Ivan the Terrible* in Mosfilm's wartime headquarters at Alma-Ata in Kazakstan. By the end of December 1944, the first part of the projected trilogy was ready for release. The film was a ferocious and monumental excursion into Russia's medieval past, with Tsar Ivan bludgeoning his way from childhood to coronation. As a cinematic history lesson, the film was complex and unsettling for audiences.

For those countries occupied by the Germans – France, Denmark, the Low Countries, Norway – there were obviously fewer opportunities to fly their own flag. German films swamped the cinemas; German film censors controlled production. But the censor's limited powers of perception sometimes allowed carefully disguised anti-Nazi sentiments to slip by. When the Danish censor sat through *Kornet Er i Fare* (1944, The Grain Is in Danger) he obviously regarded it as just a boring short about the *sitophilus granariae*, an insect gnawing its way through a whole harvest of wheat. Audiences of a different persuasion realized the insect was also the Nazi pest, gnawing its way through Europe.

France was under Nazi occupation from June 1940, though the official French government still existed at Vichy in an uneasy collaboration with the Germans. The main film studios in Paris were taken over by the German company Continental. A few films like *Les Inconnus Dans la Maison* (1942, *Strangers in the House*) betrayed German sympathies, but there was never any concerted effort to promote Nazi propaganda in the course of the film. Continental's output was noted instead for its imitation of Hollywood genre movies, since American films had been banned in France after 1942.

Many of the best French directors were then abroad – Renoir, Clair, Duvivier; those who remained took the obvious way out of their difficult situation by largely avoiding subjects with a topical edge. Simenon's crime stories, boulevard theatre comedies, Maupassant and Balzac all received uncontroversial adaptations. The bulk of film propaganda, in fact, originated from the Vichy government, whose need to foster some spirit of national pride generated a tepid trickle of features in praise of domestic life, hard work and *la patrie*.

Nevertheless, French cinema still managed to develop a special identity and a fighting spirit. New

directors as varied as Robert Bresson, Jacques Becker and Henri-Georges Clouzot embarked on their careers. Some strove to deal with France's problems allegorically: one of the period's most popular films was Jean Delannoy's *Pontcarral, Colonel d'Empire* (1942, Pontcarral, Colonel of the Empire), with its historical colonel fighting the enemy from his barricaded house at the time of the First Empire.

Equally pertinent was Clouzot's *Le Corbeau* (1943, *The Raven*), a thriller about poison-pen letters, produced by Continental. The movie was so bleak and negative in atmosphere that the director and the writer were accused of serving enemy propaganda through their analysis of a town (and, therefore, country) shaken by guilt and suspicion.

Les Visiteurs du Soir (1942, *The Devil's Own Envoy*) took the viewer back to the Middle Ages for a magical story of love conquering the wiles of the Devil, but there was no overt ideological thrust behind Marcel Carné's direction.

Other film-makers and writers (Jean Cocteau included) also luxuriated in fantasy and visual extravagance, though none could match the power and scope of Carné's *Les Enfants du Paradis* (*Children of Paradise*), a period panorama of Paris life begun during the Occupation in 1942 and released in 1945. In its length (three hours) and its lavishness, this film might almost be a symbol of the French film industry's determination not to be cowed by the war but to come up fighting. Most film industries did, all over Europe. GEOFF BROWN

Them and Us

The propaganda films of Britain and Germany had the same objectives – to denigrate the enemy and inspire the nation to greater efforts. But, in key with the national characteristics of the two sides, their films differed widely both in style and content

At the outbreak of World War II, all cinemas in Britain were closed. However, their value to the maintenance of morale was soon appreciated and they were reopened after about ten days to become one of the principal sources of recreation for the nation at war. Feature films were seen not just as providing escapist entertainment but also instruction and information. Lord MacMillan, the first wartime Minister of Information, issued a memorandum in 1940 suggesting as themes for propagandist feature films: what Britain is fighting for; how Britain is fighting; and the need for sacrifice if the war is to be won. The British cinema responded to these suggestions and in so doing achieved perhaps its finest hour.

A gentleman's game
The earliest British war film *The Lion Has Wings*, rapidly put together by the producer Alexander Korda and on view by November 1939, was a curious amalgam: part illustrated lecture (the German takeover of Europe and the nature of Nazi ideology); part dramatized documentary (the reconstruction of an RAF raid on the Kiel Canal); and part invocation of Britain's heroic past (Queen Elizabeth I's speech to the troops before the Armada). It did not work as a film – indeed pirated copies were shown in Berlin and provoked great mirth – but it did embody many of the themes which

were to be reworked by later and better films. It also established from the British point of view the images of the two sides in the conflict by intercutting scenes of the good-natured, hard-working, decent, democratic British with the regimented, fanatical, jackbooted Nazis marching in faceless formation. Equally to the point was the contrast in leadership the film demonstrated by cutting from the ranting, demonic figure of Hitler addressing a mass rally to the gentle and modest George VI singing 'Underneath the Spreading Chestnut Tree' at a Boy Scout jamboree.

The film looked both to the past and to the future. To the future in the documentary-style representation of wartime operations, and to the past in the staged sequences of a 'typical British couple' (Ralph Richardson and Merle Oberon) responding to the war – scenes which evoked the rigidly stratified class system enshrined in British films of the Thirties. Initially the cinema continued to reflect this tradition, remaining resolutely middle class in tone and values. In films like Carol Reed's *Night Train to Munich* (1940), the war was treated as a gentlemanly jape in which an upper-class hero (here Rex Harrison) runs rings round the humourless, ranting, dunder-headed Hun. The epitome of the romanticized, class-bound and hopelessly out-of-touch war film was Ealing's *Ships With Wings* (dir. Sergei Nolbandov, 1941)

Top left: Michael Redgrave in Way to the Stars *personified the courage and good humour of the British war hero. Above: unswerving loyalty and obedience were lauded in Nazi propaganda like* D III 88

an absurd yarn in which a disgraced Fleet Air Arm officer (John Clements) redeems his honour by undertaking a suicide mission to destroy a dam on an enemy-held island. It received such a hostile press that Michael Balcon, the head of Ealing studios, resolved henceforth to produce essentially realistic stories of Britain at war. He turned, therefore, to the only group in Britain familiar with the evocation of real-life – the documentarists. This group of talented film-makers, nurtured by John Grierson in the Thirties, was committed to the concept of realism in setting, mood, and content and to the dramatization of the everyday experience of ordinary people. Several members, notably Harry Watt and Alberto Cavalcanti, went to work for Ealing studios, and the documentary influence permeated feature-film production.

The image of a nation divided by class barriers was replaced by the concept of 'The People's War', the idea of ordinary people pulling together to defeat a common foe. Ealing's war films exemplified this new image: *The Foreman Went to France* (dir. Charles

Left: Olivier as the inspirational English king, Henry V. Above left: Nazi fugitives turn on a Canadian trapper (Olivier) in 49th Parallel. *Top left:* The Gentle Sex *was a tribute to the women of the ATS. Top centre: Tommy Trinder leads some kids in a sing-song in* The Foreman Went to France. *Top right: boys watch Britain's rare bird in* Tawny Pipit. *Far right:* The Young Mr Pitt's *final speech echoed Churchill: 'England has saved herself by her exertions and will, as I trust, save Europe by her example.' Above: the survivors of HMS Torrin cling to their life-raft as they see their ship go down in* In Which We Serve

Frend, 1942) told how a determined foreman (Clifford Evans) retrieves a vital piece of machinery from France, aided by two soldiers (a Cockney and a Scot) and an American secretary; *San Demetrio, London* (dir. Charles Frend, 1943) recounted the true story of the salvaging of a merchant-navy tanker by part of its crew, a cross-section of various types of men. A similar cross-section made up an army patrol pinned down in a desert oasis in *Nine Men* (dir. Harry Watt, 1943); *The Bells Go Down* (dir. Basil Dearden, 1943) dramatized the work of the Auxiliary Fire Service in London, stressing the comradeship and dedication of the team. Significantly, none of these films had an

officer hero. Indeed the personality and attitudes of the old-style officer and gentleman were comprehensively demolished in Michael Powell and Emeric Pressburger's *The Life and Death of Colonel Blimp* (1943). The title figure (played by Roger Livesey), an officer, gentleman and sportsman of the old Imperial school who would rather lose the war than resort to using the methods of the Germans, is shown as a touching but wholly anachronistic figure.

The people's war

Comradeship and cooperation, dedication to duty and self-sacrifice, a self-deprecating good humour and unselfconscious modesty characterized the films of the fighting services. The war produced a masterpiece for each service. For the navy, there was *In Which We Serve* (1942), written, produced, co-directed (with David Lean) and scored by Noel Coward, who also played the lead role. It was based on the true story of HMS *Kelly*, which had been commanded by Coward's friend Lord Louis Mountbatten and had been sunk off Crete. The film focuses on three characters: the captain, a petty officer and an ordinary seaman. Their differences of status, background and situation are submerged by their common loyalty to their ship. The army film – Carol Reed's *The Way Ahead* (1944), scripted by Peter Ustinov

and Eric Ambler – was a semi-documentary account of how a group of conscripts from all walks of life are brought together and welded into a disciplined fighting army unit. And Anthony Asquith's *The Way to the Stars* (1945), scripted by Terence Rattigan, recalled life on a single RAF station between 1940 and 1944 with its joys and losses, its tragedies and its camaraderie. The film also took in the arrival and integration of the Americans into the war in Europe.

The contribution of women to the war effort was vital, and the cinema paid tribute to them, reflecting the dramatic change in their social roles and expectations. Leslie Howard's *The Gentle Sex* (1943) was a female version of *The Way Ahead*, a realistic account of the training of a group of women from all classes and backgrounds in the Auxiliary Territorial Service (ATS). Frank Launder and Sidney Gilliat's moving and memorable *Millions Like Us* (1943) dramatized the experiences of a group of girls drafted to work in an aircraft factory.

These were films with sympathetic and realistic characters and situations to which ordinary people could relate. Much less convincing (though equally well-intentioned) were the films produced as tributes to the oppressed peoples of Europe. The plots were interchangeable – highly romanticized stories of gallant resistance fighters suffering under the yoke of Nazi oppression but doing their bit to speed the day of victory. Realism was not furthered by the casting of such resolutely British types as Tom Walls or Finlay Currie as

partisan leaders. Each country got its tribute – Belgium (*Uncensored*, dir. Anthony Asquith, 1942), Norway (*The Day Will Dawn*, dir. Harold French, 1942), Yugoslavia (*Undercover*, dir. Sergei Nolbandov, 1943), Poland (*Dangerous Moonlight*, dir. Brian Desmond Hurst, 1941), Holland (*The Silver Fleet*, dir. Vernon Sewell, Gordon Wellesley, 1943), France (*Tomorrow We Live*, dir. George King, 1942) and Denmark (*Escape to Danger*, dir. Lance Comfort, Mutz Greenbaum, 1943).

In retrospect, the most redundant propaganda features were those warning against the danger from fifth columnists – simply because there were no fifth columnists in Britain. But warnings against complacency were never wasted and the cycle produced at least two memorable films. Thorold Dickinson's *The Next of Kin* (1942) was a chilling illustration of the slogan 'Careless Talk Costs Lives', demonstrating the way in which a chain of fifth columnists and Nazi spies assemble the information enabling them to destroy a British landing on the French coast. Churchill banned the film on the grounds that it would create alarm and despondency, but a military tribunal reversed this decision. The film was widely shown, and Field-Marshal Alexander told the director: 'This film was worth a division of troops to the British Army.' Alberto Cavalcanti's *Went the Day Well?* (1942) was an equally compelling account of a group of Nazi paratroopers infiltrating and taking over an English village until defeated by the villagers.

This sceptr'd isle

Unlike the Germans, the British did not turn very often to history to point up parallels with the present – possibly because of the unpopularity of historical films with working-class audiences in the Thirties. There were a few notable exceptions. Alexander Korda produced in Hollywood *That Hamilton Woman!* (1941) with Laurence Olivier as Nelson denouncing dictatorship and appeasement with equal vigour and urging the prosecution of the war against Napoleon. In Britain, Thorold Dickinson directed *The Prime Minister* (1941), which had its propaganda value in its account of how Disraeli, Britain's Jewish Prime Minister, outwitted Germany's Chancellor Bismarck. There were definite contemporary parallels in Carol Reed's *The Young Mr Pitt* (1942), which had justly been called 'the finest historical moving picture ever to be staged in this country'. Robert Donat unforgettably played Pitt, who burned himself out leading Britain in her struggle against Napoleon. Laurence Olivier's *Henry V* (1944), dedicated to the commandos, used Shakespeare's heroic poetry as a clarion call to the nation.

Films about *why* Britain was fighting were rarer than films about *how* she was fighting, perhaps because of the difficulty of rendering ideological and philosophical concepts as acceptable entertainment. Perhaps the best programmatic account was provided by Michael Powell's *49th Parallel* (1941). Financed by the Ministry of Information and filmed partly in Canada with an all-star cast, it told the gripping story of the stranded crew-members of a Nazi submarine travelling across Canada towards neutral USA and encountering *en route* various representatives of democracy. An uncommitted French-Canadian trapper (Laurence Olivier) turns against them when they maltreat the 'racially inferior' Eskimos.

A democratic Christian community of Hutterite exiles demonstrate the workability of a system of equality and cooperation. A donnish aesthete (Leslie Howard) beats one of the Germans to a pulp when they burn his books and pictures. Finally a Canadian soldier (Raymond Massey) takes on and defeats the commander of the fugitives (Eric Portman).

Michael Powell (with Emeric Pressburger) also directed *A Canterbury Tale* (1944), a complex, absorbing fable which mystified contemporary critics. It evoked the England of Chaucer and Shakespeare, the Kent countryside, half-timbered cottages and quiet churchyards. The spirit of this England was embodied by Thomas Culpeper (Eric Portman), gentleman farmer and amateur historian, who seeks to communicate its values to a group of latter-day Canterbury pilgrims, all unseeing and unfeeling products of a modern, materialist world. It represented a sense of the living past, the beauty of the English countryside and the enduring relationship of man and the soil.

Less mystical, but no less engaging, was Bernard Miles' *Tawny Pipit* (1944), in which a hierarchical rural society, led by the squire and the vicar, bands together to preserve the nesting place of the rare British bird, the tawny pipit. 'Love of nature and animals is part and parcel of the British way of life,' declares the squire. The defence of the pipits is equated with the defence of freedom against the Germans; the villagers successfully fight off the organized power of the military, the bureaucratic machine and the criminal fraternity to ensure the survival of the pipit.

Anthony Asquith's *The Demi-Paradise* (1943) artfully demonstrated how the preconceived notions about Britain held by an earnest Russian engineer (Laurence Olivier) are dispelled by his actual encounters with the British in peace and war. The film evokes the living power of tradition and indicates what several other films divined as the British secret weapon – their sense of humour. 'If you can laugh, you can be tolerant and freedom-loving,' says the engineer.

The England that these films summoned up was essentially a mythic one – pre-industrial, timeless and hierarchical. It was the dream of a different sort of England that was to lead to the Labour victory of 1945, the logical culmination of those other films which had stressed the lowering of class barriers, the solidarity of ordinary people and the ideals of freedom and justice for the oppressed.

The cinema of hate

German propaganda features identified two sets of enemies – the enemy within (the Jews) and the enemy without (the British). It was not until the outbreak of war that the German film industry produced specifically anti-Semitic and anti-English tracts. But three major anti-Semitic films came out in 1940 and there can be little doubt that they represented the government's cinematic effort to prepare the German public for the full-scale extermination of the Jews, the logical culmination of the race policies of the Third Reich.

The first of these films, *Die Rothschilds*, directed by Erick Waschneck, is a rather dull account of how the Jewish banking family acquired wealth and power in Regency England. It can hardly have done much to stir up German wrath since the victims of the Jews in this case were the British, something

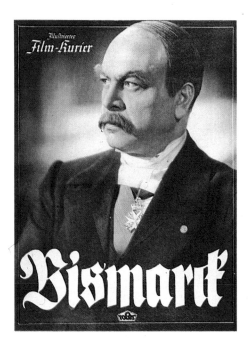

Above: Paul Hartmann as Bismarck – *authoritarian architect of a unified Germany. Centre top: Irish patriots in* Mein Leben für Irland. *Centre right: Emil Jannings as Ohm Krüger with a grotesque caricature of Queen Victoria. Right:* Jud Süss *is condemned to death by the citizens of Württemberg. Opposite page: dying for the Fatherland was extolled in both* Kadetten *and* Kampfgeschwader Lützow, *the programme of which saluted its dead pilot hero thus: 'But his ghost lives on in hundreds, in thousands. And his sacrifice will never be forgotten'*

which must have seemed akin to poetic justice. Veit Harlan's *Jud Süss* (Jew Süss) was much more dangerous, brilliantly orchestrating all the themes and archetypes of Nazi propaganda to stimulate the hatred of the audience. The central figure, Süss (Ferdinand Marian), personified the Jewish threat in all its aspects – economic, political and sexual. He acquired considerable wealth, used it to gain control of eighteenth-century Württemberg, brought in the Jews (depicted as scheming, dirty and repulsive) and raped a virtuous German girl. Eventually the honest citizens of Württemberg rose up and destroyed him.

But for sheer, concentrated nastiness, this film was exceeded by the 45-minute documentary *Der Ewige Jude* (*The Eternal Jew*) compiled by Dr Fritz Hippler. This was a systematic denunciation of every aspect of Jewry. Their appearance was shown to be always scruffy and ugly. They were accused of being responsible for all the ills which had befallen Germany since the end of World War I. They were held to be the source of all degenerate art (Expressionism, Surrealism, Cubism and jazz). Their religious practices were denounced as barbaric. The film ended with Hitler's Race Laws being flashed on the screen. There were no full-length anti-Semitic films after this, but the Jews became standard 'baddies' in conventional films.

Second only to the Jews in Nazi demonology were the British, and indeed Goebbels went so far as to describe them as 'the Jews among the Aryans'. The most memorable of the Nazi anti-British films is without question *Ohm Krüger* (1941, Uncle Kruger), directed by Hans Stein-

hoff. It was a supremely clever and utterly cynical reading of the Boer War, whose importance, so the contemporary film programme assured the audience, lay in the fact that 'for the first time the entire world of culture realized that England is the brutal enemy of order and civilization'. Modelled on Eisenstein's *Battleship Potemkin* (1925), a film Goebbels much admired, *Ohm Krüger* starred Emil Jannings as the Boer President, an all-wise and all-knowing führer-figure, leading the peace-loving Boer farmers in a just war against the military might of a greedy and cruel British Empire. The film is an object lesson in the use of archetypes and presents an unforgettable rogues' gallery of famous British figures. Cecil Rhodes is an oily schemer, his face often seen half in shadow, his voice soft, his eyes gleaming with cunning. Joseph Chamberlain is an aloof, expressionless, impeccably attired scoundrel, a monstrous caricature of British sang-froid. The Prince of Wales is an elderly lecher, ogling dancing girls while his mother lies dying. Kitchener is a beetle-browed sadist ordering total war. Churchill is a bloated despot, running a concentration camp and starving and maltreating the inmates. Queen Victoria is a whisky-sodden old wreck. English missionaries incite the natives to rise against the Boers, handing out Bibles with one hand and rifles with the other.

Much as one may admire the techniques of propaganda, one cannot but be appalled by the sheer cynicism of the exercise. The Nazis were denouncing the British for inventing concentration camps and total war at a time when they themselves were making full use of both.

Similarly, they produced two films, both directed by M. W. Kimmich, *Der Fuchs von Glenarvon* (1940, The Fox of Glenarvon) and *Mein Leben für Irland* (1941, My Life for Ireland) dealing with the oppression of the gallant, freedom-loving Irish by the tyrannical Imperialist British. The films are almost interchangeable with those made by the British depicting the struggles of the gallant, freedom-loving Poles/French/Yugoslavs against the tyrannical Imperialist Germans.

Clever attempts to rewrite the history books occurred in three other anti-British films. *Aufruhr in Damaskus* (Uproar in Damascus, dir. Gustav Ucicky, 1939), showed Lawrence of Arabia stirring up the natives of Syria against the Germans during World War I. *Das Herz der Königin* (The Heart of the Queen, dir. Carl Froelich, 1940), a film strongly reminiscent of *Mary of Scotland* (1936) – made by another anglophobe, John Ford – was a drama about the conflict between the pure, noble and romantic Mary Queen of Scots and the vicious, scheming and vindictive Elizabeth I of England. *Titanic* (dir. Herbert Selpin, Werner Klingler, 1943), a splendid re-creation of the *Titanic* disaster, featured the unsuccessful efforts of the ship's first officer – a German – to prevent the catastrophe in the face of the machinations of corrupt British capitalist aristocrats.

Führers from the past

The German cinema was also concerned to promote those qualities in the people which would sustain the war effort. Above all it promoted the idea of total obedience to an all-wise, all-powerful, all-knowing leader, and for

this purpose leading figures from Germany's history were mobilized as führer prototypes. They were invariably shown as lonely, dedicated warriors, battling for the glory, unity and future greatness of Germany. *Der Grosse König* (The Great King, dir. Veit Harlan, 1942) featured Frederick the Great (Otto Gebühr) and laid great stress on his refusal to make peace with his enemies until total victory had been achieved. Bismarck, Germany's Iron Chancellor, featured in two films directed by Wolfgang Liebeneiner, *Bismarck* (1940) and *Die Entlassung* (1942, The Dismissal) which showed him building up the army, abolishing democratic assemblies, imposing press censorship, outwitting the effeminate and cunning French and Austrians, surviving an assassination attempt by an English Jew and unifying Germany. In the end, he is dismissed by the youthful Kaiser Wilhelm II, but the moral of the film is clear – his unfinished work will be completed by Hitler.

It was not just political leaders but cultural heroes from Germany's past who were utilized to preach the message: poets (*Friedrich Schiller*, dir. Herbert Maisch, 1940), architects (*Andreas Schluter*, dir. Herbert Maisch, 1942), scientists (*Robert Koch, der Bekämpfer des Todes*, dir. Hans Steinhoff, 1939, and *Paracelsus*, dir G. W. Pabst, 1943), inventors (*Diesel*, dir. Gerhard Lamprecht, 1942), composers (*Friedemann Bach*, dir. Traugott Müller, 1941). All celebrate the struggles and achievements of solitary German geniuses, striving for perfection, refusing to compromise, and sacrificing personal happiness to attain their ultimate goals.

The German people were encouraged to dis-play at all times the qualities of discipline, obedience, comradeship and self-sacrifice. These qualities permeate such films as Herbert Maisch's *D III 88* (1939) and its sequel, Hans Bertram's *Kampfgeschwader Lützow* (1941, Battle-squadron Lützow) which deal with the exploits of the Luftwaffe in peace and war and tell virtually the same story. The comradeship of two pilots is temporarily sundered by their love for the same girl, but they are reunited in time for one of them to die gloriously in the service of the Fatherland. Their commandant tells them in *D III 88*:

'Only through frictionless cooperation and unconditional obedience can our armed forces become an instrument on which our Leader can rely totally in an emergency.'

The same message was specifically directed towards German youth in *Kadetten* (1941, Cadets), a Karl Ritter film set in 1760. It tells of the heroism of a group of boy soldiers during a sneak Russian attack on Berlin while Frederick the Great is away fighting the Austrians.

Dying for the Fatherland

The themes and archetypes of wartime propaganda came together finally in the last cinematic gasp of the Third Reich, Veit Harlan's *Kolberg* (1944). The film was designed to prepare the entire population to fight to the last man, woman and child. It was based on the heroic defence of Kolberg by its citizens against the armies of Napoleon in 1807. The führer-figure is Joachim Nettelbeck, the Mayor of Kolberg (Heinrich George) who makes endless speeches declaring: 'We'd rather be buried under the rubble than capitulate.' Under his leadership, the people pull together to achieve victory, undertaking any sacrifice, including the flooding of part of their town and a comprehensive 'scorched earth' policy to deny the enemy supplies. By the time the film was available for release in January 1945, almost all the cinemas in Germany were closed. Virtually the only people who saw the film were the garrison of La Rochelle, then completely surrounded by the Allies. A print of the film was dropped by parachute to encourage them in their resistance; they surrendered.

With a few notable exceptions, German wartime propaganda features are heavy-handed and stodgy. This is particularly true of the biographical films, staged in a leaden monumental style and replete with lengthy, wearisome Nazi rants, delivered by most of the actors as if they were on the verge of apoplexy. Significantly, the two greatest film-makers for the Nazi party of pre-war years, Leni Riefenstahl and Luis Trenker, were virtually inactive during the war. Comparing British and German propaganda features it is clear that they shared the ideas of an appeal to the heroic past and the need for comradeship, self-sacrifice and dedication to duty in the present. Where they differed was in their central ideas, with the Germans promoting the concept of total obedience to the Leader and the British promoting the concept of a common effort towards mutually agreed ends – but always with the maintenance of a degree of healthy individualism and of a sense of humour and proportion. In the last resort, that conflict of ideologies was what the war was all about.

JEFFREY RICHARDS

UN FILM DE
MARCEL CARNÉ

1ᵉ ÉPOQUE
LE BOULEVARD
DU CRIME

ARLETTY . JEAN-LOUIS BARRAULT . PIERRE BRASSEUR . PIERRE RENOIR

LES ENFANTS DU PARADIS

IMAGES DE ROGER HUBERT   avec LOUIS SALOU MARCEL HERRAND MARIA CASARÈS   SCENARIO ET DIALOGUES DE
DIRECTEUR DE PRODUCTION FRED ORAIN   JACQUES PRÉVERT

Directed by Marcel Carné, 1945
Prod co: Pathé-Cinéma. **prod:** Fred Orain. **prod man:** Raymond Borderie.
sc: Jacques Prévert. **photo:** Roger Hubert. **ed:** Henri Rust. **art dir:** Léon
Barsacq, R. Gabutti, Alexandre Trauner. **mus:** Joseph Kosma, Maurice
Thiriet, G. Mouqué. **cost:** Mayo. **r/t:** 195 minutes. Paris premiere, 9 March
1945. Released in the USA as *Children of Paradise*.
Cast: Arletty (*Garance*), Jean-Louis Barrault (*Baptiste Debureau*), Pierre
Brasseur (*Frédéric Lemaître*), Maria Casarès (*Nathalie*), Marcel Herrand
(*Lacenaire*), Louis Salou (*Count Edouard de Montray*), Pierre Renoir
(*Jéricho*), Paul Frankeur (*inspector*), Jane Marken (*Mme Hermine*), Fabien
Loris (*Avril*), Etienne Decroux (*Anselme Debureau*), Marcel Pérès (*director
of the Funambules*), Gaston Modot (*File de Soie, the blind man*), Pierre
Palau (*manager of the Funambules*), Jacques Castelot (*Georges*), Robert
Dhéry (*Celestin*), Rognoni (*director of the Grand Theatre*), Florencie
(*gendarme*), Guy Favières (*cashier*), Albert Remy (*Scarpia Borigni*),
Auguste Bovério (*first author*), Paul Demange (*second author*), Jean
Diener (*third author*), Habib Benglia (*boy from Turkish baths*).

Marcel Carné once said that *Les Enfants du Paradis* (*Children of Paradise*) was a tribute to the theatre, and indeed the film is an evocation of the stage in the days when it still belonged to the people and before it became the haunt of the fashionable upper classes. 'Paradis', in fact, is what in English we should call 'the gods' – the heights sacred to the public sitting in the gallery. And 'the children' are both the actors – beloved (or not) by that audience watching from those heavenly heights – and the audience themselves. The close relationship between public and performer has gone now. It lingered with the music-hall, but the music-

hall itself has dwindled and vanished. Perhaps the remembrance of it has helped to give Carné's piece its enormous success.

The idea for the film, it seems, belonged to the actor Jean-Louis Barrault. The second year of the Occupation saw Marcel Carné and his screenwriter, the poet Jacques Prévert, ready to begin making a new film. Working together they had enjoyed great prestige both before the war and during it; but now one of their projects had run into difficulties and they needed a fresh subject. Barrault, whom they encountered in a café in Nice, suggested a film about Baptiste Debureau, the Funambules and the Boulevard du Crime. Debureau had been the most celebrated of French mimes; the Funambules, in the Boulevard du Temple, was the theatre where he performed; the Boulevard du Temple was sometimes called the Boulevard du Crime because it was notorious for murders. Violence, the romance of the popular theatre, and a famous historical figure – everybody agreed that the possibilities were seductive, and work began on the script which, though fictional, was to be based on real-life characters – not only Debureau, but also the stage actor Frédéric Lemaître and the dandy and notorious criminal Lacenaire.

It was a work of happy cooperation. Carné and Prévert, of course, were the chief creators; the designer Alexandre Trauner assisted, as did Joseph Kosma the composer; while the actors, Barrault (Debureau), Pierre Brasseur (Lemaître) and Marcel Herrand (Lacenaire) joined in to discuss their roles. After six months preparation, Carné began shooting.

An authentic setting had to be provided to establish the relation-

1

2

ship between the two actors and their public and to revive the mood and the popular feeling of mid-nineteenth-century Paris. This posed formidable problems; because of the war, materials were scarce – indeed, everything was scarce. Yet somehow a section of the Boulevard du Temple, theatre-fronts and all, was reconstructed – stretching for a quarter of a mile. Carné employed 25,000 extras to act as the carnival crowd, with its entertainers, jugglers, tight-rope walkers and weight-lifters, and the yelling audience of the Funambules theatre.

Les Enfants du Paradis took three years to complete, and at the time was probably the most expensive film ever to be made in France. Certainly it was the grandest of Carné's films; he was never to make another as masterly. It was not a work noted for discovering new talents. Most of the players – Pierre Brasseur, Pierre Renoir, the lovely Arletty – were already established. Barrault, although he made occasional and powerful appearances on the screen, was essentially a stage actor. Only Maria Casarès went on to greater fame, playing the role of Death in Jean Cocteau's *Orphée* (1950).

The film itself, however, was a lasting triumph. For the French, just emerging from years of Occupation, the romantic brilliance of *Les Enfants du Paradis* was a testimony to survival and a reassertion of French elegance and artistry. As Carné said, it was a tribute to the theatre – a French theatre with French performers. It may also be said to have been a declaration of the resilience of France herself.
DILYS POWELL

The story of Garance, a beautiful, independent girl, and the four men who love her unfolds against a background of the popular theatre and the underworld of Paris in the 1840s (1). The girl is saved from arrest for theft by Baptiste, a mime artist, who explains in gestures that she is not guilty; the thief was her criminal companion Lacenaire. Baptiste finds her work in the theatre (2) and shelters her, but out of delicacy refrains from taking advantage of her willingness to love. She becomes the mistress of his friend, the would-be actor Frédéric; later, to save herself from a police charge (3), she accepts the protection of the Count, a rich aristocrat (4), and leaves Paris.

When she returns, Frédéric and Baptiste, now married to Nathalie, a girl from the theatre (5), are both famous. Five years have passed, but Garance and Baptiste are still in love. They are reunited (6) but betrayed by Lacenaire, who in his vicious fashion also loves Garance. He is insulted by the Count (7) and murders him (8). Nathalie discovers the lovers and her pitiful pleas drive Garance to disappear, leaving Baptiste vainly pursuing her through the crowded boulevard.

3

4

5

6

7

8

Business as usual

The French film industry survives under the Nazi Occupation, maintains production and scores some of its greatest triumphs

FERNAND GRAVEY
et
ASSIA NORIS
DANS

Le Capitaine Fracasse

On June 22, 1940, Marshal Pétain, the French Chief of State, signed an armistice with Germany. Under its terms Paris became part of an occupied zone, and was to remain so for just over four years. In June 1944 the Allies landed on the French coast; by August Paris was liberated.

However deep a resentment and humiliation the French people may have felt at their subjugation to Nazism, the French cinema flourished as never before. Something above three hundred and fifty features were made in these fifty months of occupation, including such landmarks of French film as *Le Corbeau* (1943, *The Raven*) and *Les Anges du Péché* (1943, *Angels of Sin*).

Yet there is remarkably little record of overt and willing collaboration by French film-makers with the Nazi Party and its ideologies. Indeed, a number of those artists who remained active – among them the directors Jacques Becker, Jean Grémillon, Jean Painlevé and the actor Pierre Blanchar – were responsible for the formation of the clandestine 'Committee of Liberation of the French Cinema'.

This is not to say that Goebbels did not exert comprehensive control over the French film industry. For years before the war, German films had been successfully infiltrating the French market. With the Occupation – and to an extent through the expropriation of Jewish interests – the Germans acquired complete

economic control of about a third of the industry: production, press, distribution and theatres. French film was subjected to a dual censorship by the German Propaganda Ministry, and by the German-backed Vichy government whose powers in this respect nominally covered only the so-called 'free' zone of France.

Two factors contributed to the freedom allowed to French film-makers. One was the failure of German-made pictures to attract the French public. At the start of the Occupation there was a determined effort to put German films onto French screens, but audiences tacitly boycotted them. As a result, receipts for French films rose considerably, thereby enhancing the financial prosperity of the home industry. Moreover, the Germans looked to French production to replace the films they were no longer buying from Hollywood, and so left film-makers a free hand in the field of what were regarded as purely entertainment pictures.

The only direct injection of German money into French production was through the German-owned Continental company which produced thirty of the more expensive pictures of the period. Continental concentrated particularly on 'American-style' subjects, such as Henri Decoin's light comedy *Premier Rendez-vous* (1941, First Meeting) and detective thrillers. Henri-Georges Clouzot, who had made a number of German versions of French films in Berlin in the early Thirties, scripted two of the

Above left: characters in fancy dress bring a surreal atmosphere to the contemporary setting of Grémillon's Lumière d'Eté. *Above: Gance's costume romance provided safe escapism for the people of Occupied France*

most important of these thrillers: Georges Lacombe's *Le Dernier des Six* (1941, Last of the Six) and Decoin's *Les Inconnus Dans la Maison* (1942, *Strangers in the House*), adapted from a pre-war Georges Simenon novel but turned into an attack on non-Aryans, useful as propaganda for the Vichy government.

Clouzot went on to make his debut as a director with a thriller, *L'Assassin Habite au 21* (1942, The Killer Lives at No. 21), which remains one of his best works. His next film, *Le Corbeau* (1943), based on a real-life story concerning the circulation of poison-pen letters in a French village, became the centre of a bitter controversy when the Nazis used it as anti-French propaganda in Occupied Europe.

Jacques Becker, who also began his career during the Occupation, was a pupil of Jean Renoir and worked in a realist style which combined elements from French pre-war cinema and from the American detective genre. His first film was *Le Dernier Atout* (1942, The Trump Card), a brilliant and commercially successful detective thriller. With *Goupi Mains Rouges* (1943, *It Happened at the Inn*), Becker went beyond his detective-story plot to create a rich portrayal of French rural life. *Falbala*

(1945, *Paris Frills*), completed around the time of the Liberation, was the first of the Parisian subjects on which his later fame was to rest. Set in a top fashion house, the film is a wonderfully detailed description of the French bourgeoisie under the Occupation.

A much-neglected French director, Jean Grémillon, made two of the few strictly realist works of the period. *Lumière d'Eté* (1943, Summer Light) contrasted the life of construction workers on a dam with the decadence of their employers (evidently intended to symbolize the way of life under the Vichy administration). *Le Ciel Est à Vous* (1944, The Sky is Yours), based on the real-life story of two ordinary Frenchmen who achieved a world flying record, was seen by audiences as a symbol of French aspirations towards resistance and liberation.

Other directors were able to follow their individual paths without much hindrance from the Nazis. Sacha Guitry, who was to be arrested and charged as a collaborator in 1944, celebrated his own acting talent in romantic vehicles he directed like *Le Destin Fabuleux de Desiree Clary* (1942), *Donne-moi Tes Yeux* (1943, Give Me Your Eyes) and *La Malibran* (1944). The prolific Abel Gance dedicated *La Vénus Aveugle* (1941, Blind Venus) to Marshal Pétain, and followed it with another work of characteristic romanticism, *Le Capitaine Fracasse* (1942). André Cayatte made as his first film an adaptation from Balzac, *La Fausse Maîtresse* (1942, False Mistress), and followed up with films of Zola's *Au Bonheur des Dames* (1943) and Maupassant's *Pierre et Jean* (1944).

Robert Bresson commenced a career of unparalleled, uncompromising creative independence with *Les Anges du Péché* (1943), giving cinema audiences their first encounter with his metaphysical and spiritual concerns and his severe, demanding style. It was followed by a no less austere modernization of Diderot's *Les Dames du Bois de Boulogne* (1945), scripted by Jean Cocteau and released on the day after the Liberation of Paris.

The most characteristic films from the Occupation period, however, are a handful of glittering flights into fantastic worlds or romantic periods – areas where neither Goebbels' nor Vichy's film censors could follow. The veteran Marcel L'Herbier made *La Nuit Fantastique* (1942, Fantastic Night), Jean Delannoy followed *Pontcarral, Colonel d'Empire* (1942, Pontcarral, Colonel of the Empire) – a historical drama that had clear contemporary references – with *L'Eternel Retour* (1943, Love

Eternal), a modern version of the legend of Tristan and Iseult. Both the latter and *Le Baron Fantôme* (1943, The Phantom Baron), a charming trifle directed by Serge de Poligny, were scripted by Cocteau. Claude Autant-Lara concentrated upon the decorative past in *Lettres d'Amour* (1942, Love Letters), *Le Mariage de Chiffon* and *Douce* (both 1943).

Two films above all stand as monuments of the French cinema under Nazi Occupation. Marcel Carné moved into a new phase of his career with *Les Visiteurs du Soir* (1942, The Devil's Own Envoy). Visually superb, this evocation of a medieval world, in which the Devil visits a castle at night but is unable to conquer true love, seemed to audiences a symbol of Hitler's final inability to crush the nation's spirit. *Les Enfants du Paradis* (1945, Children of Paradise) remains Carné's masterpiece and the most memorable work of the time. This fable of Love and Death, Good and Evil, is set in the Paris of the 1840s. The film's pictorial splendour and the complexity of its intertwining of life and theatre, has lost none of its attraction.

DAVID ROBINSON

Top left: Maria Casarès as a jilted mistress in Les Dames du Bois de Boulogne. *Top: disciples of the devil in* Les Visiteurs du Soir. *Above left:* Douce *starred Odette Joyeux as an ingénue. Above: in* Les Inconnus Dans la Maison Raimu *was cast as a barrister*

Occupational hazards

André Halimi, whose film *Chantons Sous l'Occupation* (1976) is a highly controversial survey of the French entertainment industry during the Occupation years, offers some reflections on the problems of making films under the Nazi yoke

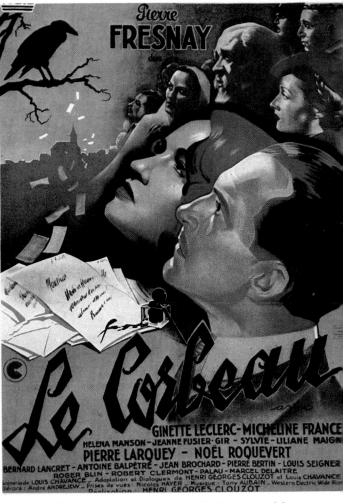

The cinema of the Occupation had certain characteristics. First, although it was subject to German censorship and, sometimes, German finance, it was dedicated to neither the glory of Nazism nor to the collaborationist policy of Marshal Pétain. It was not free in the full extent, but at least it was free to entertain. This was something in a period when the least show of resistance was ruthlessly suppressed.

On the other hand, Jews – whose influence as producers, scenarists or directors had been considerable – were all blacklisted or denied the right to exercise their profession. The critic Lucien Rebatet, in a text entitled *The Tribes of Cinema and Theatre*, included in a collected work *Jews in France*, declared:

'French films in their entirety, from production to laboratory work and down to the management of the smallest cinema, must inexorably and definitively be closed to all Jews irrespective of class and origin.'

Despite these odious, immoral laws restricting the creative opportunities of artists, a few Jewish writers managed to work under pseudonyms, though with constant anxiety and danger (and frequent changes of address).

Censorship operated at two levels: the Vichy-inspired Board of Control, consisting of representatives of the Ministries of the Family and the Interior, favoured films extolling open-air life, the family, sports and the like; the German censors naturally banned any projects of even the least controversial nature.

Two films were, however, to cause con-

Above right: in Le Corbeau, *Pierre Fresnay played a doctor victimized by a malicious letter-writer.*
Above: L'Eternel Retour, *accused of being pro-Nazi owing to the Aryan look of stars Madeleine Sologne and Jean Marais*

troversy that would haunt their makers in the years after the war. Henri-Georges Clouzot's *Le Corbeau* (1943) dealt with police informers and poison-pen letters in a French village during the Occupation. The publicity slogan for the film was 'Is the law strong enough to punish the writers of poison-pen letters?' The Germans gleefully used the film as anti-French propaganda at home and in other European countries. In France the advertising campaign was modified, as it was clearly in the Gestapo's interest to maintain an atmosphere of paranoia and mutual denunciation among the population. After the Liberation the military censorship body banned *Le Corbeau*, and both Clouzot and his writer Louis Chavance found themselves unable to work in the industry until 1947. Jean Delannoy's *L'Eternel Retour* (1943) – always considered, on account of its script, a Cocteau film – meanwhile aroused deep hostility in post-war Britain. The problem was that the English critics appeared to be unaware that the Tristan and Iseult story, on which the film was based, is an old Breton legend set down by the troubadours Béroul and Thomas: for them Tristan – particularly as played by Aryan-blond Jean Marais – could only evoke the Germanic, nationalist Richard Wagner (whose opera had celebrated the legend). The *Daily Express* branded *L'Eternel Retour* a Nazi film. Its critic wrote:

'There is a mouldy Gothic air, a death-cult mysticism about it. The hero is as blond and vacant as any one of a thousand SS paratroop prisoners I saw in Normandy two years ago. There is nothing French here, but much that is ridiculous and distasteful.'

The *Daily Mail* also spoke of the film's 'heavily Germanic spirit', while the *Daily Telegraph* commented:

'It is a pity M. Cocteau and his associate should have smeared it with marks of German ideology as blatant as so many swastikas.'

Was one obliged to work with the German 'Not at all,' replied Jean Delannoy recently. tried by every possible means to get out of and avoided problems from the start.'

Michel Duran, another scenarist wh worked during the Occupation admitted th he wrote for Continental, but added:

'I worked there by chance since it wasn't make propaganda films. My job was to wri dialogue, and I continued to do so.'

Asked why those who worked for Conti ental were condemned after the Liberation, replied:

'There was the usual settling of account Some who had not been able to work for were probably jealous of us. We never ma propaganda films at Continental.'

It was, then, a problem of conscience. The were several degrees of collaboration. Son actively collaborated with the German Others, without actually collaborating in the scripts or films, were willing to accept th finance of German companies like Continent Others abstained and preferred to rema silent. Some who did not make films, or ha problems in making them, took advantage the situation to denounce Freemasons, Jew Communists and Gaullists, hoping to step in their shoes.

Most artists worked away as if the Germa had never existed, accomplishing such maste pieces as *L'Assassin Habite au 21* (1942) a *Les Enfants du Paradis* (1945). The maste pieces will remain, long after the settling accounts and the Frenchmen who were co rupted by the Nazis have been forgotten history.   ANDRE HALIM

Hollywood goes to war

The war had been a tricky subject for American films, but after Pearl Harbor Hollywood opened up with all guns blazing

After the Japanese invaded North China in 1937, Roosevelt made a notorious speech in Chicago in which he called for a 'quarantine' of those nations who were the aggressors (or, in other words, an international embargo against Japan, Italy and Germany) lest the 'disease' of war infect the Western Hemisphere. The allegory instantly outraged a vast spectrum of opinion, both official and unofficial, and thereafter the President kept his anti-fascist feelings to himself. Hollywood, which invariably luxuriated in the warmth of the majority opinion, looked on approvingly as all the political pressures were exerted on the side of caution.

When war eventually broke out in Europe, Roosevelt began 27 months of what he later termed 'walking on eggs'. Congress was immediately called into special session to push through a clause that permitted foreign powers to buy arms from the United States, provided the munitions were paid for in cash and transported on non-American vessels. This was designed to help Great Britain who, unfortunately, had neither the money nor the ships to conform to such requirements.

This was a difficult period for Hollywood. The studio heads read Dr Gallup's poll, which announced that although 84 per cent of all Americans wanted an Allied victory, 96 per cent of them felt that their country should stay out of the conflict. The contradiction almost paralysed the film industry.

In the summer of 1939 all the studios postponed their spy, refugee or anti-Nazi stories. Warner Brothers shelved *Boycott* and *Underground Road* (eventually released in 1941 as *Underground*); Fox held up production on *I Married a Nazi* and Walter Wanger dithered over his dramatization of Vincent Sheean's *Personal History*, which finally saw the light of day as *Foreign Correspondent* (1940). It was felt that a sudden declaration of war or conclusion of peace would ruin the market value of the stories. The events of early September gave the green light to production although there remained the nagging fear, intensified in the wake of the Phoney War in the West, that peace would break out and cause the pictures to be shelved yet again.

Warner Brothers, who had made the one explicitly anti-Nazi film of the pre-war period (1939, *Confessions of a Nazi Spy*), were unofficially told by the government not to make any more such pictures. In April 1940 the news filtered back to Hollywood that several Polish exhibitors who had shown *Confessions of a Nazi Spy* had been hanged in the foyers of their own cinemas.

Warners were thus happy to mute their anti-Nazism by making such films as *The Sea Hawk* (1940) in which Errol Flynn as a swashbuckling privateer rouses a somnolent England to inflict a crushing defeat on the Spanish Armada – a simple parallel with the Luftwaffe and the Battle of Britain.

When the Phoney War of 1939 gave way to the blitzkrieg of 1940, the struggle in America between the isolationists and the supporters of intervention increased in bitterness. Charles Lindbergh, the aviator hero of the Twenties, called passionately for

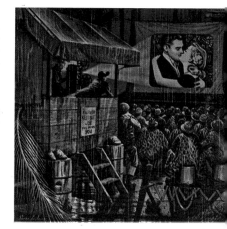

Left: support for Britain and her allies was evident in Hollywood before the USA joined the war. As well as this airborne adventure, 1941 also saw the release of A Yank in Libya, *a film with an equally contrived plot that had an American as hero of a British campaign. Above: cover from* The Saturday Evening Post *depicting the role of Hollywood in the war effort; films were shipped to all the fighting fronts and screened in improvised 'cinemas'. Below: British troops were also sustained on a diet of Hollywood cinema. Here ATC cadets attend a show of* I Wanted Wings, *an action movie about young flyers proving themselves in training*

To understand the way in which America rather tentatively entered World War II it is necessary to appreciate the horrifying spectacle of twelve million men unemployed in the bitter winter of 1932–33 and ten million as late as 1938. The shock to the American psyche was profound and would have long-term effects.

It was Herbert Hoover's contention that the Depression had originated in Europe and that the contagion had somehow been transported to America, possibly in the manner of Dracula coming ashore in Bremen. Since everybody was also aware that most of the European countries had defaulted on their war loans, the isolationist mood of the USA in general and Congress in particular remained essentially unbroken throughout the decade.

The isolationist senator Gerald P. Nye chaired the Congressional Committee which concluded that arms manufacturers, in an unholy alliance with the international bankers and businessmen, had been responsible for the entry of the United States into World War I. Consequently in August 1935 Congress passed the Pittman Neutrality Resolution prohibiting the export of munitions and the shipment of arms on American vessels to foreign belligerents.

America was hardly alone in its introspection. The assembled powers of the world were equally unwilling to act after Italy had invaded Abyssinia in 1935, when Hitler re-occupied the Rhineland in 1936, or when Italy and Germany both sent troops to fight with Franco in the Spanish Civil War.

total isolation and warned that American intervention would be a disaster in view of the invincibility of the German armed forces and the inevitability of German domination of Europe.

When President Roosevelt summarily dismissed his opinions, Lindbergh angrily resigned his Commission as a colonel in the Air Corps. Roosevelt ignored the petulant retaliation. In Charlotte, North Carolina, the residents of Lindbergh Drive renamed their street Avon Terrace.

Hitler's victories in the West were undoubtedly bad for Hollywood. In the Low Countries alone 1400 cinemas were immediately closed, representing a loss of $2.5 million in annual revenue to the American film companies. That, added to the losses previously sustained in parts of Scandinavia, Poland, Italy, Spain and the Balkans, meant that they had lost over a quarter of their annual revenue. By the end of 1940, the whole of Continental Europe was closed to US film imports apart from Sweden, Switzerland and Portugal.

Hollywood directly reflected the troubled anxieties of these confusing days. Chaplin's *The Great Dictator* (1940), though ostensibly a satire on Hitler, worked best when it was at its furthest remove from the political parallel and the film's mawkish descent into moral sentimentality in the closing sequence sat unhappily on the preceding farce.

MGM's *Escape* and *The Mortal Storm* (both 1940) doffed their caps in the direction of the horrors of Nazi Germany but they testified to Louis B. Mayer's insistence on avoiding overt condemnation of fascism for fear of political and economic reprisals.

Roosevelt's desperate anxiety to help Britain as she suffered the Blitz and the U-boat war in the Atlantic was tempered by the knowledge that he had decided in 1940 to run for President for an unprecedented third term of office. Only when he had defeated the Republican candidate, Wendell Willkie, could he afford to make sweeping demands of 'Lend-Lease', the Act of Congress which permitted complete and open aid to Britain, short of actual military involvement.

Roosevelt's increasing involvement in the war aided those Hollywood films which touched on the conflict, although most of them treated the issues lightly: there was the Bob Hope comedy *Caught in the Draft*, Abbot and Costello in *Buck Privates* and Tyrone Power and Betty Grable in *A Yank in the RAF* (all 1941). The more serious movies – Robert Taylor in *Flight Command* (1940), Errol Flynn in *Dive Bomber* (1941) and Ray Milland and William Holden in *I Wanted Wings* (1941) – were still far stronger on traditional Hollywood melodrama than ideological content.

It was, therefore, highly encouraging that the coveted place of 1941's top money-making picture was taken by the reflective Howard Hawks film *Sergeant York* (1941), which portrayed a World War I hero (an Oscar-winning performance by Gary Cooper) who overcame his pacifism when he realized that killing for one's country could be also construed as doing God's work. York's rapid elevation to the status of war hero seems to bear divine endorsement, and his decision to fight becomes, by implication, America's decision too.

The easiest way Hollywood could treat the war without offending the isolationists was to make films about Britain for whom sympathy was high in 1941. *That Hamilton Woman!* with Vivien Leigh and Laurence Olivier, was an instant success despite the limited budget on which Alexander Korda made it. The historical parallel of Britain triumphing over the threatened invasion of a foreign tyrant was particularly attractive to Winston Churchill, who took time off from conducting the war to cable Korda with 'helpful' suggestions.

Top right: Gary Cooper played Sergeant York, *the pacifist hick who takes up arms for his country in World War I. The film was a powerfully persuasive argument for American intervention in World War II. Right: it was hardly possible to forget Pearl Harbor, especially as Republic's first contribution to the war effort was released only two months after the event. Below: the film trade papers promoted new alliances (Britain, USA and USSR) through the old alliance between the film distributor and the exhibitors. Bottom: Bob Hope and Dave Willock in* Let's Face It. *Bob ended up a hero and so won a medal*

Despite the marked pro-Allied sentiments in the country at large, Congress still contained a small but significant group of die-hard isolationists. Hollywood was given conclusive evidence of this in October 1941, when Senators Nye and Clark introduced the Senate Resolution 152 which proposed the formation of a committee to investigate:

'. . . any propaganda disseminated by motion pictures . . . to influence public sentiment in the direction of participation by the United States in the . . . European war.'

Of the movies that had caused so much heart-searching in Hollywood during the previous two years, 17 were resurrected and paraded before a collection of unsympathetic politicians. Warner Brothers were condemned for making *Confessions of a Nazi Spy*, *Underground*, *Dive Bomber* and *Sergeant York*. MGM was accused of impure thoughts during the making of *Escape* and *The Mortal Storm* and Fox was keel-hauled for producing *I Married a Nazi* (eventually released as *The Man I Married* in 1941).

Hollywood resigned itself to facing the inevitable rebuke. Ironically it was saved by intervention of the Japanese air squadrons which, in the early morning of December 7, 1941, sank or badly damaged eight battleships and three light cruisers and killed 2400 Americans on the drowsy naval base at Pearl Harbor.

The Pearl Harbor disaster instantly resolved all doubts regarding America's entry into World War II. Hollywood 'enlisted' in a burst of patriotic enthusiasm and economic shrewdness. Paramount changed the title of their picture *Midnight Angel* to *Pacific Blackout* (1942) but it failed to rescue the truly awful nature of the film. David Selznick copyrighted the title *V for Victory* but never got round to using it and in March 1942 Republic Pictures emptied cinemas all over the country with a quickie entitled *Remember Pearl Harbor*.

More significant were the wartime regulations which the government imposed on Hollywood. In December 1941, only two days after Pearl Harbor, army officials moved into all the studios and commandeered the firearms used in any production which were then turned over to civil defence units. All studios were ordered onto a daylight shift of 8 am to 5 pm so that employees could get home before the blackout began and, as a result, night filming was temporarily halted. Most of these instinctive measures were only imposed in the early days of the war when it was still feared that the Japanese were preparing to invade along the vast, undefended coastline of California, but the moves were, at the same time, symptomatic of the government's new involvement in the affairs of the US film industry.

As early as May 1942, the trade paper *Variety* divulged that top-level discussions had resulted in a decision not to portray Hitler and Hirohito as personal symbols of German and Japanese evil. The American public was to be taught that the German and Japanese people were equally to blame for tolerating and cooperating with such leaders.

It was the US government that outlined for Hollywood the six basic patterns for pictures related to the war. The first was the issues of the war itself, into which category fell such diverse movies as *This Above All* (1942) and *Watch on the Rhine* (1943). The second was the nature of the enemy, as exemplified

Once America had entered the war, the Hollywood studios hurled everything into the fight – even star comics and crooners

---

in *Hitler's Children* (1943) and *This Land Is Mine* (1943). Third came the notion of 'United Nations and its Peoples' by which was meant everything from *Mrs Miniver* to *Mission to Moscow* (both 1942) and *Dragon Seed* (1944).

The fourth category focused on the pressing need for increased industrial production, and here the portrayals featured ordinary people engaged in factory work in films like *Wings for the Eagle* (1942) and *Swing Shift Maisie* (1943).

The last two categories were self-explanatory morale-boosting films about the home front and movies dealing with the fighting forces, a genre in which Hollywood had a long and successful record. Even films which were simply composed of military heroics invariably made obeisance to at least one of the categories mentioned.

No genre was excluded from the fight against fascism. The musical made a forceful entry with *Yankee Doodle Dandy* (1942), starring James Cagney as George M. Cohan, the author of the song 'Over There', the one universally acknowledged hit of World War I. Paramount's contribution included *Star Spangled Rhythm* (1943), which served as a passable excuse for a series of flag-waving and eyebrow-raising numbers. More bizarre than most war musicals was *When Johnny Comes Marching Home* (1943), which starred a heroic marine (played by the irrepressible Allan Jones from *A Night at the Opera*), the teenage wonder Gloria Jean and Phil Spitalny's all-girl orchestra.

Basil Rathbone returned to the attack as Sherlock

Holmes, chasing Nazi villains in contemporary London (where the head of the Nazi spy ring was, inevitably, Moriarty). Nazis also showed up in Maria Montez's temple (in *White Savage*, 1943) and even attacked a coonskin-clad Errol Flynn in the wilds of Canada in *Northern Pursuit* (1943). They also managed an appearance in the 1943 version of *The Desert Song*, where they signally failed to achieve either victory or a decent song.

The progress of the war itself seemed to follow the traditional narrative line laid down by Hollywood. America's initial experience was a series of desperate defeats. By New Year's Day 1942, the Japanese had made successful landings on Guam, Hong Kong, Borneo, Wake Island and the Philippines. General MacArthur was forced to retreat to the fatal Bataan peninsula from which he was removed while his troops died bravely and helplessly. The names of Bataan and Corregidor became synonymous with death and despair. On May 6, 1942, to prevent even more pointless slaughter, General Wainwright was compelled to surrender the rock with its 11,000 American defenders. It was the biggest capitulation in American history and its effect on the population was profound.

The American film industry had, therefore, to address itself to the unaccustomed atmosphere of military disaster. In an attempt to finish *Wake Island* (1942) on a rousing note, Paramount took the costly step of halting production just before shooting was due to take place on the closing sequences. In this way they hoped that the real military events would permit them a happy ending. They didn't. MGM's *Bataan* (1943) closes with the massacre of the American patrol whose fortunes we have been following, although the end caption points out that from such sacrifices sprang the victory of the Battle of Midway.

Victories in North Africa and Italy in 1943 were followed the next year by the successful invasion of France and, as military events foreshadowed ultimate victory, Hollywood's major problem became how to avoid making war movies which would be immediately outdated if the Germans surrendered before the editing was completed.

In the event it did not really matter. 1946 proved to be the most successful year in the history of the film industry. If the war had driven people into the cinemas to escape, peace sent them there to celebrate. All the major studios did their bit for the war effort, supplying propaganda and escapism in generous helpings. Spectacular profits were their reward. These were indeed the golden years of Hollywood. It was a time, so it was said, when even good pictures made money.   COLIN SHINDLER

Above: the theme and closing hymn of Mrs Miniver *was 'There'll always be an England', but there was no mistaking MGM's all-purpose 'English' mansion as Walter Pidgeon and Greer Garson's home. Below: the last defender in* Bataan. *Bottom: James Cagney helps the RAF in* Captains of the Clouds *(1942)*

On the Battlefront

Hollywood's finest war films celebrated the courage, loyalty and good humour of the ordinary fighting man, forced to pay the ultimate price of freedom

When the Japanese attack on Pearl Harbor, on December 7, 1941, finally brought the walls of American isolationism tumbling down, Hollywood mobilized for war virtually without breaking step. Encouraged and endorsed by Roosevelt's government, it proceeded to glorify the waging of war in the same way that it had happily exalted the busting of crime syndicates or celebrated the winning of the West. Hollywood's total response to the US government's exhortations and practical cooperation was spectacular: out of approximately 1700 features produced between 1942 and 1945 over 500 were war films of one kind or another.

The qualitative result, however, was somewhat less satisfying. The avowed aims of the American war film were to satisfy the public demand for information about the war, to explain its purposes and why sacrifice was sometimes necessary, and to raise home-front morale by showing, in a positive light, the husbands and sons of America in action. The problem of achieving these aims was that, in contrast to Britain and the rest of Europe, the USA was far removed from the actual theatres of conflict. This fact, combined with the official

guidelines as to what could be shown on the screen, ensured that what the public mostly got were films which (as Leif Furhammar and Folke Isaksson wrote in *Politics and Film*):

'. . . sprang less from reality than from currently popular preconceptions which, in turn, they served to reinforce. War was an exciting adventure; politics a superior form of romance; morality a matter of morale. In this treatment, death was painless, decorative and even, ultimately, a blessing.'

As the war progressed, however, the glamour and escapism began to be replaced by greater honesty and realism. Of all the types of war films that were made, perhaps those which best reflected this progression were the ones which attempted to convey the ordeal of combat, the grim necessity of fighting a 'just' war, the banality of death as well as heroism in

Above: Bataan*'s study of sacrificial heroism helped Americans come to terms with initial defeat in the Philippines. Right: Cary Grant captains the crew of the submarine that sails into the jaws of death in* Destination Tokyo. *Below: a band of heroes from all walks of life sheltered together in* Guadalcanal Diary

battle, and the one authentic legacy of the soldier – comradeship-in-arms.

The first significant attempt to treat these themes was John Farrow's *Wake Island* (1942), a stirring, semi-fictional account of a doomed, two-week defensive action in the Pacific by a handful of marines in the days immediately following Pearl Harbor.

Although one critic justifiably called *Wake Island* 'a failure in realism', pointing to its over-the-top heroics and sentimentality (represented most jarringly by the presence of a dog-mascot and its litter of puppies), it nevertheless laid the ground rules for all the subsequent successful combat pictures: the immediacy of its true-life theme and the greater confidence in its subject-matter engendered by the USA now having its own exclusive theatre of war; the fact that (because of a War Production Board ban on expensive studio sets) it was made on location and in cooperation with the US Marine Corps; and its concentration on the fighting man, which, though stressing individual characteristics, at the same time implied a oneness against the enemy and a coming-together of the many ethnic strains of American society in a common struggle.

Similar to *Wake Island* in both atmosphere and technique was Lewis Seiler's *Guadalcanal*

Diary (1943), which came close to enacting the spirit of one of the Pacific's bloodiest campaigns and the USA's first major victory. The cross-section of American social types acting in harness without losing their individuality included, this time, a saintly, courageous chaplain (played by Preston Foster).

An interesting sidelight on this and similar films about the Pacific was the image of the Japanese soldier as well-dressed, well-equipped, strong and formidably efficient, whereas later accounts (as in James Jones' *The Thin Red Line*) tell us that they were ragged, half-starved and under-resourced, but totally dedicated.

Another popular film area of operations for American film-makers was the Philippines. Among the most acclaimed films concerned with this theatre of the war was Tay Garnett's

Bataan (1943), an emotive rendering of a supposedly true account of how 13 men fought a desperate, sacrificial rearguard action to aid the withdrawal of General MacArthur's forces.

The Pacific war film also took to the air, most effectively perhaps in Howard Hawks' $3 million epic Air Force (1943), the story of a Boeing-17 Flying Fortress and its crew battling their way across the Pacific from Pearl Harbor to an Australian beach, culled by writer Dudley Nichols from factual records made available by General H. H. Arnold of the US Army Air Force. General Arnold's instruction was to tell 'how the Japs laced hell out of us at first; then tell how we fought back. Tell the whole story with its bitterness and sadness and heroism.' Hawks responded with a characteristic paeon to virility and professionalism, and with a heavy concentration on triumphant action set pieces culminating in a re-creation of the Coral Sea naval battle against the Japanese fleet.

Hollywood took particular inspiration from the Doolittle raid, the first bombing attack on Japan which occurred 131 days after Pearl Harbor. Delmer Daves opened the proceedings with his feature debut Destination Tokyo (1943), a stirring account of the submarine Copperfin's daring mission to penetrate Tokyo Bay to help set up the raid. The picture was convincing enough to be used later as a navy instructional film. Lewis Milestone followed up with The Purple Heart (1944), an indictment of Japanese atrocities against American airmen who had fallen into their hands. But most notable of all the Doolittle films was Mervyn LeRoy's Thirty Seconds Over Tokyo (1944), supervised by the leader of the raid himself, Major Ted Lawson, and chronicling all the events from preparation and attack to the final escape of the crew aided by Chinese patriots.

A recurrent problem for American war films was their impact on the British public, who periodically complained of both their quantity and their content. The film most attacked on these grounds was Raoul Walsh's Objective, Burma! (1945), the film in which, as several reviewers later described it, Errol Flynn cap-

tured Burma single-handed. Apart from one or two passing references, the film managed to omit any mention of Allied involvement in the Burma campaign, least of all the British 14th Army, made the Burmese jungle look like a national park, and so offended the British public and military personnel alike that Warner Brothers were forced to remove it from English screens. In retrospect, Warners' principal crime seems to have been one of gross mistiming: it was simply the wrong moment to present such a film to a Britain exhausted by six years of all-too-realistic warfare.

More significantly, America's three war masterpieces of 1945 received hardly any attention at all in the UK. These were the heady days of victory and the British had had enough of war particularly in films which took such a grim, melancholy view of the fighting man. John Ford's first war feature, They Were Expendable (1945), dealt with the agonized exploits of Commander John D. Bulkeley's (Brickley in the film) small squadron of PT boats in the Philippine withdrawal, coupled with implied criticism of the pre-war military leadership. Despite an apathetic reaction on both sides of the Atlantic, it has survived as a compellingly unglamorous statement of what the British film director Lindsay Anderson has described as 'the time-honoured conceptions of duty, courage and comradeship in arms', and it is now acknowledged as one of the great achievements of American wartime cinema.

Perhaps the two finest depictions of the American infantryman were The Story of GI Joe and A Walk in the Sun (both 1945). The Story of GI Joe (dir. William Wellman) was universally praised but little seen. A hymn of praise to the American soldiers who battled their way from

North Africa to Rome, via Sicily, Southern Italy and Cassino, the film was based on the writings of war correspondent Ernie Pyle (Burgess Meredith) who was later killed at Iwo Jima. There were no mock heroics, only the hunger, misery, fear, boredom and weariness of the foot-soldiers amidst a confusing nightmare of military manoeuvres. The film also dared to show the bodies of dead infantrymen in a low-key finale which was at odds with the euphoria of the time and would account for the wariness with which it was received.

For A Walk in the Sun (dir. Lewis Milestone) scriptwriter Robert Rossen took the screenplay almost verbatim from Harry Brown's original novel and conveyed fully the book's verbal cadences and almost folkloric style. The film portrays the confused progress of a single platoon during one morning between landing at Salerno and taking an objective six miles away. This was the ultimate refinement of the group motif, achieved by acute observation of individual characteristics and states of mind, from the frenetic collapse of a shell-shocked sergeant (Herbert Rudley) to the habit of another soldier (John Ireland) of composing letters home in his head as an ironic commentary on the action. In keeping with the predominant vein of Hollywood's final, masterly chronicles of the war period, the film was, as noted by the critic Penelope Houston, 'concerned with the immediate realities of a situation rather than its deeper implications.' The film appeared to accept the fact of war rather than rebel against it.

Thus the American combat film attained maturity and excellence at the very moment that the genre had suddenly become unfashionable, and the masterpieces of the war remained unsung until a later time of rediscovery and reappraisal.   CLYDE JEAVONS

Top: American airmen get help from British soldiers in Air Force. *Above right: the restrained performances of John Wayne and Robert Montgomery (centre) helped to make* They Were Expendable *one of Hollywood's finest war films. Right: George Tyne and Richard Conte in* A Walk in the Sun

21

Howard Hawks rediscovered

Hawks was a much-neglected director until the French critics of the Fifties saluted his personal style of film-making and established him as one of Hollywood's great individual talents

Howard Hawks has created some of the most memorable moments in the history of the American cinema. The problem, however, is how do these moments hang together? Is there a shaping intelligence behind them, or are they merely the accidental benefits of Hollywood movie-making? Until recently the consensus of opinion favoured the latter view. Richard Griffith's remark in 1948, in *The Film Till Now*, that Hawks is 'a very good all-rounder', is representative of the attention paid to Hawks before the French film journal *Cahiers du Cinéma* championed him as *the* American *auteur*. And even after the first rumblings of the *politique des auteurs* (the theory of authorship, by which the creative and artistic credit for a film is attributed to its director) in the mid-

Above: Hawks, seated by the cameraman, directs Gary Cooper in Sergeant York *(1941), and (left) discusses the script of* Gentlemen Prefer Blondes *(1953) with Marilyn Monroe. He was born in Goshen, Indiana, in 1896, and after graduating in engineering from Cornell University in 1917 served in the Army Air Corps during World War I. He then worked as an aircraft builder and pilot and as a racing driver before entering movies in 1922. Although Hawks continued to write, direct and produce films until 1970, flying and driving remained his great passion – revealed in such pictures as* The Air Circus *(1928),* The Crowd Roars *(1931) and* Red Line 7000 *(1965). He died in 1977 – partly from blood poisoning contracted from injuries sustained motorcycling when he was 78 years old*

Fifties, in 1959 *Sight and Sound*, the leading organ of British film culture, had no qualms about not reviewing *Rio Bravo*, a film now acknowledged as one of the great Westerns.

Prior to the *auteur* theory, the mark of a film artist in the American cinema could be found in his choice of subject-matter, in his obvious artistic aspirations, or in his personal visual style. Clearly, by these criteria, Hawks was an unambitious director. In 53 years as a film-maker he was responsible for no major cinematic innovations and was happy to produce pictures that in their sober adherence to the conventions of Hollywood movie-making lack the personal touch of a Hitchcock or the artistry of a Chaplin. Certainly Hawks was a prolific genre director: *Scarface* (1931) is a gangster film; *Gentlemen Prefer Blondes* (1953), a musical; *Land of the Pharoahs* (1955), a biblical epic; *The Dawn Patrol* (1930) and *Air Force* (1943) are war films; *To Have and Have Not* (1944) and *The Big Sleep* (1946), thrillers; *Red River* (1948) and *Rio Bravo* (1959), Westerns; *Bringing Up Baby* (1938) and *Monkey Business* (1952), comedies; and *Only Angels Have Wings* (1939) and *Hatari!* (1962) are just two of his many adventure films.

The breadth of Hawks' films and their consistent commitment to action rather than reflection blinded early critics to the clear pattern of repetition and variation that binds the films together. It was precisely the attempt to trace such a pattern in such a diversity of films directed (and, in most cases, produced) by one man that led 'auteurist' critics to propose Hawks' work as the test case of their theories, and revealed that behind the mask of Hollywood there lurked artists.

Turning from the ostensible subject-matter of Hawks' films then, it is possible to discern a clear pattern of themes running through them: the group, male friendships, the nature of professionalism, the threats women pose men. Recurring motifs include the passing and lighting of cigarettes for friends, communal sing-songs, and bizarre sexual role-reversals.

Accordingly, rather than relating *Only Angels Have Wings* to the spate of aviator movies that appeared in the Thirties, *To Have and Have Not* to Curtiz's *Casablanca* (1942), and *Rio Bravo* to the development of the Western, it is more useful to relate these Hawks films to each other, or even, as Robin Wood has suggested in his book *Howard Hawks*, to regard them as a loose trilogy in which notions of heroism and self-respect are interrogated.

Band of angels

Only Angels Have Wings is concerned with the problems of a group of mail plane flyers. From the start the group is hermetically sealed off from the outside world by storms, giant condors, mountains and highly dangerous landing-strips – and the action takes place almost entirely in the saloon-cum-office run by Dutchie (Sig Ruman). Here the group is self-sufficient with its members demanding and acknowledging support for each other's actions, as instanced in the talking down of pilots in bad weather, and details like Kid (Thomas Mitchell) passing Geoff (Cary Grant) a cigarette even before Geoff searches for one. Geoff is the leader of the group, who flies when the weather is too bad to send up his comrades.

Into the group comes Bonnie (Jean Arthur), down on her luck but asking for help from no-one. When one of the flyers, Joe (Noah Beery Jr), attempts a landing in bad weather – against Geoff's advice – to keep a dinner date with her, he crashes and is killed. His feelings for a woman have affected his judgment, caused him to behave irresponsibly and let his

Above right: Sergeant York, *based on the diary of a pacifist who eventually joined the army and became America's greatest hero of World War I. Released shortly before America joined World War II, it made a powerful call to arms. Below and below right: Hawks' films are full of sing-songs – as in* Only Angels Have Wings *with Jean Arthur and Cary Grant – and the lighting of cigarettes – as in* To Have and Have Not *with Humphrey Bogart and Lauren Bacall – and similar gestures of friendship*

comrades down by breaching the professional code that binds the flyers together and makes it possible to keep the mail-run going in the face of overwhelming odds. 'Who's Joe?' says Geoff when Bonnie berates him for his callousness in eating the steak that had been prepared for the man who has just died, and goes on to sum Joe up with the words, 'He just wasn't good enough'. The sequence finally ends, however, with the celebratory (and defiant) singing by Geoff and Bonnie of 'The Peanut Vendor', a communal act which has the double function of initiating her into the group as a professional in her own right (she is a singer) and confirming her acceptance of the rules of the game of Hawks' group of flyers.

As the story develops, and Bonnie's love for Geoff deepens, it becomes evident that although suspicious of emotional entanglements – he has been fooled once before – he is, in fact, 'in love' with Kid, his assistant, as his breakdown after Kid's death testifies. At this point the interlocking web of relationships becomes even more complex. Kid's death is, on the one hand, self-inflicted: his eyesight is failing and he flies against Geoff's instructions; but as a grounded flyer he has only a living death to look forward to. At the same time his death is caused by his taking on an important job meant for a flyer whose abilities he distrusts. The flyer, Bat McPherson (Richard Barthelmess), once baled out of a plane leaving a friend of Kid's to die, and has since determined to win back his self-respect by taking on the most hazardous flights possible. This wash of conflicting emotions and loyalties that Hawks

sees as life is only held in check by the sense of what Robin Wood calls 'the constant shadow of death', which in turn demands responsible behaviour and self-respect if the group, or the individual, is to survive.

Loners together

The pattern of relationships in *To Have and Have Not* is similar – but with significant differences. In *Only Angels Have Wings* the group comprises a leader, his friend, the failed professional who is seeking redemption, and an intruder; in *To Have and Have Not* there is the loner Harry Morgan (Humphrey Bogart), Eddie (Walter Brennan) – 'who used to be good' – as a drunken version of Kid, and Slim (Lauren Bacall) as a far more assertive and aggressive Bonnie figure. The equivalent of the McPherson character is Paul de Bursac (Walter Molnar), a man who needs physical assistance from Morgan rather than moral support. And in contrast to Geoff in *Only Angels Have Wings*, who is desperately trying to secure a mail-run contract for Dutchie, Morgan in *To Have and Have Not* is working only for himself. Despite the existence of a group, the characters in *To Have and Have Not* are much more independent and self-motivated than in the earlier film.

Although the bar run by Crickett (Hoagy Carmichael) in *To Have and Have Not* has a communal function in a similar fashion to Dutchie's, the dramatic thrust of the film is provided by the Morgan–Slim relationship. Bogart and Bacall fell in love while making *To Have and Have Not* and their scenes reflect it –

KATHARINE HEPBURN CARY GRANT in A HOWARD HAWKS PRODUCTION Bringing Up Baby

Cary Grant (above), and Elsa Martinelli in Hatari! *(below), learn what it is like to be hunted. Bottom: Cowpunchers Noah Beery Jr, Walter Brennan and Montgomery Clift enjoy a game of cards in* Red River

the world and it's certain we'll take nothing out,' recites Tom Dunson (John Wayne) dryly over a grave in *Red River*. The emotional, romantic reactions of the characters in the adventure films are similarly muted; the women go through elaborate rituals of courtship (usually confiding their love not to the loved one but to his friend) in the course of which they prove themselves as tough as men.

The heroes of the adventure films are emotionally repressed and a current of homosexuality runs beneath the male friendships – in *A Girl in Every Port* (1928) which Hawks himself has described as 'a love story between two men', and erupting closest to the surface in *The Big Sky* (1952).

In the comedies the hero is perpetually humiliated, as often as not by a domineering woman. This humiliation takes two forms: in the regression to childhood – in *Monkey Business* where Barnaby (Cary Grant) and Edwina Fulton (Ginger Rogers) take a rejuvenating drug that turns them – emotionally – back into children, and in the reversal of normal sexual roles, the extreme case being *I Was a Male War Bride* (1949) in which Grant is, for most of the picture, dressed as a woman.

Hunt the man down

In the classic Hawks comedy, *Bringing Up Baby*, the woman is the hunter. Susan (Katharine Hepburn) sees David Huxley (Cary Grant), falls in love with him, pursues him and against all odds – he is engaged to be married – catches him. *Bringing Up Baby* draws a parallel with Hawks' adventure films, extended by the big-game-hunting metaphor that runs through it: Baby (Susan's pet leopard) and a wild leopard are both let loose and hunted during the course of the film. The timid David is constantly humiliated by Susan; at one point he has to dress in a monstrously feminine negligée in order to escape – and is then confronted by a decidedly masculine aunt. But forced to keep company with Susan, he is liberated from the stultifying world of zoological research. Fittingly, the film ends with Susan climbing up the huge scaffolding surrounding the dinosaur skeleton he is completing (in another comic inversion of the big-game-hunting adventure film David 'hunts' dead animals) and bringing down the whole edifice crashing to the floor – and with it David's past dull life.

especially the one where Slim instructs Morgan to whistle when he wants her ('You just put your lips together and blow') and then exits to the sound of his whistle of surprise. They give the movie a depth of emotion that is missing from the bite-on-the-bullet stoicism of *Only Angels Have Wings*.

In *Rio Bravo* Hawks heightened emotions by having a hero who is completely sexually embarrassed. Previously Hawks had restricted the sexual humiliation theme to the string of crazy comedies he made alongside his adventure films. *Rio Bravo*, though, is a bringing together of comedy and adventure in Hawks' work, a summation of two traditions his films had established.

In his adventure films, the hero is master of all he surveys; in the comedies he is the victim, both of society and of women – who only have marginal roles in the adventure films. The adventure films occupy a world, far from society's grasp, of hunters, fishermen, aviators and so on, who lead their lives struggling against natural hazards; survival depends on every member of the group being 'good enough', and they celebrate that survival through the ritual of sing-songs. Their reaction to death is to pass over the event as quickly as possible. 'We brought nothing into

Filmography
1917 The Little Princess (some scenes only, uncredited). **'23** Quicksands (sc. only). **'24** Tiger Love (sc. only). **'25** The Dressmaker From Paris (sc. only). **'26** The Road to Glory; Fig Leaves (+prod); Honesty – the Best Policy (sc. only). **'27** The Cradle Snatchers; Paid to Love (+prod); Underworld (add. sc. only, uncredited). **'28** A Girl in Every Port (+prod); Fazil (both sound and silent versions); The Air Circus (silent scenes only). **'29** Trent's Last Case (both sound and silent versions; unreleased in USA). **'30** The Dawn Patrol (+co-sc) (reissued as Flight Commander). **'31** Scarface/Scarface, the Shame of a Nation (+co-prod); The Crowd Roars; Tiger Shark; Red Dust (add. sc. only, uncredited). **'33** Today We Live (+prod). **'34** Viva Villa! (some scenes, uncredited; +add. sc, uncredited); Twentieth Century (+prod). **'35** Barbary Coast; Ceiling Zero (+co-prod). **'36** Sutter's Gold (add. sc. only, uncredited); The Road to Glory (USA retitling for TV: Wooden Crosses/Zero Hour); Come and Get It (co-dir). **'37** Captains Courageous (add. sc.

Rio Bravo, which on the surface is a Western adventure film, has been described by Hawks himself as a comedy, but it is by no means a high farce in the *Bringing Up Baby* tradition. Nevertheless, it is inflected at every stage by the tone of the comedies. For example, there is a strong element of parody, most explicit in Feathers' (Angie Dickinson) sophisticated education of Chance (John Wayne) through a process of sexual humiliation and taunting: thus the scene when she sees a pair of scarlet bloomers being held against him and declaims, 'Those things have great possibilities Sheriff, but not on you'.

Chance meeting

Though the characters of *Rio Bravo* can be traced back to the seminal roles of *Only Angels Have Wings* – Chance to Geoff, Stumpy (Walter Brennan) to Kid, Dude (Dean Martin) to McPherson and Feathers to Bonnie – the group is no longer a natural formation. It gathers around Chance but for reasons of loyalty rather than professionalism, and at one point, in the communal sing-song that takes place, Chance is even excluded, becoming merely an observer. More significantly, the fear of old age and failing powers, introduced with Kid in *Only Angels Have Wings*, is placed much closer to the centre of *Rio Bravo* in the form of Stumpy, Chance's anarchic, nagging deputy sheriff who performs the tasks of a wife, cleaning and feeding the inhabitants of the jail as they wait for attack from outside. Colorado (Rick Nelson), the young gunman, introduces a theme of youth-versus-age that dominates later Hawks films, notably *El Dorado* (1967) and *Rio Lobo* (1970), which with *Rio Bravo* make up another loose trilogy.

In *Rio Bravo* the squabbling group eventually grows into a kind of 'family' in which the stoical rules of conduct common to previous Hawksian groups are replaced by something closer to family ties. The final shoot-out – photographed like a firework display – becomes a celebration of new-found unity.

In *El Dorado* Hawks goes further, emphasizing the superiority of filial and family loyalties to any professional ethic. But if in *Rio Bravo* Chance is 'not good enough' to overcome his enemies on his own, in *El Dorado* Cole Thornton (Wayne again) isn't 'good enough' even with help. He only kills the professional gunman who opposes him (and who had ironically

acknowledged him with the courtesy that one professional pays another) by trickery. Thornton is even denied the moral authority that Chance possesses in *Rio Bravo*. When he brings the dead body of their son to the MacDonalds – the boy committed suicide when he failed to kill Thornton – there is no shot of Thornton speaking. We simply hear him accepting responsibility for the boy's death. Returning home, he is ambushed and wounded by Maudie (Charlene Holt), the dead boy's sister; her bullet represents the pangs of conscience Thornton has already given voice to, and the paralysis it causes him is an indication of his age. In contrast to Maudie and Mississippi (James Caan) who both exact personal revenge on their enemies, Thornton and the drunken sheriff, J.P. Harrah (Robert Mitchum), have their roots in Kid in *Only Angels Have Wings*. Logically, like Kid, they should have 'grounded' themselves; instead they wearily and farcically – as in the intensely physical (and comic) curing of Harrah's drunkenness with a stomach-turning antidote, compared with the spiritual curing of Dude's in *Rio Bravo* – wend their way through the action.

In *Rio Lobo*, the age of the Wayne character, Colonel McNally, is once again central to the film, though not in the exploitative fashion of

John Wayne leads his men into action in Rio Lobo *(above) and* El Dorado *(below)*

Henry Hathaway's *True Grit* (1969). Hawks gives his 'baby whale' (the fat, aged army officer played by Wayne) the dignity of a revenge quest, as McNally finally capitulates to filial feelings for the son he never had. But Hawks also undercuts this dignity with broad farce in the activities of the group, a group held together purely by the desire for several private revenges and divided equally carefully into young and old characters. The final break from the world of *Only Angels Have Wings*, however, is signalled by the surprisingly elegant, occasionally almost abstract, photography.

Hawks' world is a limited one, lacking, say, the richness and complexity of John Ford's. But his straightforward stories about the stresses and joys of men and women working together in groups, about the nature of friendship, love and professionalism, are stamped with the consistency and highly individual authorship of a great film artist. Howard Hawks has created a body of work that in its laconic optimism is as majestic as the towering mountains Geoff Carter and his foolhardy band of pilots must fly over in the deliciously titled *Only Angels Have Wings*.   PHIL HARDY

only, uncredited). '38 Bringing Up Baby (+prod); Test Pilot (add. sc. only, uncredited). '39 Gunga Din (add. sc. only, uncredited); Only Angels Have Wings (+prod); Gone With the Wind (add. sc. only, uncredited). '40 His Girl Friday (+prod). '41 Sergeant York; Ball of Fire. '43 The Outlaw (some scenes only, uncredited); Air Force (+co-prod); Corvette K-225 (add. sc. uncredited;+prod;+sup). '44 To Have and Have Not (+prod). '46 The Big Sleep (+prod). '48 Red River (+prod); A Song Is Born (USA retitling for TV: That's Life). '49 I Was a Male War Bride (GB: You Can't Sleep Here). '51 The Thing (co-sc;+sup;+cast dir) (GB: The Thing From Another World). '52 The Big Sky (+prod); O. Henry's Full House *ep* The Ransom of the Red Chief (GB: Full House); Monkey Business. '53 Gentlemen Prefer Blondes. '55 Land of the Pharoahs (+prod). '59 Rio Bravo (+prod). '62 Hatari! (+prod). '64 Man's Favorite Sport (+prod). '65 Red Line 7000 (+co-sc;+prod). '67 El Dorado (+prod). '70 Rio Lobo (+prod).

Ingrid Bergman
As time goes by

Discovered in Sweden in the early Thirties, Ingrid Bergman rose to the rank of international star in the Forties, proving herself a brilliant partner to Bogart, Cooper, Grant and Tracy. For many years the seductions of stardom left her unmoved and she never allowed herself to become stereotyped. Today, some fifty years on, and after a series of uneven films, she still commands respect and admiration throughout the industry

Far left: portrait of Bergman in 1942. Above left: her performance in På Solsidan *attracted the interest of the American press. Above: star of Selznick's* Intermezzo, *a virtual copy of the original Swedish film. Below: although Bergman's Broadway portrayal of Joan was a triumph, her screen role in* Joan of Arc *was not well received*

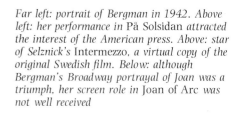

Filmography

1935 Munkbrogreven; Bränningar (USA: The Surf); Swedenhielms; Valborgsmässoafton. **'36** På Solsidan; Intermezzo. **'38** Dollar; Die 4 Gesellen (GER); En Kvinne Ansikte. **'39** En Enda Natt; Intermezzo: a Love Story (USA) (GB: Escape to Happiness). **'40** Juniatten. *All remaining films USA unless specified:* **'41** Adam Had Four Sons; Rage in Heaven; Dr Jekyll and Mr Hyde. **'42** Casablanca. **'43** Swedes in America (short) (GB: Ingrid Bergman Answers); For Whom the Bell Tolls; Saratoga Trunk. **'44** Gaslight (GB: The Murder in Thornton Square). **'45** The Bells of St Mary's; Spellbound. **'46** Notorious; The American Greed (short) (GB: American Brotherhood Week). **'48** Arch of Triumph; Joan of Arc. **'49** Under Capricorn (GB). **'50** Stromboli, Terra di Dio (IT) (USA: God's Land). **'51** Europa '51 (IT) (USA: The Greatest Love). **'53** Siamo Donne *ep* Il Pollo (IT) (USA: Five Women/of Life and Love *ep* Ingrid Bergman; GB: We Women/We, the Women). **'54** Viaggio in Italia (IT-FR) (USA: Strangers; GB: The Lonely Woman/Journey to Italy); Giovanna d'Arco al Rogo (IT-FR); Angst (GER-FR) (GB: Fear). **'56** Elena et les Hommes (FR-IT) (USA: Paris Does Strange Things; GB: The Night Does Strange Things); Anastasia (GB). **'58** Indiscreet (GB); The Inn of the Sixth Happiness (GB). **'59** The Camp (narr. only) (short). **'61** Goodbye Again (USA-FR). **'64** Der Besuch (GER-FR-IT) (USA: The Visit); The Yellow Rolls-Royce (GB); Stimulantia *ep* Smycket (SW). **'69** Cactus Flower. **'70** A Walk in the Spring Rain; Henri Langlois/Langlois (guest) (doc) (FR). **'73** From the Mixed-Up Files of Mrs Basil E. Frankweiler (GB: The Hideaways). **'74** Murder on the Orient Express (GB). **'76** A Matter of Time (USA-IT). **'78** Herbstsonate (GER) (USA: Autumn Sonata).

Born in Stockholm, Sweden, on August 29, 1915, Ingrid Bergman was brought up by her elderly uncle after the death of her parents, and at 17 joined Stockholm's Royal School of Dramatic Art where she was soon being chosen for the major roles. In 1933, she signed a contract with the Svenskfilmindustri and made her first screen appearance in *Munkbrogreven* (1935, The Count of the Monk's Bridge). By her fifth film, *På Solsidan* (1936, On the Sunny Side), she had become a star in Sweden. On this and several other occasions she worked under the direction of Gustaf Molander, who managed to bring out the full range of her talents.

Then, in 1939, David O. Selznick, to whom her growing reputation had been pointed out, brought her to Hollywood and cast her in the remake of *Intermezzo: a Love Story*, (she had already starred in the Swedish version) alongside Leslie Howard. Selznick, a great discoverer and modeller of actresses, was aware of the problems inherent in trying to 'sell' foreign stars to the American public, and astutely decided to place his bets on a fresh, natural and healthy image, relying on, in *Intermezzo*, the sort of story that he knew the public would accept. The gamble paid off and Bergman became an instant success in Hollywood.

However, after only a couple more roles as a pure and loyal woman, Bergman rebelled. Conscious of her potential, she refused to be typecast and fought for the part of Ivy, the barmaid of easy virtue, in Victor Fleming's *Dr Jekyll and Mr Hyde* (1941).

This complete role-change, however, served only to 'enrich' her screen image. Many of the subsequent Bergman heroines were two-faced and their moral irresolution made them fascinating to watch. This was true of *Saratoga Trunk* (1943), in which she played an illegitimate Creole adventuress in engaging manner, *Notorious* (1946), in which she was a lady of loose morals but admirable intentions, and *Under Capricorn* (1949), in which, while eloping, she murdered her brother who was following her. These films represent the 'black' aspect of her Hollywood character. The heroines are thrown into a booby-trapped, nightmarish world and their physical or mental degradation is all the more suggestive and convincing because the appearance of the actress seems to contradict it.

On the other hand *For Whom the Bell Tolls* (1943), *Spellbound*, *The Bells of St Mary's* (both 1945) and *Joan of Arc* (1948) – all roles in which she was taking a stand – summarize the positive aspect of the Bergman character. They highlight her idealism, her sincerity and altruism, all of which Selznick had been sensitive to. And yet the ambiguous Bergman characters are preferable to her rather 'toneless' and angelic presentations. In *Casablanca* (1942), the pull of two men, Rick Blaine (Humphrey Bogart) and Victor Laszlo (Paul Henreid), unearths a shaky division of loyalties – on the one hand there is her husband and on the other her commitment to the past.

In spite of the diversity of the studios she worked for and the types of characters she played, Bergman's American career retained a certain unity through the influence of the ever-present Selznick, whose contradictory tastes enabled him to create icy neurotics, fading madonnas and nymphomaniacs. After the break with Selznick in 1946 something was definitely lost from Bergman's style, and nothing new appeared to take its place.

The man who had finally persuaded her to make the break from Selznick was Peter Lindstrom, a Swedish dentist to whom Bergman had been married since the beginning of her career. His intelligent advice in Sweden became sadly misguided in Hollywood. *Arch of Triumph* (1948) sustained considerable losses. In the same year, Bergman saw Roberto Rossellini's *Roma, Città Aperta* (*Rome, Open City*) and, greatly impressed, wrote to him

offering her services.

Curiously, films of the Rossellini period in the Fifties, in spite of some complex narratives, were not so much a denial of the 'Bergman myth' of virginal purity than a change in its essential qualities. *Stromboli* (1950, *God's Land*), was slightly exceptional in that it still partly stemmed from Rossellini's earlier neo-realistic style. Bergman played an unhappy wife escaping from the island of the title. However, all her later films in Italy formed a link with her earlier American films. The temptations of sainthood in *Europa '51* (1951, *The Greatest Love*) are reminiscent of the religious inspiration of *The Bells of St Mary's* and *Joan of Arc*; and the marital hell in *Stromboli* harks back to the tormented wife in *Gaslight* (1944, *The Murder in Thornton Square*) – the film for which she won her first Academy Award, playing a woman blindly in love with a contemptible adventurer. But the more naturalistic approach of Rossellini was not compatible with either actress or theme. In 1950 Bergman finally divorced Lindstrom and married Rossellini, thereby legalizing a relationship that had caused a public outcry against her 'scandalous' behaviour and seriously damaged her career prospects in Hollywood. But when the strain of a series of unsuccessful films proved too much and Bergman decided to return to the stage for a while, Rossellini went to make a film in India and returned with the wife of an Indian director. In 1957, with another divorce, the 'Rossellini period' was over.

20th Century-Fox had offered her the chance of an international comeback with *Anastasia* in 1956, a story about the escape of the Tsar's daughter in 1918. It was a tremendous success, winning Bergman her second Academy Award. There followed a series of roles devised to regain her internationally popular image. In *Anastasia*, *Indiscreet* (1958, again teamed with Cary Grant) and *Inn of the Sixth Happiness* (1958, as a missionary in China), Bergman achieved respectability. Several later films, of which *A Walk in the Spring Rain* (1970) – an intimate composition in half tones, about the affair of a married and middle-aged woman – was no exception, were not suitable material and did not allow her to attain her true potential, but in 1974 she won another Academy Award, this for Best Supporting Actress, in *Murder on the Orient Express* in which she played a timid and devout missionary.

In 1978, Bergman was cast in *Autumn Sonata* as the self-obsessed mother who is totally involved in her career– the first role worthy of her since the end of the Selznick period. She bravely exposed herself to Ingmar

Above left: Bergman and Bogart, the ill-fated lovers in Casablanca. *Above: in* The Yellow Rolls-Royce, *with Omar Sharif and Joyce Grenfell, Bergman, as a widow crossing war-torn Yugoslavia, outshone in an improbable plot. Below: a lady with a guilty secret in* Murder on the Orient Express

Bergman's scrutinizing eye and achieved, with his complicity, a character of great depth and nuance; this was probably one of the most complete, moving and intelligent creations of the actress' career.

Throughout her years in the cinema, she has maintained regular contact with the stage, playing in about ten plays between 1940 and 1967, including *Joan of Lorraine* (1946), for which she was awarded the Tony Award, *Tea and Sympathy* (1956), *Hedda Gabler* (1962), and *A Month in the Country* (1965), directed by Sir Michael Redgrave at the Yvonne Arnaud theatre in Guildford. In 1958 she married a theatrical impresario, Lars Schmidt.

Ingrid Bergman's career spans a remarkable number of years; they divide into four distinct periods – Sweden, Hollywood, Rossellini and the International period. She survived the disappearance of the Hollywood studios and the Rossellini experience. She also emerged well from several miscasts, thanks to her adaptability and to a thorough discipline that even her least interesting roles exhibit. She remains a combination of femininity, distance, honour and vulnerability, that still seduces us.

OLIVIER EYQUEM

Hollywood's friends and foes

With America facing wars in Europe and the Pacific, the movie capital set about promoting the idea that the Japanese were sadists, the Germans were fools, the British lived in a land of hope and glory, and that the Russians were nearly as brave as the Americans themselves

The first Hollywood feature film to proclaim the evil of Hitler's Germany was Anatole Litvak's *Confessions of a Nazi Spy* (1939). Although the film had prompted a predictably hostile response in German official circles, it had aroused only disfavour or, at most, luke-warm public reaction in the USA.

In the awkward two years which followed the outbreak of war in Europe those movies that did portray Germany or Italy tended to do so from a respectful distance. Mervyn LeRoy's *Escape* (1940), though set largely inside a concentration camp (designed by Cedric Gibbons), even managed to avoid the mention of the words 'German' or 'Nazi'. Fritz Lang's *Manhunt* (1941), which opens with a British hunter (Walter Pidgeon) seeing if it is possible to assassinate Hitler, rapidly retreats into the story of a chase. Increasing Japanese militarism, meanwhile, made even less of an impression on Hollywood than it did on the American government before the events of December 7, 1941.

Above: The Purple Heart, *a piece of inspired guesswork about the fate that befell brave American pilots captured by the Japanese.*
Right: The White Cliffs of Dover, *regarded by* Newsweek *as 'Anglophile . . . with knobs on'.*
Far right: Casablanca, *a wartime fairy-tale*

From Hollywood's point of view the disaster at Pearl Harbor was mitigated by the fact that the studios now had a clear political line to follow. They sprang into action with such topical 'turkeys' as *Remember Pearl Harbor, Little Tokyo, USA* and *Secret Agent of Japan* (all 1942). By the end of 1942 *Across the Pacific* and *Wake Island* had indicated that the quality of films made about the Japanese was likely to improve during the course of the war – though not necessarily the view taken in them of the enemy's essentially evil and duplicitous nature. It was an attitude that reinforced the public's hostility towards Americans of Japanese extraction living in the United States; they found that their insurance policies were arbitrarily cancelled, their cheques bounced, the milkman refused to deliver and shop-keepers declined to serve them.

In 1943 20th Century-Fox made *The Purple Heart*, best of the anti-Japanese pictures. Written and produced by Darryl F. Zanuck and directed by Lewis Milestone, it was intended to strengthen public hatred of the Japanese at a time when it appeared as if the war in Europe were stealing all the headlines. The film was not finally released until 1944 when the War Department was prepared to concede officially that the Japanese had indeed been torturing American POWs. Zanuck would have been

28

quite prepared to wait until the end of the war to release his picture – so strongly did he feel about it.

The Purple Heart originated – as did MGM's *Thirty Seconds Over Tokyo* (1944) – in the sensational raid in April 1942 made by a group of B-25 bombers which took off from an aircraft carrier in the Pacific and attacked Tokyo. The damage this caused was slight but the boost to American morale was considerable. Though based on no hard factual evidence (none of course existed), the film supposes that the American flyers shot down in the raid were tried, tortured – with due emphasis on sadistic humiliation – and executed.

In a sense, the Nazis, perhaps because they were European and therefore better 'known', fared somewhat better in Hollywood as the war progressed. But their movie image did not get off to an auspicious start. Early in 1942 two comedies appeared suggesting that the Nazis were fools to be outwitted by simple tricks. Ernst Lubitsch's *To Be or Not To Be* is admittedly a very funny film, starring Jack Benny and Carole Lombard as Joseph and Maria Tura – a husband-and-wife acting team in Poland who are able to use their stage techniques to triumph over the Gestapo. Sig Ruman, the Teutonic stooge from the Marx Brothers films, plays the redoubtable Concentration-Camp Erhardt ('I do the concentrating, they do the camping'). Benny in disguise asks his opinion of Tura as an actor. 'Ah yes,' recalls Ruman, 'I saw him once before the war. Believe me, what he did to Shakespeare we are now doing to Poland.'

Perhaps not surprisingly, *To Be or Not To Be* was released to a barrage of hostile notices which declared the film to be in the grossest of bad taste. One critic went so far as to call Lubitsch's comedy 'propaganda for Goebbels'.

No such charge was levelled against Leo McCarey's *Once Upon a Honeymoon* (1942), but it was successful neither as anti-Nazi propa-

ganda nor as comedy. In the Thirties McCarey had graduated from directing Laurel and Hardy two-reelers to improvising with considerable success around the sophisticated talents of Cary Grant and Irene Dunne in *The Awful Truth* (1937). The issues of World War II proved beyond McCarey's grasp, however, and his depiction of a concentration camp in which Grant and Ginger Rogers are wrongly held made no attempt to arouse in his audience any sense of the despair and degradation that permeated such places. It was simply a setting for a case of sub-comic mistaken identity.

As the war continued, the portrait of the Nazi enemy progressed via the Nazi beast to the compliment of the 'good' German, the 'real' inhabitant of the land of Bach and Beethoven. Perhaps supreme among Nazi beasts of the cultured variety was Conrad Veidt who starred in *Escape* (1940), Jules Dassin's *Nazi Agent* (1942), and played the much loved Major Strasser in Curtiz's *Casablanca* (1942). Erich von Stroheim, who was the grudgingly admired Rommel in Billy Wilder's *Five Graves to Cairo* (1943), went on to depict another 'good', but flawed, German in Milestone's *The North Star* (1943). Also in 1943, in an adaptation of John Steinbeck's novel *The Moon Is Down*, directed by Irving Pichel, Cedric Hardwicke plays a German officer who has the hostages in a Norwegian village shot, but only with terrible feelings of guilt. The government, which kept a watchful eye on Hollywood's treatment of the war, nodded approvingly both at straightforward portraits of Nazi beastliness and at more reflective examinations of the issues of the war. *Hitler's Children* (1942), a hugely successful low-budget production directed by Edward Dmytryk, was superficially just another ramble over the territory of Nazi methods of enslavement, using the device of an attractive American girl (Bonita Granville) who was, unfortunately for her, born in Germany and is therefore subject to German authority. The masterstroke was the advertising still which showed Miss Granville in a state

Above left: Russian peasants surrounded in The North Star *which starred Erich von Stroheim (left), who had been playing cruel German soldiers since World War I, as a Nazi officer complete with scar. Bottom: Skippy Homeier as an orphaned Hitler Youth adopted by an American family in* Tomorrow the World

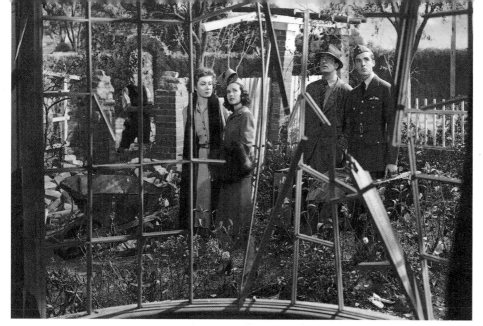

of undress being publicly flogged by the Nazis for her refusal to submit to their licentious suggestions.

The Broadway stage was perhaps a more fitting arena for a debate on the differences between democracy and fascism. Lillian Hellman's play *Watch on the Rhine* did not translate particularly well to film when it was made by Herman Shumlin in 1943; and James Gow's *Tomorrow the World* (1944), though less stage-bound in its direction (by Leslie Fenton), appealed principally through its story of the havoc created in an American household when a 12-year-old Nazi boy is brought to live there. Ironically, the dawning maturity of film audiences and their receptivity to 'ideas' persuaded Steinbeck and Hitchcock to devise *Lifeboat* (1944), in which the survivors of a torpedoed ship are cast adrift in an open boat. The film outraged critics, who saw in Walter Slezak's portrait of the sole Nazi member of the boat a more eloquent advocate of his political system than the inept quarrelsome products of democracy – his fellow passengers – were of theirs. While the best of the films dealing with the enemy came towards the end of the war, Hollywood's tribute to America's allies diminished in power as the war continued. The pro-British sentiment which had been built up in so many films of the early Forties – *The Sea Hawk* (1940), *That Hamilton Woman!* (1941) and so on – reached an all-time peak in 1942 when MGM made *Mrs Miniver*. William Wyler's universally popular, finely wrought film has undeservedly fallen into critical disrepute because of its lack of 'realism' (though this doesn't seem like much of a charge when one starts to examine *Casablanca* for *its* realism). Mrs Miniver (Greer Garson) captures a German pilot, hiding his gun behind the Welsh dresser, while Mr Miniver (Walter Pidgeon) is off rescuing British troops from the beach at Dunkirk. The village's last moments before global warfare breaks out are spent at the local flower-show where the British aristocracy in the person of Dame May Whitty is revealed as a crab apple with a core of solid gold.

Mrs Miniver opened at the Radio City Music Hall in New York on June 4, 1942. Within ten weeks it had attracted a million and a half spectators. In all it grossed $6 million in North America alone and swept the board at the Academy Awards where it took four of the top five Oscars. On an even higher level President

Roosevelt told Wyler that *Mrs Miniver* had appreciably lessened the political problems of increasing aid to Britain; and Frank Knox, Secretary of the US Navy, thought that the film was as valuable in terms of morale as a flotilla of battleships.

So pleased were MGM with their triumph that the studio ordered the same writing-production team to repeat the success. In 1944 they came up with *The White Cliffs of Dover* with Irene Dunne replacing Greer Garson as MGM's compulsory matronly heart-throb and Clarence Brown directing. Unfortunately, though equally laudable in aim and professional in execution, the film was only a pale shadow of the great *Mrs Miniver*.

Throughout the war the British remained the American film industry's favourite ally. RKO provided free facilities for the making of *Forever and a Day* (1943), basically the story of a house to which every Hollywood-based British actor donated his or her services; the proceeds went to the British Red Cross. Margaret O'Brien's glutinously compelling performance in Woody Van Dyke's *Journey for Margaret* (1942) successfully pleaded for the adoption by American households of endangered British children. There followed an instant demand for little English girls – six years old and preferably with blonde hair. It must have come as a shock to Americans when they were confronted with the offspring of Cleckheaton and Wapping.

Anatole Litvak's *This Above All* (1942), an adaptation of Eric Knight's bitter novel about an aggressive British soldier who deserts because he feels the war is being waged to preserve the stagnant and repressive British class system, is in some ways the most interest-

Above left: undaunted – an English family at war in Mrs Miniver, *starring Greer Garson, Teresa Wright, Walter Pidgeon and Richard Ney. Left: Cary Grant and Ginger Rogers in* Once Upon a Honeymoon. *Below: US envoy's daughter (Eleanor Parker) impressed by Russian ski-troops in* Mission to Moscow

Americans: Robert Taylor, as an orchestral conductor on tour of the Soviet Union in 1941, marvels at the collective wheat farm which reminds him of the Mid-Western wheat farm on which he was raised. Susan Peters plays the beautiful concert pianist with whom he falls in love – to the accompaniment of endless thunderous variations on Tchaikovsky's B Flat Piano Concerto. At some point the Germans invade the Soviet Union and unsportingly interrupt a blossoming relationship – but fortunately love conquers all, including the German Panzer divisions.

On a more serious level was Samuel Goldwyn's *The North Star* (1943), written by Lillian Hellman and originally to have been directed by William Wyler on location in Russia. Litvinov (Soviet ambassador to the USA) pointed out, when asked for permission,

Left: Ruth Warrick and Kent Smith in the Union Jack-waving Forever and a Day. *Below: Norwegian villagers prepare to face a Nazi firing squad in* The Moon Is Down. *Bottom: Robert Young and Laraine Day with William Severn and Margaret O'Brien as the British war orphans in* Journey for Margaret

ing of all the pro-British films to come out of Hollywood during the war years. Darryl F. Zanuck cast Tyrone Power as the dour Yorkshire anti-hero and, predictably, dictated that there should be a happy ending in which the soldier's patriotism is revived by his girl.

In the long run, Hollywood's films showing solidarity with the brave Russian people were to have the most dramatic impact on the American film industry. The most famous of them was *Mission to Moscow* (1943), adapted from the memoirs of Joseph E. Davies, the former American ambassador to the USSR. According to Jack Warner, the film was made by Warner Brothers on the direct order of President Roosevelt, an allegation which proved useless when Warner was under attack by the House Un-American Activities Committee in 1947.

The essence of *Mission to Moscow* is the conviction that Russians are just like Americans with fur hats, and that the ideological divisions between the two nations are more apparent than real. The film was brilliantly directed by Michael Curtiz, skilfully blending newsreel with dramatic reconstruction, but it is riddled with such political bias as to make *Triumph of the Will* look like an objective documentary. Trotsky, Nazi Germany and Japan are all conveniently linked to outbreaks of sabotage in the USSR and the Stalin purges of 1937 and 1938 are thereby justified on the grounds of national security. Even the Non-Aggression Pact with Germany is easily explained as a reaction to misguided British and French appeasement of Hitler at Munich which had left the USSR defenceless on her eastern border.

On its release, in 1943, *Mission to Moscow* aroused instant controversy, attracting violent criticism from the Right (particularly from the Hearst press) and Left (especially those who took exception to the film's pro-Stalinist attitudes). It was therefore not surprising to find that MGM's contribution to this new genre *Song of Russia* (dir. Gregory Ratoff, 1943), concentrated on Russian music and a love story. It was another film which emphasized the essential similarities of Russians and

that there was enough shooting already going on in the Soviet Union in 1943, and with Wyler's departure for the armed forces Lewis Milestone took over the direction. Despite Lillian Hellman's best intentions, *The North Star* still suffers from the idea perpetuated in all Hollywood films about the Soviet Union that the country is a slightly abnormal version of America. The villagers in *The North Star* look and sound like characters in *Oklahoma!* and the cavalier treatment of political ideology means that the Nazi invasion of June 1941 is made to seem like a cattle raid by organized rustlers.

Both *The North Star* and *Song of Russia* were cited in 1947 as evidence of Communists at work in Hollywood. Sam Goldwyn and Louis B. Mayer, like Jack Warner, maintained that such pictures were only part of the war effort and that although they were self-evidently pro-Soviet in attitude the films were simply expedient propaganda exercises.

Hollywood has usually managed to bend with the political wind. Its portraits of America's allies and enemies during World War II remain as clear evidence of contemporary official policy and wider public attitudes.   COLIN SHINDLER

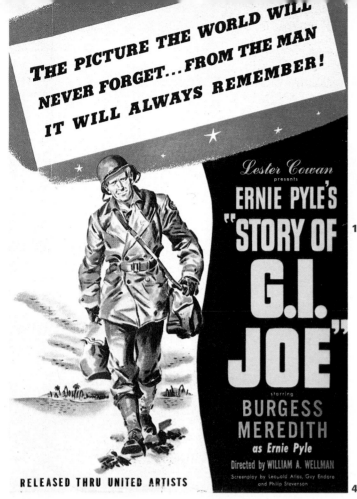

1

4

Directed by William Wellman, 1945
Prod co: Lester Cowan Productions/United Artists. **prod:** Lester Cowan. **assoc prod:** David Hall. **sc:** Leopold Atlas, Guy Endore, Philip Stevenson, from the book by Ernie Pyle. **photo:** Russell Metty. **ed:** Otho Lovering, Albrecht Joseph. **art dir:** James Sullivan, Edward G. Boyle. **mus:** Ann Ronell, Louis Applebaum. **mus dir:** Louis Forbes. **sd:** Frank McWhorter. **ass dir:** Robert Aldrich. **r/t:** 109 minutes. Re-released as *War Correspondent*.
Cast: Burgess Meredith (*Ernie Pyle*), Robert Mitchum (*Lt Walker*), Freddie Steele (*Sgt Warnicki*), Wally Cassell (*Pte Dondaro*), Jimmy Lloyd (*Pte Spencer*), Jack Reilly (*Pte Murphy*), Bill Murphy (*Pte Mew*), Tito Renaldo (*Lopez*), William Self ('*Gawky' Henderson*), Yolanda Lacca (*Amelia*), Dorothy Coonan (*Red*), 'and as themselves, combat veterans of the campaigns in Africa, Sicily and Italy'.

'Many things in the film move me to tears – and in none of them do I feel that I have been deceived, or cynically seduced or manipulated, as one usually has to feel about movies.'

So wrote James Agee in a rapturous review of *The Story of GI Joe* on its original release in 1945. And Sam Fuller, himself no mean chronicler of the brutalities of war in *Fixed Bayonets*, *The Steel Helmet* (both 1951) and *Merrill's Marauders* (1962), has commented that:

'Except for Wellman's *GI Joe*, with its feeling of death and mass murder, all war films are kind of adolescent, completely insincere.'

Today's viewers may feel a little less enthusiastic than Agee and Fuller. Vietnam brought into the open one of the rarely acknowledged facts about war: that not all officers are resourceful leaders, and that their tired and frightened men may be as likely to shoot them as to obey them. But *The Story of GI Joe*, devoting itself to the propo-

sition that Captain Walker is one of the good officers, careful and caring about the lives of his men, proceeds to demonstrate it with such quiet conviction that one feels a genuine sense of loss at his death. The closing sequence then shows Private Dondaro – last seen resentfully digging latrines as punishment for neglect of duty – weeping as he holds his dead captain's hand. Here, at least, we are being 'seduced or manipulated', not cynically but sentimentally.

In fairness to Agee, it must be remembered that in 1945, in the context of Hollywood's insistence on flag-waving and rampant heroism in all war movies, *The Story of GI Joe* came as a breath of honest, clean air with its infantryman's angle on war as a meaningless vista of mud, muddle and fatigue ending very probably in a wooden cross. And in fairness to the film itself, it should be added that the final sequence is its only serious lapse. Elsewhere, what Fuller de-

scribes as its feeling of death and mass murder comes over with an astonishing power, more effective than all the anti-war sentiments of *All Quiet on the Western Front* (1930) because the terrible carnage of war is implied, never stated.

The film's masterstroke is its use of the war correspondent Ernie Pyle as an intermediary between us and the action: his commentary supplies the emotional significance that the scenes themselves are not required to carry. Much of the film is therefore shot in documentary style, not imitating newsreel images so much as *interpreting* them while this documentary approach is barely marred by the character sketches and personal conflicts used by most war movies to ensure audience involvement.

In the film's exemplary opening sequence, for instance, we sense not so much fear as a terrible vulnerability as the men are told that they are going into the line and almost lose their talisman, a little dog. That night, vague characterizations – with nostalgia evoked by music from a radio ('This is Berlin bringing you the music of Artie Shaw') – begin to emerge with Dondaro expounding on his favourite topic of women, Murphy grieving that he is too tall to become a pilot, and so on. But by the time battle comes, after weary days of endless marching through rain and grey dawns, anonymity has taken over again; and as the shells scream, Pyle's voice speaks for all of them:

'This was their baptism of fire; it was chaos . . . each boy facing the worst moment of his life, alone.'

Thereafter, as one battle gives way to the next, the audience is chiefly aware that some faces have disappeared to be replaced by others, that familiar faces have suddenly become older and warier, that all are blanketed by an overwhelming fatigue and despair.

But Ernie Pyle is himself a participant in this drama as he wanders around with his typewriter, his next dispatch always in mind. Harassed by tiredness and the apprehension of death as he watches these men, he grows to love them and faces the almost impossible task of making sense of what is happening to them in the stories he writes for their families at home.

This explains the abrupt shift in manner with the bravura sequence in the Italian town; it begins with the snipers being cleared from the church (the last one, shot by Walker as Warnicki kneels to pray, clutches a bell-rope to toll an ironic knell as he falls), then continues with Warnicki finding a gramophone, Dondaro finding a complaisant Italian girl, and Murphy's wedding.

These scenes function as the random personal impressions out of which Pyle builds a meaningful basis for his tale of the terror of war. We hear the beginning of one of his dispatches after Murphy's death: 'He was just a plain Hoosier boy [a native of Indiana]; you couldn't imagine him ever killing anybody . . .' Sentimental, yes; but *The Story of GI Joe* cancels out all mawkishness by showing exactly why Pyle felt as he did about the GI who 'lives so miserably, dies so miserably'.

TOM MILNE

ERNIE PYLE

SOMEWHERE IN ITALY (BY WIRELESS)

I HAD LONG AGO COME TO THINK OF PRIVATE

"WINGLESS" MURPHY AS AN OLD, OLD FRIEND.

HE WAS JUST A PLAIN HOOSIER BOY.

YOU COULDN'T IMAGINE HIM EVER KILLING

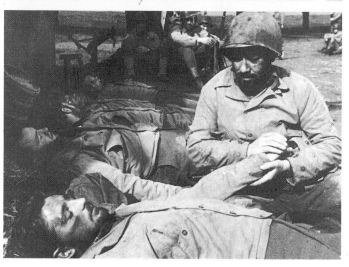

War correspondent Ernie Pyle watches as Lt Walker, leading a company of untried GIs into action, allows them to take along a pet dog (1). After sharing their miseries and their baptism of fire, while recording it all in his dispatches (2), Pyle begins to look upon the boys as his special family. He is later parted from them but, after the North African and Sicilian campaigns, they are reunited in Italy.

Entering an enemy-held Italian town, Walker (now a captain) and Sgt Warnicki (3) clear German snipers from the bell-tower of a ruined church. Warnicki, whose wife has sent him a record of his child's voice, finds a gramophone in a shattered house (4) but it has no needle. In the bombed church,

Pyle gives away the bride when Murphy and an army nurse are married by the chaplain.

Finding their way blocked by a hilltop monastery held by the Germans, the frustrated GIs dig in. Murphy is killed and Pyle's moving story about him (5) wins him the Pulitzer Prize. At Christmas, Pyle insists his 'family' get turkey and whisky (6).

Warnicki at last gets to hear his son's voice but succumbs to battle fatigue and has to be put under restraint (7). Walker leads the rest of the company in a desperate assault on the monastery. As the exhausted survivors sit on the road they have cleared to Rome (8), mules bring the dead down from the hilltop. Walker is among them (9).

Keeping Up Morale

Hollywood's instinctive reaction to the outbreak of World War II was to ignore it in the same way as it had previously glossed over other important social and political developments. However it was quick to capitalize on the impetus war gave to technology, which resulted in improvements in film-stock processing, sound recording, and lighting in colour films. The public was hungry for entertainment and the studios swung into action with renewed vigour. Each one had a different approach: MGM, for example, concentrated on family pictures and musicals; Warner Brothers preferred fast-paced war films and melodramas; 20th Century-Fox made bold, brassy colour films. By mid-1941 box-office receipts showed a noticeable increase.

But pressure from Roosevelt's government and from within the film industry itself, gradually induced Hollywood to play a more and more active role in building and maintaining morale at home and abroad. Certain stars joined the armed forces amid fanfares of publicity that encouraged the general public to follow suit. James Stewart signed up for active service in the navy when he discovered that his boss, Louis B. Mayer, head of MGM, was trying to protect his studio's 'assets' by keeping him out of the draft. The film director Woody Van Dyke, who had received a commission in the Marine Reserves in 1934, was asked to make his outfit – the 22nd Battalion Marine Corps – operational in 1940. With many Hollywood workers in its ranks, the Battalion went abroad, where Woody earned the nickname of 'Steam Engine in Breeches' for his dynamism. However he was eventually forced to resign his commission because of heart trouble (from which he later died).

Many big names took part in the Stars Over America shows, which were put on extensively at hospitals and army camps in the USA and overseas. The stars also became involved in nation-wide tours to promote the buying of War Bonds. Bette Davis, for instance, recalls one tour in Missouri and Oklahoma during which a portrait of her in *Jezebel* (1938) fetched

Above left: the million-dollar legs of Betty Grable, the forces' favourite pin-up, in their finest hour. Below left: Lt Gable of the USAAF. Below: James Stewart takes the oath of allegiance with other draftees

Hollywood movies and Hollywood stars lifted the hearts of Americans at home and in the front line, temporarily allowing them to forget the horrors of war

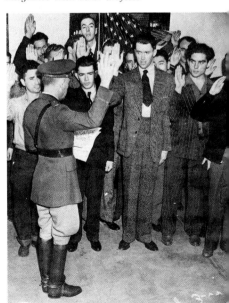

guest appearances by everyone from Harpo Marx to Gracie Fields.

After the USA entered the war in 1941, Hollywood's biggest successes were the patriotic, all-star extravaganzas – *Star Spangled Rhythm, This Is the Army* (both 1943) and *Follow the Boys* (1944). These films offered loose apologies for plots (often on the lines of boy tries to date girl) with music, and were showcases for a studio's roster of talent. Undoubtedly the finest of these musical, flag-waving celebrations was *Yankee Doodle Dandy* (1942), a glowing tribute to the patriotic songwriter George M. Cohan (played by James Cagney) and the American way of life.

Victory for all the family

Undue sentimentality marred the majority of the earliest attempts at 'serious' portrayals of the home front. A comedy like *The More the Merrier* (1943) came much closer to the truth with its depiction of the accommodation shortage which forces a working girl (Jean Arthur) to share a small apartment with two bachelors (Cary Grant and Charles Coburn). However, the following year saw the appearance of two of the most superior, polished and effective morale-boosting dramas to emerge from the American cinema during World War II – *Since You Went Away,* and *Meet Me in St Louis* (both 1944). The script of *Since You Went Away* was rewritten, updated and expanded by David O. Selznick to provide a sweeping portrait of America at war, played with genuine, tender conviction by a large cast. The film kept the more unpleasant details of war to a minimum, effectively focusing characterization and narrative on the 'unconquerable fortress of 1943 – the American family'.

Minnelli's *Meet Me in St Louis* was a classic showcase for all the virtues of a closely knit family. It was a superbly constructed musical, with fine songs and a fabulous street set that enhanced the nostalgic re-creations of a

Far left: Cagney leads a patriotic chorus in Yankee Doodle Dandy. *Top: the stars' morale-boosting work was celebrated in* Hollywood Canteen. *Left: Sgt Carl Bell, the millionth serviceman to enter the Canteen, is congratulated by (from left) Lana Turner, Deanna Durbin and Marlene Dietrich. Below: Bing Crosby in* Star Spangled Rhythm, *a musical showcase for Paramount's stars*

$250,000 worth of bonds and her autobiography $50,000. Although she raised $2 million in two days, she remained aware of the ambiguous nature of her achievement, commenting later that 'It seemed outrageous... that motion picture stars had to seduce people into buying bonds to help their country'.

Carole Lombard became Hollywood's 'first victim' of the war when the plane she was in crashed while returning from a bond-selling tour in Indiana. Shortly afterwards, amid a blaze of publicity, her husband Clark Gable joined the US Army Air Force. His fans followed him everywhere – even to the extent of keeping pace with him on the other side of the compound fence when he was on guard duty. The army was forced to announce:

'Lieutenant Gable will appreciate it if the public will not interfere in his training. He wishes to be treated like every other member of the public.'

The effect that Gable's decision to join up had on building American morale may be measured by a story – widely believed – that alleged that Göring had offered the equivalent of $5000, plus promotion and leave, to the flyer who managed to shoot him down.

In 1942, following the success of the New York Stage Canteen, the Hollywood Canteen was set up in Los Angeles. It was founded by Bette Davis and John Garfield who raised the initial capital from the sale of $25 tickets for a premiere and a party. The building was equipped and decorated by volunteers from all the guilds and unions in Hollywood, and the Canteen opened with the public paying $100 apiece to sit and watch the first troops crossing the threshold. Like its East Coast counterpart, the aim of the Canteen was to give GIs on leave some fun and relaxation. They could eat from a menu devised by the famous chef Milani and cooked by Marlene Dietrich, be entertained by Bing Crosby, and be asked to dance by Rita Hayworth – all for free. By the end of the war the Hollywood Canteen had entertained an estimated three million servicemen. The studios made sure that an even wider audience had a share of the fun (though *not* for free) by producing two films, *Stage Door Canteen* (1943), from United Artists, and *Hollywood Canteen* (1944), from Warners; the movies contained

bygone era lovingly given new life by the colour camera. The performances of Judy Garland and Margaret O'Brien injected a feeling of warmth, happiness and optimism.

At home and overseas, movies formed a staple part of the troops' ration of entertainment. Statistics in 1943 show that 630,000 men in the armed services were seeing Hollywood films each night. Some of these – including *Saratoga Trunk* (1943), and *The Two Mrs Carrolls* (1945) – were viewed by them quite a few years before their commercial release. The soldiers also provided a captive audience for instructional short films like John Ford's *Sex Hygiene* (1942), a graphically documented treatise on VD.

Perhaps fortunately, the men in the front line did not have to depend solely on the silver screen for distraction; they could still hope for the personal appearance of one of their favourite stars. After Pearl Harbor, Al Jolson immediately campaigned to be allowed to go abroad and entertain the troops, saying, 'My name's Jolson and I sing. Let me sing to the boys. I'll pay my own fare'. When the United States Entertainment Organization was formed, Jolson was one of the first to be sent overseas. He tells the story of how, on his first appearance, it had been rumoured that Lana

Above: Marlene Dietrich said, 'The war gave me the opportunity of kissing more soldiers than any other woman in the world'. Below: Al Jolson sings his heart out for the troops. Bottom: Vernon Cansino (far left) shows army buddies a photo of his sister – Rita Hayworth

Turner was to appear. The disappointment that greeted Jolson – who had not sung before a live audience for many years – when he stepped out onto the stage was immense. But he won them over, crying, 'Hallo boys – I'm Al Jolson. You'll see my name in the history books'. He sang all the old favourites – 'Dixie', 'Buddy, Can You Spare a Dime?', 'Give My Regards to Broadway' – but unless pressed by his listeners, he would not sing 'Sonny Boy' as he found that it tended to reduce audiences to tears. As was the case with all the stars who ventured abroad, stories circulated about his courage. One famous one tells of how, when sheltering during an air raid, he joked about not being scared. He was only there, he said, because 'I'd look awfully silly singing "Mammy" with just one arm'.

The voices of Hope and 'Uncle Sam'
Bob Hope and Bing Crosby (who was known as 'Uncle Sam Without Whiskers') were two tireless entertainers despite frequent narrow escapes in the air and on the ground. Not content with singing to the assembled troops, Crosby would travel round the front finding more boys to shake hands with.

Hope broadcast from a military base each week. His main problem was that as each show was received by the Allied forces everywhere, he continually had to rewrite his gags. One of his most famous openings was:

'Hallo everybody. Thank you very much. Thank you for the applause and please point your guns in the other direction.'

In the excitement of the concert, the soldiers had forgotten to disarm.

In addition to the French *Légion d'Honneur*, Marlene Dietrich received the Medal of Freedom – the highest American civilian decoration – for her efforts to 'bring pleasure and cheer to more than 500,000 American soldiers'. Her shows often began with a comedian coming on stage and announcing that Miss Dietrich would be unable to appear as she had gone to dinner with an American colonel. As a cry of disappointment went up from the audience, a voice would call out from the back of the auditorium, 'No, I'm here'. A moment later the slim, immaculate figure of Dietrich would run down the centre aisle. The highlight of her act was when she played the saw with a violin bow. She always wore khaki, and refused to pose for 'leg' pictures while 'in uniform'. She lived as the soldiers did, washing her face in snow and eating out of mess tins. Although working exclusively for the Allied cause, Dietrich was popular with soldiers on both sides during the war, so the Office of Political Warfare asked her to record her hit songs in German – but rewritten with a propaganda twist. She considered this her greatest contribution to the war effort.

A personal appearance by a celebrity was a rare release from the bitter routine of war; for the rest of the time GIs had to make do with pin-ups of their favourites. The two most popular darlings of the forces were Betty Grable and Rita Hayworth. It was considered the ultimate compliment to a star when a photograph of Hayworth in a black lace and white satin negligée was pasted on the side of the first nuclear bomb, tested on the Bikini Atoll in 1946 – a gruesome tribute perhaps, but a symbol of Hollywood's invaluable contribution to American morale during the war.
KINGSLEY CANHAM, SALLY HIBBIN

Documents of war

During the war the people back home craved information, and film was a fast, effective means of reporting the war's progress. For some documentary film-makers, it was their finest hour

From the outset of World War II, Britain, Germany, the USA, the USSR and Japan all mobilized their cameras as well as their guns in the battle to win people's minds and to stimulate morale, recalling, perhaps, Stalin's words that 'the cinema is the greatest means of mass propaganda'. As authentic records of the war, many of the official films and newsreels thus produced have still to be properly analysed. They were often composed of reconstructed material – model and studio work was mixed in with actuality footage which was itself subject to rigorous censorship – and they continue to pose problems for film historians whose task is to sort out the mock from the genuine.

Indeed one has to delve deep into the archives to find the 'real' war – unadulterated shots of sailors relaxing after D-Day, bomb-disposal experiments in London's Richmond Park, a day's activities on a British bomber-squadron airfield, and so on – usually recorded by amateur cameramen with no propaganda axe to grind.

Of course it was rarely the prime intention of the official war documentary or newsreel to present a genuine, straightforward account of combat or home-front conditions. Many of them did offer a stark portrayal of war, but in retrospect they are chiefly of interest and importance as exercises in propaganda and as reflections of national attitudes at a time of intensive crisis and global turmoil. Their purpose was not simply to record the war (which in part they did) but to 'interpret' it to the soldier and civilian on whose behalf it was being fought. It is no accident that Frank Capra's propaganda masterpiece of the war was called *Why We Fight* and not *'How We Fight'*.

In Britain the war documentary has come to be recognized as a high point in the country's cinema, a happy marriage of official need and artistic film-making which created a national cinematic identity and indigenous style. It was, in essence, the maturing of the Grierson-inspired documentary movement of the Thirties. The style appeared to thrive on austerity as well as the brilliance of its exponents, and its exposition of the war was a beguiling blend of facts and lyricism, news and motivation.

The film-makers also quickly recognized how the war had unified the British in an unusual way, lowering class barriers, providing a common cause, and engendering in the people a modest self-respect and determination to safeguard the white cliffs of democracy. Confronted with arrogant German notions of 'superiority', the British took a collective pride in being 'ordinary', and the films of the period cleverly conveyed the phenomenon of an entire populace mentally rolling up its sleeves to get down to the serious business of survival. They were also gritty, realistic, wryly humorous, informative, emotionally restrained, largely free from expressions of overt nationalism, and even relatively tolerant towards the enemy, who nevertheless had to be taught a lesson.

As the war began, the government and armed-services film units were linked together and, along

WITH THE FULL CO-OPERATION OF THE ROYAL AIR FORCE AND THE ROYAL NAVY

with the best of the independent documentary companies, were placed under the control of the Ministry of Information. Numerous instructional films were turned out, ranging from the practical (how to cope with food, health, weapons, machinery) to the political (war information, ridicule of the enemy, moral preparedness, and so forth). The Ministry of Information increased access to their films by showing them in the towns and villages of Britain (often where no cinemas existed), and even projecting them in factories, where shift-work prevented people from seeing films at normal times.

At first there was a lack of co-ordination among the documentary film-makers working under the aegis of the Ministry of Information. In the first year of the war the only projects of note were those completed on the independent initiative of the talented members of the GPO Film Unit. These included *The First Days* (1939), a mood piece depicting London's reaction to the declaration of war, made by Humphrey Jennings, Harry Watt, Pat Jackson and Alberto Cavalcanti. Watt followed this with a GPO film officially commissioned by the Ministry of Information, *Squadron 992* (1939), a simple, strikingly photographed study of an RAF barrage-balloon unit in training and protecting the Forth Bridge.

In 1940, the situation improved with the creation of the Crown Film Unit (absorbing the GPO Film Unit) which, together with many other sponsored units, such as those of the oil company Shell and Paul Rotha's independent team, settled down to a planned policy by which they would pump out propaganda in films ranging from two-minute flashes to feature-length documentaries. It is an interesting sidelight to note how many of the film-makers involved in this corporate, Establishment effort had been known in the Thirties for their radical political views.

Above: Coastal Command *was made by J. B. Holmes for the Crown Film Unit and set to music by Vaughan Williams. It showed how the RAF and the Royal Navy protected British merchant-ship convoys as they continued their hazardous work. Below: the image of a nation going about its daily business amid the bombing of the Blitz was emphasized in* London Can Take It, *a film that saw the emergence of a major new director – Humphrey Jennings*

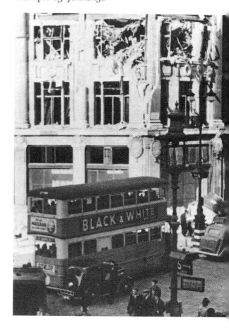

THE ACTUAL STORY OF THE ROUT OF ROMMEL BY THE BRITISH EIGHTH ARMY

DESERT VICTORY

A FULL-LENGTH FEATURE PICTURE

PRODUCED BY THE FILM UNITS OF THE BRITISH ARMY AND THE R.A.F.   RELEASED BY 20TH CENTURY-FOX

FILMED UNDER FIRE! 8 REELS OF BATTLE!

THE GOVERNMENTS OF THE UNITED STATES AND GREAT BRITAIN *Present*

TUNISIAN VICTORY

THE INVASION AND LIBERATION
OF NORTH AFRICA

AN OFFICIAL RECORD
PRODUCED BY BRITISH AND AMERICAN SERVICE FILM UNITS
DISTRIBUTED BY THE BRITISH MINISTRY OF INFORMATION
A METRO-GOLDWYN-MAYER RELEASE

"A GREAT LITTLE FILM.."
Daily Express

THE SILENT VILLAGE

Above: The Silent Village, *a portrait of a Welsh mining community, was made as a tribute to the people of the Czech mining town of Lidice who had been massacred by the Nazis in retaliation for the assassination of the SS General Heydrich. Top left:* Desert Victory, *directed by Roy Boulting, focused on the British advances through Egypt and Libya. Top centre:* Tunisian Victory *was an Anglo-American account of the latter stages of the North African campaign. It was co-directed by Roy Boulting and Frank Capra and the commentary was shared between Bernard Miles and Burgess Meredith. Top right:* The True Glory *was a résumé of the war in Europe from the D-Day invasion to the final victory. This epic documentary was given a human perspective by focusing on individual soldiers*

The poet and genius of the British documentary movement was Humphrey Jennings whose films, with their warmth and spontaneity of feeling, evoked more than any others the atmosphere of Britain and the mood of its people in wartime. He achieved this by eschewing the more pragmatic approach of his colleagues and recalling instead the sights and sounds of Britain and its people, their culture and their traditions.

Jennings made his mark as co-director, with Harry Watt, of *London Can Take It* (1940), which told the story of the first big bombing raid on London at the beginning of the Blitz. Its chief purpose was to dramatize to those abroad – particularly Americans – how their own democracy might likewise be threatened. Jennings followed this in 1941 with a trilogy of impressionistic film poems, portraying Britain at war – *Heart of Britain*, *Words for Battle* (both 1941) and *Listen to Britain* (1942). His acknowledged masterpiece, however, was *Fires Were Started* (1943), a memorial to the firemen of London which captured all the tragedy and heroism of civilians at war.

Jennings developed a more symbolic, semi-fictional technique in his next two films, *The Silent Village* (1943) and *The True Story of Lilli Marlene* (1944), with less appealing results. He then reverted to his more characteristic style with *80 Days* (1944), an account of the V-1 flying-bomb attacks on England, and *A Diary for Timothy* (1945), a picture of Britain in the last months of the war that reflected on an uncertain future. Jennings' final commentary on the war, *A Defeated People* (1946), was a characteristically sympathetic study of the German experience after the armistice.

Jennings' contribution to war documentaries may have been unique but many other documentaries of the period were notable for their style. Some films contained a pleasing leavening of satire, as in *Lambeth Walk* (1941) in which shots of Germans goose-stepping were cut in time with the famous popular song. Cavalcanti made a memorable caricature of Mussolini in *Yellow Caesar* (1940), and Len Lye's *When the Pie Was Opened* (1941) was an imaginative, lively presentation of a wartime recipe for vegetable pie. Paul Rotha's *World of Plenty* (1943) was a potent piece of film journalism which surveyed the global food problem in a style similar to the *March of Time* newsreels. Finally Anthony Asquith's *Welcome to Britain* (1943), a shrewd guide to the British for the benefit of

US servicemen, used traditional, self-deprecating British humour.

Among the best and most popular British documentaries of the war were those depicting actual operations and combat. Early examples were Harry Watt's *Target for Tonight* (1941), a reconstructed account of a routine bombing raid, and Pat Jackson's colour film *Western Approaches* (1944), a tribute to Britain's merchant seamen. Both films portrayed men facing extreme danger with calm and courage. At the same time the Services Film Units contributed a morale-boosting series of 'Victory' films: *Desert Victory*, *Tunisian Victory* (both 1943) and *Burma Victory* (1945); British director Roy Boulting worked on all three films.

The culmination of the combat documentaries was *The True Glory* (1945), an ambitious, Anglo-American collaboration, directed by Carol Reed and Garson Kanin. The film celebrated the part played by the ordinary fighting men of all the Allied Nations in the final defeat of the Germans on the Western Front. It provided a fitting climax to what might most aptly be described as Britain's finest hour of film-making.

'Documentary is at once a critique of propaganda and a practice of it' wrote Grierson, summarizing the wartime role of his former colleagues

In Germany as early as 1933 the Nazi regime had exercised strict bureaucratic control over the ideological content of every film made there. Goebbels had been shrewd enough to realize that the way to keep the cinemas well attended was to lay emphasis on escapism, but he ensured that all cinema programmes were supplemented with a regular quota of propaganda newsreels and shorts. The latter were mostly simple, direct presentations of a limited number of approved themes: anti-Semitism, Aryan superiority, war heroism, Germany's glorious past, loyalty to the Fatherland and worship of the Führer.

With the outbreak of war this efficient propaganda machine simply continued its now familiar function, although naturally the emphasis was shifted to the conflict itself, highlighting the sweep of German victories in Europe.

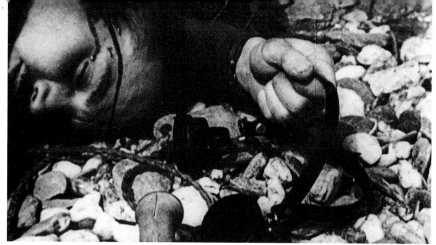

Numerous short record films described aspects of the war effort, such as the work of the Nazi Army Hospital Service or the activities of U-boats. A regular newsreel, *Die Deutsche Wochenschau* (The German Weekly Review) was produced and continued up to the end of the war. In 1940, the first German victories were celebrated in heady dynamic documentaries like H. Bertram's *Feuertaufe* (1940, Baptism of Fire) and Fritz Hippler's *Feldzug in Polen* (1940, Campaign in Poland) and *Sieg im Westen* (1941, Victory in the West). But what the public was permitted to see and what was actually filmed often differed markedly.

In addition to straight documentary there was also pseudo-documentary: Fritz Hippler's *Der Ewige Jude* (1940, The Eternal Jew) was an insidiously skilful film on 'the problems of world Jewry' that aimed to expose the alleged decadence of the Jewish people and, through explicit climactic scenes in a kosher abbatoir, their inherent barbarity. One later commentator called it 'probably the most evil film ever made'.

In the USSR, where the Revolution of 1917 had inspired the cinema's most successful coupling of artistic achievement and overtly propagandist intentions, there was rather little experience of documentary film-making to draw upon when the country finally engaged in war with Germany.

Undeterred, however, Soviet film-makers responded eagerly to the exhortations of the All-Union Cinema Committee 'to help in the moral, political and military defeat of Fascism'. Throughout the war, the Russians produced some remarkable documentaries and newsreels depicting their country's resolute defence and the defeat of their enemy.

Once at war, they shot numerous propaganda films. Outstanding talents such as Alexander Dovzhenko, Leonid Varlamov, Roman Karmen and Yuli Raizman contributed films to an ambitious cycle of documentaries. Varlamov made *Defeat of the German Armies Near Moscow* (1942). Dovzhenko and his wife Solntseva made *Victory in the Ukraine* (1945). She made *The Fight for Our Soviet Ukraine* (1943) with Dovzhenko supervising and briefing cameramen.

Karmen directed *Leningrad Fights* (1942); and other notable compilations included *Liberated France* (1945) by Yutkevich, *Defeat of Japan* (1945) by Zarkhi and Heifitz, and Varlamov's *Stalingrad* (1943). Varlamov had also supervised *A Day of War* (1942), perhaps the most elaborate of these documentaries, which was compiled from the contri-

butions of over a hundred cameramen who sent film back from the entire Soviet front.

Undoubtedly the most elating film of all was Yuli Raizman's *Berlin* (1945), photographed by Karmen and 40 other cameramen and showing the final triumphant capture of the *Reichstag* after bitter street-fighting. These films were all spectacular exercises in patriotism and Soviet audiences saw none of the retreat, disaster and death which the combat cameramen frequently recorded.

The USA also lacked a strong tradition of documentary film-making when it entered the war. As in the Soviet Union, established feature-film directors were called upon to step in and make propaganda films. For the US War Department the peculiar problem was to explain or 'sell' the war to a public that had little idea why it was becoming embroiled in something happening 6000 miles away.

At the same time there was a call for war-related films which, as one critic has put it, 'were an honest expression of national resolve and a clear indication of realities, unadorned with Hollywood hoop-la'. The US War Department not only harnessed the talents and experience of the entire American film industry, it also prepared itself to spend $50 million to ensure it got what it wanted. In the fighting areas, massive amounts of combat footage were shot and used for military study as well as being edited into newsreels for cinema consumption.

The most persuasive and influential of the US War Department's indoctrination films was Major Frank Capra's *Why We Fight* series (1942–45). It

Top: Jennings' 80 Days dealt with the German V-1 flying-bomb attacks on Southern England. The American broadcaster Ed Murrow narrated, but the most telling moments on the soundtrack were the ominous silences just before the 'doodlebugs' hit their targets. Above: Jewish profiles offered as 'documentary' evidence in support of Nazi theories on race in Der Ewige Jude. Below: the German weekly wartime newsreel

Nr. 49

Die neuesten
Frontberichte
unserer
Propaganda-
Kompanien

Der Duce besichtigt die Rüstungswerke

Graf Ciano auf dem Berg

General Antonescu in Berlin

Brennstoffnachschub für unsere Luftwaffe

Die deutsche WOCHENSCHAU

Above: The Siege of Leningrad *was a feature-length documentary showing how the city's four million inhabitants built defences in the streets and maintained a precarious food-supply line across the frozen Lake Ladoga. Below:* Stalingrad *depicted the other great siege in the history of the Eastern Front. Supervised by the director Varlamov, the film was released less than six weeks after the German capitulation. Bottom: the Soviet army of liberation in Raizman's* Berlin

was originally intended solely for military purposes but was eventually shown in cinemas throughout the USA and abroad. The aims of Capra's seven films were to counterpoint the lessons of politics and war by focusing on the key events of the conflict.

The result was an expertly sustained series of documentaries which transcended their original purposes and proved highly influential, both in terms of promoting a public 'understanding' of the war, and in terms of documentary techniques in general, whether wartime or peacetime.

The extent to which Hollywood responded to the US government's exhortations to contribute to the war effort can be gauged by the activities of one studio in particular, Walt Disney. By 1943, Disney had virtually abandoned straight entertainment films in favour of war-oriented product, turning out military and home-front propaganda films on an unprecedented scale. Disney's work at this time culminated in the extraordinary *Victory Through Air Power* (1943), a controversial hard-sell polemic for winning the war in the air.

The most enduring war documents of the period were those that stemmed from major Hollywood film-makers who were called up for the specific purpose of recording the conflict. Chief among these were John Ford, William Wyler and John Huston. Shooting often in colour, and with results which were frequently at odds with the wishes of the authorities, these directors contributed a small but remarkable group of documentaries impregnated with their creators' personal attitudes and artistic styles. John Ford led the way with *The Battle of Midway* (1942) and *December 7th* (1943). Wyler joined a USAF bombing raid over Germany to make *The Memphis Belle* (1944) and Huston set aesthetic and moral standards in his wartime film-work which have never been equalled.

As in the USA, documentary film-making was a seriously under-developed area in the Japanese cinema at the outbreak of World War II. Like the Americans, they called on their feature-film directors to service propaganda requirements. Japan's output of militaristic films was prodigious in the years immediately preceding the global conflict, but these were dramatic presentations rather than straight documentaries. Themes were heroic, and the films made strong appeals to the concept of duty, laying little stress on the issues at stake and never questioning the rectitude of Japan's position. These films did, however, avoid the super-heroism of their German counterparts, preferring to depict 'ordinary' fighting men and not shirking from the unpleasant realities of death and distress.

Japanese war films had their own distinctive style: much use of tracking shots, highly mobile camerawork, striking compositions and grainy images that added a touch of realism to battle scenes. The enemy was usually unseen and Japanese fighting units often appeared to be operating in a vacuum. There were few shots of close combat and much use of long-distance, panoramic camera-work that gave an impression of victorious advances. In contrast to American techniques, Japanese war films tended to depersonalize the war to a point which deeply impressed Frank Capra who commented, 'We can't beat this kind of thing'.

Strongly representative of these characteristics were the films of Tomotaka Tasaka, notably his fictional and somewhat ambiguous accounts of the Sino-Japanese war, *Gonin No Sekkohei* (1939, *Five Scouts*) and *Tsuchi to Heitai* (1939, *Earth and Soldiers*). Later on in the war Tasaka reverted to a more conventional format with *Navy* (1943), a depiction of military training in a camp setting. Yoshimura's *Nishizumi Senshachoden* (1940, *The Story of Tank Commander Nishizumi*) was a rare personal study of a fighting man. The film was not aggressively militaristic and was remarkable for the stark, documentary style of its war scenes and the humanistic attitude towards enemy civilians.

Cameramen did not flinch from recording the Nazi atrocities in Russia – the footage made strong propaganda for the besieged people

From 1940 onwards, the Japanese government enforced a stricter code of film-making to take account of war preparation and to encourage the 'national Japanese philosophy . . . and the spirit of complete sacrifice for the nation'. The rest of Japan's cinematographic war was dominated by nationalistic battle movies of which the leading exponents were Yutaka Abe and Kajiro Yamamoto.

Documentaries were a lesser feature of Japan's wartime film-making. The Japanese film expert John Gillett recently made a major rediscovery at the Toho studios when Fumio Kamei's *Fighting Soldiers* (1940) was unearthed. This hour-long documentary shot in China recorded conventional manoeuvre scenes but also contained moments of implicit sympathy for the Chinese peasants and refugees. Gillett has compared the film to John Huston's wartime short *San Pietro* (1944) and indeed the Imperial Japanese authorities found the film far too humanistic in its attitude to the enemy. It was banned and all copies were supposed to have been destroyed, but one print fortunately survived.

Impressive for more conventional reasons was Yamamoto's *The War at Sea From Hawaii to Malaya* (1942), half drama, half documentary, which extolled 'the navy spirit as culminated at Pearl Harbor' and was judged top Japanese film of its year. This film mixed actuality and reconstruction to great effect – the attack on Pearl Harbor being put together entirely with model work – and evidently convinced some US military advisers in Japan that it was genuine footage of the raid.

Film production units of all kinds – feature, newsreel and documentary – were mobilized to serve each nation's war effort. The results add up to a unique, unprecededly thorough record of the world's largest battle-at-arms. But this mass of reportage is also a significant compendium of differing national attitudes caught in a period of turmoil and conflict. CLYDE JEAVONS

Pulling Together

Plunged into war in 1939, the British people expended blood, toil, tears and sweat in defending their nation and defeating Germany – and the documentary film-makers were on hand to record how they did it

It is tempting to see the British documentary film-makers on the eve of World War II as a tight little group of pioneers, a family almost, working together on common principles under the stern, paternal guidance of John Grierson, and believing in cinema not as entertainment or distraction, but as the 'creative interpretation of actuality'. Grierson himself had written in 1937:

'It is worth recalling that the British documentary group began not so much in affection for film *per se* as in affection for national education.'

In other words, Grierson was suggesting that the group was not inspired by fiction and the romance of the movies, but by the romance of social advance, community and the technological society.

The truth is different. By the time war broke out, Grierson had left for Canada where he conceived, founded and guided a whole new national cinema through his invention of the Canadian National Film Board. The GPO Film Unit, base of the British documentary movement, was by then being run by Alberto Cavalcanti, much less of an ideologue, much more of an artist than Grierson. Among the talented young men working for him was the turbulent, rough-edged Harry Watt, a Scotsman, who had already distinguished himself with the classic *Night Mail* (1936), on which he collaborated with Basil Wright, and *North Sea* (1938), a vivid and exciting picture of Aberdeen fishermen battling against a storm. He didn't have much time for Grierson or his theories; his instinct was for drama. Humphrey Jennings and Pat Jackson were his young colleagues, chafing for chances.

Britain was at war, but little happened. A Ministry of Information (MOI) was formed, but it clearly had no idea how to use Cavalcanti's film-makers. In fact the first wartime 'documentary' came from the feature industry – a propaganda piece called *The Lion Has Wings* (1939), flung together by Alexander Korda in a rush of patriotism. It offered a prestigious cluster of stars and some appalling dialogue (Merle Oberon to Ralph Richardson: 'We must keep our land darling – we must keep our freedom. We must fight for the things we believe in – Truth and Beauty . . . and Kindness'). Grierson, perhaps feeling guilty from afar, spoke respectfully of *The Lion Has Wings*: 'This work of film documentation was Britain actually at war, zooming and roaring above the clouds.' But the intemperate Harry Watt more accurately called it 'a ghastly, bloody film'.

A phoney war of their own

'Nothing happened for six weeks,' Watt told Elizabeth Sussex (author of *The Rise and Fall of British Documentary*). 'We sat on our backsides looking out of the window, watching the tarts in Savile Row . . . Then Cavalcanti took it upon himself to send us out . . .'

They went out and shot a 'record of events' called *The First Days* (1939), a kind of cinematic scrapbook of London at the beginning of the war. All the film-makers at the GPO shot material, and although there is no real shape to the film, there is charm and wit and feeling in the picture they built up of evacuees and young recruits; Londoners in their braces filling sandbags; a little group on a suburban street gathered round a car radio to hear

Above: Fires Were Started, *a dramatic reconstruction of London firemen in action. Below: young evacuees with gas-masks, but few other belongings, leave London in* The First Days. *Bottom:* Squadron 992 *showed a barrage-balloon unit in training*

SCOOP!

"LONDON CAN TAKE IT!"

ONE REEL WITH ON-THE-SPOT NARRATION BY
QUENTIN REYNOLDS
OF COLLIER'S MAGAZINE
PRINTS IMMEDIATELY
AVAILABLE FROM
WARNERS!

Above and below right: London Can Take It *took the form of a news bulletin that showed the capital stoically facing up to the Blitz. Above right: the intrepid British airman, 'played' by a real member of Bomber Command in* Target for Tonight, *which dramatized a raid on Germany. The aircraft interiors were shot through holes cut in the fuselage of a wrecked Wellington brought to Denham studios*

Chamberlain announce the outbreak of war. *The First Days* captured – in the plain, ordinary faces confronting catastrophe – the poetry and pathos that Jennings in particular was to make memorable in later work.

The fight begins

The same humane, characteristically English accent distinguishes further early war documentaries: *Squadron 992* (1939), *Dover Front-line* and *Christmas Under Fire* (both 1940). The Blitz came, and the whole team collaborated on another picture under Watt's directorial supervision: *London Can Take It* (1940). This moving account of a night of raids, from sunset to sunrise, with its theme of endurance and resilience and an effective commentary narrated by the American journalist Quentin Reynolds, proved extremely successful in exciting sympathy and support in the USA. Here again there is a sharpness and sensitivity of observation, as well as a humour and understatement (much more powerful than rhetoric) which often take the picture far beyond mere record into poetry.

The Crown Film Unit, as the former GPO Film Unit had been renamed in August 1940, was soon going out beyond the Home Front, to

bring people at home the feel of the war on the battlefronts. *Men of the Lightship* (1940), *Merchant Seamen* (1941), *Coastal Command* (1942) – the titles tell the stories. Particularly rousing was Harry Watt's *Target for Tonight* (1941). 'We were getting very tired of the "taking it" angle,' Watt has recalled, and he and his colleagues decided to make a film about the war that Bomber Command was carrying into the heart of Germany. Simple, unpretentious and dramatic, this tells the story of a typical night raid – from the photo-reconnaissance that provides the planners with the necessary information, to the return of 'F for Freddie', limping home injured to land in heavy fog.

Watt did not use actors. The preface to *Target for Tonight* announces: 'Each part is played by the actual man or woman who does

the job'. But sets were constructed; the pilots changing-room was 'in a little subsidiary studio in Elstree', and the huge Bomber Command control was designed by Edward Carrick and built at Denham. A model was used to show the bombs landing on railway stock yards and real British soldiers stood in a German anti-aircraft gunners. Dialogue was written, and generally played with great naturalness and modesty by the airmen. The result was a film which caught most powerfully the courage and undemonstrative resolution of the RAF. Making his report at the end pipe in mouth, the pilot apologizes with the lightest of ironies, 'I'm afraid I didn't see very much. I was rather busy at the time'. There is nothing affected about his understatement: it has the dignity of truth, and it still has the power to move.

its impression of a Britain at war. This, perhaps Jennings' most completely successful work, got him into trouble with his colleagues, suspicious of the 'arty' and the 'intellectual'. Reviewing it in the *Spectator*, Edgar Anstey described *Listen to Britain* as 'the rarest piece of fiddling since the days of Nero', and added, 'It will be a disaster if this film is sent overseas.' Jennings' *Fires Were Started* (1943) was more safely recognizable in genre (though no less original) – a masterly tribute to London's fire service, strongly affectionate, intensely poetic, the 'public film' at its most creative. This superb sequence of documentaries closes with *A Diary for Timothy* (1945), a tender, closely-wrought, impressionist chronicle of the last year of the war.

Humphrey Jennings made more films before his tragic death in 1950 at the age of 43, but none of them really achieved the intensity of his wartime work. His colleagues were perhaps right to suspect him of aestheticism; he was certainly an intellectual. But in his war films he at least proved himself an artist, with a power of communication that has survived undiminished and which has won a place for him in the history of the British cinema.

Filming for victory

Of course, to pick out a few titles like this is to give a misleading impression of the documentary movement's contribution to Britain's wartime effort. For instance, the torrent of films produced by Basil Wright (who unfortunately spent the war years producing instead of directing) and Edgar Anstey at Film Centre, which Grierson himself had set up when he left the GPO in 1937, had great practical value and were certainly closer to Grierson's ideas. They made instructional films for Civil Defence, for the fire service, for agriculture, for the Ministry of Labour. Other units produced films for the forces, for the hospital services, for the government. The MOI distributed a new five-minute subject free to the cinemas every week, which meant that documentaries were now reaching audiences of over twenty million people. So a vast new public was introduced and accustomed to the

Target for Tonight, dramatically constructed, shows how far Crown – and particularly Harry Watt – had diverged from Griersonian principle. Pat Jackson showed a similar inclination towards the fictional with *Western Approaches*, made in 1944. This was the ambitious story of an Atlantic convoy, and a boatload of survivors from a torpedoed merchantman. Perhaps it was too ambitious, for the result somehow lacks the simple conviction of Watt's picture. All the characters are played by real seamen, but the story, involving staged scenes on a U-boat, a melodramatic climax and a last-minute rescue, smacks too strongly of artifice. And Jack Cardiff's accomplished colour photography lacks the simple black-and-white authenticity of *Target for Tonight*. Perhaps here documentary was edging too close to the theatrical.

The third of those young men who sat watching the tarts in Savile Row in September 1939 had little in common with the fictional bent of Watt and Jackson. Humphrey Jennings had an approach that was entirely his own, and one which he developed through a series of wartime films until he had become by far the most individual, imaginative and powerful of Britain's documentary directors. *Heart of Britain* (1941) was the first of these, a somewhat tentative portrait-in-miniature of the North of England at war, lyrical in feeling, personal in style. The same could be said of his next film, *Words for Battle* (1941), in which he used a collection of literary texts complemented by images of great beauty and originality to celebrate national pride. *Listen to Britain* (1942) developed the style with sounds and images alone, and is wonderfully evocative in

Above left: John Holmes' box-office success Merchant Seamen *followed the fortunes of a crew whose ship is torpedoed. Below: RAF staff in* Words for Battle *and (left) a member of the Observer Corps in* Heart of Britain *watch the war in the air. Jennings backed these films with rousing music and poetry, evoking Britain's pride in its heritage*

Above: scenes from Jennings' Fires Were Started, *which covers a night in the life of a National Fire Service unit during the Blitz. Jennings gave an affectionate portrayal of each fire-fighter in the company*

idea of a cinema of fact rather than fantasy.

Another highly successful genre was the compilation film, made up from footage shot on the battlefronts. One of the first of these, *Wavell's 30,000* (1942), showed the British advance into Libya. Cavalcanti, who had since moved to Ealing to produce features, supervised a satirical demolition of Mussolini's regime in *Yellow Caesar* (1940). And the victorious campaigns from Africa to the Far East to the Second Front were celebrated in a series of fine compilations: *Desert Victory, Tunisian Victory* (both 1943), *Burma Victory* and *The True Glory* (both 1945). Photographed with skill and daring and edited with outstanding craftsmanship, these films from the Service Film Units showed the emergence of classic documentary techniques spreading beyond Crown to inspire a whole new generation of film-makers.

Compilation provided a basis for the work of another highly individual film-maker. Paul Rotha, one of the most talented mavericks of

the British documentary movement, was an early member of the Grierson group, but his style and viewpoint were always firmly his own. Rotha set up his own unit in 1941 with the resolution not to compete with Crown on battlefield subjects but to 'make film about what was happening in Britain under the influence of a world war'. This resulted in a flow of films about public health, schools, day nurseries, education. Then came further and greater inspiration. With the writer Eric Knight, Rotha conceived the idea of a film about the problems of world food – a brave attempt to initiate debate and spread knowledge on a subject which was going to be a matter of life and death to millions in the postwar world. It was partly the nature of the subject and partly the need for economy in time and money that dictated the style of *World of Plenty* (1943). A hard-hitting script, uncompromising in its argument as well as in its statistics, was the blueprint for a powerfully effective montage of library material. It included a persuasive commentary, spoken by actors, as well as interviews with such distinguished authorities as Sir John Boyd-Orr, the nutritionist. If Rotha's plea for a world food plan, based on the right of men to eat, failed to achieve its object, the fault was certainly not in *World of Plenty*. Documentary could lead, enlighten and inspire. It could not work miracles.

What did it all mean? It was Rotha – often prickly, always outspoken – who said of the documentary movement generally: 'I don't think the films themselves are the least bit important. What is important is the sort of spirit which lay behind them.' Perhaps this reflects the anti-art impatience which, since Grierson, seemed so often and so unnecessarily to reflect documentary thinking. Rotha's view certainly plays down the documentary movement's major achievements. It is not true that all the films made in the Thirties and Forties survive today on their own terms – perhaps only *Song of Ceylon* (1934), *Night Mail, London Can Take It*, possibly *Target for Tonight*, Jennings' films from *Words for Battle* to *A Diary for Timothy*, probably a handful more – but this was work that fulfilled an honourable function in its day, and that still illuminates the moment of history that produced it.

The documentary influence

Just how influential these films were on the 'other' British cinema is another question.

During the war there were certainly instance where feature directors profited from the e perience and the understanding of the doc mentarists. Rotha claims that *Night Sh* (1942), made by his unit about women wor ing in a Welsh factory, inspired Frank Laund and Sidney Gilliat's *Millions Like Us* (1943 Carol Reed's *The Way Ahead* (1944) was deve oped out of an army training film called *T New Lot* (1942); and Basil Wright has recall how Noel Coward studied wartime documen aries when he was scripting *In Which We Ser* (1942). Films like *San Demetrio, London* (1943 too, and Asquith's *We Dive at Dawn* (1943 were certainly affected by the documenta tradition.

But it was not a lasting influence. Docume tary directors like Watt, Jackson and Jack Le who went across to features, hardly manag to make much of a dent in established trac tion; and Paul Rotha had a hard time as a independent producer of his own feature Jennings never made a fiction film, and on th evidence of dramatized documentaries like *T Silent Village* (1943) and *The Cumberland Sto* (1947), would not have been very successfu he had.

Cavalcanti claimed that 'perhaps the mo important result of the documentary mov ment' was the imposition of workers as 'dign fied human beings' on a British cinema which the working classes had tradition' been considered as fit for nothing more tha comic relief. But it is interesting to find exact the same charge being levelled, ten years aft the end of the war, by members of the Fr Cinema documentary group.

The wartime documentary movement pe formed a worthy service and made some fi films, but it did not change things. Nor did th movement go forward into peacetime wi much vitality. Perhaps one of the reasons w that, having spent the Thirties as an establishment dissidents, the survivors fou that the war had turned them into propagan ists for tradition. They were certainly no long in any sense radical. Perhaps, too, the scorn f 'intellect' and 'art', which had once signified healthy impatience with pretension, ha become too much of an excuse for co placency. When Churchill's Conservative go ernment ungratefully and unimaginative disbanded the Crown Film Unit in Janua 1952, no-one really seemed to care. Th chapter had already ended.

LINDSAY ANDERSO

Documentary Footage
Its uses and abuses

The immense amount of film shot during the war has been utilized in many ways – for propaganda, for dramatic sequences and for documentation. This article explores the ways that footage of the war has been used to mislead as well as to inform

World War II was unique in history – not only for the murderousness with which it was fought, but also for the thoroughness with which it was recorded on film. When the war ended, all the material shot, whether edited or in the form of rushes, became part of the historical record of the conflict. Though archives did their best to catalogue and identify the material entrusted to them, they were starved of funds and staff. Even today only about half the filmed record of the war has been positively identified. As with any other such records it was at the mercy of those who used it and, even in peacetime, not all film-makers are particularly fastidious.

Many scrupulous records do exist. The Wehrmacht (the German military command) painstakingly recorded its advance into Russia and shot similar footage of the campaigns in Poland, the Low Countries and France. The British recorded the Eighth Army from Normandy to the Danish border. The US Marine Corps filmed all of its amphibious operations and it recorded the invasions of Iwo Jima and Okinawa in colour. The US air force not only filmed its own operations, but recorded the advance of the American armies into southern Germany and Czechoslovakia – also in colour. There is colour film of the liberation of Prague, the link-up between the Russians and the Americans at Torgau, and of the surrender of an entire SS division to the American Sixth Army. There is also colour film of what the Americans found when they liberated the concentration camp at Buchenwald. There is even British film of bread-baking and a German film of igloo-making.

Despite the amount of resources deployed and the 500 million feet of film shot, there are unexpected gaps in the record. There is virtually no film of the British fleet in the first six months of the war. The Admiralty did not have its own film units and yet would not allow civilians to film its activities, so there is little film of the departure of the British Expeditionary Force to France or of its evacuation from Dunkirk – only a few hundred feet shot by civilian newsreel cameramen exists. The vessel carrying most of the film of D-Day back to England for processing was sunk, and there is hardly any film of the Japanese attack on Pearl Harbor from either the American or the Japanese side.

Nor is there much film of black American troops or of American service women (black or white). Their contributions to the war may not have been highly regarded. There is little Soviet film of the battle of Stalingrad – and what exists should be treated with suspicion since the army commander, General Chuikov, never allowed cameramen into the sector where the heavy fighting was. There is virtually no filmed record of the extermination of Europe's Jews and gypsies – the Nazis saw no purpose in recording that – and the victims had no opportunity to show what was happening to them. The few records which do exist are either the work of amateurs – grisly home movies dating from before the systematic ex-

Above left: picking up the pieces after a bomb attack – from British documentary footage. Below left: the Soviets re-invaded Berlin, street by street, in order to film it. Below: courage in the face of adversity – the Soviet image in films – from the Story of Stalingrad

termination began – or show conditions in transit or concentration camps, not the actual extermination camps, crematoria or gas chambers.

During the war itself the footage obtained was used in many different ways. Feature film-makers, newsreel outfits, armed forces, scientific research establishments, industries, organized pressure groups and public and private organizations of all kinds made films about the war to serve their own purposes. Not surprisingly, different groups used the footage in different ways.

The coverage of the war by various bodies on the Soviet/German battle lines is an interesting example. In Nazi Germany several powerful institutions recorded their own version of what went on. For the newsreel cameramen who were ultimately responsible to Goebbels' Propaganda Ministry, the invasion of the Soviet Union in the summer of 1941 was a classic blitzkrieg: Panzers and motorized infantry and Stuka aircraft cut through Soviet defences and raced towards Moscow. The SS slightly modified their film version of events. Wherever the fighting was toughest or the advance was swiftest, there could be found Waffen SS tanks and armoured personnel carriers. But the Wehrmacht knew better. The German army was not highly motorized. While its handful of Panzers did race ahead, the great mass of the German army fought as it had a generation before. Its units were shipped by troop train to points hundreds of miles from the front. From there they marched on foot and their supplies were brought up in horse-drawn wagons. The Wehrmacht left the job of impressing civilians to the newsreels. It was more interested in learning from its mistakes. How did equipment stand up to the heat and dust of a Russian summer? How exhausted were the troops after a week's forced march? Why could Russian ponies and iron-wheeled carts keep going in terrain that brought German draught-horses and rubber-tyred wagons to a standstill? So the Wehrmacht cameramen diligently recorded exhausted troops, broken-down machines and all the other consequences of inadequate equipment and incompetent planning; meanwhile audiences back home

Above: a British Spitfire chasing a German Heinkel in the Battle of Britain. *The Heinkels were borrowed from the Spanish air force and fitted with Rolls-Royce aero engines for the film. Below: a post-war shot of Auschwitz from* The World at War

marvelled at the speed and smoothness of the triumphal advance.

On the other side of the battle line much the same thing happened. Soviet combat cameramen recorded retreat, panic flight and disaster, while newsreel audiences behind the lines saw nothing but resolute defence, calm assurance and single-minded patriotism.

Authorities in each of the combatant countries also had the difficult task of controlling what sort of non-fictional material was shown to the ordinary cinema-going public. Every country had a centrally controlled censorship mechanism, whose interventions ranged from vague exhortations to explicit instructions. German newsreels, for instance, were never allowed to dwell on the effects of the Allied bombing offensive on German cities; to do so would be to call attention to the inadequacy of German aerial defences. But British newsreels took urban destruction as an important theme in 1940 and 1941 (carefully following government guidelines, that any pan shots of bombed-out streets should begin and end on buildings which were intact) to show that the British could take it. The Italians, who never claimed to have impregnable air defences, showed their cities in flames to rouse popular feeling against the cultural barbarism of their enemies.

The job of publicly exhibited newsreels and documentaries, though the methods varied in each country, was to support the war effort and to sustain the morale of the millions of civilians who went to the cinema each week. All other considerations were secondary. Thus, though there might be disagreement about what would best sustain morale at any given time, no-one in authority ever doubted that a film which did not do that should not be made, and if it somehow were made, it should certainly not be exhibited. This led to awesome discrepancies between the war as fought and

the war as portrayed. Harry Watt's *Target for Tonight* (1941), which used Royal Air Force air crew and ground personnel, was produced at a time when RAF night bombers were known to be unable to drop more than ten per cent of their bomb loads within an eight-mile radius of their aiming points. Yet it showed a single aircraft destroying an entire oil refinery and marshalling yards with a single stick of bombs. *Desert Victory* (1943) was made to celebrate the second battle of El Alamein which was rightly expected to be the last great land battle to be fought in the West without the assistance of the American troops. Some of it was filmed in Egypt; much of it was filmed on the back-lot at Pinewood studios. Some night shots recorded the tracer-bullet arcs of the Eighth Army in Egypt, but lighted matches thrown a few feet away from the camera looked equally impressive.

One of the most elaborate scenes from *Stalingrad* (1943), shows the link-up of the two Soviet armies who cut off the German troops besieging the city. The scene shows long lines of infantry running towards each other across snow-covered fields, embracing and cheering as they meet. But in reality the first units to link up with each other were motorized and they met in fog.

Why We Fight (1942–45) was a series of hour-long films directed by Frank Capra, to be shown to all American conscripts during their basic training. By explaining the nature of the societies of both America's adversaries and allies, it was intended to commit those young Americans who saw it to the war they were waging and the role that they were playing in it. The War Department, which sponsored it, was so pleased with the series that it was cleared for theatrical release. However, it was unwilling to allow Capra to describe in any detail the role of the Communist Party in twentieth-century China and, in order to preserve balance, decided that the activities of Chiang Kai-Shek should not be given undue emphasis either. With the most important single issue in Chinese politics simply left out of the *Battle of China* (1944), the film was crippled. Even the government came to realize this, and so withdrew it.

We do not know what effect any of these films had. Most studies of audience behaviour were conceptually unsophisticated or frankly anecdotal. What evidence there is does not support the idea that audiences were mindlessly passive or capable of easy manipulation by skilled or unscrupulous film-makers. American GIs in basic training appreciated film shows of all sorts – with the lights out they could catch up on their sleep. When German audiences left their cinemas they couldn't help noticing that their cities had been reduced to rubble. British audiences appreciated that it was difficult for RAF cameramen to film the destruction of German marshalling yards from the ground so they cheerfully accepted the destruction of a model. As always, audiences used films – they saw what they wanted to see and heard what they wanted to hear; if that coincided with what the film-makers wanted, everyone was content. It was certainly not a time for fastidious film-making.

So for thirty years Germans in tanks have continued to slice through Russia like a hot knife through butter and the Soviet Army has surrounded them with its infantry at Stalingrad under clear skies. In the BBC's *The Commanders* (1972) London was bombed with American transport aircraft and British troops were evacuated from Dunkirk with an aircraft carrier. More recently, in *The Secret War* (1977) Luftwaffe pilots blitzing Coventry in 1940 saw

beneath them fires started by the RAF when they bombed Germany in 1945. Independent television companies have been equally imprecise. In Granada Television's *Cities at War* (1968), a scene of a worker in a Leningrad factory was step printed (i.e. every third frame was printed twice) to make him appear to have slowed his pace in the bitter cold of the siege. In Thames Television's *The Hunting of Force Z* (1977) the HMS *Repulse* and the HMS *Prince of Wales*, which are sent to the bottom of the sea by the Japanese air force, were models that were first sunk in a 1942 Japanese dramadocumentary.

Films made directly for the cinema have also cut corners. Alain Resnais in *Nuit et Brouillard* (1955, *Night and Fog*) showed the horrors of Auschwitz with film taken in Holland before Auschwitz was built. In *Swastika* (1973) experts claimed to have been able to lip read what was said in Eva Braun's silent home movies and provided speeches even for guests whose backs were turned to the camera. In reality, guests facing the camera had a habit of talking more about the afternoon's entertainment than exterminating European Jewry.

It's not hard to see why such things are done. Except when making films for knowledgeable, critical specialists, most film-makers – including documentary film-makers – have never been much interested in authenticity for its own sake. They have been more concerned

with what they see as inner truths than in surface appearances. Their arguments are both practical and aesthetic. Practically, there are very few shots of advancing tanks that have been taken from the point of view of the enemy, or top shots of troops crawling on their bellies under fire, or close-ups of high-explosive shells on impact, or of the first wave of an amphibious force seen from the standpoint of the beach defenders. If such scenes are to be shown at all they must necessarily be staged. The aesthetic argument is related to this: if the point of a scene is to show cold, wet, miserable troops, it doesn't really matter whether they are filmed on manoeuvres or in combat as long as their cold and misery is genuine. What counts is the emotion, not how it is induced.

This is why documentary film-makers have always been prepared to use reconstructions, training films and even excerpts from feature films to flesh out what they see as the bare bones of their visual material. John Huston, for example, cut re-shot material into *San Pietro* (1944), Frank Capra shot Nazi classroom scenes in the United States and the Soviets refought parts of the battle for Stalingrad after the Germans surrendered, and reconquered Berlin four years after the end of the war.

Yet documentary film-makers have always been uneasy about such practices. Documentaries, after all, make claims to tell the truth and their credibility suffers if the material they incorporate is shown to be other than what it purports to be. That is why so many go to great lengths to conceal the origins of their material – even to the point of degrading picture quality to give the impression that scenes were shot under hazardous circumstances many years beforehand.

The production team responsible for *The World at War* made for Thames Television between 1971 and 1974 did not accept that documentary accounts of World War II need necessarily rely on unauthentic material or on material used unauthentically to make the film effective. The executive producer was Jeremy Isaacs, I was the associate producer and we thought it was possible to be faithful to actuality film as shot and yet make films which

Above left: in Patton *large numbers of Patton tanks converge – but they were, in fact, built long after the war had ended. Below left: the bombing of Pearl Harbor was restaged for* Tora! Tora! Tora! *Below: an American plane attacks a Japanese aircraft carrier in* Midway *– a reconstructed sequence from the film*

Above: four scenes from the original D-Day footage used in Overlord. *The makers went to great pains to use shots of the best technical quality without presenting them in contextually implausible ways*

were more than chronicles. We saw no reason why the impact of the series would be diminished if it faithfully acknowledged and critically evaluated the material from which it was made. But such positive identification of material was expensive, difficult and time consuming: it meant being systematically sceptical towards all previous use of material, and being particularly vigilant where compilation films were concerned. (Those who believe that 'if you've seen one Stuka you've seen them all' had a habit of sending the same one into action against Warsaw, Rotterdam, Biggin Hill and Stalingrad.) Though *The World at War* was a critical and popular success and earned more money for Thames than any other project it has undertaken, the challenge of its production methods does not appear to have been taken up by others dealing with World War II.

Feature film-makers have never been worried in the same way about distinctions between authentic and unauthentic material and its use. Being concerned with dramatic impact, they have had no hesitation about blurring distinctions to suit their needs. Budgetary considerations are often paramount: assembling a naval armada to invade the European continent strained the combined industrial resources of the United States and Britain, so not surprisingly producers have tended to use actual footage of the D-Day landings rather than try to re-create the whole

show. There is the question of danger as well: front-line filming is among the most hazardous possible. An explosive charge planted underground and detonated has different characteristics from one which results from the impact of a high explosive shell. The pilots of ground-support aircraft pressing home an attack will fly differently from stunt pilots doing their best *not* to kill the camera crew. No wonder *Midway* (1976) used material shot by John Ford and his crew when they were in the line of real fire in 1942.

Another use of actuality material is to propel a narrative forward or to establish locations. *La Traversée de Paris* (1956, *A Pig Across Paris*) made no attempt to suggest that it had been filmed under German Occupation: it simply used the well-known films of the German victory parade down the Champs Elysées as its title sequence to establish economically where and when the story was going to take place.

All these practices have their dangers: actuality material that is striking enough to use in the first place may end up stealing the show from the fictional material in which it is embedded. Who could take even a Francis Ford Coppola D-Day seriously once they'd seen what the real armada looked like? Could anyone feel that the studio Third Reich which collapsed around Alec Guiness' head told them more about the fall of Berlin than Soviet actuality film which punctuated his impersonation of the Führer in *Hitler: the Last Ten Days* (1973)? And could anyone looking at the brief snatches of film of Japanese aircraft taking off from their carriers to bomb Pearl Harbor – the only such film which exists – be impatient to return to the travelling matte

world of *Tora! Tora! Tora!* (1970)?

Some makers of feature films have taken that lesson to heart. There is no actual footage in *Patton* (1970) – the fictional presentation of America's most-photographed tank general. Audiences won't be tempted to wonder how he managed to win his victories with tanks which were built long after his death.

Actuality film is inconspicuous in many other war spectaculars because genuine footage could hardly be intercut with scenes in these films. For *The Battle of the River Plate* (1956), the American navy lent Michael Powell a cruiser but wouldn't let him sink it or, for that matter, replace the Stars and Stripes with a German naval battle flag. *The Battle of Britain* (1969) equipped its Heinkels and Messerschmitts with the same aero engines as the Royal Air Force had. (The Germans still lost!) The cameramen who filmed the liberation of Paris in 1944 were tactless enough to neglect their fellows who subsequently became ministers in de Gaulles' Fifth Republic, so their material was not really welcome in *Paris Brûle-t-il* (1969, *Is Paris Burning?*).

Can fiction and actuality film ever be successfully integrated? Admirers of *Overlord* (1975) think it is a model of how such a thing might be done, but if it showed a way, no-one has yet followed it. Certainly the enterprise is fraught with difficulties and there is no point even attempting it until film-makers stop thinking of archives as visual breakers' yards from which to get the odd shot of a Stuka or an invasion, and begin to think of the filmed record of World War II as something to respect. If past experience is any guide, that time might be some way off.

JERRY KUEHL

Realism, Italian-style

After the false rhetoric of the Fascist regime had been exposed, Italian film-makers went in search of the truth and found it in everyday life

When the great Italian director Roberto Rossellini was asked to define neo-realism, he said:

'For me it is above all a moral position from which to look at the world. It then became an aesthetic position, but at the beginning it was moral.'

To understand both the moral and aesthetic position which informed neo-realism, as well as the forces which helped destroy it, it is necessary to begin with the economic, political, and social context in which it was born.

There were, of course, harbingers of a 'new realism' before Rossellini's *Roma, Città Aperta*

1945, *Rome, Open City*). But when that film burst upon the international cinema scene in the immediate post-war years, neo-realism proper can be said to have begun. *Rome, Open City* was a direct product of the 'War of Liberation' taking place in Italy in 1945.

During 1943 and 1944, Italy had been torn apart. Mussolini's government had fallen, the new Badoglio government had surrendered to the invading Allied armies in the South while the Germans had occupied the North; anti-fascist Italians of every political and religious persuasion had been involved in the fighting to liberate their country and had been united by the struggle against fascism.

To film-makers and all other artists of the period it was clear that if the lies and empty rhetoric of the Mussolini government had brought Italy to agony, then a confrontation with reality, an encounter with 'truth' would save Italy. In terms of the cinema this meant the rejection of what had gone before, for although there were few blatant propaganda films made under the Fascist regime, the films that were produced in Italy during the war years had

little to do with Italian reality.

Some long-term benefits emerged from the Fascist government's control of the film industry. The huge studio complex of Cinecittà had been built and the Italian film school, Centro Sperimentale di Cinematografia, had already trained many important Italian film-makers. Not every film made under the Fascist regime was poor but none of them came close to touching the social reality of Italy; for the most part, they were slick, glossy, vacuous melodramas made entirely in the studios and featuring upper-middle-class characters. Collectively they were known as 'white telephone' films, a nickname that has come to typify film production in Italy under the Fascists.

Inspired by the 'War of Liberation', film-makers rejected the old cinema and its conventions. Their belief in showing 'things as they are' was placed in the service of the construction of a new Italy. In this way the moral and aesthetic principles of neo-realism were united. The manner and style of the new cinema was to be as much a statement as its subject-matter.

The theory of neo-realism was formulated in part from basic assumptions about the nature of cinema and its function in society, and in part from the early films of the movement. Theory and practice rarely coincided in one film and many were only superficially neo-realist films. Some astute Italian critics decried the use of neo-realist mannerisms to disguise purely commercial ventures (usually exploitative sexual melodramas) and the forcing of material which cried out for a different treatment into a neo-realist style.

Cesare Zavattini, the writer of Vittorio De Sica's major films, and a director himself in the Fifties, formulated the theory of neo-realism; cinema's task was no longer simply to 'entertain' in the usual sense of the word, but to confront audiences with

Above: Massimo Girotti in Visconti's Ossessione. *A stranger in a remote rural district, he finds casual work with a couple who run a roadhouse, seduces the wife and plots with her to murder the husband. Left: the hurried burial of a partisan in Rossellini's six-part film* Paisà, *about the resistance and liberation of Italy in 1944–45. Below: production shot from De Sica's* The Children Are Watching Us *(1943), not strictly a neo-realist film but one that anticipates the style, notably through its use of exterior shots and urban settings*

Above: a starkly realistic scene from La Terra Trema, *filmed several years before the term 'kitchen sink' was used to describe realist drama. The actors were non-professionals and the details of life in the Sicilian fishing community were totally authentic. Right: father and son (Lamberto Maggiorani and Enzo Staiola) walk the rain-soaked streets in Bicycle Thieves. Below right: Sperduti nel Buio (Lost in Darkness), a melodrama filmed in the slums of Naples, provides evidence of a realist style in Italian cinema as early as 1914. With its scrupulous attention to detail, its cracked walls and worn steps and its use of natural light, this film influenced several generations of Italian film-makers*

found in newspapers. Zavattini cited the example of a woman buying a pair of shoes to show how simple such narratives could be and how social problems – poverty, unemployment, poor housing – could be illustrated within a fiction film.

Although most of the problems presented in neo-realist films were susceptible to political solution, the neo-realists never presented a clear political programme. Their party affiliations were, after all, quite diverse: a number of writers and directors were Marxists but just as many were Christian Democrats, or held various other political ideas.

The theorists, especially Zavattini, insisted that there was a natural affinity between the cinema and 'reality', despite the fact that a camera will record whatever is in front of the lens and that the processed film will then (depending upon the skill of the film-maker) convince a spectator of the 'reality' of what he is seeing. But it was never quite so simple and Zavattini frequently made it clear that, for him, the entire question remained ambiguous, that cinematic 'realism' was merely a convention, and that the neo-realist method was only one possible approach to cinema.

Inevitably audiences become accustomed to cinematic conventions, even those as initially 'shocking' as open-air shooting on real streets with non-professional actors. In *Rome, Open City* real locations were used for almost the entire film but no-one has complained (and very few people even knew) that the priest's room, the Gestapo headquarters and one apartment were constructed entirely in a studio and therefore broke the rules of authenticity. Similarly the theoretical principle that roles be played by 'real people' – which was partly an over-reaction to the artificiality of movie stars – became a convention in itself.

In De Sica's *Umberto D* (1951), the non-actor playing the role of the unemployed government official was in real life an elderly professor. He was highly praised for the 'reality' of his performance but it was a performance; the professor had nothing in common with the character except age.

The only neo-realist film which followed the theory by having the entire cast made up of non-professionals was Visconti's *La Terra Trema* (1948,

Pure neo-realism lasted only for a few short years, although the style was soon absorbed into Italian popular cinema

The Earth Trembles). In that film, however, Visconti rehearsed his village fishermen over and over again until they delivered the performances he wanted. They were effective, not so much because they were fishermen, but rather because they had been formed into good actors.

For some critics and film-makers, 'reality' meant 'social reality' and in particular the representation of the the conditions of the poor and unemployed. Later, when directors like Rossellini and Visconti moved away from the working classes, they were denounced as 'betrayers of neo-realism', as if the middle classes were not a part of 'social reality'.

Social criticism was hardly lacking in neo-realist films, but it was rarely their major thrust. In De Sica's *Ladri di Biciclette* (1948, *Bicycle Thieves*) the camera pans along rows of pawned sheets while the protagonist attempts to pawn those belonging to his wife. Throughout the film we are made aware of the thousands of people like him, all seeking work. Yet the problem of unemployment is never analysed. Instead the story takes a dramatic turn as the protagonist steals a bicycle and is thus criminalized

their own reality, to analyse that reality, and to unite audiences through a shared confrontation with reality. The most disheartening thing for the neo-realist film-makers must have been that this basic goal was not achieved, simply because Italian audiences remained indifferent or hostile to the films, preferring instead pure escapism. They had no desire to confront on the screen the depressing reality of their everyday lives.

If cinema was to present things 'as they are', it meant that fiction, particularly that derived from novels and plays, would have to be replaced by looser, rather 'open ended' narratives, based on real experience familiar to the film-makers or, perhaps,

by his poverty. He is subsequently humiliated and finally 'redeemed'. At the end of the film we are moved by the man's plight, but we are no closer to an understanding of his social reality.

Visconti's *La Terra Trema* comes closest to being the perfect neo-realist film: it achieves a clear understanding of how the fishermen are exploited and of how this 'social reality' works to oppress people generally. Ironically, while the theory of neo-realism was fulfilled by *La Terra Trema*, Visconti violated one of Zavattini's fundamental tenets by basing the film on a novel, *I Malavoglia*, by the nineteenth-century writer Giovanni Verga, who is often mentioned by critics and film historians as one of the possible sources of Italian neo-realism.

Most of the arguments and polemics surrounding neo-realism had already been rehearsed in the nineteenth century. At that time the literary movements of the *verismo* novelists concerned themselves primarily with the lower classes and their problems. One of the stated goals of the verist writers was the social education of their readers. Such work, however, rarely reached the class which might have drawn benefit from it.

Most verist novelists, like the neo-realist directors, sought to increase their popularity by recounting routine shop-girl fantasies, cloaked in the mantle of realism. But a small core of film-makers remained faithful to the principles of neo-realism; among them were Giuseppe De Santis, who made *Caccia Tragica* (1947, *Tragic Pursuit*), a tale of robbery at a collective farm and *Roma Ore Undici* (1952, *Rome, Eleven O'Clock*), a memorable film of a real-life incident in which a staircase collapsed under the weight of two hundred girls who had all applied for the same job.

In tracing the origins of Italian neo-realism, 'realist' film styles can be detected in the early Italian cinema: even the historical spectaculars which gave Italian cinema its international reputation contain a vividly realistic streak.

The American cinema may also be evidenced as an antecedent of Italian neo-realism: it is clear, for example, that everyone working in Italian cinema of the Forties was familiar with such 'realist' classics as Vidor's *The Crowd* (1928) and Stroheim's

Greed (1924). Also influential was the so-called 'poetic realism' of Jean Renoir and his fellow film-makers in France during the Thirties. Visconti's own training as an assistant on *Toni* (1934) and his close study of Renoir's films is echoed in films like *Ossessione* (1942, *Obsession*) and *La Terra Trema*.

The 'War of Liberation' may have temporarily united Italians of diverse political beliefs and provided an inspiration for the neo-realists but the honeymoon was short-lived. After the liberation, anti-communist propaganda took root in Italy.

Although the social criticism of neo-realist cinema was essentially mild and non-Marxist, the films did illuminate problems in Italy that remained unsolved. In the immediate post-war climate, 'anti-fascist' had come to mean much the same thing as 'communist' and the government did not take too kindly to the image of the country that the neo-realist film-makers were projecting. For its part, the Church claimed that such films were unsympathetic to the clergy and even blasphemous.

Some neo-realist films had great success at the box-office, but for the most part they depended on foreign receipts to cover the costs of even the small budgets involved. The huge popularity of American films all but destroyed whatever financial basis the domestic market had for Italian films, neo-realist or otherwise. Gradually the producers, too, became hostile to the neo-realist style.

When the government appointed Giulio Andreotti as the head of Direzione Generale dello Spettacolo (an agency for overseeing the performing arts), he was given wide-ranging powers over the cinema. Andreotti controlled bank loans: he restricted them to 'suitable' films and vetoed loans on films which were 'infected with the spirit of neo-realism'. His powers went even further: Andreotti could, and often did, ban public screenings of films that he decided were 'not in the best interests of Italy'. Even more harmful were the bans on the exportation of films that maligned Italy. And it was these moves as much as anything else that brought about the demise of the neo-realist movement.

The immediate inheritance of the neo-realist movement was to be evidenced in the Fifties, the decade that also saw the break up of the original core of directors – Rossellini, Visconti, De Sica and the young Antonioni. As their careers diverged and the political realities of Italy in the Fifties went through several changes, the Italian cinema gradually shed its mantle of neo-realism.

DAVID OVERBEY

Top: in Riso Amaro *(1948, Bitter Rice)* Silvana Mangano and Vittorio Gassman *try to steal the rice crop from a small valley in the North of Italy. The film portrayed the painful labour of rice-growing with a documentary zeal, but its success at the box-office, both at home and abroad, was probably due to its erotic content (below left). Above:* Stromboli, *made in 1949, is a transitional film that bears the vestiges of the documentary style so beloved of the neo-realists, but also indicates the shift in Italian cinema towards the use of international stars in sensational dramas set against a background of rural poverty*

The films of

Roberto Rossellini

Rossellini is commonly known as the 'father' of the neo-realist movement. Yet this convenient critical label does not do full justice to a director who, in the face of widespread criticism, continually sought to redefine the relationship between the film-maker and his audience and to create a new, vital role for cinema in society

Rossellini made his first full-length feature films during the period that the Fascist regime held sway in Italy. For this reason, many of the director's later admirers were uncomfortable when he talked blithely and frankly of his work on *La Nave Bianca* (1941, The White Ship), *Un Pilota Ritorna* (1942, A Pilot Returns) and *L'Uomo della Croce* (1943, The Man of the Cross). Indeed, *La Nave Bianca* was produced under the supervision of the dedicated Fascist Francesco De Robertis at the Naval Ministry.

These films have been described as 'fascist propaganda', mostly, of course, by people who have never seen them. However, in Rossellini's defence it must be remembered that anyone working in the cinema at that time was forced to operate under tight restrictions. Obviously no anti-fascist films were made; on the other hand, few overtly propagandist features were made either (the radio was far more extensively used for such purposes). Few film-makers indulged in the kind of fascist rhetoric to be found in Alessandro Blasetti's *Vecchia Guardia* (1934, *The Old Guard*) or Mario Camerini's *Il Grande Appello* (1936, The Great Roll-Call).

La Nave Bianca is half documentary and half

fiction. A romance between a sailor and a schoolteacher-turned-nurse links the film's two sections. The first shows the sailor's ship leaving port (with a few shots indicating the power of the Italian navy), sailing into battle and being severely damaged. The second section deals with the rescue of the wounded – including the sailor – and their fine treatment on a hospital ship, where the sailor is reunited with his beloved. The film's ideological fault is not that it is openly fascist in outlook but that it achieves its aim of promoting the illusion that all is well in Italy in 1941.

Any attempt by a film-maker to present life as it was lived was bound to be frustrated

during the Fascist period, as most of the future neo-realists soon found. However, their very frustration with this state of affairs made them reject fascism on moral and aesthetic grounds; thus the neo-realist movement partly owes its origins to the disenchantment of certain film-makers with the restrictions placed on artistic freedom in Fascist Italy.

Above left: Rossellini in 1949, when rumours of his romance with Ingrid Bergman were rife. Above: an American GI meets a Naples urchin in Paisà. *Below: a village under fire in* L'Uomo della Croce, *one of Rossellini's films made during the Fascist regime*

By 1942 De Robertis and Rossellini had quarrelled – first over Rossellini's refusal to work from a detailed scenario, and then over politics. Two years later, Rossellini was in Rome, the representative of the Christian Democrats in the film branch of the Committee of National Liberation. It was then that neo-realism was born with *Roma, Città Aperta* 1945, *Rome, Open City*). Rossellini is often said to be the father of neo-realism which, considering the influence *Rome, Open City* and his next film, *Paisà* (1946, *Paisan*), had on film-makers in Italy and all over the world, is not surprising. However, it must be remembered that neo-realism had a number of antecedents, sprang from a number of sources, and that the same influences working on Rossellini were also felt by other film-makers, some of whom were already aiming at similar goals. Rossellini himself was unhappy with the title; it resulted in his work being attacked as it moved away from dealing exclusively with the Italian experience of World War II:

'It was the war itself which motivated me; war and resistance are collective actions by definition. If from the collective I then passed to an examination of personality, as in the case of the child in *Germania, Anno Zero* (1947, *Germany, Year Zero*) and the refugee of *Stromboli* 1950, *God's Land*) that was part of my natural evolution as a director.'

That 'evolution' was often branded 'involution' and 'betrayal of neo-realism' by a good many critics at the time.

Rossellini's personal life undoubtedly had a strong impact on the subsequent development of his work. One of the reasons he made *L'Amore* (1948, *Love*) was his long-standing relationship with the actress Anna Magnani:

'The phenomenon to be examined was Anna Magnani. Only the novel, poetry and the

cinema permit us to rummage through a personality to discover reactions and motives for actions.'

In the second part of the film, *Il Miracolo*, (*The Miracle*), Magnani plays a simple peasant woman who is made pregnant by a vagabond she believes to be St Joseph. It caused a scandal everywhere. Rossellini's wish to return to a 'more optimistic subject' led to *Francesco, Giullare di Dio* (1950, *Flowers of St Francis*), a film about St Francis in the form of a fable. Instead of winning back support from those who had attacked him as a blasphemer after *Il Miracolo*, the new film merely antagonized those who had liked the previous one.

Ingrid Bergman had seen *Rome, Open City* and *Paisà* in the winter of 1947–48. She wrote to Rossellini expressing a strong desire to appear in one of his films. A few months later they met to discuss the making of *Stromboli*.

Bergman was disenchanted with her marriage and career at the time and a love affair rapidly developed between her and her idol which shocked her American fans – accustomed to Bergman's 'spiritual' image – and provided good copy for gossip columnists for some time. Following the birth of a son, Bergman's husband, Dr Lindstrom, divorced her and she and Rossellini were married. The partnership led to six of his finest films, particularly *Stromboli* and *Viaggio in Italia* (1954, *Journey to Italy*). *Stromboli* has Bergman cast as a Lithuanian refugee who marries a peasant to escape from an internment camp after the end of World War II. When he takes her to his island home, she finds herself even more imprisoned. Seeking to escape, she climbs over the island's semi-active volcano, Stromboli. Exhausted and in despair she sinks to the ground and cries out to God. In *Journey to Italy*, she and George Sanders play an English couple whose marriage is gradually breaking down. They travel to Italy in order to sell a house bequeathed to them in a will. Gradually they fall under the influence of the unfamiliar Italian environment, and are ultimately reconciled during a religious parade in a small village. Both films were unsuccessful at the box-office, and have led to a great many misunderstandings about the nature of Rossellini's religious beliefs. He has pointed out that the refugee's crying out to God at the end of *Stromboli* is merely an instinctive act that anyone at the end of his strength might commit, and that the couple's reconciliation at the end of *Journey to Italy* is at best only temporary; any religious significance the scene may possess is probably ironic.

Although Rossellini's films found fewer and fewer paying customers and were often dismissed by the majority of critics who bothered to review them (with the French being a happy exception), his influence on other film-makers continued to be felt. *Journey to Italy* encouraged Michelangelo Antonioni to make *L'Avventura* (1960, The Adventure); certainly both François Truffaut and Jean-Luc Godard have admitted their debt to Rossellini during this period. Rossellini was simply a decade ahead of his time, and audiences were just not

Above: St Francis and his brother friars in Flowers of St Francis, *which explored the idea of saintliness through a naturalistic evocation of history. Right: Ingrid Bergman as Karin, the oppressed wife of a Sicilian fisherman in* Stromboli

ready to accept or understand what he was attempting to do.

For a very short period Rossellini attempted to work within the commercial cinema, making *Il Generale Della Rovere* (1959, General Della Rovere), a heavily scripted, sentimental, pseudo-realist film, and *Vanina Vanini* (1961, The Betrayer), based on stories by Stendhal. While the first did very well with audiences and critics, the second was a failure. Rossellini himself was happy with neither, and decided to give up the cinema and work in the popular medium of television, making historical and scientific meditations – which he described as 'studies of ideas as they burst upon history'. *L'Età del Ferro* (1964, The Age of Iron) was followed by *La Prise de Pouvoir par Louis XIV* (1966, The Rise of Louis XIV), which had a surprising international success in cinemas. The series continued with *Atti Degli Apostoli* (1969, Acts of the Apostles), *Socrate* (1970, Socrates), *Il Messia* (1975, The Messiah), and was to include a film on Karl Marx.

Just before his death in 1977 at the age of 71, Rossellini was looking forward to the publication in France of his book on education and society, *Un Esprit Libre ne Doit Rien Apprendre en Esclave*. In many ways that title – which in English means 'A free spirit will learn nothing from slavery' – sums up his life and career. When asked at Cannes what he thought his role and function was in world cinema, he replied with a laugh: 'As I see it my role is to be a constant pain in the ass to everyone.' And so he was – if all pejorative connotations may be removed from the phrase. He never let anyone alone; he pushed, questioned, probed, and analysed constantly. To be in his company – or viewing one of his films – invariably forced one to re-examine and reconsider everything, from the role of a director in the cinema, to current definitions of 'reality' and 'truth'.

He was constantly curious, and serious, about everything. When he began thinking about a new film – particularly in the latter part of his career when he dealt primarily with historical figures and their ideas – he would read all he could find on the subject. He would also stop people in the street and ask them detailed questions about their jobs, their ideas, and their lives. He loved to provoke others by making deliberately outrageous comments –

Above: two scenes from Rossellini's rarely-seen documentary India, *which concentrates on the relationship of Man and Nature – a theme that the director explored throughout his work. Right: Jean-Marie Patte as the all-powerful king in the TV film* The Rise of Louis XIV, *which combined opulence with a high degree of realism*

his eyes twinkling with playfulness – to stir up reaction and debate.

All the praise heaped upon him by critics immediately after his death would, without doubt, have amused him highly. He was, after all, hardly used to universal praise when he was alive. From the beginnings of his career to the time of his last feature film, *Il Messia*, he was criticized by practically everyone for practically every reason. The Left attacked his early films, calling them apologies for fascism; it also complained about *Anno Uno* (1974, Italy, Year One), an analysis of Italy after World War II based upon the remarkable career and personality of the politician Alcide de Gasperi, leader of the Christian Democrat Party. After he had made *Stromboli*, the Right claimed he was:

'. . . the head of a gang directed by the Kremlin and Mao Tse-tung which has the sole goal of destroying the brains of American filmgoers.'

His personal morality and religious views also came under fire: he had 'insulted all Italian women' and made a 'blasphemous' film with *Il Miracolo*, the second part of *L'Amore*; at the same time he was described as a 'spokesman for the Church and a slave of the clerics' when he made *Flowers of St Francis* and *Journey to Italy*. Save for a small handful of works, the general public tended to ignore Rossellini's films. As he saw his function as film-maker as partly that of a teacher who wanted people to use their brains and their eyes in new ways, he felt the lack of a popular audience keenly, though he was never surprised by it. He commented:

'As I see it, the only chance is to make films intended for a much smaller audience, to reduce costs as much as possible, and to think carefully how best to launch a film made outside the usual formula. There is always a small public who will come to see films which say something new.'

Rossellini saw film as an instrument for examining moral values in order to arrive at a definition of 'the truth'. Over the years, he came to believe that 'the truth' could only be found by allowing audiences the widest possible freedom to experience a film. From the first he distrusted traditional narrative forms, believing them to be too manipulative of emotions and ideas and falsifications of the 'cinematic reality' he aimed for. Over the years he reduced narrative to a bare minimum, presenting instead a carefully selected series of fragments which illustrated 'the movement of ideas in history'. Yet when examining a concept he never insisted on a single point of view. His idea in making *Il Messia*, for example, was to examine Christ's 'revolutionary idea that the Law was made for Man, rather than Man for the Law'. Yet by allowing his camera to roam – often with apparent aimlessness – over his reconstruction of a 'past reality' he allows the audience freedom to choose some 'stray detail' which might then set off a chain of new ideas or interpretations. Thus, in addition to

his examination of how power functions in *The Rise of Louis XIV*, a viewer could also become aware of a 'stray detail' such as the distance between kitchen and dining-hall at the Palace of Versailles, which meant that Louis probably never had a hot meal.

Although in his later years Rossellini claimed to feel little personal contact with his earlier work, he continued to maintain that there were 'constant elements' running through his films and that 'in *La Nave Bianca* I had the same moral position as in *Rome, Open City*'. He himself pointed to 'the documentary attitude of observation and analysis', to a 'perpetual return to fantasy', and to an 'effective spirituality' (as opposed to specific religious faith) as themes which recur throughout his work.

Rossellini mistrusted the use of 'the beautiful shot' for its own sake. He observed:

'A film must be well-directed; that is the least one can expect from a film-maker, but a single

Filmography

1936 Fantasia Sotto-Marina (short). '37 Prelude à l'Après-midi d'un Faune (short). '38 Daphne (short); Luciano Serra, Pilota (co-sc; 2nd unit dir. only). '39 Il Tacchino Prepotente (short). '40 La Vispa Teresa (short). '41 Il Ruscello di Ripasottile (short); La Nave Bianca (co-dir; +co-sc). '42 Un Pilota Ritorna (+co-sc). '43 L'Invasore (sup; +co-sc. only); L'Uomo della Croce (+co-sc). '45 Roma, Città Aperta (+co-sc) (USA: Rome, Open City; GB: Open City). '46 Paisa (+prod; +co-sc) (USA/GB: Paisan). '47 Germania, Anno Zero (+co-sc) (IT-GER) (USA/GB: Germany, Year Zero). '48 L'Amore: episode one/Una Voce Umana, episode two/Il Miracolo (GB: The Miracle) (+co-sc); La Macchina Ammazzacattivi (+prod) (USA/GB: The Machine That Kills Bad People). '50 Francesco Giullare di Dio (+co-sc) (USA/GB: Flowers of St Francis); Stromboli/(Stromboli,Terra di Dio) (+co-prod; +co-sc) (USA: God's Land). '51 Europa '51 (+co-sc) (USA: The Greatest Love). '52 I Sette Peccati Capitali ep L'Invidia (+co-sc) (IT-FR) (USA/GB: The Seven Deadly Sins ep Envy); Medico Condotto (sup; +co-sc. only); Dov'è la Libertà? (+co-sc) (USA/GB: Where Is Liberty?). '53 Siamo Donne ep Il Pollo (+co-sc) (USA: Five Women/Of Life and Love ep Ingrid Bergman; GB: We Women/We, the Women). '54 Amori di Mezzo Secolo ep Napoli '43; Viaggio in Italia (+co-sc) (IT-FR) (USA: Strangers; GB: The Lonely Woman/Journey to Italy; Giovanna d'Arco al Rogo (+sc) (FR-IT) (USA/GB: Joan of Arc at the Stake); Angst (GER-IT) (GB: Fear). '55 Orient-Express (sup. only) (FR-IT-GER). '59 India (+sc); Il Generale Della Rovere (+co-adapt) (IT-FR). '60 Era Notte a Roma (+co-sc) (IT-FR) (USA/GB: It Was Night in Rome). '61 Viva l'Italia (+co-sc) (IT-FR); Vanina Vanini (+co-sc) (IT-FR) (USA/GB: The Betrayer). '62 Benito Mussolini (prod; + uncredited sup. only); Anima Nera (+co-sc). '63 Les Carabiniers (co-sc. only) (FR-IT) (USA/GB: The Soldiers); RoGoPaG/Laviamoci il Cervello ep Illibatezza (+sc) (IT-FR). All subsequent films were initially made for Italian TV unless specified. '64 L'Età del Ferro (sup; +comm. sc only). '66 La Prise de Pouvoir par Louis XIV (FR) (USA/GB: The Rise of Louis XIV). '67 Sicilia: Idea di un'Isola (short). '69 Atti degli Apostoli (+co-sc). '70 La Lotta dell'Uomo per le Sua Sopravivenza (sc; +ed; +comm. only); Socrate (+co-sc) (film) (IT-FR-SP) (USA/GB: Socrates). '72 Blaise Pascal (+co-sc); Agostino di Ippona (+co-sc). '73 L'Età di Cosimo; Cartesius (+co-sc). '74 Anno Uno (+co-sc) (GB: Italy, Year One). '75 Il Messia (+co-sc) (IT-FR). '76 Concerto per Michelangelo (short). '77 Beaubourg, Centre d'Art et de Culture Georges Pompidou (short).

Above: the Apostles' first supper after the death of Jesus from Atti degli Apostoli, *which chronicles the disciples' struggles to preach Christianity. Right: Christ crucified –* Il Messia

shot need not be beautiful.' He felt instead that the most important aspect of technique – which can't be learned' – was 'rhythm': 'You feel when the point is made, how long to maintain a sequence, or you don't'.

He also mistrusted scenarios that were complete down to the last detail, saying that 'they are only useful to reassure producers'. He preferred to depend upon the 'inspiration of the moment, of the place, of the actors.'

He was the fount from which all important Italian cinema has sprung since the war, and a major force in international film-making. He had his failures – films which did not work on any level – however, as a lasting creative influence on the art of our time, he was a major figure of this century.   DAVID OVERBEY

Luchino Visconti: opening shots

A grim, compelling study of adultery and murder; a portrait of a man struggling to keep his integrity in the face of hardship and exploitation – these are the subjects with which Visconti began his career as a director

Luchino Visconti – or to give him his full title, Conte Luchino Visconti di Modrone – came from one of the most illustrious families of the Milanese aristocracy. Though he professed himself to be a dedicated Marxist, this was hardly borne out by his elegant lifestyle; he dwelt in a superb Roman *palazzo* decorated with priceless tapestries where white-gloved Sicilian servants waited at table.

In his early years he gave no sign of developing into one of the cinema's boldest and most fastidious talents. His first passion was for breeding and training race-horses.

The famous couturière Madame 'Coco' Chanel, who had been travelling back with Visconti from a race-meeting in England, had the idea of introducing him to the film director Jean Renoir. The outcome of this meeting was that Visconti became one of Renoir's assistants (the others were Jacques Becker and Cartier Bresson) on *Une Partie de Campagne* (1936, A Day in the Country) and *Les Bas-Fonds* (1937, The Lower Depths). Subsequently when Renoir, disgusted by the French reception of his masterpiece *La Règle du Jeu* (1939, The Rules of the Game), left his native country vowing to work elsewhere, Visconti co-scripted with him the ill-fated *La Tosca* (1940), on which Renoir worked for only a few days before being replaced by Carl Koch.

Visconti's first film, *Ossessione* (1942, Obsession) was a deliberate gesture of defiance against authority. Under Mussolini's totali-

tarian regime, it had been decreed that neither crime nor immorality was to be depicted on the screen so as to propagate the impression that the government had successfully eradicated these social evils. *Ossessione* was a sombre story of lust, infidelity and murder, loosely based on James M. Cain's novel *The Postman Always Rings Twice*. In the flat, bleak landscapes of the Ferrarese region of northern Italy, where the film was shot, and in the searingly accurate observation of the main characters' sordid motives and behaviour, lie the true seeds of the movement that was later to become known as neo-realism.

The tale of a casual labourer, who becomes infatuated by a woman and allows himself to become her accomplice in the murder of her middle-aged husband, pulsates with a dark sensuality rarely equalled on the screen. The depiction of the husband as an affable, trusting creature lends an added poignancy and harshness to the woman's ruthless pursuit of her own gratification. Clara Calamai plays the role of the woman to perfection; the final shots of her, dead and dangling in her lover's arms like a rag-doll, are unforgettable.

After *Ossessione* Visconti devoted himself to the theatre, and it was not until 1948 that he returned to the cinema to make an even more uncompromising work, *La Terra Trema* (1948, The Earth Trembles).

The new project was conceived along grandiose lines. *La Terra Trema* was to be the first part of a trilogy. This saga of life in a small Sicilian fishing-village was to be followed by another dealing with people in the city, with a third about workers in the fields. The general theme was the plight of humble people at the mercy both of their environment and those intent on exploiting them.

La Terra Trema was filmed entirely in the coastal village of Aci Trezza and enacted by the local inhabitants. The leading character, 'Ntoni, a young fisherman, is sick of being

Left: Visconti was 36 when he made his first feature Ossessione. *Below, far left: the lovers, Giovanna and Gino. Below: having murdered Giovanna's husband, the couple seek to escape the police, but their car goes out of control and Giovanna is killed*

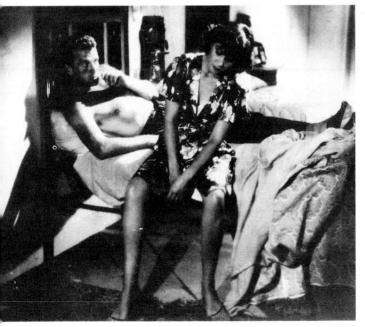

sometimes seems to detract from the force of the social protest. In his determination to show the proximity of the fisher-folk to their environment, no stone, as it were, remains unturned. Pebbles, rippling water and facial expressions are long and lovingly dwelt on to the point of over-indulgence, with the result that the film's rhythm becomes decidedly slow. But there are many sequences which achieve greatness, such as the scene in which black-cowled women, perched on the rocks like gaunt birds, await the men's return from the rough sea. Then, again, there is 'Ntoni's race through the rain in search of refuge in the little house he is about to lose.

Although the film received a prize at the Venice Film Festival for its masterly stylistic qualities, *La Terra Trema* was a failure at the

box-office and the rest of the trilogy was consequently abandoned. But one might say that Visconti was still pursuing his original conception years later with *Rocco e i Suoi Fratelli* (1960, *Rocco and His Brothers*), a tale of Sicilians fighting to survive in Milan.

Visconti was, in all respects, a law unto himself. He was frank and open about his homosexuality at a time when it was far from socially acceptable to be so. When he attended a film premiere in Rome with his entourage, one had the distinct impression that royalty had consented to grace the occasion. And at the Venice Festival, when everyone else would be staying across the water on the Lido where the event took place, Visconti preferred to remain at a patrician distance, installed in the exclusive Bauer-Grünwald hotel. News of the Festival's progress would be conveyed to him by messengers speeding across the lagoon. His sardonic wit was feared. He was also a fervent patriot. He deplored what he viewed as the Italian tendency to take their vast cultural heritage for granted and to allow their magnificent architectural achievements to fall into disrepair. 'The Italians don't deserve Italy,' he once remarked. His exhaustive quest for visual perfection often went to exaggerated lengths. When shooting *Il Gattopardo* (1963, *The Leopard*), he demanded a series of retakes under the boiling Sicilian sun because a horse, on the edge of the frame, persistently swished its tail, which, in the opinion of the Master, marred the composition of the shot.

Visconti knew how to bide his time and most of the projects he held dear he eventually managed to realize. The great exception, about which he had dreamt for years and frequently seemed close to setting up, was Marcel Proust's *A la Recherche du Temps Perdu*. That elegant work and this meticulous, director were surely meant for each other.   DEREK PROUSE

xploited by the wholesale fish-dealers and ecides to strike out on his own. He plans to alt his own fish, employ his own men and nake his own arrangements for the disposal of is produce. But one stormy night his boat is vrecked and he is deprived of his livelihood. He ries desperately to find work but the wholesale ealers boycott him to punish him for his ebellion. When he is unable to meet his nortgage dues, the bank evicts him and his mily from their house. One sister becomes a rostitute and the other, out of pride and umiliation, refuses an offer of marriage. Finlly, 'Ntoni manages to get work as a fisher-nan for one of the wholesalers but remains a tubborn outsider.

The film is superbly shot by the brilliant ameraman G.R. Aldo, but Visconti's obsesion with the creation of a formal pictorial style

hese scenes from La Terra Trema *show the lm's protagonist 'Ntoni with his son (above); Ntoni refitting his boat for a fishing expedition top); and the women of the village anxiously waiting the return of their menfolk from the ea (right)*

Directed by Vittorio De Sica, 1948
Prod co: Produzione De Sica (PDS). **prod:** Vittorio De Sica. **prod man:** Umberto Scarpelli. **sc:** De Sica, Oreste Bianco, Suso Cecchi d'Amico, Adolfo Franci, Gherardo Gherardi, Gerardo Guerrieri, adapted by Cesare Zavattini from the novel by Luigi Bartolini. **photo:** Carlo Montuori. **ass photo:** Mario Montuori. **ed:** Eraldo da Roma. **art dir:** Antonino Traverso. **mus:** Alessandro Cicognini. **mus dir:** Willy Ferrero. **ass dir:** Gerardo Guerrieri. **r/t:** 90 minutes. Italian title: *Ladri di Biciclette*. Released in USA as *Bicycle Thief*, in GB as *Bicycle Thieves*.
Cast: Lamberto Maggiorani (*Antonio Ricci*), Enzo Staiola (*Bruno Ricci*), Lianella Carell (*Maria Ricci*), Vittorio Antonucci (*the thief*), Elena Altieri, Gino Saltamerenda, Giulio Chiari, Michele Sakara, Carlo Jachino, Nando Bruno, Fausto Guerzoni, Umberto Spadaro, Massimo Randisi.

With *Bicycle Thieves*, Vittorio De Sica came very close to perfecting the kind of realist film to which he hoped to dedicate himself as a director. His previous film, *Sciuscià* (1946; *Shoeshine*) had shown him freeing himself from the theatrical influences that had shaped his earlier work, and had also established the importance of the contribution that writer Cesare Zavattini could make to his films. It was Zavattini who adapted *Bicycle Thieves* from the novel by Luigi Bartolini. 'I had liked Bartolini's book,' said Zavattini in 1980. 'I thought it would make the basis for a good film. I think it was an inspired film idea, even if it was completely different from the book which was based on the author's own experience. Later, when the film came out, Bartolini

made a bit of a fuss, prompted by someone in the bourgeois press who hated the film. But Bartolini was quite aware of what we were going to do to his story when we paid him for the title.'

De Sica had to go the rounds of the producers trying to raise money to make *Bicycle Thieves*. He acted out all the parts for them to try and catch their interest, but no-one would back his picture. He went to France, where *Shoeshine* had been very successful, but the French producers said they'd be delighted to buy the film – after they had seen it. In London De Sica met the director-producer Gabriel Pascal who kept him locked up in his country home for a weekend to prevent him from going to Korda with the film, but then Pascal only offered £5000. In

the end De Sica found three Italian businessmen who were prepared to finance him.

In order to capture the kind of 'reality' that he and Zavattini felt was essential to the telling of the story, De Sica insisted on using only non-professional actors. He had even turned down a generous offer from David O. Selznick who was prepared to finance the film if Cary Grant played the central role of the bill-sticker.

To find the right non-professional for the main part, however, was not easy. In the end De Sica used a workman, Lamberto Maggiorani, who had brought his child to be auditioned for the part of the bill-sticker's ten-year-old son.

If in *Shoeshine* De Sica could still lapse into sentimentality, particularly in the ending, in *Bicycle Thieves* he showed restraint and a firm grip of film narrative. The subject-matter is grim and De Sica lets the bare facts dictate the style of the film. He avoids sentimentality even in the fade-out with the father and son – reunited after the humiliating scene in front of the stadium – walking off into the distance with a Chaplinesque resignation to life's pitfalls.

The Rome of *Bicycle Thieves* is not that of Mussolini's heroics, or of the German Occupation, or of Hollywood's many 'Roman Holidays' to come. Though the workman's bike is stolen in a street in the centre of the city, only a stone's throw from the Spanish Steps, the Rome that De Sica shows is that of the embankments by the sluggish and muddy Tiber, the flea markets

in the rain, the ugly suburban houses. It is a harsh setting and a sad story but De Sica enlivens it often with characteristic touches of humorous observation – the scene, for example, in the restaurant when Bruno tries to manage a knife and fork and is looked down on by the well-behaved middle-class boy; the caricatures of the fortune-teller and her clients, the charity helpers in the church, and the rowdy women protecting the thief in the brothel. Despite the intensity of Zavattini's political commitment and his own social conscience, De Sica was still able to make a film that, although a powerful cry of despair, never lapses into a shout of propaganda. It was clearly the work of an artist who had mastered a medium that for so long had only given him the chance to show his professional competence. He has commented:

'What is so important about a bike in the Rome of 1948 where so many bikes are stolen every day? Yet for a worker who loses his means of support a stolen bike is a very tragic circumstance. Why should we, filmmakers, go in search of extraordinary adventures when we are confronted in our daily lives with facts that cause genuine anguish? Our literature has already explored this modern dimension that puts an emphasis on the smallest details of everyday life which are often dismissed as commonplace. The cinema has at its disposal the film camera which is the best medium for capturing this world. That's what I think this much-debated question of the new realism is all about.'

JOHN FRANCIS LANE

Antonio Ricci is an unemployed workman in his thirties, married with two children. He is offered a job as a bill-sticker on condition that he has his own bicycle. Ricci does have a bike but it is in a pawn shop. He has to pawn the family bed linen to get it out (1).

He goes to work the next day, but while he is sticking up a poster of Rita Hayworth (2) his bike is stolen (3). Many bikes are stolen every day in Rome and the police suggest he looks for the thief himself. Ricci, accompanied by his ten-year-old son Bruno, first searches the flea markets (4) where stolen bikes and parts are on sale. They see the thief talking to an old man whom they follow into an almshouse (5), but he slips away from them. Ricci takes

Bruno to eat in a smart restaurant in order to forget their problems for a while (6).

When Ricci sees the thief again he follows him into a brothel (7), but the young man denies the charge. In the street the crowd turns on Ricci and the thief has an epileptic fit. Nobody can prove anything. Ricci and Bruno sit outside the football stadium and listen to the crowd roaring inside. Ricci sends Bruno away and on an impulse steals an unguarded bike (8). He is caught immediately but the owner doesn't bring charges. Bruno has watched his father's humiliation. They walk away – at first separated, but then together as Bruno offers his hand in comfort and solidarity (9).

5

6

8

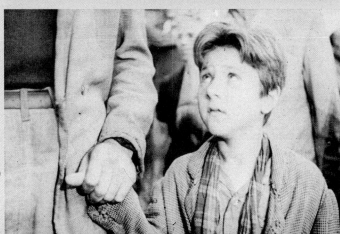

9

Vittorio De Sica

seeker of truth

Children grubbing for a living on the rain-swept streets of Rome and Naples, a bicycle thief having a fit outside a whorehouse, an old man looking for his dog among the abbatoirs – this was the 'real' Italy depicted by De Sica in his early films. One of the qualities he brought to them was a sparse but undeniable charm – which later shed its grim and gritty flavour in the glossy pictures he made with Sophia Loren

Vittorio De Sica (1902–74) was born in Sora, in the Ciociaria region half-way between Rome and Naples – the setting for his later success *La Ciociara* (1961, *Two Women*). But he was really a Neapolitan: both his father, a poor clerk called Umberto (like the old man in his 1951 film, *Umberto D*), and his mother Teresa came from Naples. De Sica began his career as an actor in films when he was persuaded to play the young Clemenceau in *L'Affaire Clemenceau* (1918, The Clemenceau Affair) which starred the great Italian film actress Francesca Bertini, and he made his stage debut (as a waiter) in 1923 with the theatre company of Tatiana Pavlova. He went on to score great successes in musicals and sophisticated comedy, and, indeed, it was as a debonair comedian that he became a star – in Mario Camerini's *Gli Uomini, Che Mascalzoni* (1932, *What Rascals Men Are!*). Between 1931 and 1940 De Sica acted in 23 films.

De Sica's debut as a director came with *Rose Scarlatte* (1940, Red Roses). He said that he began making his own films as the result of wounded pride:

'I had played in Gallone's film of *Manon Lescaut* (1940) but the critics did not like me. This hurt because I knew they were right. I had felt my own mistakes and had pointed them out to Gallone but he wouldn't listen. That's

why I felt I wanted to take responsibility for my own performance and directed myself.'

After several potboilers, De Sica made *I Bambini ci Guardano* (1943, *The Children Are Watching Us*), collaborating for the first time with writer Cesare Zavattini, thereby forming a partnership that was central to what became known as the Italian 'neo-realist' cinema – a cinema committed to the realistic treatment of the problems of urban life in impoverished, post-war Italy. Their next two films, *Sciuscià* (1946, *Shoeshine*), the story of two shoeshine boys, and *Ladri di Biciclette* (1948, *Bicycle Thieves*), about an Italian workman's search for the stolen bicycle that keeps him in a bill-sticking job, are shot in drab street-locations and concerned with the difficulties faced by the poor in simply earning enough money to survive, and despite the callous indifference of society.

'It isn't as if one day Visconti and Rossellini and the rest of us were sitting at a cafe and suddenly Zavattini came along and said "Let's create neo-realism",' De Sica has said. 'But when a producer offered me the idea of *Shoeshine*, though I didn't like the way he had conceived it, I saw its possibilities and asked Zavattini to help me get it into shape.'

In spite of the prizes and international acclaim which greeted *Shoeshine* and *Bicycle*

Above left: De Sica directs Umberto D. *Above: in* Shoeshine *the young delinquents Pasquale (Franco Interlenghi) and Giuseppe (Rinaldo Smordoni) take a brief respite from the troubles of the world before they are faced with betrayal and death. Interlenghi later turned professional and starred in Fellini's* I Vitelloni *(1953)*

Thieves, neither film opened the way for De Sica to continue making the kind of films that he and Zavattini were dreaming about. De Sica had to work for several years acting in a mixed bag of films in order to raise the money to make *Miracolo a Milano* (1951, *Miracle in Milan*). Though not all the Italian critics liked or understood the film, it was a success with the public. It also provoked a political reaction and there were vicious attacks on De Sica and Zavattini in the 'Cold War' climate of Italian politics. Even so, they managed to make *Umberto D* (1951), which was produced by Angelo Rizzoli.

Rizzoli backed *Umberto D* in the hope that De Sica would direct *Il Piccolo Mondo di Don Camillo* (1952) for him. Although De Sica – much tempted by the large sum of money Rizzoli offered him – did not accept the chore, he was, in subsequent years, to accept many compromises with producers, usually dragging Zavattini along with him. The pair had

Above: the love affair in A Place for Lovers, *with Marcello Mastroianni and Faye Dunaway, is threatened by the girl's illness. Left: Loren as a prostitute in* Marriage Italian Style. *Below left: a scene from* Lo Chiamaremo Andrea. *Below right: Giovanna (Sophia Loren) searches a Russian military cemetery for her husband's grave in* Sunflower

Top left and right: lovers Christien Delaroche and Nino Castelnuovo in Un Mondo Nuovo; *Shirley MacLaine as the wife out to get her own back on her husband in the* Amateur Night *episode of De Sica's only American film,* Woman Times Seven

become bitter about the way top-level Italian political figures had poured scorn on their work, among them future Prime Minister Giulio Andreotti, who had accused De Sica of washing Italy's dirty linen in public with *Umberto D.* The film was not included in the Italian Film Week in London in 1954 to which De Sica had been invited as the actor playing opposite Gina Lollobrigida in Luigi Comencini's *Pane, Amore e Fantasia* (*Bread, Love and Dreams*), a film that travestied the whole neo-realist idea. But a private showing of *Umberto D* for English critics resulted in rave reviews and De Sica's film eclipsed all the others that had been officially put on show by the Italians.

Although Zavattini says today that his relationship with De Sica first became strained during the making of *Un Mondo Nuovo* (1966, *A Young World*), there had been several rifts before. These were often due to compromises into which De Sica was driven by producers such as David O. Selznick on *Stazione Termini*

(1953, *Indiscretion of an American Wife*), or Dino De Laurentiis on *Il Giudizio Universale* (1962, *The Last Judgement*), or Carlo Ponti on the pictures made with Sophia Loren. There was even a rather startling collaboration between De Sica and Zavattini on *I Sequestrati di Altona* (1962, *The Condemned of Altona*), an adaptation of Jean-Paul Sartre's play, with actors like Fredric March and Maximilian Schell seeming somehow uncomfortable in De Sica's hands despite Zavattini's valiant attempt to be faithful to Sartre.

The last neo-realist film from the De Sica–Zavattini stable was really *Il Tetto* (1956, *The Roof*). At the time De Sica said:

'*The Roof* is a love story rich in poetry. Whatever people say, neo-realism is poetry, the poetry of real life. For that reason neo-realism is not dead and will never die.'

De Sica was right. Neo-realism did not die. But it was neither he nor Zavattini who were to keep it alive – either as a political manifesto or as poetry. The directors who inherited these

two aspects of neo-realism were Francesco Rosi and Ermanno Olmi who, at the end of the Seventies, were still making films about the poetry – and the politics – of real life. Yet some of De Sica's successes in subsequent years had professional dignity even if they took him and Zavattini further and further away from neo-realism. Films like *Two Women* (1961), for which Sophia Loren won an Oscar, and jovial comedies like *L'Oro di Napoli* (1954, *Gold of Naples*) and *Matrimonio all'Italiana* (1964, *Marriage Italian Style*) projected the Loren image of earthy dynamism throughout the world, doing discredit to neither actress nor director. Later on, though, De Sica seemed unable to avoid more glossy and sophisticated images of Loren, as in the unfortunate Russian-Italian co-production *I Girasoli* (1970, *Sunflower*) and *Il Viaggio* (1974, *The Journey*). And *Woman Times Seven* (1967), starring Shirley MacLaine, was a disaster – the only one of his films that De Sica ever actually admitted was bad. There was one final triumph: *Il Giardino dei Finzi-Contini* (1970, *The Garden of the Finzi-Continis*), an adaptation of Bassani's novel about Jews in Ferrara under Fascism and a film of great visual beauty and human depth. But it is for his neo-realist films that De Sica will be remembered. JOHN FRANCIS LANE

Filmography (films as director)
1940 Rose Scarlatte (co-dir; +act); Maddelena Zero in Condetta (+dial; +act). **'41** Teresa Venerdi (+co-sc) (USA/GB: Doctor, Beware). **'42** Un Garabaldino al Convento (+co-sc; +act). **'43** I Bambini ci Guardano (+co-sc) (USA/GB: The Children Are Watching Us). **'44** La Porta del Cielo (+co-sc). **'46** Sciuscià (+co-sc) (USA/GB: Shoeshine). **'48** Ladri di Biciclette (+co-sc) (USA/GB: Bicycle Thieves). **'51** Miracolo a Milano (+co-sc; +co-prod) (USA/GB: Miracle in Milan); Ambiento e Personaggi (short) (+co-sc; +act) (never shown); Umberto D (+co-sc; +co-prod). **'53** Stazione Termini (+co-prod) (IT-USA) (USA: Indiscretion of an American Wife; GB: Indiscretion). **'54** L'Oro di Napoli (+co-sc; +act in *ep* Il Giocatori) (USA/GB: Gold of Naples). **'56** Il Tetto (USA/GB: The Roof). **'61** La Ciociara (+co-sc) (IT-FR) (USA/GB: Two Women). **'62** Il Giudizio Universale (+act) (IT-FR) (USA/GB: The Last Judgement); Boccaccio '70 *ep* La Riffa; I Sequestrati di Altona (IT-FR) (USA/GB: The Condemned of Altona). **'63** Il Boom. **'64** Ieri, Oggi, Domani (IT-FR) (USA/GB: Yesterday, Today and Tomorrow); Matrimonio all'Italiana (IT-FR) (USA/GB: Marriage Italian Style). **'66** Un Mondo Nuovo (IT-FR) (USA/GB: A Young World); Caccia alla Volpe (+guest appearance) (USA/GB: After the Fox). **'67** Le Streghe *ep* Una Sera Come le Altre (IT-FR) (USA: The Witches *ep* A Night Like Any Other); Woman Times Seven (FR-USA). **'68** Amanti (+co-sc) (IT-FR) (USA/GB: A Place for Lovers). **'70** I Girasoli (IT-USSR) (USA/GB: Sunflower); Il Giardino dei Finzi-Contini (USA/GB: The Garden of the Finzi-Continis). **'71** Le Coppie *ep* Il Leone. **'72** Lo Chiamaremo Andrea. **'73** Una Breva Vacanza (IT-SP) (USA: The Holiday; GB: Brief Vacation). **'74** Il Viaggio (USA/GB: The Journey).
De Sica also acted in 153 films from 1918–74.

Left: Montgomery Clift in Indiscretion of an American Wife. *Far left: the old man (Carlo Battisti) and his only friend in* Umberto D. *Above left: father and son search for the stolen bike in the streets of Rome in* Bicycle Thieves

Tools of the trade

The refinement of film stock, the introduction of tape recording and the invention of new highly mobile cameras in the Forties revolutionized film-making

Scientific research and technical development are, as in any industry, essential features of the film business. The innovations of the late Thirties and the Forties – faster film, magnetic tape recording and reflex cameras – gave cameramen greater freedom and enabled them to achieve visual effects that had far-reaching implications for cinema.

Every picture, every frame, still told a story, but those film-makers who had mastered the innovations realized the opportunities for establishing and developing narrative and character through new effects of lighting and subtleties of composition.

One film that displays such mastery of technical innovations is *Citizen Kane*. Other films exploited the new tools of the trade, especially the sophisticated cameras, by returning to real-life locations and shooting in the streets. Either way, the 'look' of Hollywood cinema was changing once again.

The invention of reflex cameras was a major technical advance; later in the Forties, smaller, more mobile cameras like the German Arriflex brought a new flexibility to camerawork

For many years motion-picture cameras like the Mitchell NC (and the BNC model) allowed the cameraman to focus his subject by means of a 'rackover' system: the body of the camera (containing the film magazine, camera drive and motor) could be shifted sideways at the touch of a lever. This action brought into position (behind the lens) an optical viewfinder which gave the cameraman an uninterrupted view of his subject while taking the shot.

In the design of motion picture cameras one priority has always been that the cameraman should be able to have a continuous view of what he is shooting, through the taking lens during filming. This facility for 'reflex viewing' (focusing and viewing as one operation at one and the same time) was built into movie cameras in the late Thirties.

In 1937 the Vinten camera incorporated a revolutionary viewfinding system: a rotating mirror was placed in front of the film at an angle of 45°. The mirror acted as a shutter to keep out the light while the film was advanced between exposures, but at the same time the mirror reflected the image onto a piece of ground glass in the viewfinder, thus enabling the cameraman to check his focus constantly.

In 1938 Arnold and Richter, camera makers in Munich, Germany, developed the Arriflex camera whose great advantage was that it was light enough to be hand-held. It also incorporated a shutter reflex viewfinder mechanism based on the principle of the rotating mirror as pioneered by Vinten. Arriflex reflex cameras were used extensively by German newsreel cameramen during

World War II and became highly prized trophies when captured by Allied war correspondents. The basic pre-war Arriflex design has continued in production with remarkably few modifications for over forty years.

The Cameflex (as distinct from the American Cameraflex) was produced by the French Eclair company. It comprised many innovations in motion-picture camera design. The film was moved in the camera by a ratchet mechanism that gave much steadier pictures but was rather noisy to operate and did not permit the film to be run in reverse. Mounted on the front of the camera was a lens turret with three lenses attached to it; a lens of the appropriate focal length could be selected by simply turning the turret. The Cameflex also featured an eyepiece which could be rotated to any angle (so that the cameraman could view his picture even if the circumstances of shooting obliged him to work in awkward positions). Loading the camera was made easier by the invention of a 'clip on' magazine which could be attached and removed even when the camera was running. Like the Arriflex, this camera was light and portable, though Cameflex instruments were designed to be operated from the shoulder rather than held in the hand.   DAVID SAMUELSON

Tape recording as we know it today developed from a sound-recording system perfected in Germany during World War II. The German Magnetofon company developed a plastic tape coated with magnetic materials that would act as a medium for recording sounds. The implications for motion pictures were twofold: tape provided a new recording medium and a new form of soundtrack on the

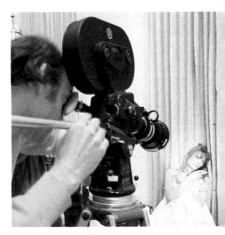

Top: the Arriflex camera, first introduced in 1938 and scarcely modified in over forty years' use. Centre: the Cameflex, with its lens turret. Above: the Vinten camera. Left: the Mitchell NC

film itself. The advantages of using tape were immediately apparent.

Magnetic sound gradually replaced the old optical system for all studio and location film-making because of its facility for instant playback, erasure of errors and re-use. No longer did a sound engineer spend a sleepless night wondering whether an expensive actor or an even more expensive orchestra had had a day's labour ruined by a technical slip in the recording. The results of their work were there on tape, to be checked and, if necessary, corrected on the spot. Magnetic tape was in experimental use in Hollywood from 1947 onwards and by the Fifties all studios were using it for their sound recording.

Magnetic recording brought greater flexibility to sound shooting and saved recordists many a sleepless night wondering about the quality of the sound

However, the adoption by the film trade of magnetic soundtracks was beset with problems. At a time when audiences were declining, cinemas were unwilling to lay out the cost of re-equipping their projectors for magnetic 'stripe' soundtracks, even though these were proved to be of higher fidelity than optical soundtracks.

When the CinemaScope revolution occurred in the early Fifties, 'directional' sound (that is, sound that came from, or moved to, a specific point on the screen) was best achieved by the use of magnetic soundtracks. The biblical epic *The Robe*, for example, was released in CinemaScope in 1953 carrying four magnetic soundtracks. The effect was moderately impressive but the cost of re-equipping 35mm projectors to reproduce magnetic soundtracks was exorbitant. The four-track, magnetic stereophonic film with its costly alteration to the projection mechanism and its hazardous maintenance, soon fell into disuse.

In the studios, however, magnetic recording was making great advances. PVC plastic was developed to make the tape more robust. The great sound trucks with their massive batteries and generators became obsolete as the highly portable tape recorders gained in usage. By the end of the Forties, optical sound was no longer used for recording during filming but released prints were of course supplied to the exhibitors with optical soundtracks just as they had always been.

Optical sound had scored at least one major success in the Forties. Disney's breathtaking *Fantasia* (1940) was released in stereophonic sound: it had three principal optical soundtracks. A fourth track carried a pattern of electronic cues and was used for control of volume levels. The sound engineers on *Fantasia* were working on the idea of making the sound come from different parts of the screen.

In 1951, the Festival of Britain's Telekinema (later to become the National Film Theatre) gave a demonstration of stereoscopic films coupled with an attempt at stereophonic cinema sound. The experiment was not wholly successful, but it provided sufficient interest to catch the attention of many cinemagoers and proved that people were beginning to care about the quality of sound that they were hearing in cinemas.   KEN CAMERON

When panchromatic film stock was introduced to motion pictures in the mid-Twenties, it marked a significant improvement in black-and-white movies: it was sensitive to all the colours of the spectrum and thus gave more faithful reproduction. In 1939, vastly improved panchromatic negative films came on the market and opened up great possibilities for the creative motion-picture cameramen of the Forties.

The new panchromatic films were more sensitive to light – in technical terms they were 'faster' and permitted photography under poor lighting conditions. They were also less 'grainy' than previous films which meant that the images looked sharper. As more and more 'exterior' scenes were being photographed indoors, using back projection and studio live action, the finer-grain, faster films greatly enhanced the quality of the images. Moreover, fast films allowed cameramen to 'stop down' their lenses, thereby increasing 'depth of field' (the distance both in front of and behind the point being focused within which other objects will remain in acceptably sharp focus).

Faster films operated under lower lighting levels. The benefits of this were several-fold: smaller, more compact lamps could be used, giving the cinematographer better control over lighting; a 50-percent saving was achieved in power consumption; and fewer lamps meant less heat on the set with a consequent improvement in working conditions.

The use of colour for motion pictures advanced at a tremendous rate during the Forties. At the start of the decade, three-colour photography was dominated by Technicolor (the system used by most of the major studios), although in the field of two-colour photography many companies (Cinemacolor, Cinecolor, Magnacolor, Trucolor) were very active. The quality of two-colour processes did not match that of the Technicolor process but they were often used for B pictures and were felt acceptable for certain subjects, especially Westerns.

In 1945 the patents of the German Agfacolor system were circulated abroad and the process was imitated by several film manufacturers. Among these derivative systems was Ansco Color, a multilayered film with three emulsions (each with differ-

Left and centre: sound recording in the Forties, showing the most portable tape recorders of the day. Above: a reel of nitrate film in an advanced state of chemical decomposition

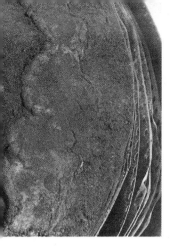

Below: Orson Welles directing Citizen Kane – *in this scene Susan Alexander makes her operatic debut. Bottom: low-key lighting and deep-focus photography in* Citizen Kane

ent sensitivities to colour), was introduced. Instead of the colour being produced from three strips of film (as in Technicolor), this process was based on one strip which was coated with three layers of emulsion, one on top of the other. It meant that standard cameras could now be used for full-colour photography. Normal processing and printing equipment was also usable, with a minimum of modification.

Black-and-white films may have been superior in quality to colour movies of the time but the increased sophistication of film stock meant that cameramen had to be more precise in judging the correct exposure. The development of exposure meters was, therefore, of major importance. The photo-electric exposure meter, for instance, was used to establish 'key' lighting (the main lighting on the set) and to maintain consistent light levels; with the commercial availability of these precision instruments, films attained a uniform standard in the printing, despite the widely varying types of lighting under which they may have been shot. Also available were new lenses coated with an anti-reflective substance that cut down light loss and thus provided further lighting controls.

The usable life of a film print was greatly extended by the introduction of a new lacquer that helped prevent abrasions and could be removed and replaced with a new coating whenever necessary.

Since the beginning of cinema, film stocks had been nitrate-based. Such film was highly inflammable and was notorious for causing fires in laboratories and projection booths. Early in the Forties, however, a gradual change to 'safety' acetate films was under way in Germany and France. Other countries followed, and in 1943 refinements were made in the chemical base of the 'safety' film.

With this increased safety came drawbacks. Acetate films were subject to a greater degree of shrinkage which caused problems in printing and projection; they also had less resistance to tearing than the old nitrate films and frequently broke during handling.

By the end of the decade, however, research into safety films resulted in the introduction of 'triacetate' films with physical properties similar to those of nitrate films. A side benefit of this development was the reduction in fire-insurance costs, but what mattered was that film had become safer to work with.   DENNIS KIMBLEY

Citizen Kane was, in many ways, the showcase of the new movie technology. And the Forties vogue for location shooting was no less important for film style

Orson Welles' original contract with RKO gave him unlimited power over any film that he directed, with the sole proviso that the studio had the right to reject any presentation of a completed script. Such unprecedented freedom accorded to a not entirely humble newcomer to Hollywood was one of the causes of the hostility directed at Welles even before he began shooting *Citizen Kane*.

Welles had proposed two scripts to RKO which they had rejected. The first was based on Joseph Conrad's *Heart of Darkness*, but its projected costs and the enormous technical problems it posed led RKO to turn it down. The second proposal, *Smiler With a Knife*, from a novel by Nicholas Blake, hit problems over the lack of a suitable leading lady.

Herman J. Mankiewicz then suggested to Welles the subject which was to become *Citizen Kane*.

Welles asked Mankiewicz to develop a treatment and a script, but the controversy is still raging as to who exactly wrote what. Nonetheless, the shared screen credit (and Oscar) seems to be just; Mankiewicz wrote the actual script but enough of Welles' ideas were incorporated during production for him to deserve at least a co-author credit.

Citizen Kane has long been hailed as original and innovative, chiefly for its synthesis of cinematic and narrative elements which had not co-existed before. Its influences, however, are worth noting too. Fritz Lang once called the film 'a scrapbook of expressionist devices' and though the judgment may be unfair, it is quite clear what Lang meant.

Welles had spent a long time studying the films of Lang, as well as those of John Ford, Frank Capra and others. There are elements of all those directors' styles in *Citizen Kane*, but the most obvious influence is the German-style lighting and the kind of camera placement to be found in Lang's films.

Gregg Toland and Russell Metty brought to the film their experience with lighting, deep-focus photography, coated lenses and the newly developed fast film stock. They devised techniques of building sets to allow for the low camera angles and the special lighting that Welles wanted.

Welles had made himself a master of sound during his work in radio, and, in many ways, the use of sound in *Citizen Kane* is the most innovative aspect of the film. The dialogue is made to overlap and thus provide continuity, and Welles creates irony out of the conjunction of sound and image. A major part of the film's success comes from the score by Bernard Herrmann who worked on the music reel by reel as the film was being edited.

The filming began before the script was actually approved by the studio. Welles was supposedly shooting 'tests' but he managed to film half a dozen sequences that found their way into the final film. These included: part of the picnic sequence, the scene in the projection room and the 'March of Time' newsreel (which was composed of old footage and newly shot material that had been specially 'aged' in the laboratories).

Even when shooting started officially on June 30, 1940, the plot of the film was meant to be a secret. It soon became an open secret, however, and the fact that it was based on the life of the newspaper magnate William Randolph Hearst excited much controversy. Ironically the relationship of Hearst to the film often gets in the way of considering the film in a fresh perspective. At the time, critics who would tear an ordinary Hollywood biopic to shreds for its departure from fact were outraged by *Citizen Kane*'s similarities to Hearst's life.

Although Hearst himself had read the script in 1940, he later became incensed over the film's alleged blackening of his name. What made matters worse was that his gossip columnist, Louella Parsons, had become hysterically obsessed by the film. At first Hearst forbade any other mention of *Citizen Kane*, or, for that matter, any other RKO films in his newspapers, although he proceeded to attack it just before it was due to open. In addition he threatened Hollywood in general, saying that he would expose immorality in the film industry and play up any scandals that were found there.

MGM's Louis B. Mayer tried to buy the original negative for $842,000 in order to destroy it. But Henry Luce, Hearst's newspaper competitor, was equally interested in buying it so that he could release it. RKO's production executive George J. Schaefer denied that *Citizen Kane* was about Hearst, and Welles mischievously added that they were nonetheless planning such a film.

The film was completed towards the end of 1940 and was scheduled to open in February 1941 but

was postponed when the RKO board over-ruled Schaefer's decision to release it.

In March, Welles called a press conference to point out that his contract gave him the right to demand that the film be released within a certain period of time, otherwise, he said, he might sue the studio. In spite of Louella Parsons' demands that the governor of New York ban the film, it did open in New York City on May 1, 1941, at the Palace cinema.

The myth that *Citizen Kane* was savaged by the critics and flopped disastrously is simply not true. The film attracted highly enthusiastic reviews and did enough business in major cities to break even. Since its first release *Citizen Kane* has, of course, proved quite profitable and is still widely shown today. It won several Oscar nominations and the Best Screenplay Award for 1941, although the film, like its maker, remained unpopular in Hollywood.

Film scholars and critics insist that *Citizen Kane* had a tremendous effect on everyone who saw it – audiences and film-makers – but exactly why it is a masterpiece is hard to define. Certainly the radically different use of narrative techniques, the deep-focus photography, the overlapping sound and the complex cutting contribute to the film's uniqueness.

Top: filming The Naked City *on the real locations where the story was supposed to have happened was a breakthrough in Hollywood style. Above:* The House on 92nd Street *also used genuine locations, but the story was routine spy fiction. Right: the poster for Jules Dassin's* The Naked City *proclaims that the movie was 'actually filmed on the sidewalks of New York'. Ironically, the cameraman was William Daniels who had been responsible for some of the most stylized photography of Garbo earlier in his career at MGM*

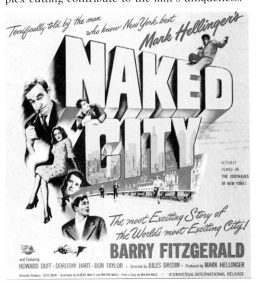

Since the cinema was invented, the majority of films were made on studio sets or on locations conveniently close to the studios which 'doubled' for places where the action was supposed to be taking place.

There was, after all, nothing which could not be duplicated, more or less realistically, with sets. Moreover, studio shooting provided complete control over every technical aspect of filming. There were always those directors who insisted that one paid heavily for that control with a loss of realistic atmosphere but, with few exceptions, they were overruled by imagined 'technical limitations' and the cost of going on location.

Whatever film-makers and audiences understood by realism – a concept that consistently defies definition – there appeared to be a direct relationship between the artificiality of sets, the lack of 'real-life' subjects and the treatment of those subjects in the majority of Hollywood films.

Veteran directors returning from their experiences in World War II with an altered perception of 'reality' were joined in Hollywood by younger directors who wanted to treat American society and its problems in a realistic fashion. Concurrently, Italian neo-realism burst upon the international film scene, with its mixture of actual locations, realistic acting and its treatment of post-war life. After *Rome, Open City* (1945) some film-makers found it impossible to return to their sets and the subjects which those sets represented. On the economic level of American film-making, the neo-realist style also made its mark: it was suddenly possible to produce good and profitable films without big stars and huge budgets, and film-makers could save money by shooting carefully on real streets in real cities.

Louis de Rochemont, throughout the Thirties the producer of the *March of Time* newsreels, clearly anticipated the new American movement towards realism with his production of *The House on 92nd Street* (dir. Henry Hathaway, 1945). This semi-documentary spy film was shot all in New York with plenty of real-life locations. Two years later he produced *Boomerang* (dir. Elia Kazan, 1947) a thriller about incompetence in municipal government. Kazan maintained much the same approach in his *Panic in the Streets* (1950), about the public health service, which was shot on the docks of New Orleans. Kazan's major contribution to the post-war realist movement was his mixture of professional and non-professional actors and to his use of young actors from the New York stage trained in the 'realist' school of acting.

Jules Dassin's treatment of a formula prison-escape story in *Brute Force* (1947) was tough and realistic and made the film seem more hard-hitting than it was in retrospect. His subsequent thriller *The Naked City* (1948) was one of the most influential crime films of the decade: the New York settings and the grimy, unromantic aspects of normal police procedure overshadowed the murder plot, and the atmosphere created by shooting in the streets and unglamorous offices and apartments paradoxically brought a freshness to the genre.

For a time, realistic shooting and settings encouraged a more-or-less realistic treatment of social problems: *Crossfire* (1947) and *Home of the Brave* (1949) dealt with racial discrimination; the problems of soldiers readjusting to civilian life were focused in *The Men* (1950); corruption in the boxing-ring was the subject of *Body and Soul* (1947) and in the political arena in *All the King's Men* (1949). Other genres, notably Westerns, benefitted from the realist trend: films like *The Gunfighter* (1950) favoured increased location shooting and a greater degree of psychological realism.

DAVID OVERBEY

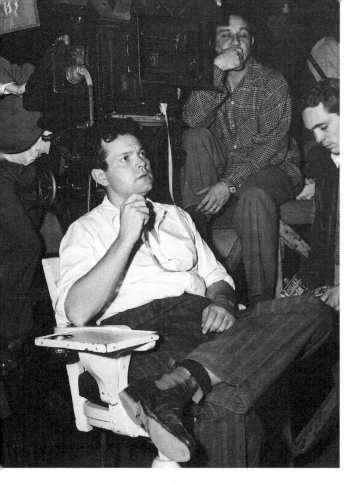

The Immortal Story of Orson Welles

'There but for the grace of God, goes God.' This famous quip by the writer Herman Mankiewicz sums up the mixture of awe and resentment that greeted the arrival in Hollywood of Orson Welles, for whom the word 'genius' seemed to have been newly minted

Orson Welles came to Hollywood having soared to prominence as a producer of stage and radio. Given *carte blanche* by George J. Schaefer, president of RKO studios, Welles was determined to create something highly personal for his film debut. He had considered and reluctantly discarded an adaptation of Joseph Conrad's *Heart of Darkness* and been forced to abandon a project based on Nicholas Blake's *The Smiler With a Knife*, owing to the aversion of Carole Lombard and Rosalind Russell – the film's potential stars – to working with an untried director.

Undeterred, Welles decided that he would play the lead in an original story, *Citizen Kane* (1940), concocted by Herman Mankiewicz and himself. Despite the risks involved, Schaefer stood by Welles and turned over the resources of his studio to him. But prior to release, the film ran into unexpected problems. Louella O. Parsons, head of the movie department of Hearst's newspaper empire, had been one of the first to view the film and had complained to Hearst that *Citizen Kane*'s story was nothing but an unflattering version of Hearst's liaison with his mistress, Marion Davies. The Hearst newspapers refused to run advertisements for

---

'The cinema has no boundaries. It's a ribbon of dream'

---

the film. As a result, *Citizen Kane* did not have a nationwide release and some cinemas even cancelled their bookings. In spite of a number of intelligent and enthusiastic reviews, it was not the runaway box-office hit the studios had hoped for.

RKO was concerned, therefore, about Welles' second venture, *The Magnificent Amber-*

sons (1942), a film version of Booth Tarkington's novel, which was already in production. Welles did not act in *The Magnificent Ambersons*, preferring to concentrate his talents on directing the picture. He was thoroughly conversant with his material; in 1939 he had played the part of the unsympathetic young hero, George Amberson Minafer, on the radio. He cast Tim Holt in this role for the film and devoted all his energies to re-creating a nostalgic picture of American life in the nineteenth century.

To those few who were lucky enough to see the sneak preview of the completed film at the United Artists Theatre in Pasadena, *The Magnificent Ambersons* was a stunning, never-to-be-forgotten event, in every way as important cinematically as *Citizen Kane*. However, the film was sent back to the editing room as the studio felt further cutting was necessary.

Welles was meanwhile staggering production on two films, *Journey Into Fear* (1942) – a version of the Eric Ambler novel, which Welles was directing with Norman Foster and also acting in – and a semi-documentary about South America made with the cooperation of the US government, *It's All True*.

The worst thing that could have happened to Welles' career in Hollywood then hit with the suddenness of a Californian earthquake: Schaefer, Welles' sponsor, was replaced as head of production at RKO by Charles J. Koerner, a man who knew how to distribute and exhibit movies, had great taste, but no patience with failure at the box-office. Welles, busy shooting in South America, was summarily fired, and all the film he had shot for *It's All True* was deposited in the RKO vaults where it remained until June 1978 when a portion of it was shown for the first time.

On July 1, 1942, *The Magnificent Ambersons*,

a third of its original length edited out – and with it much of its bitter-sweet drama – opened in Los Angeles as part of a double bill with a 'programmer' called *Mexican Spitfire Sees a Ghost* (1942). The Hollywood career of Orson Welles seemed to have ground to a halt; he was regarded as an expensive eccentric.

When *Journey Into Fear* was released it had been even more mangled by RKO's editors than *The Magnificent Ambersons*. Wisely, Welles left Hollywood. His name had been linked with the beautiful Dolores Del Rio, but when she saw what remained of her work in *Journey Into Fear*, she threw up her hands in

Above: Welles plans a scene for The Lady From Shanghai. *Below: an atmosphere of unease is superbly evoked by this angled shot from* The Magnificent Ambersons

Above: Rita Hayworth, then Welles' wife, played the beautiful, bewitching murderess in The Lady From Shanghai. Below: the killing of King Duncan in Macbeth, the first of Welles' Shakespearean adaptations

despair and returned to her native Mexico.

When Welles returned to Hollywood, he did so solely as an actor. He was cast in *Jane Eyre* (1943) as the moody Mr Rochester, who conceals his insane wife in the attic of his house. The production had been set up by David O. Selznick and then sold with two other potential Selznick productions (*Claudia*, 1943, and *Keys to the Kingdom*, 1944) to 20th Century-Fox because Selznick desperately needed ready money. Selznick had set up Robert Stevenson as director of *Jane Eyre*, and he had supervised the script prepared by Aldous Huxley and the production designs of William Pereira. From the beginning, *Jane Eyre* was to star Joan Fontaine; the role of Rochester had been styled for an older actor, such as Ronald Colman. Colman, however, was ill, and another candidate, Laurence Olivier, was in war service for his own country. Welles was an unexpected choice for the part, but was approved by all concerned. His Rochester was young and handsome, and he played the character with great theatrical bombast. Colman and Olivier might have chosen to act the part with more subtlety, but Welles invested it with a romantic fury, more closely

akin to another Brontë hero – Heathcliff i *Wuthering Heights*.

Jane Eyre was well received, and Welles ha no difficulty getting other acting roles. He wa believable in a mysterious soap-opera ro mance, *Tomorrow Is Forever*, playing opposit Claudette Colbert, and he was even allowed direct *The Stranger* (both 1946), in which h played the lead – a Nazi war criminal attempt ing to conceal his murky past. He, howeve has never thought much of that picture.

In 1947 he directed his wife Rita Haywort (they had married in 1943) in *The Lady Fro Shanghai*, an exotic melodrama – now r garded as a classic – that at the time attracted small coterie of admirers. They chose to di regard Louella Parsons when she named We les 'awesome Orson, the self-styled genius' an informed fans that he was not only 'washe up' in Hollywood, but was finished as Rita husband. She was right in her latte accusation, for Hayworth and Welles soo divorced, Miss Hayworth declaring: 'I can take his genius any more.'

> 'A film is never really good unless the camera is an eye in the head of a poet'

Welles may have been surprised to find tha Hollywood – at least his own peers – wa sympathetic to his previous misfortunes as director. His first two films had many a mirers. Vera Hruba Ralston, wife of the hea of Republic studios, Herbert Yates, is rumoure to have persuaded her husband to put bot Welles and John Ford on the Republic lists give the studio some real class. Yates let Well direct a production of Shakespeare's *Macbe* (1948), which he made in just 23 days and on remarkably low budget. It is an uneven b extremely effective picture, and one of the be presentations of the play on film.

Macbeth was Welles' last film directed with the old Hollywood studio system. His su sequent career was erratic but often brilliant a fitting reflection of this flamboyant figure idiosyncratic genius.   DeWITT BODEE

Filmography

1940 Swiss Family Robinson (narr. only); Citizen Kane (+ co-sc; + act). **'42** The Magnificent Ambersons (+ sc; + narr); Journey Into Fear (actor; + uncredited dir). **'43** Jane Eyre (actor only). **'44** Follow the Boys (actor only). **'46** Tomorrow Is Forever (actor only); The Stranger (+ act; + uncredited co-sc). **'46** Duel in the Sun (narr. only). **'47** The Lady From Shanghai (+ act; + sc). **'48** Macbeth (+ act; + sc; + co-cost). **'49** Prince of Foxes (actor only); The Third Man (actor only); Black Magic (actor only). **'50** The Black Rose (actor only); La Miracle de St Anne (short) (FR); La Disordre (narr. only) (FR). **'52** Othello (+ act; + sc); Return to Glennascaul (actor only) (short); Trent's Last Case (actor only). **'54** Si Versailles M'Etait Conté (actor only) (FR) (USA/GB: Versailles); L'Uomo, la Bestia e la Virtù (actor only) (IT); Trouble in the Glen (actor only) (GB); Mr Arkadin/Confidential Report (+ act; + sc; + cost). **'55** Three Cases of Murder *ep* Lord Mountdrago (actor only) (GB); Napoléon (actor only) (FR); Out of Darkness (narr. only) (doc). **'56** Moby Dick (actor only). **'57** Man in the Shadow (actor only) (GB: Pay the Devil). **'58** The Long Hot Summer (actor only); Touch of Evil (+ act; + sc); The Vikings (narr. only); South Seas Adventure (narr. only) (doc); Come to the Fair (narr. only)

(doc); The Roots of Heaven (actor only). **'59** Les Seigneurs de la Forêt (co-narr. only) (BEL) (USA/GB: Lords of the Forest); Compulsion (actor only); Ferry to Hong Kong (actor only) (GB). **'60** David e Golia (actor only) (IT) (USA/GB: David and Goliath); Crack in the Mirror (actor only); Austerlitz (actor only) (FR-IT-YUG) (USA/GB: The Battle of Austerlitz). **'61** I Tartari (actor only) (IT) (USA/GB: The Tartars); King of Kings (narr. only). **'62** Lafayette (actor only) (FR-IT); Le Procès (+ act; + sc) (FR-IT-GER) (USA/GB: The Trial). **'63** River of the Ocean (narr. only) (doc) (GER); The VIP's (actor only) (GB) (USA: International Hotel); RoGoPaG (actor only) (IT-FR). **'64** The Finest Hour (narr. only) (GB). **'65** La Fabuleuse Aventure de Marco Polo (FR-IT-EG-YUG-AFG) (USA/GB: The Fabulous Adventures of Marco Polo/The Magnificent Marco Polo) (USA retitling for TV: Marco the Magnificent). **'66** Chimes at Midnight/Falstaff (+ act; + sc; + cost) (SP-SWIT); Paris, Brûle-t-il? (actor only) (FR) (USA/GB: Is Paris Burning?); A Man for All Seasons (actor only) (GB). **'67** Casino Royale (actor only) (GB); Sailor From Gibraltar (actor only) (GB); I'll Never Forget What's-'is-Name (actor only) (GB) (USA retitling for TV: The Takers). **'68** Histoire Immortelle (+ act) (FR)

(USA/GB: Immortal Story); Oedipus the King (actor only) (GB); House of Cards (actor only). **'69** L'Etoile du Sud (actor only) (FR-GB) (USA/GB: Southern Star); Tepepa (actor only) (IT-SP); Barbed Water (narr. only) (doc) (GB); Una su Tredici (actor only) (IT-FR) (USA/GB: 12 + 1). **'70** The Kremlin Letter (actor only); Start the Revolution Without Me (narr. only) (USA-CZ); Catch-22 (actor only); Waterloo (actor only) (IT-USSR); A Horse Called Njinsky (narr. only) (doc) (GB). **'71** Sentinels of Silence (narr. only) (short) (English version of Mexican short Sentinelas del Silencio); Directed by John Ford (narr. only) (doc); A Safe Place (actor only); La Decade Prodigieuse (actor only) (FR) (USA/GB: Ten Days' Wonder). **'72** Treasure Island (+ act; + co-sc) (GB-GER-FR-SP); Malpertuis (actor only) (BEL-FR-GER). **'73** Get to Know Your Rabbit (actor only); Vérités et Mensonges/F for Fake/ Question Mark/Nothing but the Truth) (+ act; + sc) (FR-IRAN-GER); **'75** And Then There Were None/Ten Little Indians/Ten Little Niggers/ Death in Persepolis (GER-FR-SP-IT). **'76** Voyage the Damned (actor only) (GB); The Late Great Planet Earth (narr: + act. only). **'78** Filming 'Othello' (+ narr). **'79** The Muppet Movie (actor only) (GB).

Apart from isolated peaks of achievement, Welles' later career has failed to fulfil its early promise. He remains a charismatic figure who seems to invite audiences to reflect on what might have been had the right opportunities come his way

After *Macbeth* he began to film *Othello*. The work was to become the kind of odyssey which was henceforth to characterize Welles' life. The filming dragged on from 1949 to 1952, moving from location to location across Morocco and Italy. When money ran out, work would stop – to recommence when funds came in and the cast could be reassembled.

If the difficulties of production again show in the uncertainty of the overall conception, at least here Welles could call on more talented associates than he had been able to for *Macbeth*; his old friend and early mentor from his youthful days as an actor in Dublin, Micheál MacLiammóir, creates a wonderful, feline Iago whose malice, the film infers, is the product of sexual impotence.

Welles now seemed doomed to endless wandering, leaving in his wake a host of uncompleted or abortive projects. In 1955 he began to film *Don Quixote* in Mexico and Paris, with himself as the Don and Akim Tamiroff, one of Welles' favourite actors, as Sancho Panza, but the film was never completed. Other projects talked of along the way include the biblical stories of Noah, Abraham and Salome; two more Shakespeare subjects, *King Lear* and *Julius Caesar* (eventually produced in 1953 by an old Mercury Theatre collaborator, John Houseman, with Joseph Mankiewicz as director); *Pickwick Papers* and (ironically) *The Odyssey*; *Catch-22*, which was eventually made by Mike Nichols in 1970, with Welles himself playing General Dreedle.

Even in the days of his childhood encounters with Shakespeare, Welles showed a special affection for larger-than-life characters. *Mr Arkadin* (1954) is a monster on the lines of *Citizen Kane*, a man of great wealth and power, who, unlike Kane, hires his own investigator to reconstruct the history of his mysterious career. This is, it is revealed, a test to establish if Arkadin's ultimate secret, the past guilt he

Left: Welles as General Dreedle on the set of Catch-22. *Below: to avenge the murder of his wife, detective Quinlan (Welles) prepares to 'execute' Grandi (Akim Tamiroff) in* Touch of Evil. *He plans to throw blame for the deed on Susan (Janet Leigh), wife of Quinlan's enemy – a Mexican police chief*

Although he was to return to Hollywood once more to make *Touch of Evil* (1958), Welles' *Macbeth* (1948) may be taken to mark his final divorce, as director, from the film capital. This was the first of his series of screen encounters with Shakespeare. To admit that it is also the least satisfactory of them is not to deny that it is, at the same time, one of the most imaginative of the cinema's adaptations of the playwright, comparing with Kurosawa's *Kumonso-* (1957, *Throne of Blood*) and towering, in its imaginative force, over Polanski's later version made in 1971. But the restrictions of time and money show, and the performances are uneven. Welles' collaborators seemed to find it hard to follow his imaginative flights.

This is hardly surprising: Welles has spent sixty years of his life brooding on the mastery and mysteries of Shakespeare, and reshaping them to find new interpretations. It is said that his bed-time stories at the age of two were Charles Lamb's *Tales From Shakespeare*. At three he rejected these in favour of the original texts. By seven he knew *King Lear* by heart, and by ten he had learnt all the great tragic roles.

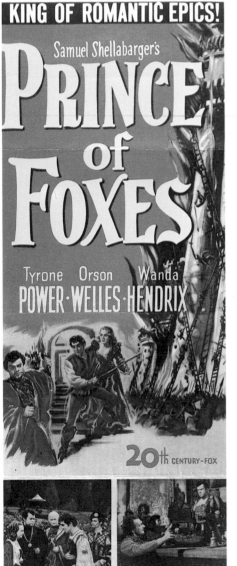

Above: Falstaff cuddles Doll Tearsheet – Welles and Jeanne Moreau in Chimes at Midnight. *Below and below right: costume melodramas like* Prince of Foxes *and* The Tartars *allowed Welles to revel in villainous roles, which he invested with sinister power*

KING OF ROMANTIC EPICS!

Samuel Shellabarger's

PRINCE of FOXES

Tyrone **POWER** · Orson **WELLES** · Wanda **HENDRIX**

20th CENTURY-FOX

with MARINA BERTI · EVERETT SLOANE · KATINA PAXINOU · FELIX AYLMER

Directed by **HENRY KING** Produced by **SOL C. SIEGEL**

Screen Play by Milton Krims
From the Novel by Samuel Shellabarger

most wants to conceal, is safe from detection. When it proves not to be, Arkadin realizes that the man must be silenced for good.

For many of Welles' admirers *Touch of Evil* (his last attempt to come to terms with the Hollywood studio system) is his masterpiece. Welles plays Hank Quinlan, a fat, decaying, crack cop, whose sense of deistic superiority leads him to frame people whom his 'infallible' instinct tells him are guilty. Welles sets the action in a border town of nightmare seediness, whose other inhabitants include Marlene Dietrich as a languidly philosophical madame, apparently a one-time flame of Quinlan's, and Akim Tamiroff as the patriarch of a bizarre gang of hoodlums.

For years *Touch of Evil* was regarded as yet another example of Hollywood's legendary humiliation of creative genius: Universal studios' editors were alleged to have butchered Welles' original version. More recently, however, this has been reconstituted, and it is arguable that the Universal conception was actually an improvement; by leaving out some too-literal explanatory scenes, the cuts enhanced the sense of mystery and metaphysic

which is the film's great attraction.

Le Procès (1962, *The Trial*), a Franco-Italian-German co-production, was shot in Paris and Zagreb. Much admired on its first appearance it now seems one of Welles' least successful works. His own evident philosophical distance from Kafka results not so much in invigorating

---

'Every time I bring out a new movie, nobody bothers to review it . . . They don't review my work, they review me'

---

tensions as in excessive debate: for an Orson Welles picture it is, unusually, often tediously talkative. Visually the film is remarkable. Much of it was shot in the abandoned buildings of the Gare d'Orsay in Paris; the old railway station, often bathed in swirling mists, provides some stunning images.

Thanks to Spanish and Swiss finance Welles was next able to return to Shakespeare with a film that may well remain, alongside

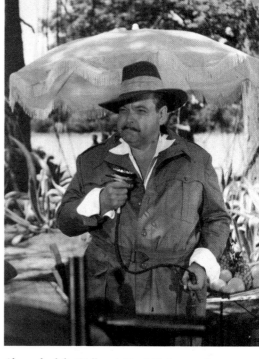

Citizen Kane, his monument – Chimes at Midnight (1966). In a textual adaptation so brilliant that even the most demanding Shakespearean cannot fault it on grounds of scholarship, Welles assembled scenes from Richard II, Henry IV Part I and II, Henry V and The Merry Wives of Windsor, along with a commentary taken from the Chronicles of the Elizabethan historian Holinshed, to create a wholly new work which might be alternatively titled 'The Tragedy of Sir John Falstaff'. Without any violence to Shakespeare's own, essentially comic, vision of Falstaff, Welles extracts a character that is heroic in his humour, generosity and goodness, flawed perhaps, but finally tragic in his incomprehension of the ingratitude of the great and powerful.

Over the years Welles acted indefatigably – often appearing in two or three films per year. Some of his roles – in Jane Eyre (1943), The Third Man (1949), Compulsion (1959) and Catch-22, for example – are memorable; all are enjoyable; none is without a conscientious intelligence. Often, however, Welles' willingness to accept parts in the most inconsiderable material – from TV commercials to Casino Royale (1967) – looks positively cynical. His majestic, unflawed performance as Falstaff, however, demonstrated that, to whatever extent he might have prostituted his talent to the service of much lesser creators, he had kept intact and pure his gifts as an interpreter.

Histoire Immortelle (1968, Immortal Story), adapted from a tale by Isak Dineson (the pseudonym of Karen Blixen), provided him with another of the monsters he loves: a man like Kane and Arkadin, rich and powerful in the worldly sense but troubled by a secret sense of incompleteness. This old man, Mr Clay, is the embodiment of the traditional sailors' legend of the rich man of Macao who invites a young mariner to sleep with his beautiful wife (played by Jeanne Moreau), and fulfil the marital function of which he is himself incapable. Brief, classical and near-perfect, this film is, to date, Welles' last completed formal story film.

His wanderings continued. He acted in Bondarchuk's Waterloo (1970) and Chabrol's La Decade Prodigieuse (1971, Ten Days' Wonder). His rich, inimitable voice and superb diction were constantly in demand for film com-

mentaries; and it was thus that he came to work with François Reichenbach. Out of their collaboration came the delicious, enigmatic Vérités et Mensonges (1973, F for Fake). Welles was fascinated by some 16mm footage Reichenbach had shot for a TV series on fakers, with the celebrated art forger Elmyr de Hory and Clifford Irving, who, subsequent to the original Reichenbach film, had become famous as the faker of Howard Hughes' 'autobiography'. To these, Welles added his own fakes (in which he included his role in the radio production of War of the Worlds which, over thirty years earlier, had fooled thousands of Americans into thinking that the USA was under attack by Martians). Welles orchestrates this material so as to entice the spectator into a fascinating labyrinth.

Old now but still exuding boyish mischief, Welles relishes his film persona of magician and charlatan, amiably deceiving his willing audience with wonderful sleight of hand. Yet his place in movie history is nearer, in reality, to one of his tragic characterizations. Potentially one of the most gifted figures of world cinema, his output in forty years has been

Above, far left: Welles abridged Shakespeare's tragic study of sexual jealousy for his version of Othello. *Here, he attends to the poisonous counsel of Iago (Micheál MacLiammóir). Above left:* F for Fake *– Welles' most recent film as director. Above and below: Welles as a TV reporter in Huston's* The Roots of Heaven, *and as the isolated Cardinal Wolsey, swept aside by the caprices of Henry VIII, in Zinnemann's* A Man for All Seasons

miserably small, a constant story of frustrated or abortive projects. This may be detected in the tale he told himself in Filming 'Othello' (1978) – his contribution to which undoubtedly went further than mere commentary and interview. In recent years the list of incomplete projects has grown. Between 1967 and 1979 he was at work filming The Deep off the Dalmatian coast. Since 1970 he has been at work on The Other Side of the Wind; but nothing of that film, either, has ever been seen publicly. 'I do not work enough', he confessed to an interviewer in 1965, in a moment of unusual self-revelation, 'I am frustrated. Do you understand?'   DAVID ROBINSON

Directed by Orson Welles, 1940

Prod co: Mercury Productions/RKO. **exec prod:** George J. Schaefer. **prod:** Orson Welles. **sc:** Herman J. Mankiewicz, Orson Welles. **photo:** Gregg Toland. **sp eff:** Vernon L. Walker. **ed:** Robert Wise, Mark Robson. **art dir:** Van Nest Polglase, Darrell Silvera, Hilyard Brown. **cost:** Edward Stevenson. **mus:** Bernard Herrmann. **sd:** Bailey Fesler, James G. Stewart. **ass dir:** Richard Wilson. **r/t:** 119 minutes. New York premiere, 1 May 1941.

Cast: Orson Welles (*Charles Foster Kane*), Joseph Cotten (*Jedediah Leland*), Dorothy Comingore (*Susan Alexander*), Everett Sloane (*Mr Bernstein*), Ray Collins (*James W. Gettys*), George Coulouris (*Walter Parks Thatcher*), Agnes Moorehead (*Kane's mother*), Paul Stewart (*Raymond*), Ruth Warrick (*Emily Norton*), Erskine Sandford (*Herbert Carter*), William Alland (*Thompson; newsreel reader*), Fortunio Bonanova (*Matisti*), Gus Schilling (*head-waiter*), Philip Van Zandt (*Mr Rawlston*), Georgia Backus (*Miss Anderson*), Harry Shannon (*Kane's father*), Sonny Bupp (*Kane III*), Buddy Swan (*Kane age 8*), Richard Barr (*Hillman*), Joan Blair (*Georgia*), Al Eben (*Mike*), Charles Bennett (*entertainer*), Milt Kibbee (*reporter*), Tom Curran (*Teddy Roosevelt*), Irving Mitchell (*Dr Corey*), Edith Evanson (*nurse*), Arthur Kay (*conductor*), Tudor Williams (*chorus master*), Herbert Corthell (*city editor*), Benny Rubin (*Smather*), Edmund Cobb (*reporter*), Frances Neal (*Ethel*), Robert Dudley (*photographer*), Ellen Lowe (*Miss Townsend*), Gino Corrado (*Gino the waiter*), Alan Ladd, Louise Currie, Eddie Coke, Walter Sande, Arthur O'Connell (*reporters*).

Charles Foster Kane utters his final word, 'Rosebud', and dies on his massive, crumbling estate, Xanadu (1).

Newsreel journalists prepare a film showing Kane's rise and fall, but it lacks an angle. A reporter is sent to find out who Rosebud may be. He interviews Susan Alexander (2) (Kane's second wife), Bernstein (3) and Jed Leland (two old employees) and Kane's butler, Raymond. Through them the jigsaw of Kane's life is pieced together.

Five-year-old Kane has inherited an immense fortune; at his mother's wish he is placed under the guardianship of banker Walter Thatcher (4) and is taken away from his Colorado home.

Thirty years later Kane buys up the New York *Inquirer* and begins his career as a scandal-sheet publisher (5). He marries Emily Norton (6) but later meets Susan Alexander (7) and establishes a love-nest with her. His attempt to run for governor (8) is shattered along with his marriage when political enemy Jim Gettys (9) exposes the affair.

Kane marries Susan and launches her on a disastrous career as an opera singer. But her failure and the set-backs he suffers during the Depression force him to retreat to his castle, Xanadu (10).

Susan, bored by the isolation of Xanadu and by Kane's autocratic behaviour, eventually leaves him. Kane dies and his chattels are disposed of, among them a childhood sled bearing the painted-on name of Rosebud (11).

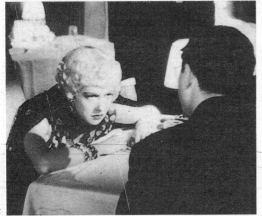

72

Up to the Forties, orthodox Hollywood camera style consisted of diffused lighting and soft focus, even for such brutally realistic films as *I Am a Fugitive From a Chain Gang* (1932). Photographed in this way a typical sequence might consist of a long or medium establishing shot with cuts to close-up shots to show detail. Orson Welles' *Citizen Kane* (1940), however, signalled the beginning of a new period in American cinema. Composition in depth, obtained by increased depth-of-field photography, meant that images on several planes could all be held in sharp focus. The dramatic effects of a scene were created by images within the composition itself rather than by editing; and because both foreground and background remained in focus, the spectator could see everything there was to see in a single shot.

Depth of field in *Citizen Kane* results from a number of factors including the use of faster film and wide-angle lenses. These lenses possess certain inherent optical properties which can dramatically affect the appearance of a composition. As well as keeping foreground and background in focus, they create the illusion of perspective by exaggerating the relative scale of objects on different planes – objects closer to the camera appear much larger than those further away.

The relationship between visual style and narrative content seems almost inseparable in the film. The character of Kane is revealed not so much by what he says and does as by how he is made to appear in the context of his surroundings.

Early in the film there is a scene where Walter Thatcher has come to Colorado to take the young Kane away with him. In one of the shots (picture 4) Mrs Kane sits reading the terms of her son's inheritance in the foreground and at the right of the frame. Thatcher is seated slightly behind and to the right of her, and Kane's father stands at the left of the frame in the middle distance. By their position and size the three figures appear to be visually and dramatically at the centre of the scene. Initially their relative sizes on the screen seem to indicate their relative narrative importance: Mrs Kane, the mother who is trying to do the best for her son, is the dominant personality; Thatcher is the interloper; and the elder Kane, ineffectively voicing his opposition, is a figure of weakness. After looking through the foreground diagonally to the middle distance, attention centres on a window at the very back of the room. Through it can barely be identified the figure of a young boy who is all but obliterated by falling snow.

The boy may at first appear to be the least important figure in the composition, but the opposite is true. Much greater dramatic coherence is given to the scene when it is scanned in reverse order, from background to foreground. The smallest figure becomes the focal point of the narrative – it is Kane's future his parents and Thatcher are discussing, *his* life that, from that point onwards, will be irrevocably changed.

Time and again in the film secondary figures are positioned to act as a frame within the film frame in order to concentrate the spectator's attention on Kane in the distance. But a point occurs during the political rally sequence where, although a similar framing technique is used, the dramatic effect is suddenly reversed. Kane is giving the supreme performance of his career: his magnificent rhetoric about protecting working men, slum children and ordinary citizens alike captivates the audience. The scene ends, however, with a shot (picture 9) that dispels this effect and signals the beginning of the end for Kane. Political boss Jim Gettys is seen standing high up in a balcony, his figure filling the right side of the frame. To the left and far below, Kane is finishing his speech to wild applause. But the exaggerated perspective and the disproportionate size of Gettys foreshadows the despairing events about to befall Kane.

Up to this point in the film Kane is depicted as being in control of space on the screen. The spectator's attention, manipulated by the expressive dynamics of the composition and lighting, is unerringly drawn to him. But from the time he loses the election to the end of the film, his presence is made to seem increasingly insignificant in relation to his surroundings. This is most noticeable in the concluding scenes of Kane and Susan's self-imposed exile in Xanadu where Kane appears dwarfed by the volume of the rooms and the sheer depth of the huge, gaping fireplace. Space in the cavernous mausoleum of Xanadu now controls Kane and isolates him in a void of darkness.

ARNOLD DESSER

5

6

10

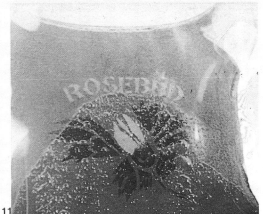

11

73

Here's looking at you

The work of the Hollywood cameramen

From our present perspective, informed as it is by the concept of a director's cinema, it is sometimes hard to imagine a time when the director concerned himself with the actors and it was the cameraman who put his signature on the finished film. In the early days of the silent cinema, however, the art of the film was founded in this close relationship between the man who directed the actors and the man whose job it was to make them look beautiful,

handsome, tragic or heroic. From this background emerged the first generation of great motion-picture cameramen.

By the Twenties, the art of the cameraman had been emphatically established. Pioneer cinematographers like Billy Bitzer and Victor Fleming had begun their careers in the movie business; others, like Arthur Edeson and James Wong Howe, had come to films from portrait photography. Now that film-making had become a highly specialized craft and, in some cases, an art form, the man behind the camera was at the very least a highly prized technician and occasionally something approaching a magician.

Cameramen had to do their own special effects and optical work. They also needed a keen sense of design and sometimes had to invent the new technology of movie-making as they went along, modifying and adapting their equipment to cope with the ambitious demands of the directors.

A good cameraman always needed a good

Above: some of Arthur Edeson's finest cinematography was seen in Casablanca *and other films for Warners during the Forties.*
Left: in The Cameraman *(1928) Buster Keaton parodied the craft of cinematography, but as a director he favoured camera movement*

director, but he also benefitted from the skills of a good designer. Cecil B. DeMille's *The Cheat* (1915), designed by Wilfred Buckland, is an early example of such collaboration. The film contains a scene where two actors are framed against what appears to be a wall in the background; the scene is dark and the actors are illuminated by one patch of light that is criss-crossed with prison-type bars. The whole effect is achieved with light and shadow and is extremely atmospheric.

In the Twenties, cameramen began using panchromatic stock which gave an excellent visual texture. The fact that film was made on a nitrate base also gave it a special luminous quality that was particularly noticeable in the black tones. Later acetate-based films never looked as rich in their blacks as did nitrate. Handling celluloid was a dangerous job for which there was no training. Most cinematographers simply coped with the hazards and taught themselves their trade.

As the variety of films in the silent era expanded – Westerns, comedies, romances, spectaculars – cameramen learned to change their style to suit the story they were making. Lighting for a domestic drama, for example, would be 'flatter' (more two-dimensional) than that designed for a lustrous, historical pageant.

This mobility between the various genres is a crucial factor in the history of cinematography. At first sight it may seem strange that the cameraman Lee Garmes, for example, could switch from Rex Ingram's exotic *The Garden of Allah* (1927) to William A. Seiter's 'realist' drama *Waterfront* (1928) and to the Eddie Cantor musical *Whoopee!* (1930), but Hollywood was an industry that made a wide range of products, and cameramen, like anyone else, were hired to make the best use of their skills on whatever film they were assigned by the studio.

If adaptability was essential to the role of the cameramen, it was also vital that he remain susceptible to new ideas. Cinematography developed so rapidly between the years 1915 and 1930 that virtually everything known about the art today was discovered in that period.

Given the flexibility of cameramen, it seems surprising that mobility of the camera was one of the last developments to be made. In the majority of silent films, motion-picture photography was just that. People and things moved in front of the camera, and highly elaborate effects were created in the camera, but the instrument itself moved comparatively little.

There were exceptions, of course, notably in the films of Buster Keaton. He conceived his comedy around a succession of dynamic, highly mobile gags: the railway engine in *The General* (1926) and the studio-built waterfall in *Our Hospitality* (1923) are fine examples of the way Keaton uses camera movement, especially tracking shots, as an integral part of the comic narrative.

The other great actor-director of the period, Erich von Stroheim, preferred static camerawork, though he displayed a great sensitivity to light and shade. Ben Reynolds was one of Stroheim's cameramen on *Blind Husbands* (1918), *Foolish Wives* (1922), *Greed* (1923) and *The Wedding March* (1928), and achieved some remarkable contrasts of opulence and poverty through his knowledge of how various surfaces reflected and absorbed light. Stroheim's sets were so elaborate that he insisted his audience be allowed the time (in the shot) to

least their eyes on the decor and to absorb all the movement going on within the frame.

The real 'liberation' of the camera took place in the late Twenties and was especially re-marked upon in the work of the German director F.W. Murnau. In this respect both *Der Letzte Mann* (1924, *The Last Laugh*), made in Germany, and *Sunrise* (1927), Murnau's first American film, are key examples of how, towards the end of the silent period, directors were making the camera work to move the film's story along.

The achievement is not solely attributable to Murnau. In France, for example, Marcel L'Herbier's *L'Argent* (1928, *Money*) contains several elaborate tracking sequences and some sequences of expertly shot, hand-held camera-work; and in Japan, Kinugasa's 'experimental' films *Kurutta Ippeiji* (1926, *A Page of Madness*) and *Jujiro* (1928, *Crossroads*) reveal a sophis-ticated awareness of camera mobility.

Ironically, the newly acquired freedom of movement in camerawork was unexpectedly interrupted, in Hollywood at least, by the arrival of talkies and the need for cameras to be sound-proofed within bulky, almost unmov-able booths. It was a retrogressive, though mercifully brief, stage in the history of cinematography.

By 1930, however, the booths were ban-ished; cameras (like the new Mitchell) were blimped and once again free to move. For the next decade the art of the cameraman was largely a refinement and sophistication of the expertise already acquired. The musicals had their heyday and, as dance-directors like Busby Berkeley designed ever more elaborate numbers, cameramen like George Folsey and Joseph Ruttenberg learned to devise new kinds of shots and angles. The movie camera had never been so mobile. At the major studios the roster of top cameramen remained as it had been in the days before the talkies. Lee Garmes and Victor Milner were at Paramount, William Daniels at MGM. The 'vocabulary' of the movie cameraman was more or less unaltered: crisp, clear shots were used for action scenes, flat-tering soft-focus for close-ups, and so on.

Perhaps the finest example of this continuity of style is evidenced in the series of 19 Greta Garbo films photographed by William Daniels. Daniels himself told Charles Higham (in *Hol-lywood Cameramen*):

'Even my lighting for Garbo varied from picture to picture. There wasn't one Garbo face in the sense that there was a Dietrich face.'

But a close comparison of the seduction scene in *The Mysterious Lady* (1928) and the bedroom scene in *Queen Christina* (1933) reveals a consistent lighting style: a fondness

for simulating firelight and candlelight, a tendency to throw shadow onto the star's eyes to increase her aura of mystery.

Lee Garmes' photography of Marlene Diet-rich in the films they made with Josef von Sternberg testifies to a similar working re-lationship, though in *Morocco* (1930), *Dis-honoured* (1931) and *Shanghai Express* (1932), the style of Sternberg's direction is more self-conscious than that of Clarence Brown in the Garbo films, and the famous 'slatted' light effects of these exotic-looking films may be more properly attributed to Sternberg than to Lee Garmes.

Nevertheless Garmes was one of the most painterly of all Hollywood cameramen. A great admirer of Rembrandt, he claimed to have borrowed the painter's technique of 'north light' – whereby the main source of light on the set always comes from the north. Garmes clearly shares with Rembrandt a predilection for low-key lighting and in a film from later in his career, *Caught* (dir. Max Ophuls, 1948), he achieves some remarkably suspenseful effects. In one scene Barbara Bel Geddes meets her lover in an old boathouse. The only illumi-nation comes from her flashlight and, as the scene develops into a quarrel, the shadows become genuinely menacing.

The partnership on this film of the versatile Garmes and the virtuoso Ophuls was one of the happy accidents of the Hollywood system. In the Thirties, Garmes had tried his hand at directing in partnership with the screenwriters Ben Hecht and Charles MacArthur, but in the

Top left: John Gilbert and Greta Garbo in Flesh and the Devil *(1927) photographed in luminous black and white by William Daniels, who created similar effects for the same duo in* Queen Christina *(top). Above: Clive Brook and Marlene Dietrich in* Shanghai Express, *shot under Lee Garmes' exotic lighting*

post-war period he returned behind the camera to work with Hitchcock, Ophuls, Wyler and Ray, among many other directors.

Whereas the Thirties and early Forties saw William Daniels' career reflect, and in some measure determine, the MGM house style, his post-war work with Jules Dassin could not have been more different. *Brute Force* (1947) and *The Naked City* (1948) were starkly realistic pictures for Hollywood, and though Daniels would later be reunited with two of his favourite directors, Clarence Brown and George Cukor, he responded with expertise and enthusiasm to the idea of shooting in the streets, over-exposing the new extra-fast film to adjust the contrast between daylight ex-teriors and (deliberately) drab interiors.

The Forties was the decade of the *film noir* whose principal visual characteristic was, as the name implies, a predominance of dark settings sparingly illuminated by 'low-key' lighting. The 'key' light is the primary light on a set (all other lamps in use are collectively termed 'fill' lighting). To position the key light as near to the floor of the set as possible was to create an effect of long, tall shadows, obscure shapes and dark enigmatic faces. The atmos-

Above: Garmes' familiar technique of filtering light through shuttered windows in Caught. *Above right: the expressionist style of lighting in* The Cat and the Canary. *Right:* Frankenstein *and (far right)* The Mask of Demetrios *both shot by Arthur Edeson*

phere evoked in this way was unique but the techniques had been around Hollywood ever since cameramen like Karl Struss, Eugen Schüfftan, Karl Freund and Franz Planer had introduced elements of the German Expressionist style into their work.

One of the earliest beneficiaries of this shadowy, often sinister, use of black and white had been Universal, whose cycle of horror films in the Thirties was clearly influenced by the German horror movies of a decade or so earlier. On the staff of Universal at that time was the cinematographer Arthur Edeson, who had begun his film career with Douglas Fairbanks Sr and had pioneered the use of filming on location with the unwieldy new sound cameras.

By the time Edeson had completed his first (war) film at Universal (*All Quiet on the Western Front,* 1930), the studio's style in horror films was a tamer version of the fiercely expressionistic films like Paul Leni's *The Cat and the Canary* (1927). Edeson photographed *Frankenstein* (1931), *The Old Dark House* (1932) and *The Invisible Man* (1933) and confirmed his reputation as one of the finest black-and-white cameramen of his generation.

When the vogue for low-key lighting resurfaced in the Forties, Edeson assimilated it to the prevalent house style at Warners, where he worked from 1936 to 1947. His camerawork on *The Maltese Falcon* (1941), *Casablanca* (1942) and *The Mask of Demetrios* (1944) bears evidence of the *noir* influence, but is at the same time a glossy refinement of the distinctive Warners visual style pioneered by Tony Gaudio and Sol Polito in gangster films and melodramas throughout the Thirties.

Another survivor from the earliest days, and a man of arguably greater talent than Edeson, was John F. Seitz. During the Twenties, Seitz was one of the highest-paid cameramen in Hollywood. An expert in the use of intense, low-key lighting, Seitz found his perfect professional match in the director Rex Ingram. The partnership yielded three extraordinary films, each of them displaying an unprecedented visual flair and sophistication: *The Four Horsemen of the Apocalypse* (1921), *Scaramouche* (1923) and *Mare Nostrum* (1926).

In the Forties, Seitz found himself working with Preston Sturges at Paramount. He photographed *Sullivan's Travels* (1941), *The Miracle of Morgan's Creek* (1943) and *Hail the Conquering Hero* (1944), but, though these comedies were minor masterpieces in the genre, they did not make exceptional demands on Seitz's unique talent for 'painting with light' (to borrow cinematographer John Alton's phrase).

Working with Billy Wilder, however, Seitz formed a relationship that was as fruitful, in its own way, as the one with Ingram in the Twenties. Their first film together was *Five Graves to Cairo* (1943) which genuinely looks as if it had been lit in a silent-film style. The whole screen is suffused with patterns of light, filtered through shutters into darkish interiors. For *Double Indemnity* (1944), Wilder's only *film noir* proper, Seitz was a logical and happy choice. The scene where Fred MacMurray calls at Barbara Stanwyck's house to discuss the insurance on her husband is a fine example of the almost tangible atmosphere Seitz's delicate lighting could create.

There followed *The Lost Weekend* (1945) and *Sunset Boulevard* (1950), in which Seitz was faced with the challenge of suggesting 'private worlds' for Ray Milland's desperate alcoholic and Gloria Swanson's faded movie star. He succeeded admirably but, looking back on her career, Seitz averred that *Five Graves to Cairo* was his favourite piece of work.

The advent of three-strip Technicolor in the mid-to-late Thirties was of major importance in the history of cinematography, but colour itself was no novelty and many cameramen had previous experience of working in the medium. On the whole, Hollywood was slow to switch to colour and it was not until the late Forties that a distinctive mastery of the new colour technology could be detected in the work of the cinematographers. There were, of course, those who had gained early experience: Ray Rennahan, for example, was the Technicolor company's full-time cameraman. He filmed the first feature in Technicolor, *Becky Sharp* (1935), and was adviser on *Gone With the Wind* (1939).

James Wong Howe shot his first Technicolor sequence in an otherwise black-and-white musical, *Hollywood Party* (1934) and in 1938 photographed his first Technicolor feature, *The Adventures of Tom Sawyer*, for David Selznick. Howe's career behind the camera had begun in 1921 and during the silent era he worked with a couple of cameramen-turned-directors – Victor Fleming and Bert Glennon. His credits in the Thirties include films with Howard Hawks, W.S. Van Dyke and John Cromwell, but it is the photography in his Forties work that is most memorable.

Howe shot some of the classics of the *film noir*: Lang's *Hangmen Also Die!* (1943), *Pursued* (dir. Raoul Walsh, 1947) and *He Ran All the Way* (dir. John Berry, 1951). *Pursued* is a dark and sombre Western that depends on effective visual devices to express childhood traumas, whereas *He Ran All the Way* is set in the rain-swept streets of New York under the pitiless ght of streetlamps. Both films demonstrate owe's versatility in black and white, but the tter film also reveals his ingenuity: for, in the urse of a scene in an indoor swimming pool, owe (standing up to his waist in water) tilized the daylight reflected from the water's urface to add a strange texture to the actors' ces. He considered this among his finest ork, but he was no less inventive when ooting *Body and Soul* (dir. Robert Rossen, 947). While a team of extra cameramen shot otage of the climactic boxing match from a istance, Howe took advantage of his height e was a little over five foot) to duck and eave in and out of the fight, even using the ld silent cameramen's trick of being pushed round on roller skates to get his close-ups.

By the end of the Forties, colour was becom-

Above: shooting The Miracle of Morgan's Creek *with Eddie Bracken and Betty Hutton; second from left is the cameraman John Seitz, at far right of film crew is the director Preston Sturges. Above right: Seitz's distinctive silent-cinema lighting for Ramon Novarro in* Scaramouche. *Right: essentially the same lighting style in* Five Graves to Cairo

ing firmly established in Hollywood. 20th Century-Fox were leaders in the field but all the major studios displayed confidence in colour. Henry King's musical *Margie* (1946), photographed by Charles Clarke, is an outstanding example and one that lacks the garishness occasionally found in other Fox musicals of the Forties. The finest cameraman on the Fox lot at the time was undoubtedly Leon Shamroy whose skills are nowhere better exemplified than in *Wilson* (1944), Henry King's biopic about the US President who fought to establish the League of Nations.

Shamroy worked closely with Technicolor's Ray Rennahan on films like *Down Argentine Way* (1940) and *That Night in Rio* (1941) and this collaboration gave him the grounding that was to make him the premier Technicolor cameraman of the Fifties: *The Snows of Kilimanjaro* (1952), *The Robe* (1953), *South Pacific* (1958) and *Porgy and Bess* (1959).

Black-and-white cinematography did not go out of fashion overnight. At some studios in the Forties 'quality' meant black-and-white pictures. It is significant, for example, that the major Goldwyn productions of the decade (*Little Foxes*, *The Westerner* and *The Best Years of Our Lives*) were all black-and-white produc-

tions and that the falling-off of the Goldwyn style appears to coincide with the growth of colour features. For black-and-white cinematography, Goldwyn's top cameraman Gregg Toland was much in demand and has become one of the art's most famous practitioners.

Toland had begun as an assistant to Arthur Edeson in the Twenties, but it was with *Dead End* (1937) and *Wuthering Heights* (1939) that he made his reputation and did much to contribute to the elegant house style of Goldwyn films.

The critical acclaim showered on *Citizen Kane* (1940) has tended to exaggerate Toland's status as a cinematographer. He did not, of course, invent deep-focus photography, which had existed from the beginnings of cinema, but he did perfect a system of adding drilled metal stops ('Waterhouse stops') to the lens in order to alter depth of focus while the camera was on the move. Toland is also to be credited with being one of the first cameramen to use the new fast film stocks introduced in the Forties and his work on *Citizen Kane* is nothing if not innovative. Camera style rarely calls attention to itself and, as a result, Toland's work tends to appear more self-conscious than that of his fellow cinematographers. In *The Grapes of Wrath* (1940), for example, the viewer is made conscious of the way the light falls across Henry Fonda's face, making a composition. *Wuthering Heights* also suffers from direction and camerawork that is inclined to strike poses rather than move the story along.

RKO was the other bastion of black and white in the Forties. The indelible image of the studio was *film noir* thrillers and the horror films produced by Val Lewton. This consistency of style is, as always, the result of several contributory factors, but since so much depends on the distinctive, chiaroscuro lighting, the work of Nicholas Musaraca on such films as *Cat People* (1942), *The Seventh Victim* (1943), *The Spiral Staircase*, (1945), *The Locket* (1946), and *Out of the Past* (1947) must be ranked alongside his more frequently praised contemporaries. The Forties was, after all, the last great period of black-and-white motion pictures. They just will not make them like that again.   MARTYN AUTY

With acknowledgments to John Gillett for his assistance

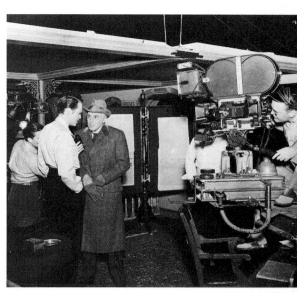

Top: James Wong Howe supervising an outdoor shot on Hombre (1967) starring Paul Newman. Top right: Gregg Toland lines up a shot on Citizen Kane beneath the extra-low ceilings that deliberately forced the camera into the corners of the set. Right: Leon Shamroy's delicate lighting on Wilson. Below: The Spiral Staircase shot by Nicholas Musuraca

Oscars for the British

In Britain in the Forties, cameramen had emerged as major creative artists in their own right. Freddie Francis, a leading cameraman in post-war Britain and director of several notable horror movies, recalls what distinguished the roles of British cameramen from their opposite numbers in Hollywood

I have been a cameraman and director all my life, but when I began in the business in 1939, the cinematographer worked for the studio first and the director second. This meant that cameramen could be taken off one production and put on another, just like that – they were interchangeable. But things did change because the studio system, such as it was, was never as rigid as that in Hollywood. And for this reason British cameramen tended to free themselves from the system sooner than their American counterparts.

When Jack Cardiff won an Oscar for his photography on *Black Narcissus* (dir. Michael Powell, Emeric Pressburger, 1947), it gave everybody hope that you didn't have to be American to win awards and those of us who were cameramen in Britain were becoming a force to be reckoned with.

Later on Robert Krasker won an Oscar for *The Third Man* (1949). He had done his training under Korda at London Films where he was camera operator on *Rembrandt, Things to Come* (both 1936), *The Four Feathers* (1939) and *The Thief of Bagdad* (1940). He was already pretty familiar, then, with the Technicolor process and made a fine job of *Henry V* (1945). On *The Third Man* Krasker took everything off level and made the film exciting for its use of odd angles. He was greatly encouraged by the director Carol Reed, in much the same way as David Lean encouraged Freddie Young. It all comes down to a director having confidence in his cameraman and then giving him the freedom to create.

On the whole the vogue for low-key lighting in Hollywood did not influence British cameramen too much, though *Brighton Rock* (1947), photographed by Harry Waxman, did favour lots of shadows and contrasting black and white. What seemed to have more influence in Britain was the continental style of Georges Périnal, who was brought over by Korda to shoot *The Private Life of Henry VIII* (1933) and stayed for the rest of the decade. Everyone loved Périnal's style and it contributed enormously to the lavish look of Korda's productions. After all, a cameraman's job is to give the director the best canvas on which to paint his picture.

From an interview with THE MOVIE, *February 1980*

Trouble in Hollywood

When the war was over the movies enjoyed a boom, but a new battle was about to be waged – this time for the political soul of Hollywood

There never was a year like 1946 for Hollywood. Servicemen waiting for demobilization were trapped in camps across America, eager for films to pass the time. When they finally got home, they were courting and going out to the movies. American cinemas sold more than 4000 million tickets – producing a box-office take of nearly $1700 million. The latter figure was not matched again until 1974, when cinemas sold only a quarter of the number of tickets. After the wonderful year of 1946, only inflation made Hollywood's take look good.

In the four years following the end of the war, however, Hollywood went from boom to nervous disarray, its structure radically altered by law, its morale shattered by paranoia, its audience thinned away. Those captive servicemen went home, married, built a suburban lifestyle away from the downtown cinemas. They wanted entertainment in the home and, when they could get it, they wanted television.

Lifestyles which had been denied by the Depression and the war were now embraced with wild relief. The women who had worked in the munitions factories went home, settled down, had babies and stopped going out to the distant, inconvenient movies.

Between 1946 and 1948, even before television was nationwide, movie admissions dropped by 16.9 per cent. In the inner councils of the industry, moguls and bankers alike saw estimates that the fall-off would exceed 25 per cent. They did not publish the figures, but they took action. In 1946, MGM had already decreed a slimming of its product. It was to be a little less long, a little less lavish. Anticipating keener competition for dwindling audiences, 20th Century-Fox concentrated its resources on fewer but bigger inducements to draw audiences back to the cinemas. Columbia and Universal, on the other hand, tried to make their product more glamorous. Everyone felt cold competition coming.

Fewer admissions were bad enough. Worse, for the majors, was the continuing interest of the US Department of Justice in the financing of Hollywood and in particular the cosy cartel operated by the big studios.

From the early Thirties, the Department of Justice had been trying to break the stranglehold of the majors over independent cinemas. Its aim was to force the film production and distribution companies to sell off their highly lucrative cinema divisions. Since most of the majors made almost all their money in film exhibition, rather than in distribution or production, Hollywood resisted as long as it could.

Cases were brought before the courts in 1938 and 1940 but the war delayed their impact. In 1946, the Department of Justice began to strip away the major privileges (and major profits) of the big-league motion-picture companies. The change was even more radical than most observers admit. Along with new tax laws (the biggest external influence on movies), the anti-trust decisions of the late Forties changed the basis and nature of movie financing, and so of movie-making.

By 1946 the pattern of the business was changing: the small-town cinema owner was no longer confronted with a salesman who would make him take everything a studio might produce, on pain of getting nothing at all. He did not have to accept prices before seeing movies and he could bid competitively. It would be naive to suggest that this made for open competition in the movie business, but it did mean movies were not automatically guaranteed success. They had to convince cinema owners first.

Independent producers now had a better chance of selling their movies. The new tax laws made it wise for stars and star directors to form themselves into independent corporations. If each movie project were a corporation in its own right, sold, when completed, to a distributor for a profit, then the profit would attract only 25 per cent capital-gains tax. The majors had to compete for these independent productions and for stars who also wanted their independence.

The majors were made to sell their cinema chains by a series of legal settlements reached between 1949 and 1959. These sales took away the largest element in profit and cash-flow from the studios. Banks were short of lending money in the immediate post-war period and were thus inclined to examine individual movie projects as well as corporate credits. In this way the idea of the 'bankable' star emerged. The strict hierarchy of first-run and second-run cinemas was shaken and this too altered the financial base of movie-making.

World War II had effectively closed most of

Above: at least the second musical remake of a mistaken-identity tale; this version was designed as a vehicle for the Brazilian star Carmen Miranda in the hope of capturing new audiences in Latin America. Below left: a contemporary advertisement (painted by John Falter) for bottled beers, showing the prominence of television in the 'average' American home at the beginning of the Fifties

Above: violence erupts during a strike by workers at the Warner Brothers studio in 1946. A similar strike at RKO (right) in the same year proved that, while the major studios were enjoying their most profitable year ever, discontent was widespread, particularly among the craft unions. Below: Adolphe Menjou, who, in 1947, warned the House Un-American Activities Committee of 'communist acting' that made propaganda 'by a look, by an inflection, by a change in the voice'. Below right: Walt Disney, who told the Committee that communists were even 'drawing' propaganda in cartoon studios

America's traditional markets for film, except Britain. Attempts were made to open up larger business in South America, notably with Carmen Miranda in musicals like *Down Argentine Way* (1940), *That Night in Rio* (1941) and *Weekend in Havana* (1944). Such moves did not, however, compensate for the loss of European markets. One of the problems with South America was the difficulty of shipping films there during wartime.

MGM had calculated rightly that the domestic US market was at saturation point in 1946. Abroad, American movies never had such a success as they did in the late Forties. But this did not bring money back to the studios.

When, in 1946, the world opened up again, only the USA had generous supplies of film stock – the raw materials with which to carry on the trade of film-making and win new markets. Alongside the 20 films made in the Soviet Union in 1948 and the mere 54 that Italy completed at the height of the neo-realist movement, Hollywood's total of 432 was staggering. Furthermore, the American film industry had a backlog of movies from the war years still unreleased in many foreign territories. Even though the US Department of Commerce announced 'only the movies which put America's best foot forward will be sent abroad', the stage was set for American domination of the world film trade.

There was a catch in this apparently open-ended market. American films covered the screens of Europe but the revenue was going back across the Atlantic and European producers enjoyed none of the profits of their cinema boom. In 1946, the French authorities conceded that three-quarters of

the nation's screen time should be filled by Hollywood product, but in 1948 they insisted that only $3.6 million out of an annual $14 million take could be sent back to the USA. For their part, the British allowed $17 million to leave the country each year but $40 million remained blocked by foreign-exchange regulations. Hollywood needed the cash but could not touch it. In time these blocked funds would form the basis of 'runaway' productions – American movies made outside America. Until this money could be made into new movies, Hollywood had a wild but profitless success on its hands.

Back in California the system was breaking up: PRC, a minor major, collapsed and United Artists tore itself apart – Pickford and Chaplin bad-mouthing each other across the nation, threatening to sell their shares and suing their absentee partner David O. Selznick. When a masterpiece of a film like *Red River* (1948) went $1 million over budget, United Artists could not support it. The production passed to an independent company. Such visible troubles did not help confidence. As a result of their experiences after 1948, at least half a dozen banks left the movie industry alone.

Labour trouble was the next problem to hit Hollywood. Post-war prices demanded new wage scales. Clean-ups in the craft unions in the early Forties had made the usual studio policy of buying off the union leaders impracticable. Those leaders were fierce and liberal, yet at the same time they included men like Ronald Reagan.

All this change and trouble and decline made for bad nerves, especially where Wall Street bankers or government support were involved. It was this nervousness that produced the sordid business of blacklists and blackmail. The political paranoia in Hollywood in the late Forties was fed by the uncertainties that abounded in the industry.

Hollywood had been blooded politically in the Thirties, with the vicious resistance to the author and screenwriter Upton Sinclair who ran for Governor of California. Prominent figures within the industry had taken part in a campaign of blatantly reactionary propaganda. Its political mood was always conciliatory to those in power, eager to avoid trouble, dissension or scandal. The flimsy wartime alliance between the USA and the USSR was terminated with the end of the war. The Left was characterized as both enemy abroad and

enemy within. It was not surprising that when the House Un-American Activities Committee, bearing the banner of the right wing, came out to investigate, Hollywood caved in. HUAC, as it was generally known, calculated quite shrewdly that Hollywood names would make headlines, and resistance would be soft. They were right.

Early investigations in 1940 had been 'promising'. In 1947, HUAC opened its attack and from the start they had help from the studios. Jack L. Warner, eager to explain away a handful of pro-Soviet movies made during the war years, warned that communist writers were 'poking fun at our political system' and picking on rich men. Adolphe Menjou alerted the Committee to 'communist acting', which made propaganda, he said, 'by a look, by an inflection, by a change in the voice'. Walt Disney told how he had been pressured by communists (in the unlikely guise of the League of Women Voters) to accept communists. His evidence, however, was such manifest and hurtful nonsense that it had to be retracted by cable.

The Committee looked and sounded absurd. The Mississippi congressman John Rankin, a man whose vocabulary depended on the words 'kike' and 'nigra', delightedly discovered that the protesting liberals had something to hide. 'One of the names is June Havoc', he reported. 'We have found that her real name is June Hovick. Another is Danny Kaye, and we found that his real name is David Daniel Kaminsky.'

The Committee was an arm of Congress. As such it was able to compel cooperation. It began to ask for names: 'I could answer that,' the screenwriter Ring Lardner Jr said, 'but I would hate myself in the morning.' Ten people refused to cooperate, and were cited for contempt of Congress. These ten witnesses, who had refused the Committee's questions, were suddenly suspended without pay; actually firing them could have led to lawsuits.

Hollywood's top moguls promised to employ no subversives; they asked for the support of the law, 'since the absence of a national policy, established by Congress with respect to the employment of communists in private industry, makes our task difficult'. The declaration also said: 'There is the danger of hurting innocent people. There is the risk of creating an atmosphere of fear.' Hurt and fear followed. The ban on ten men became a general blacklist, informally applied and therefore beyond challenge. To escape the list, a suspect had to name his 'undesirable' contacts before some self-appointed rightist like the projectionist Roy Brewer, head of the craft union IATSE. The unions joined the moguls and, as the Korean war escalated, polarizing the issue of communism, their all-industry council denounced those who refused to tell all (or invent all) for the House Committee.

Paranoia entered Hollywood's soul. It made necessary a sort of public jingoism which embarrassed almost everyone; the quietest people were suspect. It crept into movie texts, often appearing in the guise of science fiction. It curtailed the string of social melodramas which had followed the war. John Wayne hit the screen as a heroic investigator for the Committee in *Big Jim McLain* (1952). The appalling *I Was a Communist for the FBI* (1951) inflated the Cold War rhetoric and spawned radio and television versions like *I Led Three Lives*. The studios' decision to surrender to HUAC in 1947 allowed the Committee to stamp on liberals throughout the entertainment business, but once sacrifices had been made the publicity-hungry politicians clamoured for fresh victims and the more famous the name, the better. Far from escaping, Hollywood was actually setting itself up as a prime target for the witch hunts of the late Forties. By the time

Senator McCarthy arrived on the national scene in 1951, Hollywood was 'clean' politically.

If there was subversion in Hollywood in the post-war years, it was either implicit in the pessimism of the *film noir* or explicit as in the social-problem movies that dealt with racialism and allied subjects.

Edward Dmytryk's *Crossfire* (1947), for example, originally intended as an examination on homosexuality, changed its focus to anti-Semitism. The subject of Mark Robson's *Home of the Brave* (1949) was changed from hatred of the Jews to hatred of blacks. In more sentimental form, oppression of Jews surfaced in Kazan's *Gentleman's Agreement* (1947), which was mostly concerned to show that Jews are exactly like everybody else. Race also formed the dramatic problem in Kazan's *Pinky* (1949), a tale of a black girl trying to pass for white.

The idea that it might be hard to adjust to peace, a thought utterly taboo in wartime, came to the surface in *The Best Years of Our Lives* (1946). Political corruption, once completely forbidden by the Production Code, was allowed to be shown in Rossen's *All the King's Men* (1949) and also formed the subject of Kazan's *Boomerang* (1946).

Essentially, this revival of interest in social conscience had minimal political content. It was an extension of the black mood of crime melodramas and was perhaps equally romantic in nature. These films reflected a pervasive pessimism rather than activism; they spoke of subjects rather than analysed them. The Production Code would not be softened until the Fifties: in the American remake of *Le Jour se Lève* entitled *The Long Night* (1947), the criminal is obliged to surrender himself rather than commit suicide as he does in the original.

Certain subjects had, however, been opened by the war. Psychosis, induced by the strain of war, became a respectable subject because it had a visible cause. Social strain in the wake of the war was also discussed in films. This apparent liberalization was a fine illusion; it assimilated some of the uncertainties produced by the war but was swiftly reversed by the black-and-white moral certainties of the Cold War.

At the end of the decade television continued to pose a threat to Hollywood but its mass availability was delayed by various factors including the Korean War. Hollywood went about its regular work and more movies were made in 1950 than in 1946, despite the slump in attendances and the box-office gross. It was not TV that broke the movies in the Fifties and the Sixties; it was the post-war years, when Middle America established its suburban lifestyle and stopped going to the movies.

MICHAEL PYE

Below: in Edward Dmytryk's Crossfire *Robert Ryan plays a returning war veteran, pursued through New York for the murder of a Jew. The film was one of the first to hit out at racial bigotry. Bottom: in* Home of the Brave *James Edwards offers his hand to Steve Brodie but the gesture is refused by his fellow soldier – only the start of the abuse suffered by the Negro soldier in this courageous film about racism*

Are you now or have you ever been...?

After the war, the American Congress began to investigate the 'communist bias' of the film industry. Films that had once been patriotic were labelled potentially subversive. Everyone who showed the slightest left-wing views became a suspected Communist sympathizer. The witch hunt was on!

In 1947, Congressional politics invaded Hollywood. The House Un-American Activities Committee (HUAC) subpoenaed 19 'unfriendly' witnesses – writers, directors, producers and actors. From then on, the film industry was to operate in an atmosphere of a very real fear of outside control, an atmosphere that stultified creative independence and from which Hollywood never fully recovered.

Politicians wanted headlines, and votes. No congressional investigation ever achieved the sensationalized worldwide coverage in the media that became possible with an attack on the glamorous world of the stars. HUAC had been formed in 1937 and was officially re-established in 1945. It exploited public ignorance and hysteria about a 'communist-inspired conspiracy'. Officially, its members had the power only to suggest alterations to any law. In fact, they had the power to destroy

people's lives, using innuendo, hearsay and malice, under the aegis of a right-wing pres[...]

Public interest in 'the communist threa[...] had subsided during World War II, but th[...] beginnings of the Cold War made possible ne[...] opportunities to highlight and justify the hear[...]ings of HUAC. Two of the most active mem[...]bers, John Rankin, who was blatantly anti[...]Semitic, and the chairman, J. Parnell Thoma[...] who was rabidly anti-New Deal, had lon[...] memories. They recalled the 'intellectuals' [...] the Thirties: the writers, teachers and lawye[...] who had been attracted to leftist activity.

As many of these writers and lawyers we[...] now working in the film industry, Hollywoo[...] was an obvious target. The hearings open[...] privately in the spring of 1947 with th[...] appearance of helpful witnesses, like Ging[...] Rogers' mother, Lela, who revealed h[...] daughter's stubborn refusal to speak the li[...] 'Share and share alike – that's democracy', [...] *Tender Comrade* (1943). More influent[...] friendly witnesses included Jack L. Warne[...] Louis B. Mayer, Walt Disney, Gary Coope[...] Robert Montgomery, Ronald Reagan, Geor[...] Murphy, Robert Taylor and the self-appoint[...] Hollywood expert on communism, Adolp[...] Menjou. After six months of psychologic[...] pressure within the industry, the public hea[...]ings were held in October. They lasted only tw[...] weeks, with testimonies from 23 friendly w[...]nesses, and ended after 10 of the 19 unfrien[...] witnesses had been called before the Comm[...]tee. The Hollywood Ten were John Howa[...] Lawson, Dalton Trumbo, Lester Cole, Alv[...] Bessie, Albert Maltz, Ring Lardner Jr, Sam[...] Ornitz, Herbert J. Biberman, Edward Dmytr[...] and Adrian Scott.

The Ten

Writers were predominant among them. [...] that time, Lawson and Trumbo were the m[...] prominent figures. Lawson had edited a pa[...] in Rome for many years, and had also held t[...] post of publicity director for the Europe[...] division of the American Red Cross, bef[...] achieving success as a Broadway playwrig[...] After a spell as a contract writer at MGM, [...] freelanced for Wanger, Goldwyn and 2[...] Century-Fox, working on anti-fascist and[...] anti-Nazi films like *Blockade* (1938), *Sah[...] (1943) and *Counter-Attack* (1945), as well [...] melodramas such as *Smash-Up* (1947). He w[...] a founder member of the Screen Writers' Gu[...]

Trumbo was a former reporter and edit[...] who graduated from cheapies like *Road G[...] (1936) to become the highest-paid scriptwri[...] in Hollywood by the mid-Forties: *Tender Co[...]

Above left: on the picket line in support of the Hollywood Ten – the scriptwriters and direct[...] who were indicted for contempt of Congress – from the film Hollywood on Trial *(1976), which used footage that was shot during the course of the hearings. Left: the Ten and thei[...] lawyers arrive at the district court in Washington. Front row, left to right: Herber[...] Biberman, attorney Martin Popper, attorney Robert W. Kenny, Albert Maltz and Lester Cole. Middle row: Dalton Trumbo, John Howard Lawson, Alvah Bessie and Samuel Ornitz. Back row: Ring Lardner Jr, Edward Dmytryk and Adrian Scott*

Left: Humphrey Bogart, Lauren Bacall, Danny Kaye, June Havoc, Paul Henreid and Richard Conte led the protest march against the Senate investigations. Below left: John Howard Lawson refused to state whether he was a communist – 'I am not on trial here . . . This Committee is on trial before the American people'

was formed to organize the film industry's protest against the trial's infringements of the rights and freedoms of the American constitution. The chairman, John Huston, William Wyler and Philip Dunne organized a planeload of stars, including Humphrey Bogart, Lauren Bacall, Danny Kaye, Gene Kelly, and Jane Wyatt, to go to Washington and see that their people had a fair hearing. They arrived in a blaze of publicity and it was partly because of the row they caused that the hearings came to an abrupt, though temporary, halt.

The hearings

This was only the beginning. The hearing opened with Paul McNutt, special counsel for the 19, daring HUAC to list those films made in the past eight years with supposed communist propaganda content, and threatening to exhibit all those pictures immediately. Another defence lawyer directly attacked HUAC:

'The purpose of the inquiry is to build hysteria to the point of putting the power to employ or fire in the motion picture industry into the hands of this Committee, thus making the very art of producing pictures subject to political censorship.'

Led by John Howard Lawson, the Ten persistently refused to answer the question 'Are you, or have you ever been, a Communist?' and were cited for contempt of Congress. Rather than refuse to testify on the grounds that they might incriminate themselves (according to the Fifth Ammendment), they regarded the Committee itself as unconstitutional.

The Committee for the First Amendment now felt obliged to issue statements dissociating themselves from Lawson and the Ten's belligerent stance. Lawson stated in court that it was America that was on trial, not the Ten. Abraham Polonsky described in 1970 how the Committee was:

'. . . ripped asunder when the thing exploded

Dagger. Samuel Ornitz was the least known of the Ten, with *Three Faces West* (1940) as his only major credit.

There were also two directors and one producer. Herbert Biberman came to Hollywood from the New York theatre. He was a founder member of the Hollywood Anti-Nazi League, and of the Academy of Motion Pictures Arts and Sciences. He directed and/or scripted minor action films – *One Way Ticket* (1935), *The Master Race, Action in Arabia* (both 1944). Dmytryk joined Paramount in 1923, while still at school, spending the Thirties as an editor until he started directing B films in 1939, but he was well established at RKO by the mid-Forties, having worked on *Murder, My Sweet* (1944), *Back to Bataan, Cornered* (both 1945), *Crossfire* (1947). Adrian Scott also had stage experience before starting as a scriptwriter in 1940, and settling at RKO as a producer where he made *Murder, My Sweet, Cornered* and *Crossfire* all with Dmytryk.

The Committee for the First Amendment

Right: Gary Cooper giving evidence about communism – 'From what I hear, I don't like it because it isn't on the level'. Far right: Robert Montgomery testifying – 'I gave up my job to fight a totalitarianism called fascism. I am ready to do it again to fight the totalitarianism called communism'

ade, *A Guy Named Joe* (both 1943) and *Thirty Seconds Over Tokyo* (1944) were among his best-known credits.

Lester Cole was a freelancer who is probably best remembered for *Objective, Burma!* (1945). Bessie, who scripted *Northern Pursuit* (1943) and worked with Cole on *Objective, Burma!* and Maltz, who scripted *This Gun for Hire* (1942) and *Cloak and Dagger* (1946), were successful contract writers.

Ring Lardner Jr had been a reporter and publicity writer for David O. Selznick before achieving recognition as a scriptwriter. Among the films he worked on were *Woman of the Year* (1942), *The Cross of Lorraine* (1943), *Tomorrow the World* (1944) and *Cloak and*

in Washington. General Beadle Smith was sent to Hollywood and he met the important Hollywood owners. A policy was laid down to call these actors and directors off – the important ones. Pressure was put on them through their agents and the whole thing melted in about two weeks. I finally went to a meeting and Humphrey Bogart turned around and looked up a half empty room; the first meetings were held at George Chasen's, and you couldn't get in – it was like an opening night at the opera – everybody wanted to be in on this. Anyway, Humphrey Bogart looked round this room and said: "You don't think I'm going to stand up there all by myself and take a beating – I'm getting out too," and he walked out of the room. Then Huston said: "Well, it's hopeless, fellows," and left for Europe. The final meeting was held, and the only people present were Willie Wyler, the permanent secretary, myself and one other. Wyler said: "Well, I think we can use our time better than this." And it was true.'

There was no help for the victims to be had from the industry as a whole. On November 24, 1947, the Association of Motion Picture Producers met at the Waldorf-Astoria Hotel in

New York to discuss their attitude to the Ten and formulate their policy for the future. The Association declared that, since the Ten had 'impaired their usefulness to the industry', they would not be employed again until they had purged themselves of the contempt and sworn under oath that they were not Communists.

The pledge

They pledged that the industry would 'Not knowingly employ a Communist or a member of any party or group which advocates the overthrow of the Government of the United States by force, or by any illegal or unconstitutional method'. This was the beginning of the blacklist that was to grow longer and longer as the hearings continued well into the Fifties.

There were exceptions to the capitulation of the moguls. In his book, *The Hollywood Tycoons*, Norman Zierold tells how Sam Goldwyn, who loathed Russia and communism:

'watched the proceedings . . . with increased dismay because he felt this was not the American way of doing things; no Congressional committee should be the arbiter of a man's right to work. He felt that producers like Mayer, who were loudest in their outcries,

were themselves responsible if the charges were true. After all, they had made the pictures, approving each step of production. Goldwyn felt the entire industry was being hurt by the charges. He heard the Committee was planning to call his close friend Robert Sherwood in order to examine certain suspect scenes in *The Best Years of Our Lives* (1946).'

Goldwyn then sent a telegram explaining his views to J. Parnell Thomas and stating that he wished to appear before the Committee to elaborate his views personally. He threatened to make his views public if he did not get a reply from Thomas. Goldwyn's stand has been credited as a factor in Thomas dropping his investigation.

The result

Legal proceedings dragged on for more than two and a half years before any of the Ten actually served time in prison. John Berry produced and directed a short film in 1950 in their defence, entitled *The Hollywood Ten*. But, during this period, there was constant pressure from groups such as the Motion Picture Alliance for the Preservation of American Ideals to reopen the hearings, and 'clean up' Hollywood.

HUAC capitalized on the fact that, during the Thirties and Forties, there had been some card-carrying members of the Communist Party in Hollywood (including several of the Ten), and that a number of household names had contributed to liberal causes and funds, some of which had proved to be Communist 'front' organizations. These names formed the basis of the lengthening blacklist.

The Alger Hiss trial, American involvement in the Korean War, but above all, the rise to prominence of Senator Joseph McCarthy, who repeatedly threatened to name names of Communists serving in the State Department, produced a hysterical right-wing paranoia that built up in the public mind the supposed influence of these 'Reds under the beds' out of all proportion. Trash sheets like *Red Channels* began publishing the names. The people con-

cerned were put on the spot by their employers, and the HUAC hearings reopened in 1951 to examine those on the blacklist.

Box-office receipts had been declining since 1947 and were further affected by the advent of television, and expensive studio gimmicks like 3-D were failing to stem the tide, so the moguls put tremendous pressure on their employees to 'confess' or else face being blacklisted. For example, Abraham Polonsky was fired after several weeks of editorials in Hollywood papers following his being called to stand before HUAC.

The 'grey' list was also set up by the American Legion, listing names of suspected Communists or sympathizers. Every artist was by now afraid of being on somebody's 'list'. If you didn't get a job for some time, fear ate into the soul. As Polonsky commented: 'You never doubt your talent, you doubt your ability to get jobs for some strange reason.' Workers in Hollywood always faced the risk of being named by cooperative witnesses, for those on the list could 'buy' themselves off it. The 'cleaning' process required them not only to admit their own guilt, but to list publicly all their friends and colleagues who had ever shown the slightest left-wing sympathy. Clearance letters then had to be begged from the American Legion and other patriotic groups, and the price often included producing anticommunist articles. (One was John Garfield's 'I Was a Sucker for a Left Hook', written shortly before his death, with his career already totally ruined). Only then was employment once more assured.

An estimated 320 people suffered directly as a result of this cleansing process. A few brave individuals like Trumbo, Polonsky and Howard Da Silva refused to compromise or cooperate, but one of the Ten, Dmytryk, even went as far as naming John Berry, who had

Left: Cole and Bessie, who wrote the patriotic Objective, Burma! *were charged with un-American activities. Below: the miners' strike from the independent film* Salt of the Earth

Tell them that old Indian fighter got his.
Tell them I'll kill if I have to.
Tell them they'll never take me alive.

Tell them Willie Boy is here

UNIVERSAL PRESENTS Robert Redford · Katharine Ross
Robert Blake · Susan Clark
"*Tell Them Willie Boy Is Here*"
Co-starring Barry Sullivan Screenplay by ABRAHAM POLONSKY Directed by ABRAHAM POLONSKY A JENNINGS LANG PRESENTATION A PHILIP A WAXMAN PRODUCTION TECHNICOLOR® PANAVISION®

instead of the $75,000 he had earned a decade earlier, Trumbo never made less than $18,000 in any of his own depression years.'

However, Corliss admitted that the cost was more than financial:

'It would be pleasant to think that Trumbo and his blacklisted brethren wrote, under psuedonyms, the finest Fifties films. But with the exception of Michael Wilson – who had scripted *A Place in the Sun* (1950) and *Five Fingers* (1952), before being blacklisted, and *Salt of the Earth* (1954); *Friendly Persuasion* (1956); *The Bridge on the River Kwai* (1957) and *Lawrence of Arabia* (1962) afterwards – their output was prolific but hardly profound. The political and administrative pressures that obsessed most leftist writers in the Forties became murderously oppressive in the Fifties, and most of the blacklisted screenwriters' work came through subterranean channels, and went into substandard productions.'

The comeback

In the Sixties, some of The Ten had their own names back on the screen. Trumbo was the first to come out of the wilderness in 1960 when Otto Preminger gave him screen credit for *Exodus*. Herbert J. Biberman had directed the independent film, *Salt of the Earth*, but did not re-emerge until *Slaves* (1969), Lardner had to wait until 1965 for his official screen credit on *The Cincinnati Kid*, and then went on to script *M*A*S*H* (1970). Lawson had retreated to Moscow.

J. Parnell Thomas himself ended up joining one of the Ten who was still in prison, serving a sentence for fraud. Yet HUAC continued its investigations until it was formally wound up in 1975. But its ghost has never been finally laid to rest. During the Nixon administration Jane Fonda, Gregory Peck and other Hollywood celebrities found themselves named 'enemies' of the President. The year 1947 was a black one in the history of the industry. It established a precedent for effective outside control over movie content and personnel.

KINGSLEY CANHAM

Above: Abraham Polonsky did not return to film direction until 1969 when he made Tell Them Willie Boy Is Here. *Left: Zero Mostel, who was himself blacklisted, plays a comic unable to get work in television in* The Front *(1976).*
Below: Lardner's first screen credit after the trial was for The Cincinnati Kid

problems. Or he or she could use a pseudonym. Dalton Trumbo wrote *The Brave One* (1956) under the pseudonym Robert Rich, and even received an Oscar for it.

The film critic Richard Corliss admired Trumbo's 'winning combination of businessman and craftsman' which kept his career alive in the blacklisted Fifties:

'The ruin that other writers took as malefic destiny, Trumbo took as a challenge. Writing as quickly as ever, but for $3000 per script

made the film *The Hollywood Ten* in his defence! Elia Kazan, Sterling Hayden, Robert Rossen (another of the original 19) and others paraded through the witness box, and employment ended for Larry Parks, Zero Mostel, Gale Sondergaard, Marsha Hunt, Jeff Corey and many others. Actors and actresses remained out of work. Writers and directors like Berry, Joseph Losey and Carl Foreman, who had been named but refused to testify, left for Europe.

But for those writers who stayed in America, like Trumbo and Polonsky, business carried on. As Trumbo commented in *The Nation* in 1957: 'The studios, while operating a blacklist, were in the market purchasing plays and other material without crediting the authors.' Producers and directors still went to the writers they knew were competent. A writer could use the name of a friend, which often created

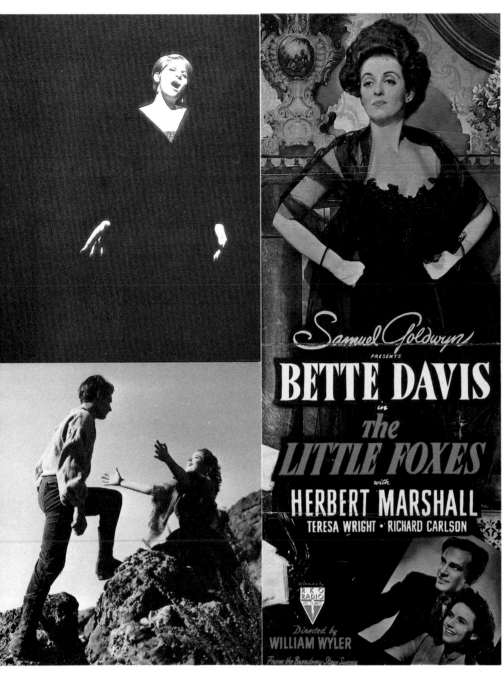

markably eclectic in his choice of subject. There appears to be no consistent philosophy of life running through his films. Often he seems to have been attracted to a theme simply because it represented a technical or personal challenge: as he had never made an epic, he might as well make *Ben Hur* (1959); since he had never made a musical, he would try his hand at *Funny Girl* (1968); because Hollywood traditionally shied away from presenting racial themes, he would tackle them in *The Liberation of L. B. Jones* (1970).

Wyler's most evident line of consistency as a director is in the development of a style based on sustained shots and great depth of field, so that something going on in the far background is just as clear as something in foreground close-up. This technique begins with *These Three* in 1936, and continues until *The Best Years of Our Lives* in 1946. Yet this style cannot be solely attributed to Wyler. *These Three*, after all, was the start of Wyler's collaboration with the cinematographer Gregg Toland and the producer Sam Goldwyn for whom most of his finest films were made during the next ten years – *Dodsworth* (1936), *Dead End* (1937), *Wuthering Heights*, *The Little Foxes*, *The Best Years of Our Lives*. (*The Best Years of Our Lives*, coincidentally, was the last time Wyler worked with either.)

At first sight it appears as if Wyler has been given credit for a collective enterprise (although certainly he did not claim it). Yet all the elements in Wyler's films hold together in a way which seems to argue that he was, at the very least, their overall guiding force. Toland may have been interested in experimenting with deep focus, but this was precisely what made him especially useful to Wyler, because shooting in that way was perfect for Wyler's treatment of actors; it accorded with his desire to produce sustained performances from them rather than shooting in short takes which

Left: Wyler is renowned for films that brought added prestige to the wide range of talents that appeared in them, including Bette Davis in The Little Foxes, *Barbra Streisand in* Funny Girl *(top far left) and Laurence Olivier and Merle Oberon in* Wuthering Heights *(far left).*
Below: Wyler became Davis' favourite director; here the pair confer during the making of The Little Foxes

The winning ways of William Wyler

William Wyler is renowned as the actor's director *par excellence* and as the supreme Hollywood craftsman, turning well-written scripts into award-winning movies with the aid of first-rate casts and technicians

There is no doubt that Wyler has done extremely well by his actors, and that they have done extremely well by him. The long succession of acting Oscars won in his films include two for Bette Davis and Walter Brennan, and one each for Olivia de Havilland, Audrey

Hepburn, Fredric March, Barbra Streisand, Charlton Heston and Greer Garson. Many actors have testified how Wyler tortured their performances out of them; although he could not or would not explain to them exactly what he wanted, somehow, mysteriously and bit by bit, it all came right. Both Laurence Olivier and Bette Davies began by detesting him and ended by adoring him. Rightly so, for they have seldom shown to better advantage on screen than in *Wuthering Heights* (1939) and *The Little Foxes* (1941) respectively.

It is undeniable that Wyler has been re-

Hopkins and Walter Huston, but comes through, in *These Three*, in the playing of Merle Oberon (a beauty, to be sure, but seldom much of an actress outside Wyler's films); then in *Dodsworth* Ruth Chatterton, a has-been making a comeback in an unromantic, middle-aged role as Fran Dodsworth, gives one of the great performances of the American cinema.

In the next few films with Toland, Wyler continued to explore the various expressive possibilities of his style (or their joint style): in *Dead End* it took on the harsh look of grimy urban realism; in *Wuthering Heights*, romantic chiaroscuro; in *The Little Foxes*, a stifling, turn-of-the-century intricacy. The two films he

Left: a tough cowboy (Charles Bickford) plays nursemaid in Hell's Heroes. *Below: Merle Oberon and Miriam Hopkins as the maligned schoolteachers of* These Three. *Bottom: Audrey Hepburn and Gregory Peck in* Roman Holiday. *Bottom left: Leslie Crosbie (Bette Davis) shoots her lover in* The Letter

rough careful editing, could later be fused to a performance.

Although the earlier part of his career remains obscure – and therefore largely ignored by film historians – Wyler was, in fact, functioning as a director in Hollywood from '26. He was born in Alsace in 1902, and educated in Lausanne and Paris (where he seemed destined to become a professional musician). He then abruptly left for the USA, following a chance encounter with Carl Laemmle, head of Universal studios. His first films were two-reel Westerns, of which, he alleges, he made nearly fifty in two years. His first film to attract attention did not come until '29 when he made *Hell's Heroes*, a shamelessly sentimental drama about three hard-

ened cowboys who find and save a baby in the desert; it impressed critics because of its (for the time) imaginative use of sound. But *These Three* and *Dodsworth* showed him at last really coming into his own.

Both had substantial subjects: *These Three* was based on Lillian Hellman's play (*The Children's Hour*) of a lesbian relationship in a girl's school; *Dodsworth* was adapted from Sinclair Lewis' novel about an American couple whose view of life is changed by a trip to Europe. Both are treated with an ease and fluidity which frees them from the curse of being stagey or bookish. Moreover, with these two films Wyler asserted his special ability in handling actors. This is not so much in evidence with reliable performers like Miriam

Above: the magnificent arena for the spectacular and fiercely realistic chariot race in Ben Hur, *which won 11 Oscars, including one for Wyler. Below: Terence Stamp as the psychopath who adds the beautiful Samantha Eggar to his collection of butterflies in* The Collector *(1965), which was based on John Fowles' novel*

made outside this collaboration, both Bette Davis vehicles for Warners, were less interesting, visually and otherwise: *Jezebel* (1938) allowed Davis to play a bitchy Southern belle; *The Letter* (1940) incited her to chew the scenery in Somerset Maugham's old shocker of adultery and murder set in Malaya. All the

same, the performances still stand up: even b this stage in her career, Bette Davis could b execrably mannered, but Wyler knew how t keep her in reasonable check.

During World War II, Wyler first foun himself making a somewhat fulsome an starry-eyed tribute to beleaguered Britain; h *Mrs Miniver* (1942) was a glossy picture whic has dated badly. He was then drafted into th US Army Air Force to make training an propaganda films. One of these, *The Memphi Belle* (1944), was generally regarded as one c the most satisfactory American official films t have come out of the war. And there is n doubt at all that Wyler's first film on his retur to civilian life, *The Best Years of Our Lives* was the finest about the home front and th veteran returning from the battlefront. Finel structured despite being on a large scale (th film ran for 160 minutes), its screenplay, b Robert E. Sherwood, miraculously avoid being sentimental, glib or patronizing. Wyle managed a large cast with consummate ease and the film represents in many respects th height of his achievement. It was loved b audiences in America and abroad, who fel that it spoke simply and unaffectedly of thei problems and emotions.

Although thereafter he operated withou the support of Goldwyn (who subsequentl produced few films of distinction) and o Toland (who died in 1948, at the age of 44 Wyler's career showed few signs of decline. Th *Heiress* (1949) put back into the simplifie

age version of Henry James' *Washington Square* some of the original Jamesian complexity, although a superb performance by Ralph Richardson as the tyrannical father was not matched by the total miscasting of Montgomery Clift as the fortune-hunting suitor. *Carrie* (1952), an intensely depressing film, contained another of Laurence Olivier's fine screen performances, and captured with astonishing accuracy the essence of Theodore Dreiser's realist novel, *Sister Carrie*. There was also much to be said for the romantic charms of *Roman Holiday* (1953), which introduced Audrey Hepburn to the American public, the knowing rusticities of *Friendly Persuasion* (1956), and the wide open spaces of *The Big Country* (1958). His second, franker version of *The Children's Hour* (1961) was a decided improvement on the first, and *Funny Girl*, on which he was assisted by Herbert Ross as dance director, was the best musical of the sixties as well as an ideal showcase for its star, Barbra Streisand.

With Wyler it has always been necessary to listen to the songs and not be too concerned with the singer. Perhaps his films *are* impersonal, but in a Hollywood where the directors are increasingly eager to be superstars in their own right, a little impersonality becomes in itself the mark of a strong and individual personality. If, in the final analysis, Wyler is not accounted a great director, there is no question but that he has made a fair handful of great films.   JOHN RUSSELL TAYLOR

Below: the grisly closing sequence of The Liberation of L.B. Jones, *in which a black undertaker becomes the brutalized victim of Southern racism as personified by a vicious, bigoted white cop*

Filmography
1923 The Hunchback of Notre Dame (ass. dir. only). '25 Crook Buster; Ben Hur (prod. ass. only). '26 The Gunless Badman; Ridin' for Love; The Fire Barrier; Don't Shoot; The Horse Trader; Lazy Lightning; Stolen Ranch; Martin of the Mounted; The Two Fister. '27 Kelcy Gets His Man; Blazing Days; Tenderfoot Courage; The Silent Partner; Hard Fists; Galloping Justice; The Haunted Homestead; Shooting Straight/Straight Shootin'/Range Riders; The Lone Star; The Ore Raiders; The Home Trail; Gun Justice; The Phantom Outlaw; The Square Shooter; The Border Cavalier; Daze of the West; Desert Dust; Thunder Riders. '28 Anybody Here Seen Kelly? (GB: Has Anybody Here Seen Kelly?); The Shakedown. '29 Love Trap; Hell's Heroes. '30 The Storm. '32 A House Divided; Tom Brown of Culver. '33 Her First Mate; Counsellor at Law. '34 Glamour. '35 The Good Fairy; The Gay Deception. '36 These Three; Dodsworth; Come and Get It! (reissued as: Roaring Timber) (co-dir. only). '37 Dead End. '38 Jezebel. '39 Wuthering Heights. '40 The Westerner; The Letter. '41 The Little Foxes. '42 Mrs Miniver (+prod). '44 The Memphis Belle (+prod; +sc; +co-photo) (short); The Fighting Lady. '46 The Best Years of Our Lives. '47 Thunderbolt (co-dir. only). '49 The Heiress (+prod). '51 Detective Story (+prod). '52 Carrie (+prod). '53 Roman Holiday (+prod). '55 The Desperate Hours (+prod). '56 Friendly Persuasion (+prod). '58 The Big Country (+co-prod). '59 Ben Hur. '61 The Children's Hour (+prod) (GB: The Loudest Whisper). '65 The Collector (USA-GB). '66 How to Steal a Million. '68 Funny Girl. '70 The Liberation of L.B. Jones.

Samuel Goldwyn

'I've always been an independent even when I had partners'

Samuel Goldwyn is remembered both as the producer of some of Hollywood's most distinguished pictures, and as a purveyor of malapropisms and *non sequiturs* known as Goldwynisms – although his family and close associates deny ever hearing him utter one. Goldwyn's eccentric language became almost as well known to the movie-going public as the familiar portly figure of Alfred Hitchcock

Samuel Goldwyn, who, to quote Bob Hope, 'did more for movies than dark balconies' had the standard movie-mogul background. Born in a Jewish ghetto in Warsaw in 1882, he arrived penniless in America at the age of 15. His real name sounded to the immigration officials like Samuel Goldfish and that is what he became.

His English, learnt in his teens, often contained a curious usage of words which, in later life, became highly publicized. He laughed at the sayings that were attributed to him (like 'Gentlemen, include me out' and 'In two words: im . . . possible') because, as he wryly put it, 'Well, I'd be the only one if I didn't'.

After prospering in the glove trade, he persuaded Jesse Lasky (who, at the time, was his brother-in-law) to go into film-making. Goldfish, Lasky and Cecil B. DeMille founded Jesse Lasky Feature Plays. They made *The Squaw Man* (1913) and discovered a new location – Hollywood. Sam sold the Lasky output to exhibitors throughout the world. The company prospered and merged with Adolph Zukor's Famous Players; the new company was later to become Paramount.

Sam clashed with Zukor and sold out. He then formed Goldwyn Pictures Corporation with Broadway's Edgar Selwyn – the company name being formed from *Gold*fish and Sel*wyn* – and, tired of the jokes associated with being a Goldfish, he took the joint name, legally, for his

own. The company lacked major stars and tried to compensate by hiring 'Eminent Authors' like Rex Beach and Mary Roberts Rinehart to write its pictures. The arrangement did not work out because the writers failed to understand the visual primacy of the silent film, but it demonstrated Sam's lifelong policy of hiring the best regardless of cost. New partners were then brought in to provide additional financing, but Sam soon feuded with them and quit the company in 1922. With

Left: Samuel Goldwyn and his wife Frances – 'She's the only real close partner I've ever had'. Below: The Kid From Brooklyn (1946) starred Danny Kaye – one of Goldwyn's many discoveries. Bottom: Roman Scandals was devised for another find – Eddie Cantor

its lion trade mark and motto '*ars gratia artis*' it went on to become Metro-Goldwyn-Mayer.

In 1923, Goldwyn, realizing that he was not endowed with sufficient patience to tolerate partners and was wealthy enough not to need them, set up in business on his own. He embarked on a series of highly popular romantic films, made a hot box-office combination

'Verbal contracts are not worth the paper they are written on'

out of Ronald Colman and Vilma Banky and invented a new slogan to celebrate his success: 'Goldwyn pictures griddle the earth!' He was now his own master.

In 1930, he made a lavish, two-colour Technicolor musical, *Whoopee!*, that brought screen stardom to Eddie Cantor, introduced Busby Berkeley to Hollywood, and led to the creation of the Goldwyn Girls. Sam had it in

unfilmable. But he outwitted his critics and remained true to the spirit if not the lesbian detail of the powerful play. Goldwyn was not allowed to retain the original title, but audiences knew full well that *These Three* (1936) was based on *that* play, due to the publicity it had received, and they were eager to see what Goldwyn and director William Wyler had made of it.

'I had a monumental idea this morning, but I don't like it'

Goldwyn's career would have been much less notable without Wyler. Despite the many films they made together, Goldwyn and Wyler were constantly feuding. 'I made them – Willie Wyler only directed them,' Goldwyn would say, while Wyler often refused to direct what he, usually rightly, considered were poor properties, happily going on suspension to back his judgment. Goldwyn could be tight-fisted: he

mind to become the Florenz Ziegfeld of the screen (Ziegfeld helped him make *Whoopee!*) and his productions of the next two decades featured a number of lightweight musical-comedy extravaganzas. He made five more with Cantor, including *The Kid From Spain* (1932) and *Roman Scandals* (1933), and he tried to start a series of annual revues with *The Goldwyn Follies* (1938). Sam rarely employed established stars, preferring to create his own. He signed up the stage actor, Danny Kaye, had his hair dyed blond, and starred him in six pictures from *Up In Arms* (1944) to *Hans Christian Andersen* (1952). Goldwyn's musicals were the profitable backbone of his output, the films most in line with his policy of providing entertainment for all the family.

But Goldwyn also made more serious pictures as part of his annual film schedule. These were almost always based on plays or novels. There was *Street Scene* (1931), a drama of New York tenement life that Elmer Rice adapted from his stage play, and *Arrowsmith* (1931), about the idealism of a doctor; *Dodsworth* (1936) about a middle-aged automobile manufacturer taking stock of himself; and *Dead End*

Top: in Dodsworth *a small-town couple visit Europe and broaden their horizons. Above: the realistic tenement building used in* Street Scene. *Left: Anna Sten, shown here in* Nana, *never became a star despite the time and money Goldwyn spent trying to build her career. She was one of Goldwyn's few failures*

(1937), another story of the slums. Such films brought the studio prestige more often than profit and probably reflect the influence of Frances Goldwyn, Sam's wife since 1925, a lady of shrewd and cultivated taste who had early on taken over the reading of books and scripts submitted to her husband.

Sam was never scared to tackle a difficult project. However, with the prohibitions of the Hays Office, he could hardly have remained faithful to Emile Zola's study of vice when he made *Nana* (1934). It was shaped as a vehicle for his new discovery, the Polish actress Anna Sten, whom audiences decisively rejected. He bought Lillian Hellman's play *The Children's Hour*, which was considered by many to be

once recovered two weeks of Wyler's salary when the director quit a picture and jokingly offered him his money back. However, Sam spent whatever it took to make a good picture and Wyler respected him for that. Wyler's greatest triumph was persuading Goldwyn to make *Wuthering Heights* (1939). It took two years to overcome Goldwyn's dislike of a story with an unhappy ending, and even then Goldwyn had the final say: just before the film opened, and without telling Wyler, he sneaked in a final shot of the film's two lovers reunited in the hereafter.

But Goldwyn also respected Wyler and rallied to his defence when Myrna Loy was reluctant to work on *The Best Years of Our Lives* (1946) with a director she had heard was sadistic towards his actors. 'That's not true,' declared Goldwyn 'he's just a very mean fellow.' Despite Hollywood's belief that there would be no interest after the war in a serious film about returning airmen's problems of readjustment to civilian life, Goldwyn staked over $2 million of his own money and was

only the Dominion Theatre was suitable an[d] was prepared to wait until he could have it[.]

Like the major studios, Goldwyn seemed t[o] lose his sureness of touch towards the end [of] the Forties. Films like *Enchantment* (1948[),] *Roseanna McCoy, My Foolish Heart* (both 1949[),] *Our Very Own, Edge of Doom* (both 1950) and *[I] Want You* (1951) failed to make a great im[-] pression on audiences, which were dwindl[ing] anyway. His star power was diminished an[d] his new discoveries, like Farley Granger an[d] Joan Evans, were not becoming major draw[s.] His subjects tended to be too American f[or] worldwide appeal. Even re-shooting key scene[s] in *Edge of Doom* after its opening failed to turn [it] into a success.

Goldwyn was 70 when his last Danny Kay[e] picture, *Hans Christian Andersen,* was release[d] in 1952. He then relinquished all his contrac[ts]

'Our comedies are not to be laughed at'

amply rewarded when the film was a box-office success and won seven Oscars.

Goldwyn was always concerned with making his films as good as they could possibly be. He stopped production on *Nana* and *The Bishop's Wife* (1947) when he did not like the rushes and started afresh with new directors, regardless of the cost. He also had Wyler re-shoot the last half of *Come and Get It* (1936) as he wasn't entirely satisfied with the material produced by Howard Hawks.

The Goldwyn studios were run in the same way as the majors but on a smaller scale. His various departments were headed by top talent, although, in fact, he and Mrs Goldwyn took charge of the story department to the chagrin of those who tried to run it according to his often contradictory dictates. It is certainly to his credit that he encouraged the brilliant cinematographer Gregg Toland, who later worked on *Citizen Kane* (1940), to experiment; part of *The Wedding Night* (a 1935 Anna Sten picture) was test shot by Toland in 3-D, and the deep-focus images of *The Little Foxes* (1941) and *The Best Years of Our Lives* came about through Goldwyn's interest in advancing technical standards. The great art director Richard Day designed almost all of Goldwyn's pictures from 1930 to 1938 – including *Dead End* with its celebrated set of a New York slum. Goldwyn was initially disappointed: 'This slum cost plenty – it shouldn't look like any ordinary slum' he complained (or so legend has it). He was concerned that audiences should have the best that money could buy. Alfred Newman was another notable figure on the Goldwyn lot, the composer or music director of nearly every Goldwyn film in the Thirties. Goldwyn could even match the major studios in such intricate, expensive areas as special effects – which he proved when he gave art director James Basevi a free hand in creating the climactic sequence of *The Hurricane* (1937).

Even more important was Goldwyn's roster

of stars. He had Gary Cooper, David Niven, Joel McCrea, Miriam Hopkins, Merle Oberon, Teresa Wright, Dana Andrews and Virginia Mayo under contract. Because of his limited output, he kept them busy by loaning them to other studios, either pocketing the profit of the transaction himself or acquiring another star in exchange. He got Bette Davis for *The Little Foxes* by providing Warner Brothers with Gary Cooper for *Sergeant York* (1941).

Goldwyn did not handle his own distribution although he was occasionally tempted to do so. In the Thirties he contributed to the success of United Artists as a member-owner, letting that company handle his pictures. In 1941, he went to RKO where his quality films propped up that ailing studio for more than a decade. Even so, Goldwyn kept a close eye on where his pictures were shown and on what terms. He even went to court to wrestle a fair deal from a circuit that was freezing his films out and helped create the climate in which the American government forced the major studios to divest themselves of theatre chains. Goldwyn's scrutiny extended overseas too: *Porgy and Bess* (1959) opened more than two years late in London because Sam decreed that

artists. There were two more special picture[s.] The first was *Guys and Dolls* (1955), whic[h] linked him for the first time with the compan[y] that bore his name – Metro-Goldwyn-Mayer [–] and which cost him an all-time record sum f[or] the screen rights to the Broadway show. H[e] daringly cast Marlon Brando and Jean Sim[-] mons in lead roles, alongside the more con[-] ventional casting of Frank Sinatra. It wa[s] expensive, but well-received both by criti[cs] and audiences.

Finally, Goldwyn made *Porgy and Bes[s]* (1959). The problems were immense: he had [to] counter black opposition to the project, fearin[g] it would be full of 'Uncle Tomism'; he had t[o] rebuild his huge Catfish Row set after a fire; h[e] changed directors and the film lost millions[.]

Not quite through with movie-makin[g,] Goldwyn made some trips to the Middle East i[n] connection with a film he was contemplating[.] But he was an old man and a series of stroke[s] confined him to a wheelchair. He died in 197[4] aged 91, leaving a fortune estimated at $[__] million. Not bad going for a Polish runawa[y] who thrived on independence and often said ['I] make my pictures to please myself'.

ALLEN EYLE[S]

Above: holding the Oscars for The Best Years of Our Lives *are Samuel Goldwyn (Best Film) – he also received the Irving Thalberg Award for services to the industry – Harold Russell (Best Supporting Actor) and William Wyler (Best Direction). Below:* Guys and Dolls *was one of Goldwyn's last films*

Picking up the pieces

In the aftermath of World War II, film industries in Europe and the Far East were resurrected and played a vital role in building new societies

On September 3, 1943, four years to the day after the outbreak of hostilities between Britain and Germany, Italy unconditionally surrendered to the Allied powers. On May 7, 1945, General Jodl signed the document of Germany's surrender. Alone of the Axis powers, Japan fought on a few weeks more. On August 6, 1945, a United States B-29 bomber dropped an atom bomb on the city of Hiroshima, and less than a month later Japan finally surrendered. The war, in which 15 million military personnel and countless civilians had perished, was over. Out of the wreckage of the old, a new world had to be built, and the men who made the movies were everywhere conscious of their role in this reconstruction.

The Liberation found the French cinema at a complete standstill. German preparations for the Allied advances had paralysed the life of Paris, closing all the city's cinemas and halting film production. Nevertheless, despite chronic shortages of equipment and energy, production did recover and rose in 1946 to 96 films – not far short of pre-war levels – though, in most cases, post-war budgets were smaller.

In the following year, however, an agreement with the Americans to relax pre-war quota controls on the importation of Hollywood films caused French film production to plummet sharply. Imported films, dubbed into French, dominated the market and handicapped home-made product for 12 months until the quota was re-established. The subsequent recovery of the cinema industry was assisted by the introduction of two government measures: the Loi d'Aide à l'Industrie Cinématographique (1949) and the Loi de Développement de l'Industrie Cinématographique in 1953.

If the French cinema's economic situation was shaky, its prestige still rated highly. A series of notable films of the Occupation period, including Marcel Carné's *Les Visiteurs du Soir* (1942, *The Devil's Own Envoy*) and *Les Enfants du Paradis* (1945, *Children of Paradise*) and Robert Bresson's *Les Anges du Péché* (1943, Angels of Sin) were all revealed after the Liberation to worldwide acclaim.

Of the pre-war masters, Jacques Feyder was dead and Jean Renoir had stayed in America. Only René Clair resumed work in France and made *Le Silence Est d'Or* (1947, *Man About Town*), an attractive and mature reflection on old age. Claude Autant-Lara rose to fame with a series of literary adaptations – the exquisite *Le Diable au Corps* (1947, *Devil in the Flesh*), from a novel by Raymond Radiguet, about a youth's first love, and *Occupe-toi d'Amélie* (1949, *Keep an Eye on Amelia*) from a play by Feydeau.

Jean Cocteau, whose wartime film *L'Eternel Retour* (1943, *Love Eternal*) had been wrongly suspected of purveying 'German mysticism', pursued his own idiosyncratic way with the magical *La Belle et la Bête* (1946, *Beauty and the Beast*) and *Les Parents Terribles* (1948), adapted from his own play.

René Clément's *La Bataille du Rail* (1945, The Battle of the Railway Workers), one of the first French films released after the war, portrayed

railway workers fighting for the Resistance and suggested, through its spare shooting style, that French films might have developed a neo-realist movement similar to that of Italian cinema in the post-war years. Clément himself followed this film with another war subject in the realist mode, but *Les Maudits* (1947, The Accursed) did not find favour with audiences and Clément's example was not followed by other film-makers.

French directors seemed, in fact, more inclined to take up where they had left off, resuming the fatalistic style of pre-war films like *Quai des Brumes* (1938, *Quay of Shadows*) and *Le Jour se Lève* (1939, *Daybreak*). Carné made *Les Portes de la Nuit* (1946, *Gates of the Night*), a drama set in the wartime black market. Clément added to the melancholic mood with *Au Delà des Grilles* (1949, Beyond the Gates), and several other films echoed the 'noir' atmosphere – doomed lovers playing out their lives in gloomy surroundings; these included: Duvivier's *Panique* (1946, *Panic*) and Clouzot's *Quai des Orfèvres* (1947, *Jenny Lamour*).

Of the French directors who came to the fore in the immediate post-war years, the most notable was Jacques Becker. His first success was a light-hearted, unsentimental film, *Antoine et Antoinette* (1946), about a lost lottery ticket. This was followed by *Rendez-vous de Juillet* (1949, Rendezvous in July), in which Becker examined post-war youth through the interwoven stories of several young actresses. *Edouard et Caroline* (1951) portrayed a Parisian, bourgeois marriage and confirmed Becker's reputation as an expert maker of everyday comedies.

The documentary film-maker Georges Rouquier

Top left: Quai des Orfèvres *(the Paris police HQ), an atmospheric thriller in which a music-hall artist is accused of a crime passionnel,* starred Louis Jouvet as a police inspector in one of his most celebrated roles. *Top:* Panique *contained an outstanding performance by Michel Simon as an aged eccentric pursued by a suspicious community. Above:* Farrebique, *a highly acclaimed story that traces the fortunes of a rural family through the four seasons of the farming year*

Top: Jean Marais and Josette Day in Cocteau's La Belle et la Bête, *a surrealistic fantasy based on the age-old fairy-tale. Above:* Le Blé en Herbe *(1954, Ripening Seed) dealt with the awkwardness and hesitancy of young love. Top right: the story of the artist Utamaro and his unique art of body-painting is told in Mizoguchi's* Five Women Around Utamaro. *Above right: Denjiro Okochi in Kurosawa's* They Who Tread on the Tiger's Tail. *The title is taken from a proverb: 'From the mouth of a serpent, they had a narrow escape. No less hard way they went, than walking on a tiger's tail'*

made a single feature-length, dramatized documentary, *Farrebique* (1947), about the life of a farming family in the Massif Central. The film owed much to the style of the American documentarist Robert Flaherty, and the same tendency was perceptible in the post-war work of Roger Leenhardt – *Les Dernières Vacances* (1947, Last Holidays) and Louis Daquin, whose outstanding film *Le Point du Jour* (1948, First Light) dealt with the lives of the miners of northern France.

However progressive these films may have been, the popular fare was bourgeois comedy in which stars like Fernandel, Bourvil and Noël-Noël were consistently popular. Alongside such traditional offerings, the debut of Jacques Tati in *Jour de Fête* (1949, Day of the Fair) – combining the influences of Chaplin, neo-realism and French rustic comedy – was a singular and welcome innovation.

The end of the war found Japan, the last Axis enemy, in a desperate situation. Most cinemas were closed, and though the studios had remained theoretically open, the shortage of materials and equipment was acute. The whole country was placed under the regulations of the Supreme Command Allied Forces in the Pacific (SCAP) whose officers drafted and implemented the rules about what films should and should not be made.

Existing films about militarism, feudal loyalty, ritual suicide and the oppression of women were placed on the banned list. As to new projects, uplifting, recommended subjects included the peaceful organization of trade unions, respect for individual rights and the emancipation of women. The latter category provided the pretext for Mizoguchi's *Utamaro O Meguro Gonin No Onna* (1946, *Five Women Around Utamaro*). Meanwhile

the SCAP authorities industriously burned negatives and prints of some 225 forbidden films, which included works by outstanding directors like Kinoshita, Ichikawa and Kurosawa. Many prominent people in the industry were condemned as war criminals and removed from their posts as a result of SCAP investigations. Industrial troubles and strikes further undermined the structure of the Japanese film industry in the late Forties, most seriously affecting the giant company Toho.

Under the Occupation, subjects and styles of filmmaking changed radically. The period film practically disappeared, though old chivalric stories were often updated as modern gangster films, to which SCAP registered no objections. The much-favoured films about the new, emancipated woman resulted in some major works like Mizoguchi's *Joyu Sumako No Koi* (1947, *The Loves of Actress Sumako*) and Kinugasa's *Joyu* (1947, *The Actress*). Kurosawa's *Tora-no-o* (1945, *They Who Tread on the Tiger's Tail*) had the distinction of being banned both before and after the defeat of Japan. But Japan's recent past was examined in the same director's *Waga Seishun Ni Kuinashi* (1946, *No Regrets for Our Youth*).

Other major directors analysed post-war society, its problems and its victims: Mizoguchi in *Yoru No Onnatachi* (1948, *Women of the Night*) and Ozu in *Kaze No Naka No Mendori* (1948, *A Hen in the Wind*).

The Occupation brought one incidental but novel revolution to the Japanese cinema – the kiss. By the late Forties it had become an essential, sensational ingredient of any film with box-office ambitions. But even despite such dramatic Western innovations, the full revelation and flowering of post-war Japanese cinema was delayed until *Rashomon* (1950) brought Japan to the attention of the moviegoers abroad.

Germany was defeated, destroyed, demoralized and artificially divided into zones under the control of the British, American, French and Soviet conquerors. By the end of the war the number of operative cinemas had dwindled to a fraction. But, as the occupying powers realized, the value of cinema in the rehabilitation of a defeated people, they set about reopening movie houses and promoting production.

In the American zone the entertainment permitted to the Germans was strictly limited to Hollywood escapism. There was little reminder or re-examination of the recent war. Production, too, was closely supervised by the military government, which was rigorous in excluding suspected ex-Nazis.

In 1947 production was licensed at the Geiselgasteig Studios in Munich and at the old Templehof Studios in Berlin. Apart from some footage shot for

Hollywood films like *Berlin Express* and *A Foreign Affair* (both 1948) and a notable success with Robert Stemmle's *Berliner Ballade* (1948, *The Ballad of Berlin*), a satire on post-war Germany, no truly distinguished films emerged from the Berlin studios in this period.

The British Control Commission was more relaxed about the film entertainment permitted the defeated people. Old German films were allowed, if they were thought to be clean of Nazi content. Foreign films, too, were re-introduced after their long wartime absence and were shown in both subtitled and dubbed versions; among them were British war pictures like *The Foreman Went to France* (1942) and *San Demetrio, London* (1943).

A number of German productions dealt frankly with recent history and contemporary problems. Wolfgang Liebeneiner, who had been an active director during the war years, portrayed a young woman's gradual disillusionment with Hitler in *Liebe '47* (1947, *Love '47*): she falls in love with a man suffering from war wounds and her faith in humanity is restored. Rudolph Jugert's *Film Ohne Titel* (1947, *Film Without a Title*) adopted a humorous approach by posing the question of how to make a comedy for German audiences who were suffering the tribulations of the post-war period. On the other hand, Arthur Brauner's *Morituri* (1946, *Those About to Die*) confronted the reality of the death camps.

Although these films used plenty of location footage and adopted a straightforward shooting style, they were never part of the mainstream of neo-realism. One German film, however, can be properly termed neo-realist: Rossellini's *Germania, Anno Zero* (1947, *Germany, Year Zero*), a grim and desolate description of a young boy's degradation in the social conditions of the defeated land.

The Eastern zone, under Soviet control, began with considerable advantages. The newly formed Defa (Deutsches Film Aktiengesellschaft) inherited

Above: the legacy of the Nazi regime was shown in Stronger Than Night, *a film that revealed how communists were interned in concentration camps. Left: Robert Stemmle's* The Ballad of Berlin *made post-war German society and the occupying forces objects of satire. Gert Frobe played 'Otto Nobody', a 'little man' picking his way through the black marketeers, the rationing and the rubble of Berlin. Below: cold-war politics prompted a succession of anti-American films; the Soviet* Meeting on the Elbe *was typical of such propaganda*

German film-makers – whether in the East or the West – seemed more preoccupied with the legacy of the war than with plans for peacetime

the old Ufa organization, the Neubabelsburg and Johannistal Studios and the Agfa laboratories along with the Agfacolor process. Everything received full state backing. In the immediate post-war years some of the best and most progressive German directors were attracted to work for Defa. Wolfgang Staudte's *Die Mörder Sind Unter Uns* (1946, *The Murderers Are Among Us*) examined varying attitudes to former war criminals and was perhaps the best of the group of films set in the ruins of Berlin that earned the generic name *Trümmerfilme* ('rubble films'). Other notable examples were Gerhard Lamprecht's *Irgendwo in Berlin* (1946, *Anywhere in Berlin*), a film about the plight of children in the aftermath of defeat, and Kurt Maetzig's *Ehe im Schatten* (1947, *Marriage in the Shadows*), based on the story of the famous actor Gottschalk who, together with his Jewish wife, committed suicide in Nazi Germany.

Slatan Dudow, who had directed *Kühle Wampe* (1932, *Whither Germany?*), from a Brecht scenario, before fleeing from Nazi Germany, returned to make *Unser Tägliche Brot* (1949, *Our Daily Bread*), a somewhat schematic film about socialist reconstruction. Dudow was later to direct a striking feature, *Stärker als die Nacht* (1954, *Stronger Than Night*) about Nazi oppression of communists.

Defa was now headed by the Moscow-trained Sepp Schwab. Bureaucracy took root and the best of

the directors, who had provided a brief renascence in East Germany, crossed to the West: Arthur Maria Rabenalt, Gerhard Lamprecht, Erich Engel and finally – after completing three more films for Defa – the gifted Staudte. Even after the death of Stalin in 1953, the revival of East German cinema was to be slow and reluctant.

The developments in East Germany, paralleled throughout the whole of socialist Europe, were primarily the result of the strengthening influence of the Soviet Union. In the USSR the ending of the war brought a renewal of the grim repressions that had marked Stalin's domination in the Thirties. A. A. Zhdanov, a prominent member of the Politburo, had become Stalin's mouthpiece and led the campaign to bring art and artists into order, making them serve the precise and immediate needs of the Party. A Resolution of the Central Committee in September 1946 condemned the second part of Leonid Lukov's film *A Great Life* (1946) for its realistic treatment of the people of the Donbas coal basin during the war. What was now officially required was an idealized image of Soviet history.

Other films came under attack: Kosintsev and Trauberg's *Plain People* (1945) was alleged to have dealt too frankly with the war, and V.I. Pudovkin suffered criticism for his historical biography of *Admiral Nakhimov* (1946). Eisenstein, too, was a victim of the prevalent ideology. In the second part of *Ivan the Terrible* (1946) his portrait of the Tsar as an iron ruler surrounded by a secret army was evidently too close to being a likeness of Stalin. The

Above: Polish Resistance fighters defend their ground in Border Street, *a re-creation of the Warsaw ghetto uprising of 1943. Below: Adám Szirtes in* The Soil Beneath Your Feet, *a man with marital problems. Below right:* Somewhere in Europe, *about a band of homeless Hungarian children who wander from town to town amid the rubble of post-war Hungary*

film was suppressed (it finally emerged more than a decade later). The intended third part was finally abandoned. Eisenstein never worked again and died, at the age of 50, in 1948.

The films that did meet with approval were, for the most part, historical fabrications. Highly favoured, of course, were those that deified Stalin like Mikhail Chiaureli's appalling *The Vow* (1946) *The Fall of Berlin* (1949) and *The Unforgettable Year of 1919* (1951). Other films, like Abraham Room's *Court of Honour* and Mikhail Romm's *The Russian Question* (both 1948), Alexandrov's *Meeting on the Elbe* (1949) and Chiaureli's *Secret Mission* (1950) attacked the American character and US imperialist aims, as well as 'cosmopolitanism' in general.

Under Zhdanov's control Soviet film production dropped gradually until 1952 when only five feature films appeared in the year. The preference was more and more for apparently 'safe' subjects and this explains the seemingly endless output of idealized historical biographies, direct records of stage productions (favoured by Stalin, who liked the theatre but had become increasingly paranoid about appearing in public), children's films and technical novelties like a version of *Robinson Crusoe* (1946) made in 3-D.

The Polish cinema was nationalized in November 1945, with Aleksander Ford, a notable pre-war director, as head of the new organization called Film Polski. The first post-war Polish feature Leonard Bucskowski's *Forbidden Songs*, did not appear until 1947 but fast became a great hit at the box-office. The film popularized folk ballads that had been banned under the Nazis and is still one of the most successful films ever made in Poland.

Bucskowski followed it with a contemporary story of post-war reconstruction, *Skarb* (1948, *The Treasure*). This film, starring Danuta Szaflarska who had appeared in *Forbidden Songs*, dealt in a gently humorous manner with the acute housing shortage in post-war Poland. Aleksander Ford, himself a Jew, made *Ulica Granicza* (1948, *Border Street*) about the solidarity of Jews and Poles which culminated in the Warsaw ghetto uprising of 1943.

Wanda Jakubowska drew on her own recent memories of Auschwitz for *Ostatni Etap* (1948, *The Last Stage*). This small group of films was a remarkable start of a new-born industry, but in 1949 the Polish Workers Party assumed power and a congress of film-makers at Wisla laid down the new, strict dogmas of socialist realism: interest in imaginative and stylistic devices was condemned along with the portrayal of introspective characters; instead 'the positive hero of the new Poland' was to be made the subject of films that dealt with everyday life in the new socialist state.

In Hungary the path of cinema history, from euphoria to reconstruction and from reconstruction to disillusion, was very much the same, if more complex. Production had continued in Budapest during the war, though by 1945 it had fallen to only three films a year. After the war the great film theorist Béla Balász returned from a quarter of a century of exile to teach at the newly founded Academy of Dramatic and Film Art. The classic Soviet films were shown in Hungary for the first time and film-makers also had the chance to see large numbers of Hollywood films. But from 1947 film production permits were granted only to the leading political parties. Two outstanding films resulted from this period: István Szöt's *Enek a Búzamzökröl* (1947, *Song of the Cornfields*) and Géza Radványi's *Valahol Europábán* (1947, *Somewhere in Europe*). The latter was scripted by Béla Balász and told the story of a group of delinquent war orphans through a touching, idealistic fantasy that owed much to the Soviet film *The Road to Life* (1931).

In March 1948 the Hungarian film industry was

In the post-war period, the film industries of Eastern Europe revived, but the films' subject-matter was often dull and dogmatic

nationalized and the first films produced by the state were auspicious: Frigyes Bán's *Talpalatnyi Föld* (1948, *The Soil Beneath Your Feet*) Imre Jeney's *Egy Asszony Elmdul* (1949, *A Woman Makes a New Start*) and Felix Mariassy's *Szabóné* (1949, *Anna Szabó*) which dealt compassionately with problems of adjustment to the new socialist world.

Soon, however, Hungarian film-makers, too, found their work forced into the schematic moulds of socialist realism. The script, which had to be approved in advance, became paramount. Béla Balász was removed from his post at the Academy. Pudovkin was sent from Moscow as an adviser on film affairs and Hungary moved into the most sterile period of her long film history.

No other Eastern European cinema began the post-war period with greater optimism than that of Czechoslovakia. A well-established film industry had survived the war and was nationalized in August 1945. A body of expert and experienced directors was assembled, among them Otakar Vávra, a specialist in historical and literary subjects. Jiří Weiss returned from London, where he had worked with the Crown Film Unit, and made his first feature film *Uloupená Hranice* (1947, *Stolen Frontier*). The Czech cinema was given a great moral boost when Karel Steklý's *Siréna* (1946, *The Strike*) won the Golden Lion at the first post-war Venice Film Festival.

Similar patterns evolved in the Romanian cinema (nationalized in 1948 but barely past the stage of primitive comedy and socialist morality films) and the Bulgarian film industry, though in 1948 the celebrated Soviet director Sergei Vasiliev was loaned to the Bulgarians to make *Geroite na Shipka*, *Heroes of the Shipka*) about the liberation of Bulgaria from Turkish rule in the nineteenth century.

In post-war Yugoslavia it had been necessary to create a national cinema from scratch – rather as the state itself had been established. The separate republics that made up Yugoslavia had their own languages and their own cultural character. In the summer of 1945 a state film enterprise was established. Promising young people were sent abroad to film schools and film centres were established in Belgrade and in the major cities of the six republics.

The first productions of this newly-formed in-

dustry were documentaries, but in 1947 a feature film *Slavica* (dir. Vjekoslav Afrić) was released. The film dealt with the partisans' struggles against the Nazis and this theme has remained a dominant preoccupation of Yugoslav cinema. Similar partisan films from the same period included Radoš Novaković's *Decak Mita* (1948, *The Boy Mita*) and Vojislav Nanović's *Besmrtna Mladost* (1948, *Immortal Youth*). Despite the break with the Soviet Union in 1948, Yugoslavia itself evolved a dogma of socialist realism, though here it was defined as 'national' realism. Whatever the name, the image of Eastern European cinema in the late Forties was one conditioned by the political situation – namely the Cold War. DAVID ROBINSON

Top: a dramatic scene from Stolen Frontier, *a post-war Czech account of the German occupation of the Sudetenland. Above: the wives of striking steel workers in the Czech film* Siréna; *the film was based on a novel by the popular author Marie Majerova. The end of the war saw the start of a feature-film industry in Yugoslavia; the aspirations of the new country were often expressed in films about youth;* The Boy Mita *by Radoš Novaković (below) was typical of this trend*

Cinema of the Rising Sun

Against all odds, the Japanese film industry made a dynamic recovery in the years after the war. Its commercial progress was matched by the new cultural and artistic trends set by directors like Ozu, Kurosawa and Mizoguchi, who were making bold attempts to reflect contemporary attitudes in their films

The dropping of the atomic bombs on Hiroshima and Nagasaki in August 1945 brought an already weakened Japan to its knees. Within a few days the American occupying forces under the leadership of General MacArthur had accepted Japan's surrender and commenced the process of 'democratizing' what the Allies regarded as an essentially feudal state. This entailed breaking down all the old feudal allegiances in commerce, politics and society in general, and the establishing of equal rights for all. The changes in the structure and operation of industry that were forced on the defeated country affected virtually every aspect of life. The cinema did not escape the upheavals.

Japan had tended to depict its long tradition of a highly structured, feudalistic society very firmly in its films. Prior to the war many films had been made which roused and reinforced the people's loyalty to the Emperor and the ideals of the nation. During the war such movies had become more overtly propagandist, and it was these to which the new American censors turned their attention. Of the 554 films from the war years, 225 were judged to be feudal or anti-democratic and were ordered to be destroyed. The Occupation forces not only censored completed films, but also kept a watchful eye on new scripts. Kon Ichikawa's puppet film *Musume Dojiji* (1946, *Girl at the Dojo Temple*) was burned simply because he had not submitted the script for approval.

At the start of the war all Japanese film companies had been amalgamated, but afterwards they were allowed to start up production as independent studios again. Censorship control was handed to the Civil Information and Education Section (CI & E) of MacArthur's Supreme Command Allied Forces in the Pacific (SCAP) in March 1946. Japanese films were subject to its rulings for the next four years but, freed from this yoke, production exploded in the Fifties and Sixties. Another reason for this boom was the physical rebuilding of the industry, especially the cinemas. In October 1945 there were only 845 cinemas in operation; more than half of the pre-war cinemas had been destroyed in the bombing, although the majority of the studios had miraculously escaped damage. By January of 1946 the number had increased to 1137 cinemas; this rate of building continued so that by 1957 it had reached the astonishing total of 6000.

There were, however, negative and destructive influences at work, including the search by the CI & E for war criminals. The task of naming these was given to the Japanese Motion Picture and Drama Employees Union; but the Americans, failing to realize that this union was largely communist-controlled, thereby unleashed a wave of political revenge rather than justice, and many who were banned from the industry had to fight for twenty years or more for reinstatement.

Meanwhile, the democratization process (which gave workers the initiative to seek greater powers), coupled with a colossal, crippling tax on the box-office returns, caused

Left: poster from Hiroshi Inagaki's Musashi Miyamoto *(1954–55, Samurai), a three-part colour remake of his 1941 version. The earlier film was one of the better-quality Japanese films to survive the post-war censorship purge by the American occupying forces*

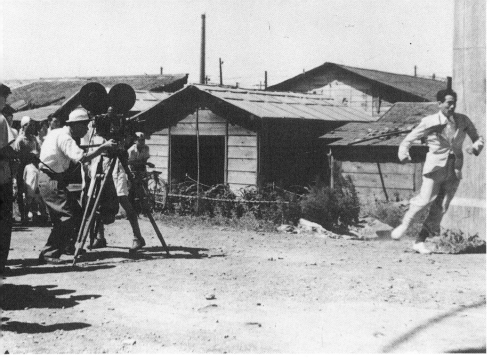

errible strife in the studios and strikes resulted. Toho, the company that gained a virtual monopoly after the war, suffered a spectacular 'work-in' in 1948 which was eventually broken by two thousand police supported by a cavalry company, seven armoured cars and three planes from the US Eighth Army. Few films were produced during this period and it was not until 1949 that a balanced pattern emerged with five major companies carving up the market between them; these were Toho, Toei, Shochiku, Daiei and Shin Toho. Toho, for example, became the main distributors for period films. Daiei had previously specialized in military films, so obviously, in the post-war climate, had to seek new material; the choice of films full of sex and violence may not have made them readily exportable, but their product was sufficiently popular at home to allow the company to rebuild its finances. Shochiku survived on domestic comedies, but in the Fifties these lost favour with audiences and the studio suffered a few lean years until it developed its enormously popular *yazuka*, or gangster films. With these new trends, Japanese film production expanded from 67 films in 1946 to the staggering total of 547 in 1960, by which time 18 companies were in business (the five majors plus a series of small independent companies).

After the war, all the precepts by which the Japanese had lived were being questioned, and writers, artists and film-makers had to cope with new ideas imposed by the West. Some indulged in recrimination; some, like Yasujiro Ozu, retreated to the conservatism of what might be called an essentially Japanese view of life; while others, like Akira Kurosawa, sought to find a balance between old and new values. Despite the problems they faced, some of the greatest talents in Japanese – and world – cinema worked throughout this period and prepared the ground for the glories of the Fifties and Sixties.

Whereas before and during the war the predominant mode of thought in Japan was of group identity (nation, family or company), the post-war turmoil generated what was for the Japanese an unfamiliar concept: that each person had to work out his or her own future. Film-makers started to examine the new ideo-

logies, and the radical importance of this can only be fully appreciated in realizing the strength of the traditionalist views of parental power in Japan, of the obedience of children and the veneration of the family as a unit, and especially the great extent to which pre-war cinema had upheld these beliefs.

Ozu acknowledged the fragmentation of the traditional group ethic in *Nagaya Shinsi Roku* (1947, *Record of a Tenement Gentleman*) in which a boy, roaming the streets amongst physical and moral disorder, seeks and finds his father. The failure of the family to provide the virtues of stability are exemplified in the boy's rejection of his father and the foster mother's 'un-Japanese' reaction to the loss of the boy (in setting up a home for war orphans she moves outside the accepted family support structure). Yet at the same time the family group remains the only hope there is for stability and order. *Kaze No Naka No Mendori* (*A Hen in the Wind*), made the following year, is a melodramatic story of a mother, awaiting the return of her husband from the war, who is compelled to become a prostitute to support her sick child. It was not until 1949 with *Banshun* (*Late Spring*) that Ozu returned to the narrative style that he had begun to develop before the war. His best films have little or no story but examine a quality that has been

Above left: the filming of Kurosawa's crime story Stray Dog. *Above: a father (Chishu Ryu) prepares to give away his daughter (Setsuko Hara) in Ozu's* Late Spring. *Below left: prostitutes in* Women of the Night. *Below right: a political prisoner in* My Love Has Been Burning. *Both films were typical studies of women by Mizoguchi.*

termed *mono-no-aware* – an acceptance of things as they are. This view of life is not fatalistic but depends rather on a calm belief in a world that changes slowly around one. At the end of *Late Spring*, a daughter has gone to be married and her father is left alone, resigned but content. The quiet, controlled style of this and other Ozu films was to become better known in the West after the success of *Tokyo Monogatari* (1953, *Tokyo Story*).

Daisuke Ito had previously specialized in the period film, but after the war he became one of the first directors to expose the resurgence of the gangster in urban life in his film *Oshó* (1947, *The Chess King*). Tadoshi Imai, who had shown his support for Japanese Imperialism in such films as *Boro No Kesshitai* (1943, *Suicide Troops of the Watch Tower*), turned against the feudal code with *Minshu No Teki* (1946, *An Enemy of the People*), a call for communist-based political action. A more humanistic approach was evident in his later film, *Aoi*

Above: Ito's The Chess King. *Above right: Imai's* Blue Mountains, *which explored the generation gap in post-war Japan. Below: Kinoshita's* Broken Drum, *which traced the breakdown of parental authority. Below right: Toshiro Mifune in* Drunken Angel

Sammyaku (1949, *Blue Mountains*), which examined teenage love and parental authority. The popularity of this particular film may have resided in its attack on the rigid views of the parents – a stance unthinkable before the war – and thereby on the basis of the family. Keisuke Kinoshita's *Yabure-Daiko* (*Broken Drum*), made the same year, showed the futility of a father trying to hold a family together with feudal authority. Kinoshita had attacked traditional family values two years earlier with *Kekkon* (1947, *Marriage*), showing that a girl can make up her own mind to marry the man of her choice.

Part of the search for new ideas – some of which bordered on the anarchic – led to the reconsideration of the woman's place in Japanese society. Directors such as Kenji Mizoguchi had long been concerned with the plight of women, but few had dared to make honest exposés of their subservient position. The new post-war freedom encouraged the fight for women's liberation. Mizoguchi in *Joyu Sumako No Koi* (1947, *The Loves of Actress Sumako*), and Teinosuke Kinugasa, in *Joyu* (1947, *The Actress*) both celebrated the heroic figure of Sumako Matsui, an actress who had earlier struck a major blow for the emancipation of women by playing Ibsen heroines in the newly formed *Shingeki* theatre. This had been the first entry of social drama into a traditional theatre dominated by *onnagatu*, male actors playing female roles.

Already famous before the war for his studies of women in such films as *Naniwa Ereji* (1936, *Naniwa Elegy*), *Gion No Shimai* (1936, *Sisters of the Gion*) and *Zangiku Monogatari* (1939, *The Story of the Last Chrysanthemums*),

Mizoguchi had avoided the worst excesses of nationalism during the war by setting his stories back in history and making them intensely personal. During the immediate post-war years he made *Josei No Shori* (1946, *Women's Victory*), a long-promised film about women fighting for and gaining professional posts with the law courts, and *Waga Koi Wa Moeru* (1949, *My Love Has Been Burning*), dealing with the part played by women in active politics. The competence and strength of women is a subject that threads its way through many of Mizoguchi's films, particularly those with a modern setting.

Even his *Utamaro O Meguro Gonin No Onna* (1946, *Five Women Around Utamaro*), the story of a famous artist set in feudal times, deals with the way in which women are exploited, and his most famous film of this period, *Yoru No Onnatachi* (1948, *Women of the Night*), is an unsentimental portrayal of the life of post-war prostitutes – a film largely instrumental in changing the laws governing prostitution.

Kurosawa, after an apprenticeship with Kajiro Yamamoto, directed his first film, *Sugata Sanshiro* (1943, *Sanshiro Sugata – The Judo Story*), during the most nationalistic period. Immediately after the war he made a series of films each of which concentrated on an individual having to work out a course of action for him or herself. There is much of the humanist in Kurosawa, but there is also something essentially feudal. In his early films the *sensei-deshi*, or master-pupil, relationship on which many, but not all, of his later films were to pivot is clearly discernible. Perhaps Kurosawa's greatest gift, supporting his great narrative strength, is his psychological insight into character. It is rare to find clearly defined 'good' or 'bad' people in his films.

Waga Seishun Ni Kuinashi (1946, *No Regrets for Our Youth*) looked back to the political turmoil that had preceded the war and centred on a young woman who, when her illusions of people are shattered and the man she loves dies in prison, chooses to live the life of a peasant

with the man's parents. The villagers turn out to be as harsh and unjust as those people she had known in politics, yet she makes a conscious choice to stay and carry out what she sees as her duty.

The conflict between will and honour or duty, the key to much Japanese literature, is turned by Kurosawa, in his films, into a modern, self-determined driving force. *Yoidore Tenshi* (1948, *Drunken Angel*) tells the story of a gangster (the first starring role for Toshiro Mifune) befriended by an alcoholic doctor who tries to cure him of his tuberculosis; the action centres round a festering pond that symbolizes the rotting heart of the lower depths of society. At the end the gangster is killed and, although little seems to have changed, along the way the story gives several lessons in humanity by showing how, though morally tarnished, people still help each other. *Shizukanaru Ketto* (1949, *The Quiet Duel*) is about a doctor (Mifune) who, during an operation, becomes infected with syphilis from a patient. From this point his own life has to be reassessed as he turns away from the woman he loves and tracks down the infected man. It is a flawed film, however, lacking the psychological strength evident in his next film, *Nora Inu* (1949, *Stray Dog*). This is based on a true story of a detective (Mifune again) whose gun is stolen. With his section chief (Takashi Shimura), he follows a chain of clues deeper and deeper into the criminal underworld. The thief is not seen until the end of the film, yet it is the relationship between the three characters that opens up aspects of human will and perseverance. After a fight in a paddy field the detective eventually captures the thief but, by this time, they are all so covered with mud that 'good' and 'bad' are indistinguishable. This fine film, with its questions about who is really on the side of law and justice, was a precursor to *Rashomon* (1950), the film with which Kurosawa entered a new decade and thrust the Japanese cinema before a worldwide public once more.　　　　　RICHARD TUCKER

Rank and film

The late Forties were years of success and optimism for the British cinema: two moguls, Korda and Rank, fought for the rich rewards offered by the American market

The British film industry entered the post-war period in a spirit of optimism. Annual attendances at British cinemas in 1946 climbed to 1635 million, a figure which was to be an all-time high. The statistic is all the more remarkable since, out of 5000 cinemas, as many as 230 remained closed owing to bomb damage and, because the limited supply of building materials was reserved for more essential uses, no new cinemas could be built.

It was not until April 1949 that cinemas were allowed to switch on their front-of-house display lighting once again. But despite a certain dinginess, the cinema was still an attractive escape from the austerity of post-war Britain with its fuel crises, rationing and various other shortages.

The major cinema circuits – Odeon and Gaumont (both controlled by J. Arthur Rank), and the rival ABC (Associated British Cinemas) – were prevented from further expanding their share of the market by the Board of Trade. It was a time for smaller companies like Granada, Southan Morris and Star to expand by taking over independent cinemas. The biggest single growth, however, occurred in Sol Sheckman's Essoldo circuit which more than tripled in size between the end of the war and the end of the decade.

The traditional low esteem accorded to home-produced films by British audiences had vanished. J. Arthur Rank, an established producer in the late Thirties, was encouraged by the popularity of such pictures as *Madonna of the Seven Moons* (1944) and *A Place of One's Own* (1945) and embarked on a great crusade to put British films on an equal footing with Hollywood product throughout the world. There were new markets to be won in the formerly occupied countries, long deprived of Hollywood and British films, and Rank's salesmen were there, trying to earn money vital to Britain's post-war economy.

Rank also had his eye on the lucrative North American market. In 1944, he bought a half-interest in the circuit of 80 Odeon cinemas in Canada, and a year later he was contemplating building a new Odeon to seat 2500 people in New York's Times Square.

Rank was the largest shareholder in Universal pictures and set up a new company in partnership with them to distribute eight Rank pictures a year in North America. These films were block-booked with new Hollywood films to make a package acceptable to the American circuits. But the US government had for some time been opposed to the system of block-booking and Rank was forced to change his plans. He eventually persuaded the five major American circuits to book British pictures on their own merits.

Britain could not afford to let all the money earned by Hollywood films in the UK leave the country – unless British films could earn more money in the USA to help redress the balance. At the same time the British market was vital to the American studios. In 1946, for example, it was worth $87 million and provided 60 per cent of their

foreign income. The American circuits were controlled by the big Hollywood companies who realized that they would have to play their fair share of British films in order to keep their side of the bargain. Expensive and prestigious Rank productions like *Henry V* (1944) and *Caesar and Cleopatra* (1945), as well as the more modestly budgeted *The Seventh Veil* (1945), were already making inroads into the American market.

In 1946, six British pictures shared 11 Academy Award nominations. Among the Oscar winners were Laurence Olivier, with a special award for *Henry V*, Clemence Dane for the story of *Perfect Strangers* (1945) and Muriel and Sydney Box for their original screenplay for *The Seventh Veil*. Success in America continued into 1947 when Rank's production of *Great Expectations* (1946) played at the mighty Radio City Music Hall in New York, and *Odd Man Out* (1947) appeared at another important Broadway cinema. The following year *Hamlet* (1948) won the Oscar for Best Picture and Best Actor, marking further triumphs for Olivier. *The Red Shoes* (1948) was also nominated for Best Picture. Hollywood smarted under charges that it was losing its artistic initiative.

Rank built up his British studio on Hollywood lines. He established an animation unit with David Hand, a recruit from Disney; he started a two-reel documentary series *This Modern Age* to rival the *March of Time*; he founded the 'charm school' at his Highbury studios to develop new talent.

As an exhibitor, Rank extended his empire. By the end of 1947, he had an interest in 725 overseas cinemas with more than a hundred in five countries – New Zealand, Canada, South Africa, Italy and Australia – and strong representation in Eire, Ceylon, Holland, Egypt, Jamaica and Singapore. In Britain, his two cinema circuits formed the prime outlet for the Hollywood majors (except Warners and MGM who had distribution ties with the ABC circuit) and at the same time Rank was programming British cinemas with his own films.

ABC had no overseas cinemas and were, therefore, a smaller concern than Rank. Furthermore

Top left: J. Arthur Rank and some of the starlets from his Highbury 'charm school'; among them are Sally Gray and Jean Kent. Top: trade ad celebrating Rank's reception in the USA as a film salesman. Centre: the man with the gong; Rank's trade mark. Above: another famous British logo, the Gainsborough Lady

Above: post-war realism characterized Robert Hamer's It Always Rains on Sunday. The film was set in London's East End, amid the street markets and railway yards, and told the story of an escaped prisoner who is sheltered by his former girlfriend (now married) but is rounded up and recaptured – all in the space of a Sunday. Above right: Robert Donat as the QC who defends a young naval cadet accused of stealing a postal order in The Winslow Boy. *Above centre: Ann Todd and James Mason in* The Seventh Veil *as the young concert pianist and her jealous, embittered guardian. Below: David Lean's Oliver Twist was remarkable for its detailed evocation of the squalor of Dickensian London and for the performances of Alec Guinness and Robert Newton*

they were substantially owned by Warner Brothers and had no-one of J. Arthur Rank's drive and zeal at the helm.

The only potential opposition to Rank's dominance of the British film industry was Alexander Korda, but he did not have the benefit of a cinema circuit. During 1943–45, Korda worked in association with MGM but he only produced one picture, *Perfect Strangers* and the chance to curb Rank's power was lost. MGM called off their deal with Korda; he re-established London Films and took over Shepperton studios.

Korda never became a prolific producer on the scale of J. Arthur Rank. In 1948, he was in severe financial difficulties following losses on two very expensive pictures, *An Ideal Husband* (1947) and a new version of *Anna Karenina* (1948). His extravagant spending on *Bonnie Prince Charlie* (1948), filmed over nine months, only made matters worse.

Fortunately, productions like *Mine Own Executioner* (1947) and *The Winslow Boy* (1948) were more economically filmed and Korda's company made some profit from distributing several of the upper-class romances that Herbert Wilcox pro-

duced and directed starring his wife Anna Neagle and Michael Wilding. These films – *The Courtneys of Curzon Street* (1947), *Spring in Park Lane* (1948) and *Maytime in Mayfair* (1949) – reflected Wilcox's opinion that audiences were sick of 'gloomy horrors' and 'wanted films about nice people'.

Associated British had some successes with the Boulting Brothers' production of *Brighton Rock* (1947) and *My Brother Jonathan* (1948). The first of these was adapted from Graham Greene's crime thriller and starred Richard Attenborough as the teenage gangster Pinky; and the second film had Michael Denison playing an ambitious young doctor in a northern industrial town.

Most of the notable British films of the late Forties were backed, produced or released by Rank

Rank also backed the independent producers' company Cineguild, formed in 1942 by David Lean, Ronald Neame, Anthony Havelock-Allan and Noel Coward. It was this team that produced *This Happy Breed* (1944), *Blithe Spirit* and *Brief Encounter* (both 1945). David Lean directed all three films and went on to make his two celebrated adaptations from Dickens, *Great Expectations* and *Oliver Twist* (1948), under the Cineguild banner.

Gainsborough, the production company of the Gaumont empire, specialized in costume melodramas about gypsies, bandits and brutality featuring such stars as Margaret Lockwood, James Mason and Stewart Granger. Despised by the critics, films like *They Were Sisters* and *The Wicked Lady* (both 1945) and *Caravan* (1946) were adored by the public. Thereafter, Gainsborough appeared to lose its popularity and eventually the company ran into financial losses with *Christopher Columbus* (1949), a tedious historical drama starring Fredric March as the intrepid explorer.

Michael Powell and Emeric Pressburger, one of the most prolific production teams of the period, formed their own company, The Archers, which was also backed by Rank, and it was Rank that released their idiosyncratic, widely discussed films: *I Know Where I'm Going* (1945), *A Matter of Life and Death* (1946), *Black Narcissus* (1947) and *The Red Shoes* (1948). Frank Launder and Sidney Gilliat's Individual Pictures company (also linked to Rank)

ROBERT NEWTON, ALEC GUINNESS
KAY WALSH
FRANCIS L. SULLIVAN
with HENRY STEVENSON

J. ARTHUR RANK presents
"OLIVER TWIST"
by Charles Dickens
A CINEGUILD PRODUCTION
EAGLE-LION DISTRIBUTION

and introducing
JOHN HOWARD DAVIES as "Oliver Twist"
Directed by DAVID LEAN
Produced by RONALD NEAME
Screenplay by DAVID LEAN and STANLEY HAYNES

made a number of accomplished films that brought credit to the parent company: *The Rake's Progress* (1945), *I See a Dark Stranger* (1946) and *The Blue Lagoon* (1949). The latter film was handicapped by interference on the part of Rank who insisted that it be shot in the studio rather than on location, thus forcing the film beyond its budget.

One of the fiercest critics of Rank's monopoly was Michael Balcon, the production chief and head of Ealing Studios, but even he was obliged to turn to Rank for distribution from 1944 onwards. The immediate post-war period was not a notable time for Ealing despite the critical successes of *Dead of Night* and *Pink String and Sealing Wax* (both 1945) and the acclaim given to *Hue and Cry* and *It Always Rains on Sunday* (both 1947). But in 1949 the company brought out *Passport to Pimlico*, *Whisky Galore!* and *Kind Hearts and Coronets* in rapid succession. The era of Ealing comedy had truly arrived at last.

Rank was making headway as an independent businessman selling his films in the USA when the British government intervened and placed a 75 per cent *ad valorem* tax on American films imported after August 1947. The result of this measure was twofold: Hollywood stopped sending new films to Britain, and American circuits were no longer disposed to show British films. Overseas sales, like those that Rank was pursuing, became harder to achieve. In Britain, cinemas were soon reduced to playing reissues of old films and to extending the runs of new British films. By the spring of 1948 the film business was in a bad way.

Rank's response to the crisis was to launch a crash programme of production at a cost of over £9 million, drawing on the spare funds of his highly profitable Odeon circuit for the first time. But the new Rank pictures spread the available talent too thinly and the quality of these films was not high enough to guarantee profits. At the same time, the Chancellor of the Exchequer, Sir Stafford Cripps, arranged for the original import tax on Hollywood films to be repealed in May 1948 in exchange for an agreement on the part of the Americans to limit the amount of earnings removed from the country to an annual figure of $17 million. The remainder of this revenue was to be reinvested in British film production. Hollywood, not surprisingly, unleashed a backlog of 265 pictures and the new British films were swamped under the competition. Once again the government tried to take remedial steps. It raised the quota of British features to

be shown in cinemas throughout the land from 20 to 45 per cent. The new figure made impossible demands on the British film industry even though Rank kept up production in an attempt to fulfil the quota. Hollywood was once again handicapped as the various studios scrambled for the limited playing time the new British law left them.

In the summer of 1949, Rank's £86 million empire had a £16.25 million overdraft and had lost £3.35 million in production, resulting in an overall year's trading loss of £750,000. J. Arthur Rank ordered savage cut-backs. No future Rank film was to cost over £150,000 – a far cry from the half-million spent on the two Olivier/Shakespeare films. Rank stopped making cartoons, terminated *This Modern Age*, closed the studios at Highbury (and the 'charm school'), Islington and Shepherds Bush and cut back on production activity at Denham. Pinewood was to be the main base for Rank production but the economies had forced many film-makers away, most of them joining up with Korda, a popular and cultured figure with whom artists felt at home.

Investment in production was no longer the

Above left: James Mason carries off Margaret Lockwood in The Wicked Lady. *This historical romance, about a noblewoman who teams up with a highwayman, was typical of the 'Gainsborough Gothic' style. Above:* London Belongs to Me *(1948) was made at Pinewood by Launder and Gilliat for Individual Pictures. Launder said, 'It was well acted and well directed but its overall drawback to my mind was too many characters in too many stories, and not enough stars.' Nevertheless it helped Richard Attenborough on his way, providing him with another working-class role, and Alastair Sim had fun with the part of the fake medium. Below: the fanciful allegory* A Matter of Life and Death *told how a young airman was judged in a celestial court.*

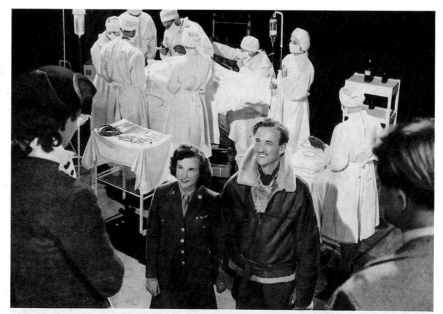

Written, produced and directed by MICHAEL POWELL and

DAVID NIVEN · ROGER LIVESEY · RAYMOND MASSEY in

A Matter of Life and Death

A PRODUCTION OF THE ARCHERS

IN TECHNICOLOR

Above: setting up a shot (involving interiors and exteriors) for Whisky Galore! *on location in the Outer Hebrides. Above right: one of several adaptations from the novels of Graham Greene in the Forties, the Boulting Brothers' version of* Brighton Rock *was, for its time, an unusually violent film. Above, far right: publicity picture of Anna Neagle and Michael Wilding, who together made half a dozen films; in* Piccadilly Incident *(1946) they were wartime lovers, then came* The Courtneys of Curzon Street, Spring in Park Lane, Derby Day *(1952) and* Maytime in Mayfair. *Below: Neagle and Wilding's penultimate film together in 1951*

attractive gamble it had been to financiers in the Thirties. Instead the government of the day created the National Film Finance Corporation which began in October 1948 with £5 million to loan to producers who proposed safe-looking projects for films. Rank made no attempt to borrow NFFC money, not wanting to increase his organization's debts, but Korda seized the opportunity and borrowed £3 million for a variety of productions.

The money gave Korda a new lease of life. He engaged Carol Reed to make *The Fallen Idol* (1948) and *The Third Man* (1949). The latter film was partly financed by the Hollywood producer David O. Selznick who supplied Joseph Cotten and Alida Valli from his roster of stars. Selznick also collaborated with Korda on Powell and Pressburger's *Gone to Earth* (1950), a melodrama set in the Shropshire countryside with spectacular hunting scenes. This film prompted an argument between Korda and Selznick over the quality of the close-ups of Jennifer

Jones and Selznick had the scenes featuring Jones re-shot in the United States before releasing the film as *The Wild Heart*.

In contrast to Ealing's eccentric style, the Neagle–Wilding films offered an image of elegance

Associated British responded to Rank's cut-back with the announcement of a major production programme in association with Warner Brothers. One of the products of this collaboration was *The Hasty Heart* (1949) starring Richard Todd. The film was directed by Vincent Sherman from a script by Ranald MacDougall and co-starred Patricia Neal; all three were Warners stalwarts from Hollywood. Associated British also drew on Hollywood talent for their lavish, American-style musical *Happy-Go-Lovely* (1951): the film was directed by H. Bruce Humberstone and starred David Niven, Vera-Ellen and Cesar Romero.

Other Hollywood companies were actively involved in British production, using up some of the frozen assets created by governmental restrictions. 20th Century-Fox made *Escape* (1948) and *Britannia Mews* (1949), a period romance written by Ring Lardner Jr. In 1949, MGM filmed *Edward My Son* and the Cold War thriller *Conspirator*, starring Robert Taylor and Elizabeth Taylor, as well as establishing its own studio at Borehamwood.

At the end of the decade, the British film industry was badly battered. The high hopes of the post-war revival were dashed. In 1949, the government set up the British Production Fund which has always been known as the Eady Plan after Sir William Eady who devised the scheme. Briefly, the fund was the product of a levy on the price of cinema admission which would be returned to producers in direct proportion to the performance of their films at the box-office. The Eady levy placed a premium on financial success and British film producers felt it keenly. In the same year as the Eady Plan was introduced, the government reduced the quota of British films exhibitors were obliged to play to 40 per cent. This move may have eased the pressure on British production but the industry would never again enjoy the financial stability of the mid-Forties.
ALLEN EYLES

Carol Reed

After several impressive films in the Thirties, Carol Reed came into his own after the war with four great triumphs – dark, brooding tales of intrigue that powerfully caught the prevailing mood of disillusion. These and other pictures reveal Reed as one of the cinema's master story-tellers

In the immediate post-war period Britain had no film director more highly regarded than Carol Reed. For three successive years the British Film Academy singled out his films as the best native product: *Odd Man Out* in 1947, *The Fallen Idol* in 1948, *The Third Man* in 1949. He was knighted in 1952, a rare honour for a director working full-time in the cinema. And he was knighted with reason, for he had achieved what had long seemed an impossible dream for the British cinema – to make films that could stand up internationally with both audiences and critics.

Like many other talents working in the British film industry, Reed began his career in the theatre. He was born in London in 1906, and by 1923 he was carrying spears and

touring in repertory. Eventually he found permanent work with crime-writer Edgar Wallace who was engaged in organizing theatrical versions of his stories. Reed served as an all-purpose aide – acting, stage-managing and looking after touring companies. When Wallace joined the board of the newly established British Lion film company in 1927 Reed became his cinema aide too, keeping an eye on the day's activities at Beaconsfield studio where film versions of Wallace's successes were put into production. From Reed's own films it is clear what he learned from his days with Wallace – a firm belief in telling a good yarn and a delight in the murkier side of life.

After Wallace died in 1932, Reed joined Associated Talking Pictures (later to become

Ealing). In 1935 he directed his first film, *Midshipman Easy*, a full-blooded maritime adventure with 15-year-old Hughie Green (the future television star) leaping about the high seas with disarming glee. For most of the Thirties Reed moved rapidly from one studio project to another, gaining some critical attention for the energy of his shooting style. *Laburnum Grove* (1936) was based on J.B. Priestley's play about English suburban life; *A Girl Must Live* (1939) was a jolly show-business comedy featuring the charms of Margaret Lockwood and a mordant Frank Launder script. More substantial were *Bank Holiday* (1938) and *The Stars Look Down* (1939), both of which tempered their melodramatic elements with realistic atmosphere. *Bank Holiday* followed the fortunes of a nurse (Lockwood), her fiancé (John Loder) and a cockney family spending an August holiday weekend among the crowds on the South Coast. *The Stars Look Down*, adapted from A.J. Cronin's novel, was the story of a young idealist (Michael Redgrave) and his fight for nationalization of the mines and better working conditions – a struggle climaxing in a full-scale pit disaster. Reed handled the subject with great skill, but no deep political commitment. 'One could just as easily make a picture on the opposite side,' he said in a rare interview in 1971.

Reed continued to make proficient entertainment films during the war. *Night Train to Munich* (1940) was a breezy thriller benefitting from a Launder and Gilliat script but burdened by some terrible model work (Reed himself admitted that the mountains in the final chase-scenes looked like ice-cream). *Kipps* (1941), adapted from H.G. Wells' novel, and *The Young Mr Pitt* (1942) were both let down to some degree by Reed's fastidiousness; Robert Donat played Pitt as a worthy dullard, while Wells' upstart hero became just a bland charmer with Michael Redgrave badly miscast as Kipps.

The Young Mr Pitt was a rare British example of propaganda by historical parallel: Pitt's Britain was threatened by Napoleon just as Churchill's was by Hitler. But Reed later

Above left: Carol Reed masterminds the action of The Third Man, *with Joseph Cotten and Orson Welles (back to camera). Below left: Hughie Green and Robert Adams in* Midshipman Easy, *Reed's first film. Below: Lilli Palmer and David Burns (with Margaret Lockwood behind them) in* A Girl Must Live

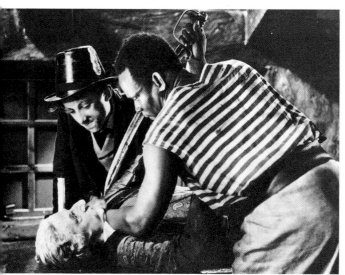

narrative strands tightly together, concluding with action in North Africa and the torpedoing of a troop ship. Reed's sense of narrative and his editing skills are also apparent in *The True Glory* (1945), a record of the Allied victory compiled from combat footage and co-directed by the American Garson Kanin.

Like the characters in *The Way Ahead*, Reed emerged from the war a stronger figure, more prepared to give his projects an individual stamp. And he found the right kind of projects. His adaptation of F.L. Green's novel *Odd Man Out* was not like *The Stars Look Down*, where Reed was uncommitted to Cronin's hero: the fate of Johnny (James Mason), the Irish revolutionary wounded in a robbery to secure funds for the IRA, interested the director deeply. This is reflected in the film's visual conception: vertiginous camera angles and masterly shadow effects create a baroque world of disordered perception, fear and nightmare. (Indeed, tilted camera angles were so much a part of Reed's style in this film and its successors that the American director William Wyler gave him a spirit level to put on top of his cameras.) Johnny totters about helplessly, dripping blood and bandages, from air-raid shelter to house, to horse cab, to builder's yard, to pub, to inevitable death.

With *The Fallen Idol*, Reed began a fruitful

moved on to a genre Britain made its own – the documentary-slanted survey of life in various branches of the fighting forces. In 1942 he made *The New Lot*, a 45-minute film produced by the Army Kinema Corporation, aimed at helping recruits find their feet. And it was such a success that Reed subsequently made a feature-length version – *The Way Ahead* (1944), one of Britain's finest war films. Like *Bank Holiday*, the film follows the fortunes of a motley group of characters, but there is little room for melodrama here: Eric Ambler and Peter Ustinov's careful script sensitively charts the gradual moulding of seven civilians into a fighting team, while Reed's direction binds the

Above: Orson Welles as Harry Lime. Right: Ralph Richardson as Baines and Bobby Henrey as the boy who worships him in The Fallen Idol. *Below right: Burt Lancaster, Gina Lollobrigida and Tony Curtis in the American circus melodrama* Trapeze. *Below: Wendy Hiller and Trevor Howard in the sultry, moody* Outcast of the Islands

Above: Charlton Heston as Michelangelo in Reed's epic The Agony and the Ecstasy. *Left: the Oscar-winning musical* Oliver! *starred Harry Secombe as Mr Bumble and Mark Lester as Oliver Twist*

tribal jealousies and the attractions of the native girl Aissa (Kerima). Reed documents his decline into complete depravity with dogged skill.

Reed made ten more films before his death in 1976, but none reached the level of this post-war quartet. As the British film industry itself declined, he spent most of his time either going over old territory or venturing into uncongenial new areas, plying his trade as he did in the Thirties with more craftsmanship than commitment. *The Man Between* (1953), a thriller set in Berlin, only summoned up fond memories of the far superior *The Third Man*. In films like *Trapeze* (1956) and *The Agony and the Ecstasy* (1965) Reed lost all trace of his personality in the face of international stars, wide screens, big budgets and silly stories.

Our Man in Havana, however, reunited him with Graham Greene, who supplied a script from his own novel about yet another muddled innocent wading into deep water – a salesman-cum-British spy (Alec Guinness) who sends his superiors drawings of imaginary missiles closely resembling the vacuum cleaners sold in his shop. Greene's story involved all the elements that Reed had successfully built on before, and the film is consistently entertaining, though pitched at a lower level than its predecessors. The one complete success of Reed's last years was *Oliver!* (1968). He had always weaved children into his best films (his adult heroes often behaved with childlike innocence too). A child was the hero of *A Kid for Two Farthings* (1955), a Wolf Mankowitz story set in the East End of London and overstuffed with sentimental whimsy. But Reed filmed Lionel Bart's musical about Oliver Twist with bracing élan. His clinical style of directing, with its strong emphasis on editing, may have been old-fashioned by the late Sixties, when more free-wheeling styles were in vogue, yet it proved exactly right for the subject: Bart's songs and routines were put across with all their excitement and charm still intact. And at last Reed won another award – an Oscar for Best Director.   GEOFF BROWN

distorted camera angles and bizarre spatial compositions to suggest the disordered perceptions of the main character – an odd boy out, isolated in an adult world he cannot properly comprehend. Greene's own script, from his story *The Basement Room*, is strikingly witty.

The hero of *The Third Man*, filmed from an original Greene script, is another odd man out – a hack writer of Westerns, Holly Martins (Joseph Cotten), who stumbles naively around a post-war Vienna criss-crossed with zones and black markets, trying to uncover the truth about the death of his friend and meal-ticket Harry Lime (Orson Welles). The quest brings many dilemmas for Martins, for he finds Lime is a murderous racketeer and not dead at all but slinking about the city's doorways and sewers. Once again Reed's camera tilts crazily, fashioning strange landscapes from the bombed Vienna exteriors; Anton Karas' zither music and Orson Welles' appearances, tantalizingly delayed until the last third of the film, are both haunting and enigmatic.

But for all the film's distinction there now seems something strained about Reed's direction; the effort that went into his visual effects is all too apparent. Perhaps Reed sensed this at the time, for his subsequent films look positively staid by comparison, though *Outcast of the Islands* (1951) bristles with tension – generated less by camera tricks than the fevered tempo of acting and editing. This film took him away from Graham Greene into the world of Joseph Conrad, another writer who loved making his characters' lives as morally complex as possible. The outcast – one more odd man – is Willems (Trevor Howard), an arch-sensualist who is given control of an East Indian river village by his protector Captain Lingard (Ralph Richardson) only to fall prey to

ollaboration with the distinguished writer raham Greene, who as a film critic had raised Reed's work in the Thirties. They were ell suited: like Reed, Greene has always lished a strong story, and also likes to hinge ents on moral dilemmas.

Most of their work together also reveals a ndness for exotic or eccentric locations – ienna in *The Third Man*, Cuba in *Our Man in avana* (1959). The action of *The Fallen Idol*, owever, takes place in workaday London, but e drama is still sparked off by the strange rcumstances of its characters. The boy Felipe obby Henrey) lives in an unidentified em-assy and idolizes the butler Baines (Ralph chardson), whose tall stories of derring-do rn sour when his wife is found dead. Aware at Baines' real affections lie elsewhere, Felipe esumes that he murdered his wife, but the y's blatant attempts to cover up for his hero ly alert the police. Once again Reed uses

Filmography

1929 The Flying Squad (actor only); Red Aces (actor only). '32 Nine Till Six (dial. dir. only). '34 Autumn Crocus (ass. dir. on location filming); Sing As We Go! (ass. dir. only); Java Head (2nd unit dir; + some scenes). '35 It Happened in Paris (co-dir); Midshipman Easy (USA: Men of the Sea). '36 Laburnum Grove; Talk of the Devil. '37 Who's Your Lady Friend? '38 Bank Holiday (USA: Three on a Weekend); Penny Paradise. '39 Climbing High; A Girl Must Live; The Stars Look Down. '40 Night Train to Munich (USA: Night Train). '41 The Girl in the News; Kipps (USA: The Remarkable Mr Kipps). '42 The Young Mr Pitt; A Letter From Home (short, never shown in GB); The New Lot (short). '44 The Way Ahead. '45 The True Glory (doc) (co-dir). '47 Odd Man Out (+ prod). '48 The Fallen Idol (+ co-prod). '49 The Third Man (+ prod). '50 Appeal Film for National Playing Fields Association (short). '51 Outcast of the Islands (+ prod). '53 The Man Between (+ prod). '55 A Kid for Two Farthings (+ prod). '56 Trapeze (USA). '58 The Key. '59 Our Man in Havana (USA). '63 The Running Man (+ prod). '65 The Agony and the Ecstasy (+ prod) (USA). '68 Oliver! '70 Flap (USA) (GB: The Last Warrior). '71 Follow Me (GB) (USA: The Public Eye).
Reed worked on other films 1929–34 but there are no reliable listings

The Third Man

Directed by Carol Reed, 1949
Prod co: (Alexander Korda, David O. Selznick for) London Films. prod: Carol Reed. assoc prod: Hugh Perceval. sc: Graham Greene. photo: Robert Krasker. add photo: John Wilcox, Stan Pavey. ed: Oswald Hafenrichter. art dir: Vincent Korda, Joseph Bato, John Hawkesworth. mus: Anton Karas. sd: John Cox. ass dir: Guy Hamilton. r/t: 104 mins.
Cast: Joseph Cotten (*Holly Martins*), Orson Welles (*Harry Lime*), Alida Valli (*Anna Schmidt*), Trevor Howard (*Major Calloway*), Paul Hoerbiger (*porter*), Ernst Deutsch (*Baron Kurtz*), Erich Ponto (*Dr Winkel*), Wilfred Hyde White (*Crabbit*), Bernard Lee (*Sergeant Paine*), Siegfried Breuer (*Popescu*), Geoffrey Keen (*British policeman*), Annie Rosar (*porter's wife*), Hedwig Bliebtrau (*Anna's 'Old Woman'*), Harbut Helbek (*Hansl*), Alexis Chesnakov (*Brodsky*), Paul Hardtmuth (*hall porter*).

Left: Carol Reed directs the chase scene in the sewers

After they had completed *The Fallen Idol* (1948), director Carol Reed and writer Graham Greene dined with Alexander Korda, who was anxious for them to work on a new film together. Although they agreed on a setting – post-war Vienna – they were stuck for a story until Greene produced an old envelope on which years before he had written a single sentence:

'I had paid my last farewell to Harry a week ago, when his coffin was lowered into the frozen February ground, so it was with incredulity that I saw him pass by, without a sign of recognition, among the host of strangers in the Strand.'

This became the basis of Reed's *The Third Man*, a film that was to take the Grand Prix at the Cannes Film Festival and earn him a third successive British Film Academy Award for Best Picture.

Greene drafted the story as a novel and then, working closely with Reed, turned it into a screenplay. Although it is in many ways a classic Greene tale, with its themes of guilt and disillusionment, corruption and betrayal, Greene himself has been quick to accord to Reed credit for many of the film's memorable qualities. It was Reed who insisted on the bleakly uncompromising ending where Anna, as she leaves Harry's funeral, walks not into Holly's arms in the conventional final clinch, but passed him, staring impassively ahead. It was Reed who discovered the zither-player, Anton Karas, whose 'Harry Lime theme' gave the film a special haunting quality. It was Reed who prevailed on a reluctant Orson Welles to play the comparatively small but pivotal part of Harry Lime. Welles became so enthusiastic about the film that he contributed to the script a much-quoted justification of Harry's criminal activities:

'In Italy for thirty years under the Borgias they had warfare, terror, murder, bloodshed. They produced Michelangelo, Leonardo da Vinci and the Renaissance. In Switzerland they had brotherly love, five hundred years of democracy and peace. And what did that produce – the cuckoo clock. So long, Holly.'

It was, of course, also Carol Reed who gave remarkable visual life to Greene's brilliantly wrought script, a perfect marriage of word and image, sound and symbol. Holly's odyssey in search of a truth that is to destroy his oldest friend, the girl they both love and, in a sense, Holly himself, is conducted against the background of post-war Vienna, unforgettably evoked by Robert Krasker's powerful chiaroscuro photography which won him a deserved Oscar. The vast, echoing, empty baroque buildings that serve as military headquarters and decaying lodging houses are a melancholy reminder of the Old Vienna, the city of Strauss waltzes and Hapsburg elegance, plunged, in the aftermath of war, into a nightmare world of political intrigue, racketeering and murder. The shadowed, narrow streets and the jagged bomb-sites are the haunt of black marketeers, vividly portrayed inhabitants of a dislocated society. There is a powerful symbolism, too, in the places where Harry makes his appearances: a giant ferris wheel from which he looks down contemptuously at the scuttling mortals, and the Viennese sewers where, after a breathtaking and sharply edited final chase, he is cornered, rat-like, and dispatched.

The angled shooting, atmospheric locations, and sombre shadow-play eloquently convey the pervading aura of tension, mystery and corruption. It is an aura enhanced rather than dissipated by flashes of black humour, such as the sequence in which Holly, bustled by strangers into a car and believing himself kidnapped, discovers he is being taken to address a cultural gathering, the members of which think he is a famous novelist.

The cast is superlative, with the four stars outstanding: Joseph Cotten as decent, dogged, simple, faithful Holly; Alida Valli as the wonderfully enigmatic Anna; Trevor Howard as the shrewd, determined, quietly spoken military policeman Calloway; and Orson Welles as the fascinating Harry Lime. *The Third Man* was one of the peaks of post-war British filmmaking and remains a flawlessly crafted, timelessly perfect work of art.   JEFFREY RICHARDS

DAVID O. SELZNICK and ALEXANDER KORDA PRESENT

THE 3RD MAN

by GRAHAM GREENE

Hunted by MEN...
Sought by WOMEN!

JOSEPH COTTEN
VALLI
ORSON WELLES
TREVOR HOWARD

PRODUCED AND DIRECTED BY CAROL REED   A SELZNICK RELEASE

Holly Martins, a writer of hack Westerns, arrives in Vienna to look for his friend Harry Lime, only to be told that Harry has been killed in a street accident. Holly attends the funeral (1) and is questioned by military policeman Major Calloway (2), who tells him that Harry was a racketeer selling penicillin so diluted that it caused the deaths of sick children.

Holly sets out to find the truth and visits Harry's girlfriend, actress Anna Schmidt (3), who suggests that Harry's death may not have been accidental. An elderly porter reports seeing a mysterious third man at the scene of the accident (4); next day the porter is found dead. Holly is chased by two thugs but escapes. Leaving Anna's apartment, he sees Harry in the shadows (5) and realizes he is 'the third man'. Harry's coffin is exhumed and found to contain the body of a police informer.

Harry arranges to meet Holly and offers to buy his silence (6). But when Calloway arrests Anna (7) (who has a forged passport) and plans to deport her behind the Iron Curtain, Holly, who is in love with her, betrays Harry to the police in return for her release. A chase through the sewers underneath the city (8), ends with Holly shooting Harry dead. Anna attends the funeral and then walks away past Holly without speaking to him (9).

Michael Powell is one of the cinema's true iconoclasts, one of its great romantics. A brilliant director, he has pursued a lone pilgrimage in search of 'truth, beauty and the heart of Englishness'

Michael Powell is the most extreme and the most elusive director in the English cinema. He may be the best, if you are prepared for the best to be so unsettling. Yes, Hitchcock is English too, but two-thirds of his work was produced in America, and he treated the English facetiously; in his films, ridiculous British manners veil an indifference to everyday experience. Powell is less devious and more rooted than Hitchcock, less nerve-racking but more troubled. His Englishness is a matter of imaginative ecstasy or pain living inside grim composure and common sense. Powell stayed in England and eventually languished because of his loyalty. Hitchcock was even knighted, rewarded for a commercial astuteness that Powell has been too proud or too reckless to maintain.

The director's tale

Powell was born in 1905 near Canterbury, the site of one of his strangest films, *A Canterbury Tale* (1944). It is a parable about materialism and idealism, with Eric Portman as a classic

Left: the land-girl (Sheila Sim) wonders if the JP (Eric Portman) can be the mysterious 'glueman' in A Canterbury Tale. *Above left: Churchill considered* The Life and Death of Colonel Blimp *'propaganda detrimental to the morale of the army' and tried to ban it*

Powell spokesman: abrasive, lofty towar women, but a spire of cold purpose. As a youn man, Powell was rescued – from a routine jo in a bank – by the hotel his father owned at Ca Ferrat, near Nice. While working there, he fe in with the director Rex Ingram at the Vic torine studio. Ingram, an outcast genius from Hollywood, worked in France and Nort Africa on movies that sweltered with his love o artifice, with Islamic atmosphere and th influence of Aleister Crowley, the model fo *The Magician* (1926), in which Powell had small comedy part.

The heady example of Ingram and the blaz of the Mediterranean never deserted Powell i the austerity of Britain in the Thirties. H worked during that decade as a director quickies, none of which won special attentio Yet he was learning his craft and resisting th creed of documentary that John Grierson ha spread through British pictures. In 1937, like Grierson disciple, he went to the Northern Isl to make *The Edge of the World*, but he returne with a Celtic myth, not a study of dam fishermen. It was the war that further e flamed Powell's imagination and brought hir his vital collaborator, Emeric Pressburger.

Pressburger (b. 1902) was a Hungarian wh had worked as a screenwriter in Europe. came to Britain in 1938 and was introduced Powell by another Hungarian, Alexand Korda. Powell and Pressburger began workin together on *The Spy in Black* (1939), abo Germans trying to penetrate the British nav base at Scapa Flow, with Conrad Veidt Powell's first study of German decisiveness. seemed unlikely that, as war drew nea Powell and Pressburger would choose to e plore the German personality, but this wa absolutely characteristic of the perverse orig nality they cultivated. They formed their ow

ell
progress

Left: the deceased doctor (Roger Livesey) appeals to the heavenly court in A Matter of Life and Death. *Above: a moment of calm before the storm in* Black Narcissus. *Below: ballerina Moira Shearer in* The Red Shoes

roduction company, The Archers, in 1942. heir logo, an arrow smacking into a bull's-e, combined the aura of Robin Hood with a st warning to voyeurs – voyeurism and its le in the act of watching films was one of owell's major preoccupations, to be defini-ely treated in *Peeping Tom* (1960).

They worked together until 1956, usually aring credit for writing, direction and pro-ction. Pressburger is still living in England d the pair remain friends. Their separation as no reflection on a partnership that seems have been a blessing to two very talented t independent men.

arallel lines

he war revitalized British movies. The Min-try of Information 'advised' on scripts and gineered films to back the war effort. Powell gan full of team spirit, but it testifies to ritain's quixotic sense of propaganda that his ar movies are so equivocal. In *49th Parallel* 941), a German submarine is wrecked on the anadian shore. Its survivors roam the land, nfronting a series of Allied attitudes to the ar. Eric Portman was the German captain: utal, efficient, and animated by his cause, a lain but a figure of heroic will.

Far more satisfying as a film, and far more xing to Winston Churchill, was *The Life and eath of Colonel Blimp* (1943). Blimp was a rtoon character, the embodiment of crusty action in the British military, created by avid Low. Churchill was mortified that a itish film might perpetuate this satirical rtrait during hostilities. But Powell and essburger adore their Blimp – Clive Candy oger Livesey) – and show him in three fferent periods: 1902, 1914 and 1942. He is t the brightest man, and he is certainly not ruthless as Portman's captain in *49th*

Parallel. But he has all those aspects of English-ness cherished by Powell: Tory values, a stiff upper lip, and a fond heart. Moreover, Candy has a German friend (Anton Walbrook), and there is the haunting allure of a woman who appears in all three episodes. As played by Deborah Kerr she is the natural but impossible love object for all Powell heroes: red- or auburn-haired, classy and controlled, yet with a hint of abandon that brings both sweetness and unstated passion to a single close-up. *Blimp* was also two-and-a-half hours long. Despite Churchill's opposition, it was seen and loved by a people who always respond well to a gracious celebration of their foibles.

Blimp was outrageously original and a heartfelt statement against the wartime stress on realism and obedience. Powell's films around 1945 were equally personal reactions against the new socialist tide in Britain. Although *I Know Where I'm Going* (1945) and *A Matter of Life and Death* (1946) are love stories, they are also political statements wilfully set against the grain of the time. Their unruliness shows the difficulty Powell has had in being a man for his own time; but their spirit proclaims

his loyalty to gentlemanly values, values buried in his sense of English tradition. Thus they look better as time passes, their strange-ness turning into a poetry such as the silent screen understood.

Heaven can wait

The post-war love stories depict desire lurking within a restraining code, the lovers tossed about between common sense and irrational lyricism. Women are nuisances, helpmates or familiars who intuit the power of spell and fantasy. The films move violently yet serenely from reality to hallucination. *A Matter of Life and Death* has a bomber pilot 'killed' in action. But he claims a reprieve in heaven because he fell in love with a radio operator just before dying. Reality is given gorgeous colour, and the socialist utopia of heaven is insipid black-and-white. Although David Niven as the pilot is chatty and matter-of-fact, he is a poet too. He lands on a beach that looks like a Magritte painting, and the film is without rival in British cinema for its evocation of the eerie calm of Surrealism. Though it ends happily, it has unnerving moments in which it hovers on the edge of order and chaos. It was also the first evidence of Powell's characteristic Chinese-box structure, in which some actions are the shadows of others – the trial in heaven being a version of an operation on the pilot's brain.

Peace probably frustrated Powell. Instead of

Above: the alcoholic's nightmare in The Small Back Room, *with David Farrar. Top: the film-maker as voyeur – Carl Boehm in* Peeping Tom. *Top right: Robert Helpmann in the musical* The Tales of Hoffmann *(1951)*

a splurge of joy and release in Britain, there were ration books and shortages. He responded with the exotic *Black Narcissus* (1947), made in a studio re-creation of Nepal, about the thunder of denied sexuality in a convent. It was picturesque, fevered and half-crazy: Gothic romance has often beckoned Powell. The sensual potential of David Farrar, Deborah Kerr, Kathleen Byron and the young Jean Simmons is viewed with flinching ecstasy, as if

the film had been made by a hysterically abstinent nun.

David Farrar and Kathleen Byron play the couple in *The Small Back Room* (1949). He is a crippled, alcoholic bomb expert. His tin foot is ridiculed by a new German weapon he must learn to dismantle and by the giant whisky bottle he wrestles with in a dream sequence. Farrar – a dark, Gary Cooper-like actor, apparently too moody to seize the stardom that Powell believed would await him – is an ideal Powell hero: passionate but introverted. *The Small Back Room* is a remarkable *film noir* love story. Sexual longing hides in every shadow, as if hoping to refute the loneliness implicit in the title.

Dance crazy
The Red Shoes (1948), on the other hand, is an explosion of colour – garish, undried, and vibrant with the feeling that is bitten back in the story and the playing. Revered by ballet lovers, *The Red Shoes* was the demonstration of Powell's craze for total cinema – colour, story, design, music, dance.

If anyone ever bought dancing shoes because of the film, that's fine. It seems more impressive for its relentless artiness, for its cinematic equivalent of the Andersen fairy-tale and its rapture with art. *The Red Shoes* captivates young people because its zeal is so close to nightmare: the ballerina cannot stop dancing, and the impresario urges her to perform at the cost of her life and the love he cannot even admit. *The Red Shoes* is theatrical and fanciful, but Anton Walbrook's rendering of the Diaghilev figure reflects Powell's conception of the artist as outcast, scold, and prophet to an indolent world. The artist's dedication is

close to destructiveness: his vision is nev‹ more romantic than when it refuses to yield ‹ real obstacles; he is most tender and wounde‹ when he cannot share the sentiments of oth‹ people. For all its rainbow dazzle, *The Red Sho‹* glorifies the pained but magnificent isolation ‹ the artist.

The camera murders
Which brings us finally to *Peeping Tom*, a fil‹ that received violent abuse and loathing, an‹ virtually ended Powell's British career. *Peepir‹ Tom* is more naked than *The Red Shoes* becau‹ the ecstasy it depicts is so damaging, yet fir‹ by the same desperate search for a perfectio‹ that might redeem the mess of life. The hero ‹ a young man, 'taught' terror by his fath‹ (played by Powell himself), whose voyeurist‹ compulsion is in filming the dying spasms ‹ the young women he has murdered. Mar‹ Lewis (Carl Boehm) works in the film indust‹ as a focus-puller, but by night he is a dead‹ *auteur*, alone and in command. Powell nev‹ condemned the 'sick' young man: that's wh‹ repelled audiences in 1960. Further, he admi‹ now that he sympathized with him and wit‹ the way he represented all film directors ‹ their creation of a seen world that surpasses a‹ reality.

In Susan Sontag's words, *Peeping Tom* dea‹ with 'the central fantasy connected with th‹ camera' – that seeing is more potent tha‹ participating. As the reflection on a career, ‹ enacts Powell's rueful belief in the need ‹ sacrifice life to art. *Peeping Tom* is a tribute ‹ the artist as self-destructive terrorist.

DAVID THOMSO‹

Condensed material from an article in The Boston Phoen‹ *Section Three, February 12, 1980.*

Filmography
1926 The Magician (actor only) (USA). **'27** The Garden of Allah (actor only) (USA). **'30** Caste (sc. only). **'31** 77 Park Lane (co-sc. only); Two Crowded Hours; My Friend, the King; Rynox (+co-sc); The Rasp; The Star Reporter (+add. photo. **'32** Hotel Splendide; C.O.D.; His Lordship; Born Lucky. **'33** Perfect Understanding (sc; +2nd unit dir. only); The Fire Raisers (+co-sc). **'34** Red Ensign (+co-sc) (USA: Strike!); The Night of the Party (USA: The Murder Party); Something Always Happens; The Girl in the Crowd; Crown vs Stevens. **'35** Lazybones; The Love Test; The Phantom Light; The Price of a Song; Some Day. **'36** The Man Behind the Mask; Her Last Affaire; The Brown Wallet. **'37** The Edge of the World (+sc). **'39** The Spy in Black (USA: U-Boat 29); The Lion Has Wings (co-dir). **'40** Contraband (+co-sc) (USA: Blackout); The Thief of Bagdad (co-dir). **'41** An Airman's Letter to His Mother (short) (+prod; +sc; +co-photo); 49th Parallel (+prod; +co-sc) (USA: The Invaders); One of Our Aircraft Is Missing (co-dir; +co-prod; +co-sc; +act)*. **'43** The Silver Fleet (co-prod. only); The Life and Death of Colonel Blimp (co-dir; +co-prod; +co-sc)* (USA: Colonel Blimp); The Volunteer (doc) (co-dir; +co-prod; +co-sc; +act)*. **'44** A Canterbury Tale (co-dir; +co-prod; +co-sc)*. **'45** I Know Where I'm Going (co-dir; +co-prod; +co-sc)*. **'46** A Matter of Life and Death (co-dir; +co-prod; +co-sc)* (USA: Stair-way to Heaven). **'47** Black Narcissus (co-dir; +co-prod; +co-sc)*; The End of the River (co-prod. only). **'48** The Red Shoes (co-dir; +co-prod; +co-sc)*. **'49** The Small Back Room (co-dir; +co-prod; +co-sc)* (USA: Hour of Glory). **'50** Gone to Earth (co-dir; +co-sc)* (USA: The Wild Heart); The Elusive Pimpernel (co-dir; +co-sc)* (USA: The Fighting Pimpernel). **'51** The Tales of Hoffmann (co-dir; +co-prod; +co-sc)*. **'55** The Sorcerer's Apprentice (short) (+prod); Oh, Ro-salinda!! (co-dir; +co-prod; +co-sc)*. **'56** The Battle of the River Plate (co-dir; +co-prod)* (USA: Pursuit of the Graf Spee). **'57** Ill Met by Moonlight (co-dir; +co-prod; +co-sc)* (USA: Night Ambush). **'58** Luna de Miel (co-dir; +co-prod; +co-sc) (SP-GB) (GB: Honeymoon). **'60** Peeping Tom (+prod; +act); The Queen's Guards (+prod). **'66** They're a Weird Mob (+prod) (AUS-GB). **'67** Sebastian (prod. only). **'68** Age of Consent (+co-prod) (AUS). **'72** The Boy Who Turned Yellow.
* *co-dir. co-prod. co-sc. collaborations with Emeric Pressburger.*

Ealing's glory

The brightest illustrations of the optimism of post-war British cinema
were the dramas and comedies produced at Ealing Studios

There have been few famous film companies in the world whose headquarters could truthfully be described in these terms:

'It somehow had the air of a family business, set on the village green of the queen of the London suburbs. The administrative block looked like a country cottage and was separated from the studios proper by a neat little rose garden, tended, between office crises, by Balcon's secretary, Miss Slater.'

That was how Ealing Studios appeared in 1938 to Monja Danischewsky, appointed by the new head of production Michael Balcon to look after publicity. The country cottage which contained the administrative offices was Regency in style; behind it had once been apple orchards, ruefully cut down by Balcon's predecessor Basil Dean to make space for the studios themselves. Yet even without the apple trees, the Ealing environment made other British studios, not to mention Hollywood's factories, look like dark, satanic mills.

Behind Ealing's unique appearance lay some special qualities. To the general public, the other major studios in and around London – at Denham, Elstree, Shepherds Bush, Islington – were merely buildings where films were made. But Ealing was always much more than a geographical location. The word effortlessly conjures up an entire roster of performers and directors and a whole school of film-making, with a characteristic way of treating comedy, drama and all the gradations in between.

Ealing's way with comedy caught the public attention, both in Britain and all over the world. Think of Ealing and one automatically thinks of comedy scenes: the car in *The Lavender Hill Mob* (1951) careering about the streets with 'Old Mac-Donald Had a Farm' blaring out of its radio and a policeman on the running board singing along; Alec Guinness' succession of d'Ascoynes meeting their fate in *Kind Hearts and Coronets*; the Scottish

islanders in *Whisky Galore!* (both 1949) frenziedly concealing their favourite tipple from the excise officials' prying eyes.

With such fond memories it is easy to forget that comedies made up only a small part of Ealing's large output. Out of the 95 films Michael Balcon produced during nearly twenty years in control, the hard core of classic Ealing comedies only amount to nine. And Ealing had been established as an important production base seven years before Balcon arrived.

There had been some film activity near Ealing's village green in the early silent days, but fully equipped studios were constructed only in 1931. Under the auspices of Associated Talking Pictures (ATP), Basil Dean, the theatrical producer-turned-film magnate, had supervised the construction of the studios which were the first in Britain to be custom-built for sound. At the time the Weather Bureau claimed that Ealing was the least fog-bound place in London; as Dean was particularly keen on outside filming, the site suited him well.

Dean was the first theatrical personality to support the new talking pictures (the majority of his colleagues shrank from them in horror), yet for all his enthusiasm and his advocacy of location shooting, he remained closely tied to theatrical and literary traditions in his choice of subjects for filming. ATP produced well-groomed versions of plays such as Galsworthy's *Loyalties* (1933), C.L. Anthony's *Autumn Crocus* (1934), J.B. Priestley's *Laburnum Grove* (1936), along with versions of firmly established novels like *The Water Gypsies* (1932), *Three Men in a Boat* (1933), *Lorna Doone* (1934) and *Midshipman Easy* (1935). Many were directed by Dean himself.

In the mid-Thirties Dean tried to establish a repertory company of actors to stock both his film and stage productions. The scheme collapsed, but some theatrical talent did move over permanently

Top left: the homely façade of Ealing Studios. Top: an aerial view of the studios showing the leafy suburban location with fields to the rear. The building at extreme left housed the model stages; the scenery stores, workshops and main sound stages were housed in the large central block. Above: Basil Dearden (left) and the bespectacled Michael Balcon deep in conversation during the shooting of Saraband for Dead Lovers *(1948)*

113

Above: Florence Desmond and Gracie Fields in Sally in Our Alley, *an early comedy hit from ATP before it became Ealing Studios. Top: the inimitable Formby grin was prominent in* No Limit; *this fast-moving farce about a Lancashire lad and his love of motorcycle racing was another ATP success. Top right: a typically imaginative Ealing poster for* Painted Boats, *a story of life aboard the barges on England's canals. Below: Aldo Ray at the centre of the action in* The Siege of Pinchgut. *This film about a convicts' riot was chiefly made on location in Australia by the documentary-trained Harry Watt*

to the new medium: directors Carol Reed and Basil Dearden both emerged from Dean's theatre staff. Ealing under Balcon had little to do with the eminently respectable kind of cinema Dean liked to promote, yet the two regimes still had many similarities and points of continuity. Both men were concerned to make the studio's product characteristically British. The words of the plaque erected on the studio buildings in 1955, when they were sold to the BBC, put the matter in a nutshell:

'Here during a quarter of a century were made many films projecting Britain and the British character.

Dean projected Britain largely through the pictorial image of the country. ATP's films were not restricted to the fog-less fields around Ealing: *The Water Gypsies* took audiences on a tour of canals; *Three Men in a Boat* took them up and down the Thames; *Sing As We Go!* (1934), one of the company's Gracie Fields vehicles, featured the bustling holiday crowds of Blackpool.

Balcon never neglected the country's pictorial image either: *Hue and Cry* (1947), the film that ushered in the classic comedies, strikingly explored the blitzed landscapes of London, while one semi-documentary feature, *Painted Boats* (1945), was completely given over to canals. Yet his projection of Britain went considerably deeper than the details of urban and country landscapes. The best of Balcon's films use national characteristics as a springboard for their very plots. Through their stories of community endeavours, of quirky individuals tilting at unwieldy officialdom, we receive a clear picture of the imagined makeup and habits

of middle-class, mid-century England.

Another link between the two periods is the importance given to comedy. If ATP had made only genteel films of Galsworthy plays, they would have been out of business in no time. As it was, the company's early years were financially shaky. They pulled through partly because of continuing financial support from the businessman Stephen Courtauld, and partly because of the box-office allure of Gracie Fields. Her first husband, Archie Pitt, positively shoved her into a film career with *Sally in Our Alley* (1931), but no-one regretted it. Provincial audiences lapped up the boisterous Lancashire comedy, sentiment and music in her films. When Dean became distressed by their lack of polish, he brought in a respectable name, J.B. Priestley, to work on the scripts. Then, in 1935, another Northerner, George Formby, joined the studio for a series of equally popular farces – beginning with *No Limit* (1935) – that mixed slapstick and buffoonery with Formby's suggestive ditties sung to a ukelele.

In 1938 many changes took place at Ealing. Balcon replaced Dean and the actual name of Associated Talking Pictures was phased out in favour of Ealing Studios, previously used as the name of the company who owned the studio space. By this time Gracie Fields had been lured to Hollywood with the offer of a higher salary, but the production of Formby films continued until 1941. The popular tradition of low-brow, low-budget moneymakers was then taken over by Will Hay, who had worked for Balcon at Gaumont-British and transferred his activities to Ealing from 1941 until 1943, when ill-health curtailed his career.

With the end of the war, however, Ealing's conception of comedy changed decisively. Instead of producing films shaped round comic stars with permanently established personalities, Balcon started to make films designed for a motley collection of versatile performers superbly adept at comedy: Alastair Sim, Alec Guinness, Margaret Rutherford, Joan Greenwood and Cecil Parker. Ealing comedies were now created by a team for a team.

In a way, this development was in line with another Ealing tradition that went back to Basil Dean's days – the cultivation of a family atmosphere at the studio. The air of a 'family business' which Danischewsky found in 1938 had been carefully fostered from the start. To avoid any hint of drab regimentation, Dean called the studio canteen 'The Inn' and decorated its walls bright red to keep everyone happy. Ealing personnel also found happiness at the local pub, the Red Lion. The sense of being pioneers in difficult times helped spread cameraderie amongst Dean's staff, and the

studio's chief star Gracie Fields was highly adept at rollying people along.

Balcon continued and intensified Dean's tradition of benevolent paternalism. Signs with legends like 'The studio with team spirit' hung from the walls. Balcon was also careful to encourage the individual talents within his team. Future producers and directors began as editors (Robert Hamer, Charles Crichton), assistant editors (Seth Holt), writers (Alexander Mackendrick), art directors (Michael Relph). Danischewsky himself rose from publicist to writer and associate producer.

The studio, in fact, became exactly the kind of isolated community it loved to celebrate in its films. It was populated by a closely-knit group of talents all proudly united in a common goal and somewhat suspicious of outsiders or anyone 'different'. Once established at Ealing, people tended to stay there. Certainly those who moved away, such as Henry Cornelius and Alexander Mackendrick, were very much the exceptions.

Balcon's team was drawn together during the war years, when, in common with British films of the period, Ealing's output testified to a new strength, character and sense of purpose. *Convoy* (1940) was one of the most popular films of its time – a sturdy drama of life on board a convoy ship. Its publicity slogan was 'Entertainment with authenticity'. But at this early stage of the war the authenticity in *Convoy* lay chiefly in its location footage. The director Pen Tennyson (killed in an air crash the following year) shot so much background material on the high seas that subsequent Ealing directors constantly returned to his footage to fill out their own maritime features and shorts. The attitudes of Tennyson's characters were, however, less authentic: the officer class paraded on deck with binoculars while the humble workers stoked the fires and checked the gauges down below, both social groups carefully keeping each other at a respectful distance.

But the pull of the war's events – and the influx of documentary-trained talent, like the director Harry Watt – helped Ealing films reflect Britain's new spirit of comradeship, all layers of society working together with courage and good humour. By the time of *San Demetrio, London* (1943), authenticity of emotional content was plainly considered more important than authenticity of location.

With the war drawing to a close, Ealing prepared for peacetime production. A deal with J. Arthur Rank's empire in 1944 gave the company security for the future and a guaranteed release in Rank's cinema chain for all their films. But what kind of films would these be? Balcon made an extravagant statement about this in the trade magazine *Kinematograph Weekly* in January 1945:

'British films must present to the world a picture of Britain as a leader in Social Reform, in the defeat of social injustices and a champion of civil liberties . . . Britain as a questing explorer, adventurer and trader . . . Britain as a mighty military power standing alone and undaunted against terrifying aggression.'

One could just about squeeze *Scott of the Antarctic* (1948) into that scheme, but it hardly accounts for Ealing's anthology of supernatural stories *Dead of Night* (1945), the rural romance of *The Loves of Joanna Godden* (1947) or the rush of comedies that followed in the post-war period.

It is not in the British character, despite Balcon's declaration in 1945, to use films to confront big issues and to conquer all and sundry. Ealing realized this and instead settled for small issues, small communities and characters too humble to stride anywhere, except in their dreams.

In comedies and dramas, Ealing kept the community spirit of the war still burning brightly: London's East End was featured in *It Always Rains on Sunday* (1947), Paddington Green in *The Blue Lamp* (1950). Other films looked at a cross-section of society: the varied frequenters of a London dance hall in *Dance Hall* (1950), a group of seamen on weekend leave in *Pool of London* (1951).

This is unquestionably Ealing's richest period. The famous comedies emerged, three of them in 1949 (*Passport to Pimlico, Whisky Galore!, Kind Hearts and Coronets*), all subtly different in tone. Robert Hamer's *Kind Hearts and Coronets*, in which Dennis Price undertook the disposal of the d'Ascoyne family, was distinguished by its black humour, highly literate script and an elegant visual precision unique in Ealing's output. Alexander Mackendrick's *Whisky Galore!* provided a caustic look at human foibles as Hebridean islanders and a pompous British resident (played by Basil Radford) clashed over a consignment of whisky rescued from a wrecked boat. Henry Cornelius' *Passport to Pimlico*, with a script by the Ealing stalwart T. E. B. Clarke, presented a boisterous picture of another community eager to abandon constraints and which established the London district of Pimlico as an independent, ration-free state after a dusty document revealed the area to be an outpost of the Duchy of Burgundy.

Ealing's dramas of the period, like *The Blue Lamp*, also celebrated community life, although the population and officialdom were now seen working together to combat the anti-social elements that threatened its smooth running. Jack Warner played P.C. Dixon, a personification of the British bobby – cheerful, homely, fond of his darts and his garden plants. When he is fatally wounded during a bungled robbery, even the underworld fraternity unite with the authorities to trap the killer (played by Dirk Bogarde) amongst the happy crowds at a greyhound stadium.

As the Fifties moved on, however, Ealing's projection of British life began to falter. Comedies and dramas repeated the familiar formulas with diminishing returns. Comedies became increasingly pallid with *The Titfield Thunderbolt* (1953) and *The Maggie* (1954), and reached the height of whimsicality in *Barnacle Bill* (1957) when a sea captain, played by Alec Guinness, kitted out a rundown pier as an ocean liner. At least *The Ladykillers* (1955), where Mackendrick and his writer William Rose made a virtue of Ealing's obsession with the quaint and decrepit, was fully up to standard. The Ealing dramas turned equally limp: *Dunkirk* (1958) presented all the emotions and situations of the past war in a manner so cold that they instantly congealed into clichés.

After Ealing's home territory was sold to the BBC in 1955, production continued at MGM's Borehamwood studios. Their final film was *The Siege of Pinchgut*, released in August 1959. The company may have run out of steam during the Fifties, yet its influence was still widespread. The output of Group Three, a company supported by a large government subsidy, chiefly consisted of meek little comedies in a debased Ealing manner, celebrating quaint happenings in quaint places. Many of Ealing's talents migrated to television but the mature, vintage Ealing films of the Forties and early Fifties remain unique.
GEOFF BROWN

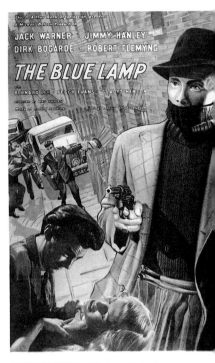

*Above: examples of Ealing posters.
Top:* The Blue Lamp *marked a new mature style in British crime films. Below: Diana Dors in* Dance Hall.

The discreet charm

of Alec Guinness

During the 1979 British Academy Film and Television Arts awards, Sir Alec Guinness, coming forward to collect the Best Actor prize for his brilliant portrayal of secret service man George Smiley in the BBC's *Tinker, Tailor, Soldier, Spy*, seemed daunted at the prospect of addressing the audience and the TV cameras. When, shy and diffident, he eventually stepped up to the microphone, his hurried thank-you suggested all the embarrassment of a school-boy at a prize-giving, not the charismatic ease of a much-fêted star acknowledging another tribute to his genius. But then Alec Guinness is a supreme example of the actor who hides behind the mask of his characters and who prefers to let his performances speak for him. Consequently he is an unknown quantity. Very few critics have penetrated the makeup; the nearest that biographer Kenneth Tynan came was when he described Guinness as 'a master of anonymity . . . the whole presence of the man is guarded and evasive'. Guinness himself has remarked, 'I was always rather embarrassed with me personally, and I was glad to go into a thin cardboard disguise.'

He was born in London in 1914 and educated at private schools in the South. At 18 he took a job as a copy-writer in an advertising agency, but the stage beckoned and in 1934 he won a scholarship to the Fay Compton Acting

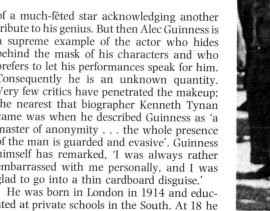

Top left: Guinness as Fagin in Oliver Twist. *Top: as Emperor Marcus Aurelius in* The Fall of the Roman Empire *(1964). Above: winning his first Oscar as the colonel in* Bridge on the River Kwai *(his second was an honorary award in 1980). Left: with Noel Coward and Burl Ives in* Our Man in Havana *(1959)*

School. John Gielgud saw him, was impressed and gave him his first break as Osric in *Hamlet*, by 1938 Guinness had the lead in the Old Vic's modern dress version of the play. He joined the Royal Navy in 1941 and quickly became an officer.

After the war he returned to the stage and in 1946 began his film career as Herbert Pocket in David Lean's *Great Expectations*. It was a character well known to him – he had played Pocket in his own stage adaptation of Dickens' novel in 1940. Lean next cast him as Fagin in *Oliver Twist* (1948). If the revered *Kind Hearts and Coronets* (1949), which followed, was to establish Guinness as the screen's most perceptive and refined interpreter of English idiosyncrasy, his Fagin first revealed him as a

(1972, *Brother Sun, Sister Moon*). Guinness was himself received into the Roman Catholic Church in the mid-Fifties.

He was reunited with Lean in 1957 and won the Best Actor Oscar for *The Bridge on the River Kwai*. Guinness has probably never been more intense, more fierce: his Colonel Nicholson, leader of British POWs held by the Japanese, is a fanatic, a figure of iron will perverted by blind pride: the skill and endurance of his men in building a bridge for the enemy means much more to him than the need to win the war.

In spite of a dozen roles in international blockbusters of the Sixties and Seventies, Guinness remains an anonymous figure, enigmatic, thoroughly discreet (he turned down the opportunity to play Anthony Blunt in a scheduled feature about the KGB mole), thoroughly elusive. Fagin, the eight d'Ascoynes of *Kind Hearts* and Colonel Nicholson apart, he will most likely be remembered as the clerkish, mild-mannered, middle-class 'little man' of Ealing days. Not the man for the big occasion perhaps – but therein lies his strength.

GRAHAM FULLER

Filmography

1934 Evensong (extra). '46 Great Expectations. '48 Oliver Twist. '49 Kind Hearts and Coronets; A Run for Your Money. '50 Last Holiday; The Mudlark. '51 The Lavender Hill Mob; The Man in the White Suit. '52 The Card (USA: The Promoter). '53 Malta Story; The Captain's Paradise. '54 Father Brown (USA: The Detective); The Stratford Adventure (doc; as himself) (CAN). '55 To Paris With Love; The Prisoner; The Ladykillers; Rowlandson's England (doc; narr. only). '56 The Swan (USA). '57 The Bridge on the River Kwai; Barnacle Bill (USA: All at Sea). '58 The Horse's Mouth (+sc). '59 The Scapegoat; Our Man in Havana. '60 Tunes of Glory. '61 A Majority of One (USA). '62 HMS Defiant (USA: Damn the Defiant!); Lawrence of Arabia. '64 The Fall of the Roman Empire (USA). '65 Hotel Paradiso; Situation Hopeless, but Not Serious (USA-GER); Doctor Zhivago (USA). '66 The Quiller Memorandum. '67 The Comedians (GB-GER-FR). '70 Cromwell; Scrooge. '72 Fratello Sole, Sorella Luna (GB: Brother Sun, Sister Moon) (IT-GB). '73 Hitler: the Last Ten Days (GB-IT). '76 Murder by Death (USA). '77 Star Wars (USA).

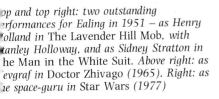

*op and top right: two outstanding
erformances for Ealing in 1951 – as Henry
olland in* The Lavender Hill Mob, *with
tanley Holloway, and as Sidney Stratton in
he Man in the White Suit. Above right: as
evgraf in* Doctor Zhivago (1965). *Right: as
he space-guru in* Star Wars (1977)

aster of disguise. An extraordinary study in
ervous, jealous avarice masquerading as
vuncular warmth, the fumbling, hook-nosed
ld Jew – sketched straight from Cruikshank's
lustrations – his beard matted and his heavy-
dded eyes sparked with cunning, repels and
emands sympathy at the same time. Guiness' remarkable performance was regarded as
nti-Semitic in 1948 and the American release
f *Oliver Twist* was long delayed.

The Ealing comedies and more stage-work
ccupied Guinness for the next few years and
e became a major star. He was the detective-
riest in *Father Brown* (1954), and a cardinal
eld captive in *The Prisoner* (1955); perhaps the
ogical conclusion to this sequence was his
'ope Innocent III in *Fratello Sole, Sorella Luna*

Kind Hearts

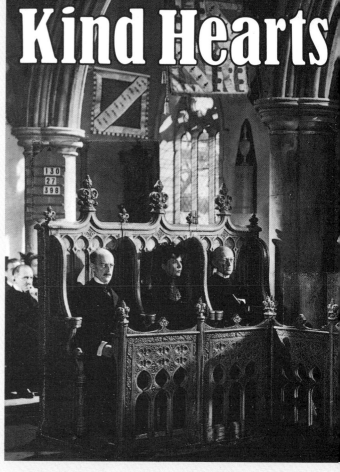

Few films make effective reading when their words are divorced from their images. And if one is found that does, the tendency is immediately to assume that there must be something wrong with it. Certainly *Kind Hearts and Coronets* has often posed this kind of a problem: it allows such weight to the spoken word that it has often been thought of as literary and uncinematic. And yet, at this distance of time from its first appearance in 1949, it stands out as the least faded, most indubitably alive of all the British films of its era. And, perhaps because cinema criticism is now a lot less hidebound by simplistic theories of what is or is not 'cinematic' than it once was, it would probably not occur to anyone seeing the film for the first time to query its 'summit meeting' of words and images or worry about how it could somehow be made to fit into a world-view shaped by neo-realism.

The corollary of this is that today's audience would not realize how exceptional the film was in its time; but part of Robert Hamer's stated principle in making it was that it should be 'a film not noticeably similar to any previously made in the English language'. Hamer had

been a film editor, then a writer, then – as one of Michael Balcon's bright young men at Ealing – a director, making his debut with an episode in the composite picture *Dead of Night* (1945). He had followed it with a couple of solo features, *Pink String and Sealing Wax* (1945), a period murder story, and *It Always Rains on Sunday* (1947), a downbeat study of working-class life which he also wrote; the elegance of the first and the social perceptiveness of the second retrospectively provide a hint of what was to come. No-one, however, could have guessed what Hamer was up to when he discovered and began to adapt the little-known Edwardian novel, *Israel Rank* – a rather self-consciously decadent piece written by Roy Horniman (a follower of Oscar Wilde) – having decided that it had the makings of a film comedy.

In adapting it Hamer remained true to the period of the story and to the allegiance to Wilde. Otherwise, only the basic plot of the novel was retained: the plight of a young man whose mother has married beneath her and been cast out by her family, and his determination to get revenge and repair his spoilt fortunes by murdering his way through a

1

When the younger daughter of the Duke of Chalfont runs off with a penniless Italian singer her family disowns her. She tells her son Louis about his grand forbears but, denied any aid from her family, he has to work in a draper's shop. Stung by the family's refusal to recognize kinship with his mother – even when she dies – he determines to get his own back and to impress his suburban girlfriend Sibella (1)

by disposing of all who stand between him and the family title.

First, he murders his most obnoxious cousin (2) during a dirty weekend at Henley, and then blows up another cousin, an amateur photographer (3). A cleric uncle is poisoned (4); a suffragette aunt it shot down in her balloon (5); a soldier uncle is booby-trapped while recounting his most famous campaign (6); and a sailor uncle goes down

2

3

4

7

8

9

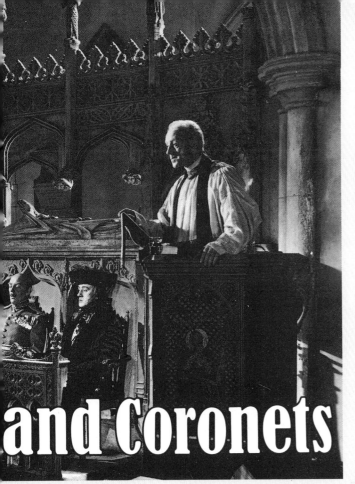

and Coronets

Directed by Robert Hamer, 1949
Prod co: Ealing. **prod:** Michael Balcon. **assoc prod:** Michael Relph. **sc:** Robert Hamer, John Dighton, from the novel *Israel Rank* by Roy Horniman. **photo:** Douglas Slocombe, Jeff Seaholme. **sp eff:** Sydney Pearson, Geoffrey Dickinson. **ed:** Peter Tanner. **art dir:** William Kellner. **mus:** Ernest Irving, extract from Mozart's *Don Giovanni* played by The Philharmonic Orchestra, conducted by Ernest Irving. **cost:** Anthony Mendleson. **sd:** Stephen Dalby, John Mitchell. **ass dir:** Norman Priggen. **r/t:** 106 minutes.
Cast: Dennis Price (*Louis Mazzini*), Valerie Hobson (*Edith d'Ascoyne*), Joan Greenwood (*Sibella*), Alec Guinness (*Ethelred, Duke of Chalfont; Lord Ascoyne d'Ascoyne; The Reverend Lord Henry d'Ascoyne; General Lord Rufus d'Ascoyne; Admiral Lord Horatio d'Ascoyne; Ascoyne d'Ascoyne; Henry d'Ascoyne; Lady Agatha d'Ascoyne*), Audrey Fildes (*Mama*), Miles Malleson (*hangman*), Clive Morton (*prison governor*), John Penrose (*Lionel*), Cecil Ramage (*Crown Counsel*), Hugh Griffith (*Lord High Steward*), John Salew (*Mr Perkins*), Eric Messiter (*Burgoyne*), Lyn Evans (*farmer*), Barbara Leake (*schoolmistress*), Peggy Ann Clifford (*Maud*), Anne Valery (*girl in the punt*), Arthur Lowe (*reporter*).

with his ship after a collision at sea (7). This makes Louis heir apparent to the Chalfont title, and the accepted fiancé of Edith (the photographer cousin's widow).

Just as Louis is achieving his goal by shooting the present duke (8) – whereupon the last remaining uncle expires on hearing he has succeeded to the dukedom – Sibella's husband dies in suspicious circumstances and he is charged with the one

Above: two down, six to go – the funeral service for the second d'Ascoyne cousin

murder he didn't do. Sibella agrees to get him acquitted if he will dispose of Edith and make her the next duchess (9). All goes according to plan, but there is still the problem of Louis' compromising memoirs (10) which he has absent-mindedly left in his prison cell on being freed (11) . . .

whole family of unspeakable relatives on his way to a dukedom. In the novel this involves a lot of Nietzschean attitudinizing on the part of the self-styled superman hero; in the film it is all distilled into an exquisitely subversive comedy of manners, decorated with a constant sparkle of verbal wit such as Wilde himself would not have disowned.

But that is not all. The film's visual wit perfectly complements the verbal. If the tone is established primarily by the dialogue and by the ruthless Louis' voice-over commentary on the action, it is still true that the best effects are produced by a knowing counterpoint of word and image. A typical example of this is when Louis' tea-time conversation with his cousin's chilly wife (soon to be his) is accompanied by the gradual appearance of a column of smoke indicating that something nasty has happened to his cousin in the woodshed. Elsewhere Hamer's precise selection of what details to show us in the behaviour of his characters lets the audience know just how to read every move in this cool but by no means unemotional game.

The performances are, of course,

superb. Dennis Price as the dandyish, but under it all slightly demonic, Louis was never better, and neither were Joan Greenwood and Valerie Hobson, perfectly cast as the two contrasting women in his life. Alec Guinness' extraordinary feat, playing eight members of the d'Ascoyne family, has been much remarked on, but the most remarkable thing about it is that it is virtually unnoticeable. So exactly is each member of the family portrayed that, while seeing the film, the spectator is aware only of the diversity and believability, not of the one actor who achieves it. But, first and foremost, the film is the personal creation of Robert Hamer, as close to a genuine *auteur* film as the British cinema has ever come.

Though some of Hamer's later films were enjoyable – notably *Father Brown* (1954), which re-united him with Guinness and Greenwood – he never had another comparable chance to express his elegant, uncomfortable wit in the context of a generally conservative British cinema. A pity – but at least *Kind Hearts and Coronets* remains a masterpiece, and unique.

JOHN RUSSELL TAYLOR

5

6

10

11

Backing Britain

The producer Michael Balcon was dedicated to creating a firm national identity for British cinema. Convinced that high quality entertainment could be made on low budgets, he became the moving force behind many of the industry's greatest triumphs of the Thirties, Forties and Fifties

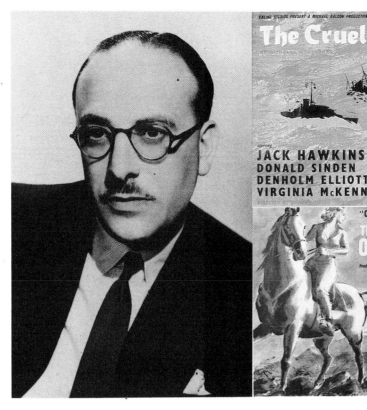

Michael Balcon is thought of as the most stubbornly British of all film-makers; the legend, in an industry where image-making is daily routine, is simple truth. Balcon, whose personal life centred on his Sussex home and his family, was the most English of men. Although he travelled widely and had a multitude of overseas friends, he was never much attracted to the international film scene. There was nothing chauvinist in this: he was an admirer of French and early German cinema and, above all, of the flair and inventiveness of Hollywood, but saw their qualities as deriving from firm national roots; he wanted the same for Britain.

Born in 1896 into a middle-class Birmingham family rather down on its luck. Balcon entered film production, with Victor Saville and a joint capital of £200, soon after World War I. They made their first features at Islington studios which Balcon was later to acquire for his Gainsborough company. It was here that he became impressed with the efficiency and enthusiasm of the young Alfred Hitchcock, giving him his first chance to direct a feature film – *The Pleasure Garden* (1925).

A doomed partnership

In 1931, Balcon took over production at Shepherds Bush for the newly-formed Gaumont-British Picture Corporation, while his Gainsborough programme, with such successes as *The Ringer*, *The Ghost Train* and *Sunshine Susie* (all 1931), overflowed into rented accommodation at Elstree. Hitchcock's films, such as *The Man Who Knew Too Much* (1934) and *The Thirty-Nine Steps* (1935), together with Korda's internationally acclaimed productions of the same period, raised British cinema to world class. The euphoria faded in 1936, when pressure from Hollywood and internal troubles threw Gaumont-British into disarray. Balcon made the bold decision (naive, he called it later) to accept an offer from Louis B. Mayer of MGM for a co-production deal. Mayer was to

provide money for mutually agreed subjects which would be produced in Britain by Balcon who was guaranteed creative independence. Balcon spent six months in Hollywood, where his appreciation of production efficiency was offset – indeed overwhelmed – by his loathing of Mayer's despotism and the abject sycophancy of his 'court'. Absurd as Mayer's antics were, a man of Balcon's sensitivity could not laugh them off; he felt that they outraged human dignity. The project was doomed before it began and Balcon, back in London, completed only one picture, the somewhat vapid *A Yank at Oxford* (1938), before walking out on the partnership.

Doubts and divisions

He walked into the arms of his old friend Reg Baker, the administrative chief at Basil Dean's Ealing Studios, and joined the company as head of production.

The move to Ealing in 1938 was most timely. Balcon was going through a period of self-appraisal, ever more conscious of the shortcomings of the British cinema he had done so much to build and sustain.

What distinctive contribution had it made to the art and influence of film? Justly proud of the more cinematic of his films, such as Hitchcock's thrillers, the best of the Hulbert comedies, and individual classics like *Rome Express* (1932) and *Man of Aran* (1934), Balcon saw that British films on the whole were unadventurous and over-dependent on theatre and the dying tradition of music-hall.

Above: two of Michael Balcon's most successful post-war Ealing productions, The Cruel Sea *and* The Overlanders. *Below: a black stoker (Paul Robeson) helps keep the mines open in* The Proud Valley, *a Balcon film that confronted serious social issues*

ALEC GUINNESS · CECIL PARKER
HERBERT LOM · PETER SELLERS · DANNY GREEN
as

THE LADYKILLERS

Colour by Technicolor
Ealing Studios present
a Michael Balcon Production

Left: the sinister gang of The Ladykillers, *one of the finest Ealing comedies. Above: Albert Finney as the hero of* Tom Jones (1963), *a multi-Oscar winner and the last major film with which Balcon was associated*

There were more disturbing self-doubts. The imminence of war cast a harsh light on the relevance of British cinema to the vital issues of the day. The chaos of inflationary post-war Germany, which Balcon had witnessed at first hand, and unemployment and the General Strike in Britain, the Wall Street Crash, German rearmament and the Spanish Civil War had found no place in the minds of film-makers preoccupied with the politics of Wardour Street. Balcon observed:

'Truly we were operating in a vacuum, making our contribution to the provision of what was no more than entertainment opium for the masses . . .'

Ealing's war

Early in 1939 he submitted a memorandum to Whitehall on 'How to put films to work in the national interest in wartime' and merely received an acknowledgment slip. Meanwhile, his first Ealing schedule included several films dealing with social concerns, among them the successful *The Proud Valley* (1939), with Paul Robeson. When war came the film industry was left to improvise; Balcon adjusted rapidly to this new state of affairs, and by 1940 Ealing's first war films were under way, *Convoy* leading the line. In 1941, alongside its quota of Ministry of Information shorts, Ealing put out *Ships With Wings* and began production on Thorold Dickinson's powerful *The Next of Kin* and Cavalcanti's *The Foreman Went to France* (both 1942), while maintaining its traditional comedy output – Will Hay and Tommy Trinder having joined George Formby in that department. The imaginative treatment of war themes was further developed in films like *Went the Day Well?* (1942), *Nine Men* and *San Demetrio, London* (both 1943) and *Johnny Frenchman* (1945). Government lack of interest (earlier Balcon had resisted a Whitehall proposal to commandeer Ealing Studios for storage accommodation) was now replaced by Churchill's almost embarrassingly close personal attention; he held up *Ships With Wings* and *The Next of Kin*, lest they occasioned alarm and despondency, until the chiefs of the armed forces secured their release.

Seen as a chapter in film industry, the interest of these films lies in their fusion of the narrative and documentary modes. An admirer of Griersonian documentary – it was Grierson who had brought Flaherty to him – Balcon now recruited documentarists to Ealing as a matter of deliberate policy. He made the perceptive comment that documentary is less a style than 'an attitude of mind', a useful gloss on Grierson's well-known definition of documentary as 'the creative interpretation of actuality'.

Happy anarchy

Ealing's finest hour, however, still lay ahead. The post-war comedies have a significance beyond that of the war films, whose matter and purposes were largely defined by the war itself; the comedies were necessarily and brilliantly original. Conceived during the years that had seen the rejection of Churchill as peacetime leader, films like *Hue and Cry* (1947), *Passport to Pimlico* and *Whisky Galore!* (both 1949) unerringly caught the public mood. 'There was a mild anarchy in the air,' said Balcon, and his team of talented writers – T. E. B. Clarke, William Rose, Michael Pertwee, Robert Hamer, Henry Cornelius – devised a series of ingenious and witty variations on the theme of the struggle of ordinary people against bureaucratic authority. Though writers' films, they depended less on dialogue than on action and incident, and what had been learnt in the war about filmic reality and the use of locations lent conviction to their make-believe.

The anarchy, let it be admitted, was always well under control and the assaults on the Establishment 'sallies' rather than 'onslaughts', and a reaction by younger men with more trenchant things to say about the state of the nation was inevitable. Yet the Ealing comedies, for all their indulgence, emerged from the experience of their generation and had their own unassailable authenticity; they had vitality, too, and a sense of social discovery.

Mr Balcon's academy

Post-war Ealing opened up other new areas to British cinema, literally in the case of *The Overlanders* (1946) and the other Australian and African films, such as *Eureka Stockade* (1949) and *Where No Vultures Fly* (1951). Charles Frend's *Scott of the Antarctic* (1948) and *The Cruel Sea* (1953) further extended the narrative-documentary style, while dramas such as *Against the Wind* (1948) and Charles Crichton's fine *The Divided Heart* (1954) stemmed from the war and its aftermath.

Ealing, lacking financial reserves, had always lived from film to film. Disaster struck in 1955 when a bank overdraft led to the sale of assets, of which the studio was the chief. Deprived of a base, Balcon's central principles of production, continuity and community no longer obtained. Stressing the importance of common purpose and free exchange of ideas, he had once described a production unit as 'a sort of Soviet'. His witty and well-loved colleague the writer and producer Monja Danischewsky characterized Ealing, with a different emphasis, as 'Mr Balcon's Academy'. There is no contradiction: that there was a genuine exchange of ideas, without regard to hierarchy, under Balcon, is undoubted; that the headmaster had the last word no less so.

Although Balcon's career did not end with the passing of Ealing, his later years were largely taken up with the politics of survival for independent production in Britain. During his retirement he gave much of his time to the encouragement of young film-makers. He would listen to the views of some young aspirant with the same attention he would have shown to Antonioni or Jean Renoir.

He died in Sussex in 1978.

STANLEY REED

David Lean

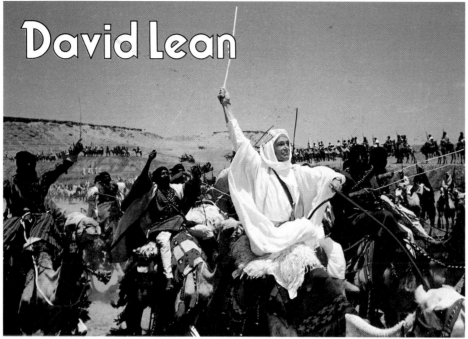

In Search of New Horizons

Lean's fascination with the effect of natural environment on character and motivation has led him to the wildest parts of the globe – a restless quest that is reflected in the powerful, contradictory emotions that sway his protagonists

David Lean is at once the most prestigious and most mysterious British film director; he is also perhaps the least understood, having an unenviable reputation among the most influential British and American critics. Lean's films, especially his later ones, attract huge audiences and win Academy Awards, yet the majority of commentators dismiss him as a brilliant technician without a personality, squandering needlessly inflated budgets on calculatedly tasteful spectacles. Rarely interviewed, Lean is widely regarded as remote and outmoded.

Lean has not been a prolific director but has preferred to be highly selective and to control every aspect of his productions; his perfectionist techniques have become legendary. His last three films have brought him much personal wealth, enabling him jealously to guard his privacy and leaving him free to travel extensively to research new projects. He is an intensely likeable man, very distinguished-looking, disarmingly modest about his own achievements and generous and perceptive in his praise of other people's.

The lonely sea and the sky
When asked what had attracted him to his latest project, an authentic account of the mutiny on the HMS *Bounty* and its bloody aftermath, Lean offered three reasons: the surprising youth of the protagonists (Fletcher Christian was 22 and Captain Bligh was 33 when the *Bounty* set sail), the fact that a mere three hours before taking the ship Christian had no such intention (in truth, he was intending suicide), and, most revealingly, his fascination with the terrible beauty of the empty ocean and the desperate struggle for

sanity and survival upon it.

These are important keys to the meaning of Lean's work which, since his breakthrough film *Brief Encounter* (1945), has dealt obsessively with the conflict between discipline and individualism, between a peculiarly British emotional reticence and Romantic excess. The widely contrasting locales of his later films – the jungle in *The Bridge on the River Kwai*

(1957), the desert in *Lawrence of Arabia* (1 the icy wastes of *Doctor Zhivago* (1965) wild Irish coastline in *Ryan's Daughter* (19 are no mere pictorial backdrops. Lean's acters are shaped by their social and phy environments and are constantly in co with them. They are placed in necess alien, inhospitable and challenging lands that offer a source of escape and self-disco

Lean's heroes and heroines are compu fantasists and fanatics, whether they be f in suburban railway stations, in deca

Above: David Lean behind the camera. Abo left: Lawrence (Peter O'Toole) leads his Be allies into battle in Lawrence of Arabia. *Below: Pip (Anthony Wager) encounters N Havisham (Martita Hunt) in Lean's fine adaptation of Dickens'* Great Expectations

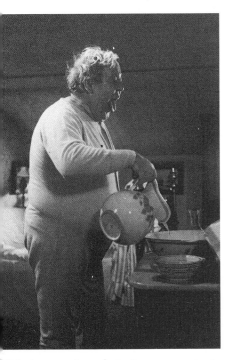

Victorian mansions, designing supersonic aircraft, on holiday in Venice, building bridges in Burma, forging myths from the sands of Arabia, or dreaming of escape from an Irish village torn apart by racial hatred and religion.

Running parallel to these assertive and tragic characters are the precisely delineated societies founded on class barriers, discipline, traditional values and moral complacency, all of which are challenged yet remain indomitable. Lean's is a deeply pessimistic vision, as evidenced by the fates of his characters: Laura, in *Brief Encounter*, renouncing love for drab security; Pip finding disillusionment in *Great Expectations* (1946); Mary, in *The Passionate Friends* (1949), driven, like Laura, to near-suicide and then a living death; *Madeleine* (1950) ostracized and condemned by the courts to spiritual limbo; Ridgefield, in *The*

Sound Barrier (1952), sacrificing a son for an obsession; Jane, in *Summer Madness* (1955), slipping back to her grey life; Nicholson, in *The Bridge on the River Kwai*, realizing, at the moment of his death, that the very quality that made him such a good leader – his iron fixedness of purpose – has made him a traitor to his country; Lawrence, in *Lawrence of Arabia*, destroyed by his own legend; Lara and Zhivago, in *Doctor Zhivago*, frozen into anonymity; Rosy Ryan, ostracized and damned, with a suicide and several shattered lives resting on her conscience. The few happy endings are equivocal, undermined by the compromises which make such endings possible.

Lean's films are pessimistic, but never grim. He is first and foremost a master story-teller, an entertainer with a fine sense of drama and humour, an ironist – a poet and imagist, as his frequent collaborator the playwright and screenwriter Robert Bolt has called him.

Lean was born on March 25, 1908, in Croydon, Surrey, the son of a comfortably-off accountant whose strict Quaker principles led him to regard film-going as a sinful waste of time and money. But when Lean went to a boarding school at Reading he spent hours at the local cinemas and took up photography. After briefly following his father into accountancy, he was encouraged by his mother and an aunt to take a job as a teaboy and general dogsbody at Gainsborough studios. This was in 1927, so Lean witnessed at first hand the arrival of talking pictures. He minutely observed how films were made (Anthony Asquith was one of the directors he studied) and quickly realized the importance of editing and how ability in that department might lead to direction.

By 1930 he had left Gainsborough to become

Above: Henry Hobson (Charles Laughton) wakes with a king-size hangover in Hobson's Choice – *a rare excursion into comedy for Lean, and his last black-and-white film. Below: Lean's Oscar for* The Bridge on the River Kwai *was the first won by a British director*

assistant editor of British Movietone News, then its editor, and in 1934 he joined Paramount-British where he cut 'quota quickies'. Lean's talents were recognized by the Hungarian emigré director Paul Czinner who invited Lean to cut *Escape Me Never* (1935). This success led to further prestigious assignments – Asquith's *Pygmalion* (1938), Gabriel Pascal's *Major Barbara* (1941), Michael Powell and Emeric Pressburger's *One of Our Aircraft Is Missing* (1941) among them – which earned Lean respect within the industry and a range of technical experience that was to form the backbone of his work as a director.

Utterly English

Lean's next big break came from Noel Coward who wanted someone to help him direct *In Which We Serve* (1942), which Coward had written and would star in. Coward sought Britain's most skilful editor and Lean found himself directing virtually the entire film since Coward apparently soon tired of the chore. Coward acted as producer and screenwriter in three further collaborations with Lean. *This Happy Breed* (1944) gave Lean his first solo director's credit and *Blithe Spirit* (1945) allowed him to experiment with comedy; but it was the third, *Brief Encounter*, that enabled Lean to impose his own essentially cinematic style and thematic emphases over Noel Coward's story. One of the British cinema's enduring masterpieces, it is open to a variety of interpretations, but is immaculate in its detail and depiction of a certain strata of British society.

Great Expectations and *Oliver Twist* (1948) both furthered Lean's reputation as a director and remain the best adaptations of English literature ever filmed. It is difficult to choose between the two, but if *Great Expectations* is the more profound work, echoing Dickens' growing maturity and brilliantly evoking the darkness surrounding the characters in its combination of fairly-tale and social realism, *Oliver Twist* is the more ambitious, with some vivid characterizations – particularly Alec Guin-

Above: part of the magnificent half-mile-long set of the Moscow streets designed for Doctor Zhivago. *Below: Sarah Miles as the romantic dreamer Rosy Ryan in* Ryan's Daughter

ness' Fagin – and some stunningly executed sequences, such as the climax with Sikes on the roof which utilizes both Russian montage theories and German Expressionism.

Based on H.G. Wells' novel, *The Passionate Friends* re-examines some of the themes found in *Brief Encounter*. The film starred Trevor Howard and Lean's actress wife Ann Todd (they divorced in 1957). *Madeleine* is a visually striking Victorian melodrama in which Ann Todd plays an upper-middle-class girl who is accused of poisoning her former lover, a destitute Frenchman. Madeleine is tried for murder but the case against her is 'unproven'. It is a bleak, unresolved story that contains Lean's most elaborate attempt to examine the hypocrisies of 'polite' society.

These early films were produced by Cineguild, a company founded by Lean, producer Anthony Havelock-Allan and cameraman Ronald Neame. In 1952, Cineguild was disbanded and Lean went to Alexander Korda's ailing London Films to make *The Sound Barrier*, written by Terence Rattigan and starring Ralph Richardson as a typical Lean hero driven by an obsession (designing a supersonic plane) which consumes both his family and his humanity. After *Hobson's Choice* (1954), a delightful Victorian comedy with the incomparable Charles Laughton as a drunken bootmaker whose chauvinism is successfully challenged by his eldest daughter, and *Summer Madness*, another return to *Brief Encounter* territory with Katharine Hepburn as an

American schoolmarm frightened by romance in a gloriously visualized Venice, Lean teamed up with producer Sam Spiegel to make *The Bridge on the River Kwai*.

One of the key British films of the Fifties, this film uses the basic framework of the 'war is futile' genre for an exemplary study of military codes and conduct. While confined in a remote Japanese POW camp, Lean's extraordinary hero Colonel Nicholson builds a bridge to boost morale among his dejected troops, to show the enemy what British soldiers are made of and,

finally, to justify a meaningless life in enforce[d] exile. His moment of self-revelation come[s] when he attempts to foil an Allied raid on h[is] beloved bridge, resulting in the deaths [of] several of the commandos taking part. His cr[y] 'What have I done?' is a tragic epitaph.

Lawrence of Arabia, scripted by Robert Bolt, [is] perhaps Lean's greatest film. Far from being a[n] objective analysis of Lawrence the film project[s] his *legend*, his contradictions and tortured sou[l] as a subjective Homeric adventure. The film [is] arranged as a continuous mirage, showin[g] Lawrence's self-delusion as an almost biblica[l] hero – if not a god – who achieves th[e] impossible and has power over life and deat[h]. Rich in characterization and social obser[v]ation, it also united Lean with cameram[an] Freddie Young, whose 70mm composition[s] and colour texturing are astonishing.

Epics of passion

Lean, Bolt and Young turned *Doctor Zhivag[o]* into MGM's biggest hit since *Gone With th[e] Wind* (1939), which it closely resembles in i[ts] love story engulfed by the tide of history (th[is] time the Russian Revolution). *Doctor Zhivag[o]* might lack the neurotic qualities that chara[c]terize Lean's best work but it still leave[s] cinemas awash with tears.

The pantheist imagery of Lean's work wa[s] most fully realized in *Ryan's Daughter*, a[n] ambitious and prohibitively expensive fil[m] mostly shot on location on the awesome wes[t] coast of Ireland and which was approximatel[y] three years in the making. Bolt's origina[l] screenplay reworks Hardyesque formulas int[o] a story about romantic excess and mora[l] cowardice, set during the Troubles of 1916 an[d] complete with overbearing priest, village idio[t] crippled war hero and sexless schoolteacher. I[t] is Lean's most extreme film, for his admirers [a] masterpiece and for his detractors the las[t] straw.

In 1980, despite financial difficulties and th[e] illness of his screenwriter Robert Bolt, Lean'[s] *After the Bounty* looked like getting off th[e] ground with Sam Spiegel producing, promis[ing] that Mr Christian, Captain Bligh and a ne[w] film by David Lean would soon grace ou[r] screens.   ADRIAN TURNE[R]

Filmography
1934 Java Head (ed. only). **'35** Escape Me Never (ed. only). **'36** Ball at Savoy (ed. only); As You Like It (ed. only). **'37** The Wife of General Ling (ed. only). **'38** Pygmalion (ed. only). **'39** Spies of the Air (ed. only); French Without Tears (ed. only). **'41** Major Barbara (some scenes only, uncredited; +ed); 49th Parallel (ed. only) (USA: The Invaders); One of Our Aircraft Is Missing (ed. only). **'42** In Which We Serve (co-dir. only). **'44** This Happy Breed (+co-sc). **'45** Blithe Spirit (+co-sc); Brief Encounter (+co-sc). **'46** Great Expectations (+co-sc). **'48** Oliver Twist (+co-sc). **'49** The Passionate Friends (+co-sc) (USA: One Woman's Story). **'50** Madeleine (USA: The Strange Case of Madeleine). **'52** The Sound Barrier (+prod) (USA: Breaking the Sound Barrier/Star Bound). **'54** Hobson's Choice (+prod; +co-sc). **'55** Summer Madness (+co-sc) (USA/GB) (USA: Summertime). **'57** The Bridge on the River Kwai. **'62** Lawrence of Arabia. **'65** The Greatest Story Ever Told (some scenes only, uncredited) (USA). **'65** Doctor Zhivago (USA). **'70** Ryan's Daughter. **'79** Lost and Found – The Story of Cook's Anchor (co-dir; co-prod; +narr. only) (NZ) (doc).

Down these mean streets

Raymond Chandler's famous quotation defines the world of the private eye in the Forties – and the movies of that decade have done much to popularize detective fiction over the years

Scholars are fond of pointing out that the earliest detective thriller was Sophocles' *Oedipus Tyrannus*, and indeed the play has every ingredient that was later to constitute the classic film thriller: nothing is what it seems, a secret (usually violent, often sexual) returns to haunt the present, and the corruption which is connected to that secret permeates society to the highest levels.

For all its classical antecedents, however, the film thriller has its roots in more recent culture. It was an accident of history that the birth of cinema coincided with the great age of detective fiction, but both were essentially popular art forms and movies soon drew on the weekly magazine thrillers for story material.

Arthur Conan Doyle's tales of Sherlock Holmes were hugely popular in Britain, while Edgar Wallace's sensational novels and stories tended to appeal to a less critical readership, though in France and Germany they were favoured reading among intellectuals.

The Sherlock Holmes stories are based around feats of logical deduction and therefore provide more 'polite' thrills. In the cinema, however, Sherlock Holmes movies were relatively classless in their appeal. From 1903 there have been few years without some screen adventures of Holmes and Watson. Although a good many actors played the roles, filmgoers remember best the teaming of Basil Rathbone and Nigel Bruce, as the sleuth and his trusty doctor friend. The partnership began at 20th Century-Fox with the highly atmospheric *The Hound of the Baskervilles* and *The Adventures of Sherlock Holmes* (both 1939) but the remainder of the Rathbone–Bruce films were made for Universal in the Forties.

Perhaps because spy stories were in vogue during wartime, the Victorian detective seemed out of step with the times. This may explain why Universal modernized its Sherlock Holmes films – like *Sherlock Holmes and the Secret Weapon* (1942) and *Sherlock Holmes in Washington* (1943). The films had little in common with the original Conan Doyle stories but there was a certain flair in the writing, and the two actors played their roles with a touch of humour.

The influence of Edgar Wallace, whose novels featured 'master criminal' types, can be seen in the early German and French thrillers. Fritz Lang's *Die Spinnen* (1919, *The Spiders*) and *Dr Mabuse der Spieler* (1922, *Dr Mabuse, the Gambler*) owe their conception of a supremely professional, diabolically gifted villain to Wallace and this notion was later to be returned to Anglo-Saxon culture when the German Expressionist film-makers emigrated to Hollywood and worked in the horror and thriller genres.

A simultaneous development of thrillers in the USA can be traced through the early American cinema. As early as 1912, D.W. Griffith looked forward to many of the motifs and themes found in later film thrillers. His short film *The Musketeers of Pig Alley* (1912) is set in a cul-de-sac where two gangs terrorize the already miserable inhabitants, daily victims of violence and civil corruption.

Griffith's interest in crime and corruption was not unique in this period. Thomas Ince's *The Girl and the Gambler* (1912) tells how a policeman infiltrates a gang in order to uncover the real boss, and George Irving's *The Wakefield Case* (1920) features a brutal detective who puts out a man's eye by shooting him at point-blank range.

With Prohibition, the nature of the thriller film changed radically. Organized crime became a major theme in the movies. On January 16, 1919, the 18th Amendment to the American Constitution became law. It prohibited the making, the sale and the transportation of alcoholic beverages in the USA. By 1933, when the law was modified, it had long become clear that Prohibition was unenforceable. Bootleggers and racketeers became organized nationally for the first time. As gangs fought over territorial monopolies, violence in the streets became an everyday affair. Citizens lost respect for the law by defying the rules on Prohibition and began to hold governmental and law-enforcing agencies in contempt for their impotence and inner corruption.

The city streets were the territory of the criminal and his constant companion, the detective. Only S. S. Van Dine's popular hero Philo Vance – usually played on the screen by the suave William Powell – still inhabited a rarified world where blood and violence remained unseen. It was the detective writer Dashiell Hammett who took crime out of the drawing room and thrust it into the streets. Those streets were not merely mean, they were savage places where blood, brutality and survival were the names of the game.

Hammett's first stories appeared in the pulp magazine *Black Mask* in 1922. Other contributors to this key source of later film stories included Raymond Chandler, Frank Gruber, Horace McCoy and James M. Cain.

Hammett's detective Sam Spade first appeared on

Top: Hollywood's versions of Conan Doyle's detective thrillers bore little relation to the originals, but Basil Rathbone as Holmes and Nigel Bruce as the good Doctor Watson were popular characterizations. Above: physical violence is no new phenomenon in thriller films; Fritz Lang's Spione *(1928, Spies) excels in the use of terror to manipulate the audience. Left: Lang's 'super-villain' Dr Mabuse (played by Rudolph Klein-Rogge) was modelled on the villains of Edgar Wallace's fiction, which exerted a powerful influence on the generation of German émigré directors in Hollywood who virtually dominated the genre of movie thrillers in the Forties*

Top: the epitome of the debonair detective was William Powell's portrayal of Philo Vance. Above: Siodmak's The Suspect *(1944), loosely based on the notorious Crippen murders, gave Laughton one of his finest roles. Above right: William Powell as Philo Vance, solving the mystery in* The Kennel Murder Case *(1933). Right: the killing of the diplomat in Hitchcock's* Foreign Correspondent *(1940)*

the screen in *Satan Met a Lady* (1936), an early version of *The Maltese Falcon*, but the time was not quite right for the tough, hard-boiled detective who moved through a thoroughly corrupt world. Hammett realized this and instead launched his famous Thin Man series of novels featuring the husband-and-wife detective team of Nick and Nora Charles. On the screen they were played by William Powell and Myrna Loy in a series of polished 'whodunnits' beginning with *The Thin Man* (1934).

In some cases the 'gentlemen' detectives like Philo Vance and Nick Charles provided a moral balance to the working-class gangster heroes of the great Thirties crime movies. Audiences could thrill to the actions of villains in *The Public Enemy* (1931) and *Scarface* (1932) but the last words of Tom Powers as he lies dying in the gutter in *The Public Enemy*, 'After all, I ain't so tough,' might stand as a moral judgment on all Thirties thrillers. On the other hand, the veneer of sophistication of *The Thin Man* style of thriller with its moral warnings and its sense of social reform appealed to the more optimistic mood of audiences in post-Depression America.

By the Forties, the era of the private eye had arrived. The figure was created and given flesh and blood by the writers Dashiell Hammett and Raymond Chandler. The private eye is the key figure of American cinema of the Forties; his task is to probe the dark areas of the American psyche. In the minds of most filmgoers the private eye, whether incarnated as Sam Spade or Philip Marlowe, is associated with the figure of Humphrey Bogart – to

Suave sleuths gave way to puzzled, probing private eyes in the thriller films of the Forties

the extent that it is no longer possible to read the novels or stories without seeing Bogart in the mind's eye and hearing his snarling tones.

In the novels of Hammett and Chandler, as well as in the films made from their work, the 'truth' is always something other than the supposedly all-important answer to the mystery. In *Murder, My Sweet* (1944), from Chandler's novel *Farewell, My Lovely* published in 1940, Philip Marlowe sets out to find a woman named Velma but is drawn into a murder mystery that, for most of the film, has little to do with his original mission.

The 'whodunnit' is, therefore, the superficial motivation of the thriller. Alfred Hitchcock used the world 'MacGuffin' to describe this motivational device: the subject in a film or novel about which the characters care intensely but for which we, as readers or viewers, care very little. Hitchcock's own relationship to the pure detective thriller is a fairly distant one. For him the fascination lies with the thrills of suspense not the who-did-what. *The Man Who Knew Too Much* (1934), *The Thirty-Nine Steps* (1935) and *North by Northwest* (1959) all revolve around spy rings, but the viewer's attention is diverted away from such conspiracies and towards the various kidnappings, chases and murder attempts through which Hitchcock manipulates his audience.

The detective novels and movies of the Thirties and Forties are full of 'MacGuffins' and viewers who complain that they do not understand who killed whom and for what reasons (in, for example, *The Big Sleep*, 1946) are on the wrong track. The 'truth' for Sam Spade and Philip Marlowe resides in what they find along the way and how they behave in the face of it.

Chandler himself described the detective better

than anyone else has done:

'He has a sense of character, or he would not know his job. He will take no man's money dishonestly, and no man's insolence without a due and dispassionate revenge. He is a lonely man and his pride is that you will treat him as a proud man or be sorry you ever saw him. He talks as a man of his age talks – that is, with rude wit, a lively sense of the grotesque, a disgust for sham and a contempt for pettiness.'

When the novels and films begin, the detective is already aware that things are not what they seem. Subsequently, he may be beaten, drugged, shot at, lied to, betrayed, threatened with everything from losing his licence to losing a limb. Yet he will survive, almost as if he were forced to undergo physical tests to prove that his code works, in the same way that he is obliged to produce moral proof of his incorruptibility in turning down bribes of money, power and sex.

He is not, however, perfect. In *The Maltese Falcon* for example, Spade has already betrayed his partner Miles by conducting an adulterous affair with Miles' wife. When Miles is shot, he suddenly rejects the wife and continues the investigation – in part motivated by feelings of guilt but also to avenge Miles' death. He is a hero of a sort but flawed and human – used, abused, tired and without many illusions, but still moving forward in an attempt to live up to his own code and justify it to himself. He is sexual, but not romantic in the usual sense of the word. He knows where that particular illusion leads, he can play the game but is nobody's fool.

The most accurate definition of the moral impulse behind the thriller novels also came from Chandler:

'Down these mean streets a man must go, who is not himself mean, who is neither tarnished nor afraid.' As the decade wore on, however, those streets got darker and meaner, and the men and women who had to go down them frequently became more than a little tarnished by the *noir* around them.   DAVID OVERBEY

Knights in Dark Armour

Students of Raymond Chandler, and of literary detective affairs generally, are inclined to complain that Chandler's novels have been degraded by their screen treatment. Yet, judged purely as films, of the eight major adaptations four are highly successful entertainments and two more are genre masterpieces. Chandler's hero, Philip Marlowe, is their common denominator

The main titles end. Immediately there is a harsh white light. The camera pulls back. A blindfold man is trapped in the glare. No establishing shots, no preparation for this sudden jump into the middle of a scene. Is the man a good guy or a bad guy? What has he done? Who the hell *is* he?

In its original context, for its contemporary audience, this was a splendid way for Edward Dmytryk's *Murder, My Sweet* (1944), also known as *Farewell, My Lovely*, to show Dick Powell, the pop-eyed crooner and romantic lead, moulding a new tough screen image. In retrospect, what better way to introduce Raymond Chandler's character of Philip Marlowe to the screen.

Dashiell Hammett's private eyes, Sam Spade and 'The Continental Operator', are cynical, and as complicit in the corrupt world as the racketeers and venal cops; but Chandler's Marlowe, though cynical, is a modern knight. Chandler directs us to this view in the opening of the first Marlowe novel, *The Big Sleep*. Over the entrance doors to his client's mansion is a stained-glass panel:

'. . . showing a knight in dark armour rescuing a lady who was tied to a tree . . . if I lived in the house, I would sooner or later have to climb up there and help him.'

For critic Gavin Lambert, he is the epitome of

Above: poster for Farewell, My Lovely. *starring Robert Mitchum, as the over-age Marlowe, and Charlotte Rampling. Right: Dick Powell in* Murder, My Sweet, *one of the first crime-films to depict the seamier side of detection*

Right: Bogart immortalized Marlowe in the highly successful film The Big Sleep. *Far right: lobby-card for* Lady in the Lake

ive should outrank the plot 'in the sense that
good plot . . . made good scenes'.

Hawks' film is packed with them, mo
involving Bogart and, curiously for a har
boiled movie, many of the most memorable ar
idiosyncratic love scenes between Bogart an
Lauren Bacall. Yet there is mayhem abroa
and a cloying sense of malevolent evil oozin
around in the movie which the passages
humour serve to intensify, never to diminis

Bogart's reliability, however, is rarely i
doubt. As much as Marlowe helped Bogart t
crystallize his own image, he made Marlow
an immortal.

Robert Montgomery directed himself an
elected to tell the story of the *Lady in the La*
(1946) entirely in a first-person camera styl
We see what Marlowe sees, so we only see hir
– and then rarely – as a reflected mirro
image. In theory this may have merit in tha
it attempts to duplicate the reading of a firs
person novel, but it is virtually the antithesis o
'direction', especially when Marlowe/th
camera looks at everything in slow pans an
at a lumbering crawl. The Chandler wis
cracks seem absurd when spoken by a di
embodied voice, and when we do see Marlow
he looks sleek, smug and far too happy. Reall
he isn't Marlowe at all.

Above: perhaps the least effective of the
Marlowe films, The High Window *starred*
former stunt man George Montgomery. Right:
James Garner probably used Marlowe *as a*
model in The Rockford Files. *The earlier film*
featured the up-and-coming actor Bruce Lee

an American good guy, fighting the evils of
power and greed:

'Marlowe wears loneliness and a monthly
income of maybe $400, like the badges of an
honest man, but knows the allure of the other
side.'

It is these qualities which make Marlowe the
screen private eye *par excellence*.

With Dick Powell's Marlowe, we sense a
layer of quality, of a 'good' family background
and upbringing, yet he seems more eager to
make a fast buck than some of his successors.
At times it's as though he is merely playing
detective for a bet. He greedily eyes *femme
fatale* Claire Trevor, ignoring the conversation
around him, as if in surprise at this unexpected
bonus. Then comes a drug-dream sequence.
Mists of confusion swirl round him when he
comes to – stubble-chinned, trying to keep
upright – and suddenly he gets angrier than
any other Marlowe, disgusted with himself for
being duped, so that the façade falls away and
the genuine Marlowe emerges for our
admiration.

Murder, My Sweet achieved Powell's aim of
turning his career around. He went on to
make other hard-boiled films in similar vein.
In 1953 he was back playing Marlowe in a
television version of *The Long Goodbye*.

Nowhere does Chandler ever really describe
Marlowe. The closest we get to a firm portrait
is more about the inside than the outside:

'I brushed my hair and looked at the grey in
it . . . The face under the hair had a sick look. I
didn't like the face at all.'

To most fans, Powell's successor had absolutely the *only* face 'under the hair'. The
director Peter Bogdanovich described how:

'His expression was usually sour and when
he smiled only the lower lip moved. There was

a scar on the upper lip . . .He held his cigarette
(a Chesterfield) cupped in his hand. He looked
right holding a gun.'

Humphrey Bogart, of course. If Marlowe is
the private detective *par excellence*, Bogart – in
The Big Sleep (1946) – is the Marlowe *par
excellence*, the touchstone for all others to
emulate or transcend. *The Big Sleep*, directed
by Howard Hawks, is a masterpiece. One of
the writers, Leigh Brackett, said of it:

'I did witness the historic occasion upon
which everybody began asking everybody else
who killed Owen Taylor, and nobody knew. A
wire was sent to Chandler, and he sent one
back saying, "I don't know". And, really, who
cared?'

Ms Brackett was absolutely right. This be-
wildering film demonstrates Chandler's own
dictum that the immediate scene in a narrat-

For *The High Window* (1947), also known a
The Brasher Doubloon, 20th Century-Fox cas
a young contract actor, George Montgomery
However, although he sports a moustache fo
'maturity', Montgomery is hopelessly out o
his depth with the subtle Marlowe characte
To be fair, though, little subtlety remains i
the script for him to work with. In contrast t
The Big Sleep there is virtually nothing *but* pl
and only a few good scenes in *The Hig
Window*.

The next Marlowe novel, *The Little Siste*
was published in 1949 but nobody rushed t
film it. *The Long Goodbye*, begun in 1950 an
published in 1953, had no initial takers eithe
Playback, published in 1958, is the weakest o
all the novels, and has still never been filmec
The movies' love affair with Marlowe wa
effectively over for twenty years.

Left: the original artwork for the poster of The Long Goodbye, *starring Elliot Gould. Above: the 1978 version of* The Big Sleep *paid homage to the Forties, many scenes being re-created from the Bogart film*

In 1959, the year Chandler died, Philip Carey appeared in a 'Philip Marlowe' television series. But memories of its one-year run are dim, save that Marlowe, virtually the inspiration for succeeding TV private-eye series, seemed more like a boy among men than the father-figure he effectively was.

The dark knight was losing his battle. Standards, attitudes, morals had changed in the twenty years since his creation. It was ten years before James Garner appeared as *Marlowe* (1969), adapted from *The Little Sister*.

Garner is a splendid actor, and in the Thirties would have given Cary Grant more than a run for his money, but in the Sixties and Seventies the Garner style was out of favour. Films like *The Skin Game* (1971) show him at his best but the suspicion remains that his true worth will only be fully appreciated as he becomes older, more of a 'character'. Even so, *Marlowe* is a successful attempt to update the book to the hedonistic Sixties. The film, however, concentrating as it does more on freaky frolics than forlorn failings, looks like an uncanny first-run for Garner's excellent television series *The Rockford Files* (1974–1980), which adopts the dark knight ethos quite brilliantly at times. In attitude Rockford *is* Marlowe, and as Garner *is* Rockford you can't get much closer.

Next came Elliot Gould, in *The Long Goodbye* (1973). This is the most contentious and – to purists – blasphemous adaptation. For, judging the literary Marlowe to be a relic from the dead past, director Robert Altman makes no attempt merely to adapt the book. When he has finished, Marlowe has been destroyed.

If *Murder, My Sweet* had a brilliantly apposite opening sequence for its time, so too does *The Long Goodbye*. From this shambling Marlowe – obsessed with feeding his cat the right brand of food – we instantly know not to expect anything Bogartian. This Marlowe is a lunatic: a moralist in an age of amorality, a romantic in an age of realism, an idealist in the age of Watergate, exactly as he is in the novels. The true Chandler feeling is more of an issue than ever before.

The film is as much a pastiche of the genre as it is a critique, has many moments of wit along with a sense of evil rarely matched in any of the other films, and a true sadness. Gould's performance is brilliant, and, appropriately, it was Leigh Brackett – a creator of the Bogart Marlowe – who wrote this iconoclastic adaptation, and said of it:

'Gould's Marlowe is a man of simple faith, honesty, trust and complete integrity. All we did was strip him of the fake hero attributes.'

The latest Marlowe, who has been more favourably received than Gould, is Robert Mitchum in *Farewell, My Lovely* (1975) – Dick Richards' remake of *Murder, My Sweet* – and in Michael Winner's remake of *The Big Sleep* (1978). The latter title transposed Southern California in 1939 to Southern England forty years on, taking full advantage of 'enlightened' censorship to explore the abhorrent sexual undercurrents which Hollywood had only been able to hint at in earlier versions. Most critics thought the result was 'ludicrous'.

Richards' film blithely ignores the conclusions drawn by Altman and sets its narrative in the Forties to return Mitchum to the ambiance of the *film noir* which first attracted attention to him. Although Richards' film opts to make Marlowe more sentimental in his dealings with the 'underprivileged' characters, and Mitchum's bulk and height are not really in keeping with the previous Marlowe incarnations, he is an unqualified success as the script chooses to emphasize the dark and bitter side of the character – made possible, and logical, by the fact of Mitchum's age.

Thus Marlowe on screen has come almost full circle, but surely Altman/Gould rather than Richards/Mitchum are showing us more of 'the truth'.   CHRISTOPHER WICKING

129

John Huston: Teller of Tall Tales

After forty years as a director, during which a bare half-dozen of his films have been acclaimed as masterpieces, Huston is today reckoned as little more than a story-teller. But posterity may well agree with James Agee that he was 'the most inventive director of his generation'

One of John Huston's most engaging character creations is Huston himself: the tall, craggily handsome, elegantly loping, irresistibly charming man with an insatiable zest for life – for horses, women, booze, gambling, adventure, work, reading, art, the Irish, and for almost everything else in the world.

It must be confessed that Huston's incorrigible love for a character and his seductive gift as a story-teller may have slightly obscured the record of his early life; and pleasant tales like that of the grandfather who won and lost townships at poker seem to have only flimsy foundations.

The clear facts are that Huston was born on August 5, 1906, in Nevada, Missouri, and christened John Marcellus. His father Walter Huston (1884–1950) moved from engineering to vaudeville and by the Twenties became a distinguished stage actor. With the coming of sound, the elder Huston drifted, inevitably, to

Hollywood. John's parents separated when he was still a child and he divided his boyhood between his father's theatrical lodgings and the hardly less erratic life of his mother, a newspaper-woman with a passion for travel and horses which she passed on to her son. As a child he was delicate; he once told the critic James Agee that he had cured himself – and at the same time acquired his life-long delight in adventure – by breaking out of a sanatorium nightly to plunge into an icy stream and shoot a waterfall.

In his teens he was a boxing champion. At 20 he made the first of several marriages. On account of his horsemanship he briefly held a commission in the Mexican army. He wrote a book which retold the story of *Frankie and Johnny* and is said to be a mature and accomplished work; this led to the publication of several of Huston's short stories in major magazines. Still restless, he lived as a café sketch artist in Paris, moved in the fringes of the Bohemian set in London, acted a bit, edited a New York magazine and finally arrived in Hollywood, where he married for the second time, in 1931.

Thanks to the influence of his father, who had so risen in the ranks of Hollywood actors as to have played the title role in D.W. Griffith's *Abraham Lincoln* (1930), Huston was taken on as a writer at Warners. His first assignment was to work on the script of *A House Divided* (1932) directed by William Wyler, who was only four years his senior but whom he came

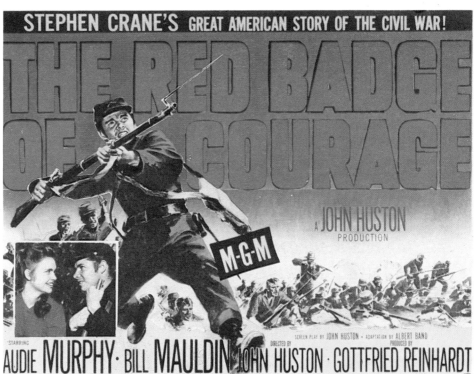

STEPHEN CRANE'S GREAT AMERICAN STORY OF THE CIVIL WAR!

THE RED BADGE OF COURAGE

A JOHN HUSTON PRODUCTION

M-G-M

SCREEN PLAY BY JOHN HUSTON · ADAPTATION BY ALBERT BAND · DIRECTED BY · PRODUCED BY

STARRING AUDIE MURPHY · BILL MAULDIN · JOHN HUSTON · GOTTFRIED REINHARDT

Far left: Huston the actor as Noah in The [Bi]ble – In the Beginning. *Above left: the 1948 [cl]assic* The Treasure of the Sierra Madre *in [w]hich Huston's father Walter (far left) teamed [up] with Bogart. Above: another of Bogart's [ro]les was in* Key Largo, *Huston's last film for [W]arners. Left: Bogart and Katharine Hepburn [o]n board* The African Queen. *Right: The Red [B]adge of Courage launched Audie Murphy's [br]ief career. Below: Captain Ahab (Gregory [Pe]ck) loses his battle with the white whale in [M]oby Dick*

regard as his master. The list of scripts on [w]hich Huston worked at Warners was im-[p]ressive: Robert Florey's *Murders in the Rue [M]orgue* (1932), Wyler's *Jezebel* and Anatole [Li]tvak's *The Amazing Dr Clitterhouse* (both [19]38), William Dieterle's *Juarez* (1939) and *Dr [E]hrlich's Magic Bullet* (1940), Raoul Walsh's [Hi]gh Sierra *and Howard Hawks'* Sergeant York [(b]oth 1941). Henry Blanke, who produced [se]veral Huston films, remembered him on his [ar]rival in Hollywood as 'just a drunken boy; [ho]pelessly immature. You'd see him at every

party . . . with a monkey on his shoulder. Charming. Very talented, but without an ounce of discipline in his make-up.'

By 1941, however, Huston had clearly convinced Warners that he was mature enough to be trusted with direction. Jack Warner told him that if he could make a screenplay out of Dashiell Hammett's *The Maltese Falcon* – already filmed twice before – he would let him direct it. Huston's version of the story is that as a first step he and the writer Allen Rivkin began simply breaking the novel into separate scenes and dialogue, but eventually left the task to Huston's secretary. This mechanical breakdown fell into the hands of Jack Warner, who pronounced it 'great' and told Huston to go ahead. Huston undoubtedly likes to give the impression that his work has been the result of this kind of 'accident' and chance and gag; but it seems a tallish story – particularly since on other occasions, more recently in *Wise Blood* (1979), Huston has avoided reworking to an unrecognizable degree the work of famous authors, but has chosen novels from which he can cleanly extract his scripts.

More convincing is Huston's account of the advice of his producer Henry Blanke: 'Shoot each scene as if it is the most important one in the picture. Make every shot count. Nothing can be overlooked, no detail overlooked.' The advice was evidently followed; the casting was perfect and Huston's first feature film remains, after 40 years, a classic.

Huston's succeeding films did not sustain the first promise. *In This Our Life* (1942) was a Bette Davis vehicle hurried out in the wake of the success of *Jezebel* and *The Little Foxes* (1941). *Across the Pacific* (1942) was a spy comedy-thriller reassembling most of the team from *The Maltese Falcon* to no great effect. Huston was then called to war service and made three short films for the army – *Report From the Aleutians* (1943), *San Pietro* (1945) and *Let There Be Light* (1946). The last, which dealt with mentally affected war veterans, was never shown; but it did provide Huston with valuable material and inspiration when he

came to make *Freud* (1962) 16 years later.

He returned to Warners to make another classic in 1948. *The Treasure of the Sierra Madre*, based on a novel by the mysterious writer B. Traven, had a theme which recalled *The Maltese Falcon* story and recurred throughout Huston's later work – a group of people in passionate, even murderous, quest for some object which will in the end prove only an illusion. Humphrey Bogart was teamed with Walter Huston in his most memorable performance. Huston's last assignment for Warners was *Key Largo* (1948), which had a fine cast (Bogart, Lauren Bacall, Edward G. Robinson and Lionel Barrymore) but remained an essentially stagebound adaptation of a pre-war play by Maxwell Anderson.

Huston's next film, *We Were Strangers* (1949), was less than successful, although a good deal of vitality remains in its story of Cuban revolutionaries tunneling, for slightly obscure reasons, through a graveyard. At MGM Huston enjoyed some success and won Oscar nominations for *The Asphalt Jungle* (1950), a taut story of urban crime filmed in the hard realistic style of the period. MGM, despite Louis B. Mayer's reservations, next permitted Huston to direct a favourite novel – Stephen Crane's *The Red Badge of Courage* (1951). Lillian Ross's book *Picture*, a day-by-day account of the making of the film, tells how it fell victim to studio politics in the days of MGM's decline, eventually emerging in a heavily cut 69-minute version. Still, much of the quality survives in the portrait of a boy's reactions to war and in the performance of Audie Murphy, a World War II veteran who was launched by the film into short-lived stardom.

The African Queen (1951), scripted by Agee from C.S. Forester's novel – with Bogart as the boozy riverboat captain and Katharine Hepburn as the starchy missionary who becomes his unlikely ally against the German army in Africa – was to be one of Huston's most successful films. It was also the first of several times that cast and crew suffered from his delight in adventure. He insisted on filming in

Above: The Asphalt Jungle – *which included Marilyn Monroe and Louis Calhern – won Oscar nominations. Above right: Richard Burton confronts Sue Lyon in the film of Tennessee Williams' play* The Night of the Iguana. *Far right:* The Misfits *was to be the last film for Clark Gable – here enjoying the company of Monroe*

the Congo, despite the heat, insects and disease which afflicted the unit – though not, apparently, the director. Errol Flynn, Trevor Howard and the unit of *The Roots of Heaven* (1958) were later to suffer even more in Chad.

Established as a major Hollywood director, from this point Huston seemed to lose clear direction and cohesion. Despite his feelings for art, the next film *Moulin Rouge* (1952) – with José Ferrer stumbling about on his knees in impersonation of the stunted Toulouse Lautrec – was a conventional Hollywood biopic. *Beat the Devil* (1953) – evidently seeking to retrieve the lost times of *The Maltese Falcon*, with Bogart, Peter Lorre and Robert Morley as a latter day Sydney Greenstreet – had the sort of slackness that has sometimes seemed symptomatic of Huston's tendency to see a film as a personal party. *Moby Dick* (1956), despite Huston's subsequent loyal defence of Gregory Peck's wooden performance, was a pale shadow of Herman Melville's novel. The bold experiments with colour, made in collaboration with the English cameraman Ossie Morris, were to be developed later in *Reflections in a Golden Eye*.

Huston's next major achievement was *The Misfits* (1961), which emerged from a stormy and much publicized production period as a

sad, elegaic drama of doomed people – a divorcee and three men hunting mustang in Nevada. Perhaps only Huston could have survived the constant attention of the press and nursed his ailing cast through Arthur Miller's script. There was Marilyn Monroe, suffering from acute personality disorders and drug dependence; Montgomery Clift in a comparable condition; and Clark Gable who was to die from a heart attack almost immediately after shooting was completed.

Huston also directed Clift in the actor's last major film role, *Freud* (1962), which failed to gain critical or commercial success. *The List of Adrian Messenger* (1963) was a gimmicky thriller; but Huston's adaptation of Tennesse Williams' *The Night of the Iguana* (1964) had at least a picturesque cast (Richard Burton, Ava Gardner and Deborah Kerr) and a good deal of vitality. Thereafter Huston lent himself to two costly commercial follies: Dino De Laurentiis' production of *The Bible – In the Beginning* (1966) and the James Bond film *Casino Royale* (1967), on which he was one of five directors.

Just when it seemed he was no longer an artist to be taken seriously, however, Huston returned to the peak of form with the haunting *Reflections in a Golden Eye* (1967), in which he won memorable and complementary performances from Elizabeth Taylor, Marlon Brando, Brian Keith and Julie Harris. Of the two failures that followed, *A Walk With Love and Death* (1969) had at least ambition to commend it – which *Sinful Davey* (1969), a prankish period comedy, did not. *The Kremlin Letter* (1970) was a comedy-thriller in the style of the period.

Then in 1972 came the second of the intermittent masterpieces which have marked

the latest period of Huston's career. The virile elegaic *Fat City* (with marvellous performances by Stacy Keach, Jeff Bridges and Susan Tyrell) is a very personal reminiscence of Huston's youthful period in the world of professional boxing. Huston remained curiously erratic, following up the film with the too easy-going *The Life and Times of Judge Roy Bean* (1972) – for once a writer, in this case John Milius, complained that Huston had betrayed his script – and an indifferent thriller *The Mackintosh Man* (1973).

Huston nevertheless responded to a chance to film a long-cherished project – *The Man Who Would Be King* (1975). Rudyard Kipling had been his favourite boyhood reading; he had planned to film the book several times before – intending it, in turn, for Walter Huston, for Gable and Bogart, for Sinatra, for Richard Burton and Peter O'Toole. The parts of the two English soldiers in India who briefly become rulers of a lost kingdom were finally played (after Paul Newman had turned down one of the roles) by Sean Connery and Michael Caine.

At the age of 74 Huston was to emerge as the director of a new and majestic work – *Wise Blood* (1979) – adapted from Flannery O'Connor's novel about the Southern 'Bible Belt' and with a script that follows its original almost as loyally as the scenario for *The Maltese Falcon*, made four decades before.

Huston, who began his career as a writer has retained a deep respect for the script. His best films have been taken from writers of the first rank and adapted with sincere appreciation and understanding of the originals. After Huston had filmed *A Walk With Love and Death*, its author Hans Koningsberger commented

Real books are seldom seen circulating in the movie world; its dealings are with the story outlines . . . Huston wanted to film a novel; not the movements of the people in a story, but the idea of the book.' Koningsberger found, indeed, that Huston's critical analysis put the book and its author to strenuous tests.

Journalists around a Huston set are always annoyed because there is really nothing of Huston's direction to see. The director tends to stand on the edge of the crowd and apparently leave things to the first assistant and the cameraman. 'I see my role', he said at the time of The Mackintosh Man, 'as that of the innocent bystander.' The fact is that his creative contribution to the performances starts early. 'The trick', he told Karel Reisz who interviewed him on the set of The African Queen and remarked how he simply left Hepburn and Bogart to get on with their performances on their own, 'is in the casting'. Whether dealing with a major star like Hepburn or comparatively unknown faces like Audie Murphy in The Red Badge of Courage or Brad Dourif in Wise Blood, with major roles or one-line supports, the very confrontation of the actor's personality and the part is a creative action. Marilyn Monroe, who played a small role at the start of her career in The Asphalt Jungle and made her last

screen appearance in The Misfits, said with characteristic perception: 'John watches for the reality of a scene, then leaves it alone.'

Part of this skill is no doubt due to his massive, affectionate curiosity about people and his delight in eccentrics – whether in real life or in fiction. And this quality is one aspect of his dominating gift as a story-teller. Like Hitchcock, his own curiosity infects the spectator, forcing him into a hunger to know more about each character, a compulsion to know what happens next – the true purpose of suspense.

When Agee wrote a Life profile of Huston – 'Undirectable Director' – in 1950, he had few reserves: 'The most inventive director of his generation, Huston has done more to extend, invigorate and purify the essential idiom of American movies, the truly visual telling of tales, than anyone since the prime of D.W. Griffith.'

'To put it conservatively,' he wrote elsewhere in the article, 'there is nobody under 50 at work in movies, here or abroad, who can excel Huston in talent, inventiveness, intransigence, achievement or promise.'

Agee was perhaps too close to his subject: he was shortly to start work with Huston on the script of The African Queen (1951); still, most critics of that period would have endorsed, more or less, his view. Thirty years and twenty-four films later, critical opinion has shifted. For the critic Robin Wood, Huston is only a story-teller; no artist because 'an artist must impress himself as a particularized individual voice, whether through style or through recurrent or developing themes; usually both'. So Huston falls short.

Agee saw certain dangers for Huston, it is true. He called him 'one of the ranking grasshoppers of the western hemisphere', who had 'beaten the ants at their own game'. He saw the dangers of a dilettante approach, saw qualities in his work that were 'free and improvisatory' and yet which could lead to a 'startling irresponsibility in so good an artist'. In the long view of history it seems likely that Huston's best work will be valued nearer to Agee's qualified acclaim than to the severer contemporary view.   DAVID ROBINSON

Filmography
1928 The Shakedown (extra only). '29 Hell's Heroes (extra only). '30 The Storm (extra only). '32 A House Divided (dial. only); Law and Order (dial. only); Murders in the Rue Morgue (dial. only). '35 Death Drives Through (co-sc. only) (GB). '38 Jezebel (co-sc. only); The Amazing Dr Clitterhouse (co-sc. only). '39 Juarez (co-sc). '40 Dr Ehrlich's Magic Bullet/The Story of Dr Ehrlich's Magic Bullet (co-sc. only). '41 High Sierra (co-sc. only); Sergeant York (co-sc. only); The Maltese Falcon (+sc). '42 In This Our Life; Across the Pacific (some scenes only). '43 Report From the Aleutians (doc) (+sc). '45 San Pietro/The Battle of San Pietro (doc) (+sc; +narr; +co-photo); Three Strangers (co-sc. only). '46 Let There Be Light (doc) (+co-sc; +co-photo) (restricted Service showings only). '48 The Treasure of the Sierra Madre (+sc; +act); Key Largo (+co-sc). '49 We Were Strangers (+co-sc; +act). '50 The Asphalt Jungle (+co-sc). '51 The Red Badge of Courage (+co-sc); The African Queen (+co-sc). '52 Moulin Rouge (+prod; +sc). '53 Beat the Devil (+co-sc) (GB-IT). '56 Moby Dick (+co-prod; +co-sc). '57 Heaven Knows, Mr Allison (+co-sc). '58 The Barbarian and the Geisha; The Roots of Heaven. '60 The Unforgiven. '61 The Misfits. '62 Freud (+co-sc; +narr) (GB: Freud – The Secret Passion). '63 The List of Adrian Messenger (+act); The Cardinal (actor only). '64 The Night of the Iguana (+prod; +co-sc). '66 La Bibbia (+act; +narr) (IT) (USA/GB: The Bible – In the Beginning). '67 Casino Royale (co-dir; +act) (GB); Reflections in a Golden Eye; The Life and Times of John Huston, Esq. (doc; appearance as himself only). '68 Candy (actor only). '69 Sinful Davey (GB); A Walk With Love and Death (+act); De Sade (actor only) (USA-GER). '70 The Kremlin Letter (+co-sc; +act); Myra Breckinridge (actor only); Bridge in the Jungle (actor only) (USA-MEX). '71 La Spina Dorsale del Diavolo (actor only) (YUG-IT-USA) (USA/GB: The Deserter; retitling for TV: The Devil's Backbone); Man in the Wilderness (actor only) (USA-SP). '72 Fat City; The Life and Times of Judge Roy Bean (+act). '73 Battle for the Planet of the Apes (actor only); The Mackintosh Man (GB). '74 Chinatown (actor only). '75 Breakout (actor only); The Wind and the Lion (actor only); The Man Who Would be King (+co-sc) (GB). '76 Hollywood on Trial (doc; narr. only). '77 Tentacoli (actor only) (IT-USA) (USA: Tentacles); Angela (actor only) (CAN). '79 Wise Blood (+act) (USA-GER); Jaguar Lives (actor only).

Below, far left: Marlon Brando and Elizabeth Taylor in an intimate scene from Reflections in a Golden Eye. Below left: Brad Dourif (right) and Harry Dean Stanton in Wise Blood. Below: Stacy Keach as the albino villain of The Life and Times of Judge Roy Bean. Right: The Man Who Would be King was based on a novel by Kipling – Huston's favourite author

The Maltese Falcon regularly attracts the accolade – rarely disputed – of the best thriller ever made. It is a prototype of the Forties *film noir*, a model of movie narrative; and in the short term it launched a whole series of pictures with Peter Lorre and Sydney Greenstreet as a kind of Laurel and Hardy of crime.

It was John Huston's first assignment as a director, the reward of ten years' outstanding work as a scenarist at Warner Brothers, during which time he had collaborated on a notable run of scripts including *Murders in the Rue Morgue* (1932), *The Amazing Dr Clitterhouse*, *Jezebel* (both 1938), *Juarez* (1939), *Dr Ehrlich's Magic Bullet* (1940) and *High Sierra* (1941), in which Humphrey Bogart had his first real starring role.

Huston – in his early years a soldier, bum, boxer, playboy, ham and writer by turns – could hardly fail to be sympathetic to the author of the original novel. Dashiell Hammett had left school at thirteen and had been a newsboy, freight-clerk, stevedore, advertising manager and Pinkerton Detective (he worked on the Fatty Arbuckle case) before turning to writing when struck by tuberculosis. As a novelist he revealed, through the improbable medium of pulp detective stories, a major literary talent.

The Maltese Falcon provided Huston with a theme that was often to recur in his subsequent films: a motley and dubious group of characters in passionate search of a treasure that, in the outcome, proved illusory. (It had been a popular literary theme at least as far back as Chaucer's *Pardoner's Tale*.)

Hammett's *The Maltese Falcon* had already been filmed twice before: in 1931 by Roy del Ruth, with

Directed by John Huston, 1941

Prod co: Warner Brothers. **prod**: Hal Wallis. **sc**: John Huston, from the book by Dashiell Hammett. **photo**: Arthur Edison. **ed**: Thomas Richards. **mus**: Adolph Deutsch. **mus dir**: Leo F. Forbstein. **r/t**: 100 minutes.
Cast: Humphrey Bogart (*Sam Spade*), Mary Astor (*Brigid O'Shaughnessy*), Sydney Greenstreet (*Kasper Gutman*), Peter Lorre (*Joel Cairo*), Elisha Cook Jr (*Wilmer Cook*), Gladys George (*Iva Archer*), Barton MacLane (*Lt of Detectives Dundy*), Ward Bond (*Detective Tom Polhaus*), Walter Huston (*Captain Jacobi*), Jerome Cowan (*Miles Archer*).

Bebe Daniels and Ricardo Cortez, and in 1936, as *Satan Met a Lady*, by William Dieterle, with Bette Davies and Warren Williams. Only Huston's version is now remembered.

George Raft had been offered the role of Sam Spade, but the actor was not prepared to risk his reputation with a new director; so Huston accepted Bogart instead. (In *High Sierra*, too, Bogart had succeeded to a role rejected by Raft.) Bogart had had a decade of gangster roles – in his first 34 pictures for Warners he was a jailbird in nine, electrocuted or hung in eight, and riddled by bullets in thirteen. *The Maltese Falcon* released him from this role and established his lasting image as the sardonic, romantic private detective, operating in a shadowy and seedy world of urban crime, thus launching the major period of his career.

One of Huston's later dicta was 'The trick is in the casting' and *The Maltese Falcon* proved this. Mary Astor, already 35, with twenty years of films behind her and near the end of her starring career, was cast as Brigid. She brought her great intelligence to the role:

'She was a congenital liar ("I am a liar. I've always been a liar") and slightly psychopathic. And that kind of liar wears the face of truth, although they send out all sorts of signals that they are lying . . . One of the tip-offs is that they can't help

A beautiful woman walks into the office of Spade and Archer (1), private investigators, with an assignment to follow a man, Floyd Thursby, whom she alleges (not very convincingly) has eloped with her sister. That night, Miles Archer, tailing Floyd Thursby, is shot dead. So, a few hours later, is Thursby. Sam Spade investigating the murders, is fascinated and attracted by the beautiful client (2) even though her mendacity extends to grave uncertainty over her name, which *may* be Brigid O'Shaughnessy.

Brigid proves to be one of a mixed group of shady characters: the others are the effeminate Joel

Cairo (3), Wilmur, a dim-witted young hood (4), and Gutman, the 'fat man' (5) – all in pursuit of a priceless antique; a jewelled falcon that once belonged to the Knights of St John of Malta. After complex deceits, counter-deceits, violence and murder, Sam Spade comes into possession of the Falcon (6). The machinations and the bargaining all prove fruitless when the bird turns out to be a fake (7). Realizing that it was Brigid who killed Thursby, Spade, with mixed emotions, hands her over to the police detectives Dundy and Polhaus (8), along with the rest of the gang.

2

3

breathing rather rapidly. So, I hyperventilated before going into most of the scenes. It gave me a heady feeling of thinking at cross purposes . . .'

The Hungarian-born Peter Lorre had been a favourite character actor in both America and Britain since his flight from Nazi Germany. Sydney Greenstreet had – after a brief period as a Ceylon tea planter in his youth – spent a lifetime as a stage actor. This was his first film, and at 62 he approached it nervously. The first scene he had to shoot was the demanding sequence in which Gutman spins out the history of the Maltese Falcon while anxiously watching Spade for the effects of the drugs he has given him.

Walter Huston, the director's father, made an uncredited appearance as the seaman who staggers into Spade's office with the Falcon and then drops down dead. The

elder Huston complained that this short scene demanded not only a whole day's work but left him black and blue from twenty takes and twenty falls.

However so many takes were exceptional. Huston had precisely scripted and pre-planned the film, the work went quickly and effectively with no changes or improvisations on the set, and The Maltese Falcon was brought in well under budget. Mary Astor recalls that on one occasion the complicated shot scheduled for a day was finished in seven minutes and two takes and the company spent the rest of the day at the pool. The picture was largely filmed in sequence, which relieved the company's general confusion about the complex plot – in which all the loose ends are, nevertheless, very neatly caught up by the end of the film.

Already Huston's self-effacing style was clear. The camerawork

has been appreciatively described by the critic (and later writer of The African Queen, 1951) James Agee:

'Much that is best in Huston's work comes of his sense of what is natural to the eye and his delicate, simple feeling for space relationships: his camera huddles close to those who huddle to talk, leans back a proportionate distance, relaxing, if they talk casually. He hates camera rhetoric and the shot-for-shot's sake; but because he takes each moment catch-as-catch-can and is so deeply absorbed in doing the best possible thing with it, he has made any number of unforgettable shots.'

It is perhaps that readiness in Huston to use methods not because they are orthodox, or modish, but because they are *right*, which gives his most memorable films the quality of always improving with time, rather than dating.

DAVID ROBINSON

7

8

'Bogie'

Left: the quintessential Bogart 'look'. Top: the almost universally forgotten A Devil With Women (1930), co-starring Mona Maris, was Bogart's second feature film. Shortly after making it, he vowed never to return to Hollywood. Above: the vampiric title role in The Return of Dr X (1939) was Bogart's only flirtation with the horror film

The name perhaps means more things to more people than that of any other Hollywood hero. Bogart's ugly-handsome face, perpetual cigarette and rasping voice bespoke a man who was nobody's fool, a loner but never an outcast

Humphrey Bogart was born in New York on January 23, 1899. His father, Dr Belmont DeForest Bogart, was one of the city's most eminent surgeons. His mother, Maud Humphrey, was a magazine illustrator. After completing his studies at Trinity School, Bogart entered Phillips Acadamy in Andover, Massachusetts. Expelled for bad behaviour, he joined the US Marines in 1918 and served several months. On his return to civilian life, he was hired by the theatrical producer William A. Brady, who made him his road manager and encouraged him to try his hand at acting. His first appearances were somewhat unconvincing, but Bogart persevered and gradually learned to master the craft.

In 1929 he was spotted by a talent scout in *It's a Wise Child* and put under a year's contract by 20th Century-Fox. At this period he was just a young stage actor with no particular following; the studio, uncertain how best to use him, tried him out in an assortment of genres. The results were uneven and unpromising and Bogart, after being loaned out to Universal for a brief appearance in *Bad Sister* (1931) – as a man-about-town who leaves his young wife in the lurch – returned to Broadway, convinced that he was through with the cinema for good.

In December 1931, however, he signed a short-term contract with Columbia and left the stage to star in *Love Affair* (1932), a comedy directed by Thornton Freeland. He then moved to Warner Brothers where he made, for director Mervyn LeRoy, *Big City Blues* and *Three on a Match* (both 1932), the second of which provided him with his first gangster role. He then returned to the theatre.

The decisive turning-point in his hitherto erratic career came in 1935 with Robert E. Sherwood's play *The Petrified Forest*, in which, for more than seven months, he played the gangster Duke Mantee opposite Leslie Howard.

When asked to repeat his role on the screen the following year, Howard insisted on Bogart fo his co-star. And so it was that, at the age of 3: Bogart finally gave up the theatre and began profitable career as a supporting actor unde the aegis of Warners, for which he would mak almost all his films until 1948.

Plug ugly

He made an average of one film every tw months for the studio, which filed him from th start under 'bad guys'. In four years he ha completed an impressive number of gangst roles, supporting such established actors a Edward G. Robinson, James Cagney an George Raft. The parts he played – frequentl double-crossers condemned to die an ignom nious death – were most often used to set th main star off to advantage. These character backgrounds remained obscure and their ps chology was extremely primitive. Several yea had passed since *Little Caesar* (1930) and *T Public Enemy* (1931); the gangster was n longer seen as a romantic figure, he was ju the flotsam of a sick society. Bogart, above a played the kind of small-time loser who cou always be outwitted by a strong adversary.

A few films, however, enabled him to escape from type-casting: *Isle of Fury* (1936), in which he was a reformed fugitive; *China Clipper* (1936), for which he donned the uniform of an ace pilot; and *Two Against the World* (1936), in which he played the manager of a radio station at odds with his unscrupulous employer. In *Marked Woman* (1937) he was a tough but kindly district attorney who succeeded in breaking up a gang of racketeers with the help of a nightclub hostess (Bette Davis); and in *Crime School* (1938), he was the liberal head of a prison, who established more humane relations between his staff and the troublesome young inmates.

These dissimilar roles, however, were not sufficient to modify the actor's predominant image, and it was not until Raoul Walsh's *They Drive by Night* (1940) that he was able to break out of the stereotype which had been imposed on him. Although his role was secondary to George Raft's, his playing of a truck-driver contending with the everyday problems of

Above left: as chief warden in Crime School *he had all kinds of problems with the Dead End Kids. Above right: in the gangster film* Brother Orchid *(1940) Bogart played his then usual role of a double-crosser. Right:* High Sierra *gave him the chance to show a human side. Below left: Bogart made a rare appearance in Western garb for* The Oklahoma Kid

travel fatigue and lack of money was concrete and recognizable. It reflected a realistic and documented context, and it embodied, however modestly, certain new attitudes to screen characterization.

In 1941, Bogart's luck suddenly changed for the better. He was given the lead in Walsh's *High Sierra* in place of George Raft (who had turned the part down). Although Ida Lupino had top billing (and gave one of her finest performances), it was Bogart, in the role of Roy Earle, an ageing and disillusioned gangster, who was the discovery of the film. For the first time he revealed a human dimension and depth which went beyond the requirements of the plot. Caught between loyalty to his old boss (who engineers his escape from prison for one last job) and the desire to start afresh with the young woman (Joan Leslie) whom he naively believes is in love with him, Roy is neither a hero nor a villain. He has a *history*, a past which weighs heavily on his present existence and offers him freedom only at the price of his own death.

The lone wolf

The Forties saw a radical change of direction in Bogart's career. As a result of the general anxiety caused by the war, the cinema gained in maturity, acquiring a new kind of gravity and urgency. *Film noir*, an eminently sceptical and ambiguous genre, came to the forefront and sought out heroes who would measure up to this increasingly troubled context. It was no longer an age for defying authority and not yet one for collective commitment. Neither gangster nor cop (but a little of both), the private eye asserted himself as one of the dominant heroic figures of the decade.

In 1941 this epitome of virile scepticism took on the features of Sam Spade. The character created in 1929 by the novelist Dashiell Hammett had already been twice adapted for the screen but without success; however the third version of *The Maltese Falcon*, which was more faithful than the others to Hammett's novel, hit the jackpot. Surrounded by a brilliant cast, Bogart perfectly illustrated the ethics of the private eye. Intransigent, totally independent, indifferent to the police yet wholly unself-serving, his Spade had absolute authenticity. The

Bogartian character had suddenly found its true physiognomy. He was, and would remain, a man who concealed his own needs behind a hard-bitten exterior, who rejected all higher principles and distrusted all abstract causes. He was a loner, who did not ask help from anyone.

Casablanca (1942) and *To Have and Have Not* (1944) both cast him in the midst of a cosmopolitan and divided world. In these films, fascists, Gaullists and refugees of every kind attempt to obtain his support but Bogart remains very much his own man. He acts solely according to his own inclinations: out of loyalty to a woman he has not forgotten (Ingrid Bergman in *Casablanca*) or to keep the love of the girl who has succeeded in winning his heart (Lauren Bacall in *To Have and Have Not*).

Cherchez la femme

Walsh had endowed Bogart with humanity in *High Sierra*; Huston gave him morality and the means to defend himself in *The Maltese Falcon*; Curtiz, in *Casablanca*, added to these a romantic dimension and a reason for living. At the beginning of the film, Rick, the hero, is shown to have taken refuge behind a mask of cynicism, in keeping with the unscrupulous political climate of wartime Casablanca. The unexpected arrival of the woman he has loved painfully reawakens his emotions, forcing him to renounce his pose of disinterested spectator. The film concludes with the need for commitment, one which concerned not only the hero but the whole of America. This moral framework reappears in *To Have and Have Not* in

Left: Bogart meets Bacall in To Have and Have Not. *Above left: with Ann Sheridan and George Raft in* They Drive by Night. *Above right: the moment in* Casablanca *when Bogart almost said 'Play it again, Sam' to Dooley Wilson. Right: in* Dead Reckoning *(1947) he finds that the trail of murder leads to the door – and the arms – of a femme fatale*

Carrolls. These off-beat performances had only a limited impact in comparison with *The Big Sleep* (1946), in which Bogart, once more working with Hawks and Bacall, played another mythical detective: Philip Marlowe.

Trouble is his business

Created by Raymond Chandler in the late Thirties, Marlowe was a more romantic character than Spade. More directly implicated in the action, more conscious of the values which he represented, he was engaged in a quest for 'hidden truth'. Without being a paragon of virtue he had a rigorous conception of honour. No other actor would catch as precisely as Bogart this character's blend of strength and derision, or his equivocal pleasure in venturing down the 'mean streets' and daily facing death.

As Bogart himself became a mythical figure, he would meet up with replicas of his former self. In *Key Largo* (1948) Bogart played, opposite Lauren Bacall, a role analogous to Leslie Howard's in *The Petrified Forest*, while Edward G. Robinson played a mean gangster reminiscent of Duke Mantee. There was the same kind of allusive interplay in *The Treasure of the Sierra Madre* (1948), in which John Huston offered Bogart one of the most unusual roles of his career: as an adventurer on the skids, who sets off in search of gold and meets a squalid death, a victim of his own greed. The casting of Bogart against type disconcerted audiences when the film was released but, little by little, the actor managed to make himself accepted in character roles.

The last seven years of his career saw him gradually abandon heroic parts. With the exception of *Beat the Devil* (1953), in which Huston attempted a parodic approach to Bogart's screen persona, the majority of his films were well-received, proving that the actor had established a lasting and authentic relationship with his fans.

As the producer at the head of his own company, Santana Pictures, Bogart made *Knock on Any Door* (1949), a socially conscious film which took a firm stand against capital punishment. Then, after two conventional action films, *Tokyo Joe* (1949) and *Chain Lightning* (1950), he played the part of a disenchanted

which the hero, Harry Morgan, is caught between the temptation of detachment and the need to struggle against fascism. But the motives for which Harry finally resolves upon action remain strictly personal. The director Howard Hawks, as was his custom, reduced plot and action to the minimum and emphasized the romantic banter of Bogart and Lauren Bacall. As their on-screen romance became genuine love, Hawks reworked entire sequences day after day to explore their remarkable chemistry. The narrative thus gives a marvellous impression of authenticity and intimacy, and the film remains one of the highlights of Bogart's career.

In 1945 Bogart, whose previous wives had been actresses Helen Menken, Mary Phillips and Mayo Methot, married Lauren Bacall, who was then 21 and would be his greatest partner. Since 1943 and the box-office triumph of *Casablanca*, Bogart had become one of the top ten Hollywood stars. The end of the war saw him return to *film noir*. In 1945 he twice played the role of a murderer: opposite Alexis Smith in *Conflict* and Barbara Stanwyck in *The Two Mrs*

Hollywood screenwriter who is subject t attacks of murderous violence in Nichola Ray's *In a Lonely Place* (1950). In *The Enforc* (1951) he was a district attorney up again Murder Inc. Shot in the semi-documentar style typical of Warners, it became a *film no* classic, particularly remarkable for the comp lexity of its editing and its powerful scenes violence. (Twenty years later it was discovere that the film's direction, credited to Bretaign Windust, was the work of Raoul Walsh.)

After the fourth, last and most disappointin film for Santana, *Sirocco* (1951), Bogart worke with Huston on *The African Queen* (1951). Ha comedy of character, half adventure movi totally and unashamedly implausible, th whole film was constructed on the confron tation of two personalities. Bogart gave one his most colourful performances as a grouch alcoholic transformed into a hero by a frigi devout spinster (Katharine Hepburn) in th throes of her first amorous stirrings. That yea the actor received an Oscar, a reward honou ing 20 years of a richly successful caree Modestly Bogart declared: 'I've been around

ong time. Maybe the people like me.'

With *Deadline USA* (1952), a vibrant plea for he freedom of the press, Bogart, with the lirector Richard Brooks, returned to the delnocratic inspiration of *Key Largo* and *Knock on ny Door*. The following year, Brooks cast him n *Battle Circus* as a sceptical and gruff military loctor, overfond of women and alcohol. In *The 'aine Mutiny* (1954), an ambitious Stanley kramer production directed by Edward Dmyt-yk, Bogart took on the part of Captain Queeg, i neurotic, dictatorial officer forcibly removed 'om command by his subordinates. The film vas an ambiguous reflection on power and esponsibility, in which the actor created an inusual character role. In Billy Wilder's *Sabina* (1954) he was the sarcastic heir of a rich amily in love with his chauffeur's daughter Audrey Hepburn). Made in the same year, oseph L. Mankiewicz's *The Barefoot Contessa*, ne of the most fascinating evocations of the vorld of Hollywood, definitively made Bogart n outsider, a witness. He plays a film director, Iarry Dawes, who watches the dazzling rise to tardom of a Spanish dancer (Ava Gardner)

and her tragic involvement with an impotent aristocrat. The narrator and spectator of action in which he cannot intervene, Dawes is the voice of Mankiewicz himself, the director's disillusioned double who embodies the magic of a vanished Hollywood. The actor's creased, serene face and understated performance brought both an exceptional resonance and a poignant sense of authenticity to the subject.

The commercial failure of the film, which was considered too literary at the time, led Bogart to return to more conventional roles in films of less interest: in Curtiz's *We're No Angels* (1955) he was a comic convict in company with Aldo Ray and Peter Ustinov; in Dmytryk's *The Left Hand of God* (1955) a sham priest taking refuge in a Chinese mission-house to escape the tyrannical war-lord whose adviser he has been. In William Wyler's *The Desperate Hours* (1955), already ravaged by the illness of which he was to die, Bogart played his last gangster role.

The long goodbye

In 1956 Mark Robson's *The Harder They Fall* cast him once more as a journalist, this time denouncing the boxing racket. Similar in mood to *Deadline USA*, it ended his career, if not in glory, then on an appropriately high note.

Bogart's relatively slow start was rapidly compensated for by the depth and variety of his roles from 1941 onwards. If the war years stand out by virtue of *The Maltese Falcon*, *Casablanca* and *To Have and Have Not*, after the war he was much freer in his choice of roles and was equally brilliant in socio-political films, thrillers and comedies. His last films reveal an actor totally identifying with his roles, enriching them with his own maturity, his unique capacity for understatement and irony.

Humphrey Bogart died of cancer on January 14, 1957. During the Sixties his reputation never ceased to grow until it reached the proportions of a cult. He possessed elegance, courage and insolence, and knew how to efface himself when necessary. Aggressive, precise, economical, his acting was astonishingly modern. Bogart remains today linked with the best that the American cinema has had to offer.
OLIVIER EYQUEM

Filmography
1930 Broadway's Like That/Ruth Etting in Broadway's Like That (short); Up the River; A Devil With Women. '31 Body and Soul; Bad Sister; A Holy Terror. '32 Love Affair; Big City Blues; Three on a Match. '34 Midnight. '36 The Petrified Forest; Bullets or Ballots; Two Against the World (USA retitling for TV: One Fatal Hour) (GB: The Case of Mrs Pembrook); China Clipper; Isle of Fury; The Great O'Malley. '37 Black Legion; Marked Woman; Kid Galahad (USA retitling for TV: The Battling Bellhop); San Quentin; Dead End; Stand-In. '38 Swing Your Lady; Men Are Such Fools; Crime School; Racket Busters; The Amazing Dr Clitterhouse; Angels With Dirty Faces. '39 King of the Underworld; The Oklahoma Kid; You Can't Get Away With Murder; Dark Victory; The Roaring Twenties; The Return of Dr X; Invisible Stripes. '40 Virginia City; It All Came True; Brother Orchid; They Drive by Night (GB: The Road to Frisco). '41 High Sierra; The Wagons Roll at Night; The Maltese Falcon. '42 All Through the Night; The Big Shot; Across the Pacific; Casablanca. '43 Action in the North Atlantic; Thank Your Lucky Stars (guest); Sahara. '44 Passage to Marseille; To Have and Have Not. '45 Conflict; The Two Mrs Carrolls; Hollywood Victory Canteen (guest) (short). '46 The Guys From Milwaukee (uncredited guest) (GB: Royal Flush); The Big Sleep. '47 Dead Reckoning; Dark Passage; Always Together (uncredited guest). '48 The Treasure of the Sierra Madre; Key Largo. '49 Knock on Any Door; Tokyo Joe. '50 Chain Lightning; In a Lonely Place. '51 The Enforcer (GB: Murder Inc.); Sirocco; The African Queen. '52 Deadline USA (GB: Deadline). '53 Battle Circus; Beat the Devil (GB-IT). '54 The Love Lottery (uncredited guest) (GB); The Caine Mutiny; A Star Is Born (voice only); Sabrina (GB: Sabrina Fair); The Barefoot Contessa. '55 We're No Angels; The Left Hand of God; The Desperate Hours. '56 The Harder They Fall.

Top left: an experienced prospector (Walter Huston) frowns grimly as his partner (Bogart) exhibits all the symptoms of gold fever in The Treasure of the Sierra Madre. *Below left: a 25-year gap in their ages did not prevent the marriage of Humphrey Bogart and Betty (Lauren) Bacall from being one of the happiest between two stars. Below: the cast of* The Caine Mutiny *(including Bogart, left, and Van Johnson, right) joke between takes*

John Garfield

Reading about the life and work of John Garfield can be a depressing experience. He died young in tragic circumstances and his reputation seems to have hardened into a set of tired clichés: East Side kid makes good; the first angry young man; the original rebel without a cause; the forerunner of Brando and Dean . . . and so on. There is now a heavy layer of glib journalistic varnish over his whole career and it has become difficult to believe in a real man

that the young love to hear but seldom dar act on. Above all he was attractive passionate, intense, sullen, even insolent, vitality and his sexual drive almost burst ou the screen. *This* is what he had in comr with the young Brando, with Dean, v Valentino in his day and with the Finne *Saturday Night and Sunday Morning* (1960

His success as Micky inevitably led to sim roles – a boxer on the run in *They Made M Criminal* (1939), an ex-reform-school boy *Dust Be My Destiny* (1939) and a broke impractical inventor in *Saturday's Chilc* (1940). But he also played a variety of ot parts from the war-blinded veteran of *De nation Tokyo* (1943) to Lana Turner's murc ous lover in *The Postman Always Rings T* (1946). He formed his own production c(pany for a brief period during which time starred in *Body and Soul* (1947) as a bc corrupted by success.

But the rebel label stuck, and his unha experiences with the House Un-Americ Activities Committee, which arose mai from his habit of supporting liberal cau (while not actually accused of anything, was blacklisted as an unfriendly witne sealed the stereotype. Unable to obtain wor Hollywood he returned to the theatre ironically achieved his ambition to play lead in *Golden Boy* only a few weeks before death of a heart attack at the age of 39.

Garfield was a serious, hard-working ac who might well have matured into a charac player in the Tracy class. He deserves to remembered as a talented and engaging m not merely as a symbol of adolescent rebelli
BRENDA DAV

As so often happens the publicity and press stories about Garfield had a basis in fact. He was born Jules Garfinkel (Julie to his friends) on New York's Lower East Side in 1913. His parents were Jewish immigrants from Russia and his mother died when he was seven. He came close to becoming a juvenile delinquent before being influenced by a brilliant teacher who was able to channel his excess energy into acting. As a youth he bummed across the States with a friend, taking whatever job came up and learning the realities of working life.

He then returned to New York and joined the Group Theatre in 1934. He was featured in many of their productions, but when they produced Odet's *Golden Boy* in 1937 Garfield, who had originally been offered the lead, was relegated to a supporting role. This disappointment led to his signing a seven-year contract with Warner Brothers who had been making him offers for some time. He insisted, however, that he should be allowed to make a return to the theatre every year.

At 24, therefore, he was on his way to Hollywood, a successful young actor in line for featured roles with a big company, his theatrical career safeguarded by contract. Within a year he was a star, thanks to Warners who cast him as the rebellious young musician Micky Borden in *Four Daughters* (1938).

This was where the Garfield legend began –

John Garfield – the loser – in We Were Strangers *(top)*, They Made Me a Criminal *(above) and* He Ran All the Way *(right)*

the interweaving of fact and fiction that led, in the end, to such a confusion between the actor and his roles that his name now stands for an attitude rather than a man. Garfield himself had little reason to be bitter or rebellious. He had had a tough childhood, he had seen the poverty and distress of the Depression years and his association with the Group Theatre indicated his left-wing sympathies. But he had been very lucky, was happily married and enjoyed his work. It was Micky Borden who was bitter and twisted. Micky was a cynical no-hoper who believed that the world was against him and who proudly wore an outsize chip on his shoulder. His eruption into the sweetly antiseptic world of *Four Daughters* was nicely calculated but far from new. He was the 'Heathcliff figure' that recurs regularly in romantic fiction and his appeal to young girls, both in the film and the audience, had little to do with his views or his talent but everything to do with sex. Micky was the personification of a teenage (at the time the word would have been 'bobbysoxer') dream. Scruffy and unshaven, a cigarette drooping from his lip, he sat at the piano despising everyone and articulating all the anti-authority arguments

Filmography

1933 Footlight Parade (extra). '38 Four Daughters. '39 Blackwell's Island; They Made Me a Criminal; Juarez; Daughters Courageous; Dus Be My Destiny; Four Wives. '40 Castle on the Hudson (GB: Years Without Days); Saturday' Children; Flowing Gold; East of the River. '41 The Sea Wolf; Out of the Fog; Dangerously They Live '42 Tortilla Flat. '43 Air Force; Thank You Lucky Stars; The Fallen Sparrow; Destination Tokyo. '44 Between Two Worlds; Hollywoo Canteen. '45 Pride of the Marines (GB: Forever in Love). '46 The Postman Always Rings Twice Nobody Lives Forever; Humoresque. '47 Body and Soul; Daisy Kenyon (guest); Gentleman' Agreement. '49 Force of Evil; Jigsaw (USA retit ling for TV: Gun Moll); We Were Strangers. '5(Under My Skin; The Breaking Point. '51 He Ran All the Way.

n the shadows

The dark, sordid and guilt-ridden world of *film noir* reflected the uncertainty and paranoia that gripped America in the Forties

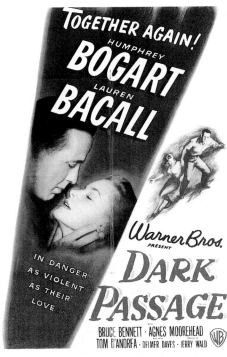

Film noir is primarily a visual style in cinema. It has its distinctive sounds – usually a plaintive, urban-bluesy soundtrack – but it is the look of *film noir* that most effectively defines it. The rain falling on the night-time city streets forms slick surfaces which catch and reflect the feeble light of street lamps and neon signs from cheap hotels, all-night diners and dubious bars. Through the rain and dimly diffused light, nothing can be seen clearly. Perspectives are distorted and the surfaces of the surrounding buildings conspire in an angular composition to give the impression of a claustrophobic trap. The slabs of shadow heighten the sinister atmosphere. This is a landscape fraught with danger, full of corruption, where moral and intellectual values are as ill-defined and murky as the streets. Nothing is what it seems, and the people who inhabit or move through the landscape pursue guilty secrets and dark motives that would not bear scrutiny under sunlight.

These images, distilled from American films of the Forties, made their impact most forcibly on French filmgoers and critics in the latter half of the decade. Throughout the Occupation American films were banned in France, but in 1945 a wave of Hollywood movies hit French cinema screens. Lacking a term of description, the French movie critics borrowed one from literature. The French editions of Raymond Chandler and Dashiell Hammett were published by Gallimard under the label *série noire* ('black series'). This prompted the term *roman noir* to be applied to hard-boiled detective novels in general and the use of the epithet *noir* with film was merely the next step.

It was, however, more than chance that an

aspect of American cinema should have appealed to French tastes. The mood of these films not only matched the despairing, nihilistic view of the world offered by French existentialist writers like Jean-Paul Sartre and Albert Camus, but it also recalled the romantic despair that characterized French cinema of the pre-war years.

In post-war America, the contrast between the dark distortions of *film noir* and the gaudy, buoyant Technicolor musicals of the late Forties reflected the shifting moods of a society rocked by a world war and stunned by the awesome potential of its new acquisition – the atomic bomb.

Sociologists have suggested that *film noir* may be read as a metaphor of 'the American nightmare' (the underside of 'the American dream'). To illustrate the theory, various social changes may be invoked: the disillusionment with pre-war values brought about by the direct experience of war; the exploding of accepted sexual and economic roles, as soldiers returned to confront a measure of female emancipation; and the realization that the peace and security so recently acquired was riddled with uncertainty and political paranoia.

One of the earliest examples of the *film noir* style, however, dates from the year the USA entered the war. *Stranger on the Third Floor* (dir. Boris Ingster, 1940) recounts a murder in a New York boarding-house committed by a stranger whom only the hero, Michael, can identify. When Michael is himself arrested for the crime, it is left to his girlfriend to track down the stranger, played by Peter Lorre in a performance which recalls Fritz Lang's *M* (1931). When his identity is revealed he is pursued through the streets until he is hit by a street-cleaning truck

Above left: Dark Passage *(1947) exploited with outstanding success the winning partnership of Bogart and Bacall. Above: not one review of* Scarlet Street *(1945) complained about Johnny (Dan Duryea) going to the chair for a crime he did not commit; the torture was for Chris (Edward G. Robinson) to go on living. Below: Lana Turner is the femme fatale from the roadside diner who gets her lover (John Garfield) to murder her husband in* The Postman Always Rings Twice *(1946)*

and makes his confession dying in the gutter.

All the key ingredients of *film noir* are present in this forgotten B movie, especially the atmosphere of unease and paranoia that hangs over the film's protagonists. For the next 15 years the *noir* style was set, and though it was most commonly seen in crime thrillers, it was also to manifest itself in other genres – melodramas, Westerns, horror films and even musicals. Although a case can be made for certain colour films, like Fritz Lang's *Rancho Notorious* (1952), to be classified as *film noir*, the *noir* style was more or less confined to black-and-white films until the late Sixties and early Seventies.

The 'look' of *film noir* was largely achieved by lighting, and the cameraman John Alton deserves the credit for adapting the techniques of German Expressionism to the 'realist' style of Hollywood in the Forties. Most scenes in *film noir* are lit for night. Shades are pulled down, ceiling lamps hang low and desk lamps diffuse harsh light at waist level – obscuring facial features and expressions. The use of oblique and vertical lines in the settings, lighting and framing (as opposed to the classic, horizontal tradition of American cinema) creates images of instability. As the critic and film director Paul Schrader wrote in his definitive essay on *film noir* (*Film Comment*, Spring 1972): 'No character can

speak authoritatively from a space which is continually being cut into ribbons of light.'

Figures are thrown into shadow by the use of low-key lighting and the main character is often directed to play his part and deliver his lines from the shadows, frequently blending into the urban landscape around him. In the camera direction of *film noir* other important changes can be detected. As Schrader put it:

'A typical *film noir* would rather move the scene cinematographically around the actor than have the actor control the scene by physical action. The beating of Robert Ryan in *The Set-Up* (1949), the gunning down of Farley Granger in *They Live by Night* (1948), the execution . . . of Brian Donlevy in *The Big Combo* (1955) are all marked by measured pacing, restrained anger and oppressive compositions.'

Finally, the use of flashback is often a crucial device in *film noir*. The main action has already happened. It is too late to change anything. Fate has taken its course and often the films, like the aptly named *Out of the Past* (dir. Jacques Tourneur, 1947), trace their own histories like a curse working itself out. In *Double Indemnity* (1944), for example, Fred MacMurray is bleeding to death, telling us what has happened as he dies. There is no question that anything is going to change. The trap was sprung before the film began. The device of the flashback or 'confessional' narration involves further ironies: the facts of the narration and the more objective images of the flashback scenes do not always tie up. When we listen to Fred MacMurray telling us of his first encounter with Barbara Stanwyck, he seems to be throwing much of the moral blame on her, but the images we are offered in the flashback scene are more ambiguous, the guilt is not easily attributable to one person.

The antecedents of the *noir* style can be traced back to the great period of German Expressionism, particularly in respect of lighting and settings and a heavily accented use of shadows. Thematically, the conflict between the 'interior' world of the individual and the 'exterior' world that repels him is one of the links between Germany of the Twenties and America of the Forties. Another, more direct connection is the presence in Hollywood of the director Fritz Lang, one of the architects of German Expressionist cinema, and of his 'inheritors': Billy Wilder, Josef von Sternberg, Robert Siodmak, Edgar

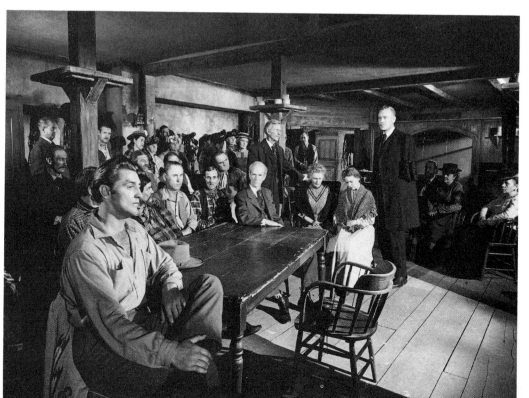

Top left: Laird Cregar and Alan Ladd in This Gun for Hire *– a detective movie that is shaped by the mood of* film noir. *Top: Robert Mitchum as the private eye whose past catches up with him in* Out of the Past. *Above: Gloria Grahame as the gangster's girl and Glenn Ford as the crusading cop in Fritz Lang's corrosive thriller* The Big Heat. *Left: Robert Mitchum as Jeb Rand with the lynch mob in* Pursued, *a Western filmed in typical* noir *style by cameraman James Wong Howe*

G. Ulmer, John Brahm, Otto Preminger, Max Ophuls, Douglas Sirk, Anatole Litvak and Rudolph Maté.

Film noir also derives from the influence of the French directors Carné and Duvivier, and it is interesting that, during his spell in Hollywood, Jean Renoir made an unusual contribution with *A Woman on the Beach* (1946). Another precursor of the *noir* style is the Hollywood gangster film, especially in the darkening, actual and metaphorical, of the Warner Brothers house style of the Thirties. Furthermore, it was from re-screening and closely studying these kinds of film that Orson Welles conceived and shaped the visual style of his masterpiece *Citizen Kane* (1940), the most significant of all the precursors to *film noir*.

The early manifestations of the *noir* style occurred in the hard-boiled thrillers of the early Forties: *The Maltese Falcon* (1941), *This Gun for Hire* (1942), *The Woman in the Window*, *Laura* (both 1944) and *Spellbound* (1945). But it was in the latter half of the decade that the sardonic tone of the music really jarred the nerves and the shadows began to cut their jagged path into the visual space. The viewer

---

In *film noir*, degradation and death seem to lurk in every nightmare alley, behind every venetian blind in every seedy apartment

---

Top right: Orson Welles and Charlton Heston in Touch of Evil *(1958), a thriller set in Mexico that testifies to the survival of the* noir *style into the Fifties. Above right: Eddie Constantine as secret agent Lemmy Caution interrogating a witness in Godard's* Alphaville, *a mixture of thriller and science fiction that clearly reveals its debt to Hollywood film noir. Right: Glenn Ford, an archetypal* noir *actor, on the familiar rain-swept streets in* The Money Trap

found himself on dangerous ground (a phrase that would serve as a symptomatic title of a later *film noir* by Nicholas Ray).

Seduced by the deadly sexuality of the *femmes fatales* (whom the critic Raymond Durgnat has termed 'black widows'), lured into the shadows by the calculating cinematography of John Alton, Nicholas Musuraca and John Seitz, and haunted by the desperate-sounding voice-over narrations, the filmgoers of the Forties could be forgiven a certain paranoia as the thrillers became darker.

Two crime films, both dating from 1949, *White Heat* (dir. Raoul Walsh) and *Gun Crazy* (dir. Joseph H. Lewis), make for an interesting comparison. In the first, James Cagney plays a psychopathic gangster, Cody Jarrett. Jarrett is clearly defined as a self-destructive criminal with a clinical history and a mother fixation, and shown to be on the path to his own apocalypse (self-immolation on top of a fuel tank). The protagonists of *Gun Crazy*, however, are a free-wheeling, Bonnie and Clyde-style couple who take to crime for no other reason than that it is seductive. Lewis offers neither reasoning nor excuses for their criminality; he merely lets it happen on the screen. *Film noir* protagonists are not 'explained', either by the films' narrative or

through the actors' performances. Explanations are of little value in a world of shifting moralities and crumbling certainties. Everything is suspect.

The protagonists frequently betray each other. Sam Spade (Humphrey Bogart) sends Brigid (Mary Astor) to jail in *The Maltese Falcon* because he sees through her manipulation of emotions and refuses to be her dupe. O'Hara (Orson Welles) leaves Elsa (Rita Hayworth) bleeding to death at the end of *The Lady From Shanghai* (1947) rather than play her fool. Glenn Ford, a detective in Lang's *The Big Heat* (1953), is an honest cop until he seeks revenge for the death of his wife, at which point he crosses over the moral line. The same actor plays a cop in *The Money Trap* (1965) where he goes on the take so that he can make enough money to keep his young wife happy. The Robert Mitchum character in *Out of the Past* leaves his nice girl for a romance with the *femme fatale* (Jane Greer) and lives to regret it. Perhaps most memorable of all is the betrayal of Joan Crawford in *Mildred Pierce* (1945). She plays a mother who sacrifices herself for her daughter only

to witness the daughter seduce her husband and destroy him. In this role Crawford is placed in the position of the betrayed, but in *film noir* it is usually the men – Richard Widmark, Robert Ryan, Richard Conte and, above all, Robert Mitchum – whose faces reflect the bewilderment of the audience; for the viewer, as much as the protagonist, is confused and double-crossed by the plot and cut off from the black-and-white morality of heroes and villains.

Even in the Forties Western, the last outpost of the 'good guys vs bad guys' formula, *film noir* made its presence felt. Raoul Walsh's *Pursued* (1947) – another highly significant title – explores the psychological roots of violence and vengeance as Robert Mitchum relives a childhood trauma and attempts to avenge his father's murder. Other genres exemplify the intersection of the *noir* style with contemporary interest in psychological problems: the cycle of horror films produced at RKO by Val Lewton collectively probe the human subconscious at a variety of levels. The most markedly *noir* of these movies is *The Seventh Victim* (1943); here the suicidal neuroses of the Jean Brooks character are used to remarkably chilling effect in this story of modern diabolism set in the boarding houses,

apartments and streets of New York.

Film noir continued well into the Fifties and wa in some measure, strengthened through its implic opposition to the coherent, comfortable image the world that President Eisenhower's admini tration sought to promote. Films like *On Dangerou Ground* (dir. Nicholas Ray, 1951) and *The Big Hea* by undermining the institutions of law and orde challenged the social values of the Fifties' con sumerist society, while *Kiss Me Deadly* (195 literally blew them apart.

Significantly, when *film noir* reappeared in th late Sixties and early Seventies in movies like *Poin Blank* (1967), *Klute* (1971), *The Long Goodbyr*, *Mea Streets* (both 1973), *Chinatown* (1974) and *Nigl Moves* (1975), the political situation was a clos parallel to that of the late Forties/early Fiftie America was engaged upon a faraway war agains communism – only the location had changed fron Korea to Vietnam. Back home, Watergate took th place of McCarthyism as the nation's longes running scandal and the movies once against sug gested that betrayal and corruption lay just beneat the surface.

Other national cinematic traditions of the Fortie passed under the shadow of *film noir*, notably th French, the British and the Japanese. The Frencl *nouvelle vague* and the so-called New Wave of Wes Germany in the Seventies both testified to renewe interest in *film noir*. Movies like Godard's *Alphavil* (1965) and Fassbinder's *Gorrer der Pest* (1970, *Goa of the Plague*) represent both a reworking of thei native *noir* traditions and a conscious evocation even tribute, to that dark era in American cinem so recently illuminated by contemporary criticism

DAVID OBERBE

Above: street violence in Martin Scorsese's Mean Streets, *a return to the sleazy underworld of* film noir. *Top left: Elliott Gould and Nina Van Pallandt in Robert Altman's* The Long Goodbye, *an idiosyncratic version of the Chandler story that reinvented a* film noir *context yet shifted some of its action away from urban settings. Top right: a more conscious evocation of Forties* film noir *in* Chinatown. *Jack Nicholson and Faye Dunaway could simply have changed places with Robert Mitchum and Jane Greer from* Out of the Past. *Right: Gene Hackman as the private eye Harry Moseby in* Night Moves, *Arthur Penn's modern* film noir.

Lovely Rita

Woman of mystery or happy-go-lucky girl-next-door? Rita Hayworth somehow blended the attributes of both in her screen personality. The result was irresistible

In John Huston's madly haphazard but inspired *Beat the Devil* (1953), Humphrey Bogart is led off by Arabs to a seemingly certain death. When next seen, however, he is in cosy conversation with the local sheikh who smiles benignly and says, 'And so you really know the lovely Rita?' while behind him hang dozens of glittering photographs of the star. The joke would not have been half as amusing had it not been founded on fact. From the Gulf of Aden to Brooklyn (where she was born in 1918), Rita Hayworth was *the* love goddess of films, the incarnation of eroticism in the post-war years.

That image of the free-living, sleekly sophisticated, sexual animal – fully realized for the first time in *Gilda* (1946) – was, nonetheless, consciously created by Hayworth and various collaborators, and was almost a decade in the making. In spite of her apparent defiance of convention – her much publicized series of marriages, divorces and romances – Hayworth and her co-workers have often denied that the image has much connection with her real personality. This denial is summed up by her

Above: this publicity shot of Hayworth taken in the early Fifties bears out Orson Welles' comment that 'she was one of those whom the camera loved and rendered immortal'. Right: in her first A film – Only Angels Have Wings

most oft-quoted statement. In an attempt to explain the failure of several of her marriages she once said: 'They all married Gilda, but they woke up with me.'

The lovely señorita

Hayworth started her career as a rather dumpy 13-year-old, dancing with her then-famous father Eduardo under her real name, Margarita Carmen Cansino, in various nightclubs, primarily in Mexico. Trained by her father, she became an accomplished dancer, especially to Latin rhythms. Joseph Cotten once commented later that 'no matter how bad the rest of the film, when Rita started to dance it was like seeing one of nature's wonders in motion.'

She was discovered by Hollywood in 1933. Warner Brothers turned her down after a test because she was overweight and her hairline was too low, but Winfield Sheenan, head of production at Fox, signed her; he was impressed with the way she held herself and her grace of movement. As Rita Cansino she danced briefly in a club sequence in *Dante's Inferno* (1935) and appeared in four mediocre films. When Fox merged with 20th Century Films, the new head of production, Darryl F. Zanuck, replaced her in the title role of the Technicolor *Ramona* (1936) with Loretta Young, and then cancelled her contract.

Hayworth freelanced her way through the tepid *Meet Nero Wolfe* (1936) and four forgettable Westerns.

Those of her admirers who claim with hindsight to be able to perceive all Hayworth's later qualities in those early appearances do her a disservice by disregarding the years of hard work and professional craftsmanship which made her a star. In these first films she was adequate in parts that called for little. The profile was there, as was a certain exuberance, but not much more.

A head start

Her husband, Edward C. Judson, then took a hand in her career. He insisted that she take diction lessons, put her on a diet, changed her makeup and way of dressing, and sent her to an electrolysist to have her hairline raised, therby broadening her forehead. Harry Cohn, boss of Columbia studios, saw her and liked what he saw. He signed her at $250-a-week (to rise to $1750 over seven years), changed her name – in part to conceal her past film work – and put her in a dozen programmers to let her gain experience and to find out what might be made of her. She was ambitious, patient and anxious to learn. When a good part in a good film came along, she was ready for it.

She got her chance in Howard Hawks' *Only Angels Have Wings* (1939). She was cast as the second female lead, playing Richard Barthelmess' flighty but ultimately loyal wife. She was good enough to be noticed by audiences and critics, and at least held her own with Cary Grant and Jean Arthur, the film's two main stars. George Cukor, a director with a keen instinct for a talented actress, had tested Hayworth in 1938 for the female lead in *Holiday* (subsequently given to Katharine Hepburn), but had felt she was too inexperienced. He remembered her, however, and borrowed her from Columbia for MGM's *Susan and God* (1940), starring Joan Crawford. Her role was not large but it was glamorous. The public quickly responded. Columbia began to churn out publicity photographs to satisfy her growing following; Cohn was aware that he had found a star, but he was not sure quite what to do with her.

He tried her in two A films: *The Lady in*

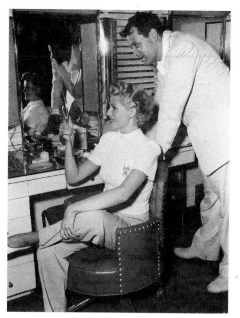

Question, (1940), which was the first time Hayworth was directed by Charles Vidor who would later collaborate on three of her biggest hits, and *Angels Over Broadway* (1940). The reviews were good, including those for Hayworth, but neither film did much business. Two other studios then showed Cohn Hayworth's real possibilities.

Warner Brothers had planned *The Strawberry Blonde* (1941) for Ann Sheridan. When she refused to do it at the last moment, the studio looked for an available second-level star whose size and colouring (in spite of the film being shot in black and white) would fit the costumes designed for Sheridan. Hayworth, who dyed her black hair to its now famous red, was thus given the role of the sunny gold digger out to steal dentist James Cagney from nice Olivia de Havilland. The film was a smash, as was Hayworth. After a minor comedy at Warners she was then loaned to 20th Century-Fox to replace Carole Landis (who refused to dye her hair red or to play an unsympathetic part) in Mamoulian's Technicolor *Blood and Sand* (1941). As Dona Sol, the noblewoman-temptress who temporarily steals bullfighter Tyrone Power from Linda Darnell, Hayworth was ravishing to look at. The film, quite rightly, was not very popular, but Hayworth received a great deal of attention. Between 1941 and 1942, her face appeared on the front cover of 23 magazines.

Naughty but nice
Although she played an unfaithful wife in one episode of Ben Hecht's *Tales of Manhattan* (1942), it was the lighter side of her role in *The Strawberry Blonde* that was emphasized in five films over the next four years – during which she established herself as a major star. She managed to be beautiful and erotic, in a 'nice' way – a girl-next-door whom women could admire and not worry if their men admired her as well, for she was never a conscious threat. She also returned to her origins as a dancer, becoming connected in the mind of her public with musicals. Until the late Fifties, audiences would eagerly await her big

Top: a young dentist (Cagney) manages to get a date with the girl of his dreams in The Strawberry Blonde. *Above, far right: Hayworth (left) in the musical* Down to Earth. *Right: both she and her then husband Orson Welles look pleased with her new, short, blonde hair-do created for* The Lady From Shanghai.

number(s) no matter what kind of film she was appearing in. Unfortunately her singing voice was weak, so that her songs were always dubbed (a closely guarded secret during her Columbia days). *You'll Never Get Rich* (1941) and *You Were Never Lovelier* (1942) had everything that musicals of the time needed for success – except colour – including songs by Cole Porter (for the former) and Jerome Kern (for the latter), with Fred Astaire appearing in both.

The plot of *Cover Girl* (1944) is silly and clichéd (will girl dancer make it on talent or beauty, remain with the poor dancer who loves her or run off with a wealthy playboy?), but that hardly matters, even when the film is seen today. Never more beautiful in colour (cameraman Rudolph Maté worked with Hayworth on her next four films and remained her favourite), she was teamed with Gene Kelly and 'sang' and danced to songs by Kern and Ira Gershwin. The film was the biggest hit of Hayworth's career up to then.

Down to Earth (1947) was planned before the release of *Gilda* and put into production just 18 days before that film's release. In it she plays a goddess (Terpsichore, the muse of dancing) who comes down to earth to help a young stage producer (Larry Parks) succeed on Broadway. The film was lavishly shot in colour. Hayworth looked beautiful and the

box-offices did good business. But the film w overshadowed by *Gilda*, which had provid Hayworth with a new image more in keep with the prevailing attitudes of post-w America. She had also discovered a n maturity as an actress. As the far-fro innocent *film noir* 'heroine' she was asked to a good deal more than simply look beauti and dance well. Although she would appe from time to time, in less demanding roles indifferent films, from *Gilda* until *The Mo Trap* (1965), there is a seriousness of intent a achievement in Hayworth as an actress oft overlooked by critics.

The thrill is gone
After *Gilda*, Hayworth's career slowly began fade. She continued to have box-office hits another seven years, but much of the exci ment and erotic charge of *Gilda* was lacki During those seven years, however, s made one of her finest films with her th husband Orson Welles, *The Lady From Shan hai* (1947). It was a financial failure when was first released, partially because it was

Welles film and not a Hayworth vehicle: h hair was cut and bleached; there were n dances (and just one, ironic, song); and he character did not even have the sympathet qualities that Gilda had possessed. Yet, wi *Gilda*, it is vintage Hayworth, and one of th finest films Hollywood made in the Forties. *Th Lady From Shanghai* cuts through every rom antic illusion and 'civilized' institution o which American society rests. The film wa years ahead of its time, and Hayworth rightl regards it as one of the best things with whic she has ever been associated.

Under a new Columbia contract (in whic she stipulated that she must always be pre sented sympathetically on screen), she becam a fun-loving, misunderstood Carmen in *Th Loves of Carmen* (1948), beautiful (in colou but unconvincing (especially with a woode Glenn Ford as her Don José). She returned t the screen after an absence of four year (during which she married and separated fro Aly Khan) in *Affair in Trinidad* (1952), a fade remake of *Gilda*. Entering the then popula

146

blical sweepstakes, she played a sympathetic, misunderstood *Salome* (1953) who dances to save John the Baptist. In the same year, obviously fighting a weight problem but full of mature sexuality, she played *Miss Sadie Thompson* in colour and 3-D. The inferior and splashy *Salome* made money, the delightfully flashy *Miss Sadie Thompson* did not.

At odds with Cohn, she turned down a project entitled *Joseph and his Brethren*, but made *Fire Down Below* (1957) playing very much third string to Robert Mitchum and Jack Lemmon. After her role as an older woman who loses Frank Sinatra to Kim Novak in *Pal Joey* (1957), she left Columbia (although in 1959 she did an interesting Western, *They Came to Cordura*, for the studio).

Right: Hayworth freshens up in Pal Joey, *which marked the end of a distinguished musical career. Below: GIs drool and Hayworth looks cool in* Miss Sadie Thompson, *one of several versions of Somerset Maugham's* Rain. *Bottom: Hayworth and Gary Cooper in a tender moment from* They Came to Cordura

'Zip', her delightful tongue-in-cheek strip in *Pal Joey*, also marked the end of her musical days. She now turned to drama as an ageing actress (*Separate Tables*, 1958), a suffering wife on trial for murder (*The Story on Page One*, 1959), and a suffering mother (*Circus World*, 1964), and to comedy (*The Happy Thieves*, 1962). The first was popular and got good reviews; the rest were failures with the critics and the public (although Hayworth herself was not bad in any of them). The old romantic team of Hayworth and Glenn Ford worked well in *The Money Trap*; the director, Burt Kennedy, generated a good deal of excitement in their scenes together. In the film, a dishonest cop (Ford) visits his old flame (Hayworth) who has fallen on hard times. Still beautiful, Hayworth fills her brief scenes with pain and an undercurrent of still-smouldering eroticism. The film was a commercial failure; when it was released for TV, Hayworth's intelligent performance had been cut for time. That, unfortunately, is the print which re-entered theatrical distribution.

Since then, Hayworth has worked in half a

dozen low budget films in the USA, Italy and Spain. Two – *I Bastardi* (1968, *Sons of Satan*) and *Sur la Route de Salina* (1970, *Road to Salina*) – are of more than passing interest because of her fine performances of what are similar parts, a drunken ex-actress and a down-at-heel café owner. Hayworth is now in semi-retirement, although she occasionally appears at various festivals. Whether she will work again is a moot point. Although she is willing, it is unfortunately true that good parts for actresses of a 'certain age' are few. Nonetheless, if she never returns to the screen, a good many of us can sit contentedly in our tents and take pleasure in the fact that we once had the privilege of knowing 'the lovely Rita'.

DAVID OVERBEY

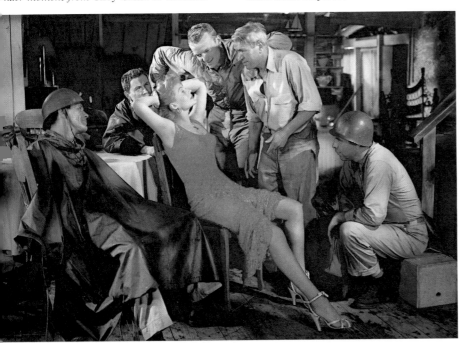

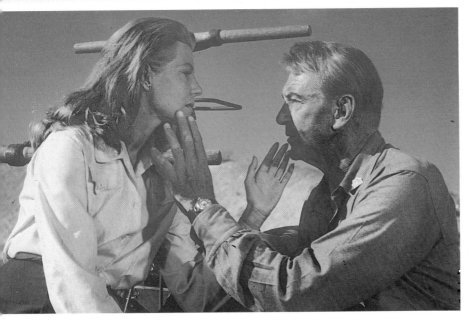

Filmography
1926 untitled short on folk dancing. '35 Cruz Diablo (extra) (MEX); promotional film for studio Spanish-language versions (short); Under the Pampas Moon; Charlie Chan in Egypt; Dante's Inferno; Paddy O'Day. '36 Human Cargo; Meet Nero Wolfe; Rebellion. '37 Trouble in Texas; Old Louisiana/Louisiana Girl (GB: Treason); Hit the Saddle. '37 Criminals of the Air; Girls Can Play; The Game That Kills; Paid to Dance (USA retitling for TV: Hard To Hold); The Shadow (GB: The Circus Shadow.) '38 Who Killed Gail Preston?; There's Always a Woman; Convicted (CAN); Juvenile Court; The Renegade Ranger (CAN). '39 Homicide Bureau; The Lone Wolf Spy Hunt (GB: The Lone Wolf's Daughter); Special Inspector (CAN); Only Angels Have Wings. '40 Music in My Heart; Blondie on a Budget; Susan and God (GB: The Gay Mrs Trexel); The Lady in Question; Angels Over Broadway. '41 The Strawberry Blonde; Affectionately Yours; Blood and Sand; You'll Never Get Rich. '42 My Gal Sal; Tales of Manhattan; You Were Never Lovelier. '43 Show Business at War (short). '44 Cover Girl. '45 Tonight and Every Night. '46 Gilda. '47 Down to Earth; The Lady From Shanghai. '48 The Loves of Carmen. '51 Champagne Safari/Safari So Good (doc). '52 Affair in Trinidad. '53 Salome; Miss Sadie Thompson. '57 Fire Down Below; Pal Joey. '58 Separate Tables. '59 They Came to Cordura; The Story on Page One. '62 The Happy Thieves (GER-SP). '64 Circus World (GB: The Magnificent Showman). '65 The Money Trap. '66 Danger Grows Wild (United Nations) (USA: The Poppy Is Also a Flower). '67 L'Avventuriero (IT) (USA: The Adventurer; GB: The Rover). '68 I Bastardi (GER-IT-FR) (USA/GB: Sons of Satan/The Cats). '70 Sur la Route de Salina (FR-IT) (USA/GB: Road to Salina); The Naked Zoo. '72 The Wrath of God.

Deadlier than the male

The *femme fatale* has always loomed large in the imagination of the tempted, tormented, lovelorn male, the creation of his own misgivings and inadequacies. He has projected her onto the screen as well, and in the Forties she found her rightful place in *film noir* – less as a tempest-tossed love goddess than as a sullen, heartless broad waiting in the dark to ensnare some faint-hearted fool with her slinky, seductive ways . . .

The *femme fatale* was always a fake. She lied, and made the husky, sincere whisper seem like a knife in the groin. But the men who created her lied too. Their bitter regrets about her duplicity, her corrupt loveliness and the need to send her to the electric chair were all a cover-up for the fact that they really wanted to live alone without thinking less of themselves.

She sauntered into innocent or weak lives, asking for a light but requiring the soul. She spread scent, languor, a mystically ultimate sophistication or depravity, her silky legs and the legend that some crime undertaken in the

Above left: Lola-Lola (Marlene Dietrich) lures the Professor (Emil Jannings) to his doom in The Blue Angel. *Above: Lulu (Louise Brooks) and one of her victims in* Pandora's Box. *Left: Rita Hayworth shows the dark, voluptuous side to her beauty*

dark would be as thrilling and as sweet as the unlimited, intricate experience she offered herself. That vicious, velvet spiral was the innovation that made masochism a new pleasure in the male sexual fantasy. Despite man's best efforts, the *femme fatale* was thinking of something else:

'But all of a sudden she looked at me, and I felt a chill creep straight up my back and into the roots of my hair. "Do you handle accident insurance?" '

She's not asking whether he's using a French letter; instead, there's a rich, stupid husband that they could remove. Taken from a James M. Cain novel, *Double Indemnity*, published in 1936, the she is Phyllis Nirdlinger and he is Walter Huff. Those are depressive names. Moviegoers know them better as Phyllis Dietrichson and Walter Neff: the man edgier, more deft and alert than his literary counterpart; the woman (related to that most iconographic enchantress, Marlene) so authoritative that she carries off the role as a burnished blonde.

We know Phyllis better still as Barbara Stanwyck, the Glendale Medusa in Billy Wilder's 1944 film version of *Double Indemnity*, the epitome of the *film noir* dark lady – all sexual innuendo and glamorous dishonesty. She seems sticky, alive with heat, a collection of surfaces begging to be touched – most of all the anklet she wears and which Fred MacMurray as Neff imagines 'biting into her leg'. That cunning detail was invented for the film – by the screenwriters, Wilder and Raymond Chandler – and it is the perfect promise of pain in pleasure, of jewellery being a mark of slavery, of narcissism as flirtation.

Who thought of the anklet? Wilder probably. So many of his other films have narrators like Neff who improve upon the visuals by verbalizing their inner thoughts. Yet Chandler's contribution to the film is surely significant, for his private-eye novels are gloomy with the conviction that good-looking dames are dishonest. Then again, it is important to remember that Cain's original novel is far more pessimistic than the movie. Cain had the illicit lovers go free. But their stew of evil and guilt is so intense that they are about to act out a suicide pact as the book ends, if Walter can trust Phyllis to keep her word. He contemplates her – the woman who has wrecked all their lives with her murderous scheming:

'She smiled then, the sweetest, saddest smile you ever saw. I thought of . . . the three little children, Mrs Nirdlinger, Nirdlinger, and myself. It didn't seem possible that anybody that could be as nice as she was when she wanted to be could have done all those things.'

The language is sentimental, nearly maudlin, which may be why Cain adopted such tough attitudes: the hard-boiled style is so often the disguise for a soft centre. Similarly the *femme fatale* is the creation of romantic dismay. She emerges from the rueful sense of the failure or impossibility of love. Thus she has her movie origins less in the quaint vamping of Theda Bara and other silent wantons than in the romantic agony of Germany in the Twenties and in the Surrealists' awareness that love yearned for is purer than love enjoyed.

America in the Twenties hardly dreamed of dark women. The *femme fatale* needs sound, so that she may say very little; silent heroines have to act out their good intentions. The city woman in Murnau's *Sunrise* (1927) is one

_bove: the devil in a black negligée – Hazel
_rooks in Sleep, My Love. Above right: sultry
_inda Darnell with Percy Kilbride and Dana
_ndrews in Fallen Angel. Right: ice-cold
_eronica Lake's first film with Alan Ladd.
_elow: Lizabeth Scott, sulky and ruthless, with
_umphrey Bogart in Dead Reckoning

_xample of allure; otherwise, Janet Gaynors
_ourished. And Louise Brooks had to go to
_ermany to make Die Büchse der Pandora
_1929, Pandora's Box), a film in which the
_ctress transcends the director G.W. Pabst's
_aution and reclaims the original author
_rank Wedekind's fascinated anguish for the
_lea of an anti-social goddess of ecstatic chaos.
_rooks may still be the greatest _femme fatale_
_ecause she is the least sinister or mannered. It
_s her compulsive vitality that is most danger-
_us. Although the men in _Pandora's Box_ are all
_er victims – prostrate, cowering or devastated
_y her energy – Brooks never makes Lulu two-
_aced. The film is _her_ tragedy, for her stunning
_ensuality can only rest after self-destruction.
_y the Forties, the dark woman was so much
_nore restrained, secretive and brooding: the
_ig sleep hiding beneath her fur coat was so
_minous a haven. But Lulu's preoccupation
_vith life and the moment makes all the men

look feeble, stilted or malicious.

Only one year later, in Germany still but
about to be transported to Hollywood, Marlene
Dietrich's enigmatic smile understood all too
well. Dietrich moved more slowly than any
other actress, taunting the viewer to see the
absurd, delirious fatalism, and covering her
mischief with the pretence of helplessness.
Clearly it is not her fault, Lola-Lola suggests in
song at the end of _Der Blaue Engel_ (1930, _The
Blue Angel_), if the men who dote on her get
hurt – men like the professor who, destroyed,
creeps away to end the life she has exposed as
bogus. But when Josef von Sternberg brought
her to America, Dietrich altered. Weight and
spontaneity fell away like worry. Sternberg
willed a colder, more serene image and, in his
own words, 'disguised her imperfections and
led her to crystallize a pictorial aphrodisiac'. In
terms of plot, some of her Paramount films
could be called happy (or fulfilled), but their
thematic consistency is the amusement that
knows the thought of love and sex – the
aphrodisiac image – is greater than the thing
itself. Sternberg made love-letter movies that
always end with a sighing 'alas' and Dietrich's
face like a light burning in the memory.

Together they made the word _fatale_ resonant: their best films – _Morocco_ (1930), _The

Scarlet Empress (1934), _The Devil Is a Woman_
(1935) – are superbly taut constructions in
which desire faces futility. There is less cruelty
in them than there had been in Twenties films,
and far less moroseness than there would be in
Forties films, just the delicious realization
(torture but bliss) that looking and dreaming
are more romantic than embracing. No
wonder the cinema's greatest surrealist, Luis
Buñuel, remade _The Devil Is a Woman_ more
than forty years later as _Cet Obscur Objet du
Désir_ (1977, _That Obscure Object of Desire_), with
the man's mixed feelings of lust and love
manifested by two actresses in the central role.

_'How can a man be so dumb . . . I've been
waiting to laugh in your face ever since I
met you. You're old and ugly and I'm sick
of you – sick, sick, sick!'
Joan Bennett in_ Scarlet Street

Sternberg's Dietrich seemed too cynical, or
too enlightened, for America in the Thirties.
The great majority of movie women loyally
aspired to the commercial code of romance.
There were 'bad' women – Bette Davis, most
notably – but they were ugly-pretty villain-
esses who got their just deserts. Vivien Leigh's
Scarlett O'Hara may have helped secure the
place of conniving beauty, but it was only in
the Forties that the Hollywood _femme fatale_
came into her own as a deceitful beauty who
lures men to their doom. Why was this? Was it
the accumulated loss of confidence of the
Thirties with the new male dilemma of being
overseas, wondering what the women were
doing at home, and dreaming of betrayals that
would prove only to be suspicions? Or was it a
reflection of deeper fissures in American sexual
relations? This becomes a distinct possibility
when you consider the chronic self-pity that
beholds the _femme fatale_, and because the acts
of treachery are the first signs of an independent woman coming onto the American
screen. Jane Fonda as a latter-day _femme fatale_
in _Klute_ (1971) is an interesting example of the
woman men cannot trust growing into someone who controls her own destiny.

It is important to see how far the bitch had
been defined in the Thirties in the work of
writers like Cain, Chandler and Dashiell Hammett. Their misogynist distaste is actually
more hostile than anything filmed. Indeed,
they can hardly conceive of women as anything other than loyal doormats or snakes in
the grass; Mary Astor as the scheming Brigid
O'Shaughnessy in _The Maltese Falcon_ (1941)

149

was too old and too stable for the part – as if Hollywood had not yet quite understood the fickleness of such women.

Ida Lupino had actually given a far better performance in *They Drive By Night* (1940) where she plays a woman of many moods and radiant falsehood. Lupino played good girls too – and she was seldom exotically glamorous – but she had no equal at taking on men.

So many actresses in the Forties responded to the low-key of *film noir* by adopting the same image. Veronica Lake also looked mysterious – in *This Gun for Hire*, *The Glass Key* (both 1942) and *The Blue Dahlia* (1946) – but there was nothing substantial behind the lock of hair. Ann Sheridan – in films like *They Drive By Night*, *Nora Prentiss* (1947) and *The Unfaithful* (1947) – often looked as if she had been slow-cured in cigarette smoke. Rita Hayworth was a crazy-eyed traitress for her baby-faced husband, Orson Welles, in his *The Lady From Shanghai* (1947), and was otherwise cast as

temptresses and reptiles. The stealthy apparition that was played by Joan Bennett in *The Woman in the Window* (1944) was a lovely throwback to the Germanic dread of a woman who will lead the settled bourgeois gentleman astray; surely Fritz Lang, who directed the film, appreciated her in this and *Scarlet Street* (1945), and Bennett herself enjoyed the lazy animal frivolity of the parts. She had the cutest pout until Gloria Grahame came along.

There are others, less well-known, but worth recalling: Jean Brooks in Mark Robson's *The Seventh Victim* (1943); Linda Darnell in Otto Preminger's *Fallen Angel* (1945); Lizabeth Scott in John Cromwell's *Dead Reckoning* (1946) – beguiling until she talks; Jane Greer in Jacques Tourneur's *Out of the Past* (1947); Hazel Brooks in Douglas Sirk's *Sleep, My Love* (1948); and maybe even Gloria Swanson in Wilder's *Sunset Boulevard* (1950), the ultimately grotesque distortion of female glamour.

And Lauren Bacall? Well, yes and no. Bacall

Above left: Ann Sheridan, who was known as 'the Oomph Girl', with Robert Alda in Nora Prentiss. *Above: the tarty, conniving 'Lazy Legs' (Joan Bennett) sneers at Chris Cross (Edward G. Robinson), the man she has led on and lived off in* Scarlet Street

in *To Have and Have Not* (1944) and *The Big Sleep* (1946) plays the *femme fatale*, but the framework of the films makes it clear that she is only pretending in order to be one of the boys. Howard Hawks and Humphrey Bogart never ask a moment of unkindness from her; they both recognize that she is a grown-up adolescent 'hiring out to be tough'. It is the cleverest compromise: the girl-next-door pretending to be the angel of death, sophistication without threat. Yet in both these two early Bacall films she was the invention of male dreams – just as the *femme fatale* was always a phantom that men invoked to justify their own fears.

DAVID THOMSON

They lived by night

The hero of the *film noir* was usually in a place where he knew he shouldn't be, perhaps lurking in the shadows of a dark street – the rain glistening, a harsh neon sign flashing – ready to keep an assignation with his intended victim, or maybe his own death. If he wasn't the dupe of some woman, of his own shady past, or just a guy entangled with fate, then he was probably a cold killer with a twisted smile . . .

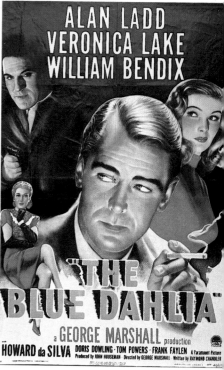

Above: in The Blue Dahlia *Ladd is a man suspected of his wife's murder and Lake is a woman who picks him up. Left: time runs out for Jeff (Robert Mitchum), trapped by his ex-girl (Jane Greer) and her gangster-lover (Kirk Douglas) in* Out of the Past

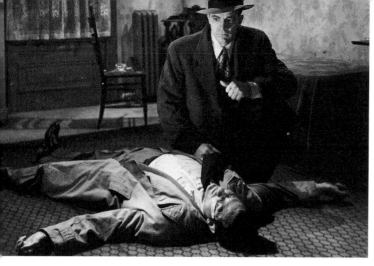

Above: Dana Andrews as the brutal cop who accidentally kills a murder suspect in Where the Sidewalk Ends. Above right: Clifton Webb, as the suave murderer Cathcart, with William Bendix in The Dark Corner. Far right: Dan Duryea as the pimp in Scarlet Street. Below: Tommy Udo (Richard Widmark) and Nick Bianco (Victor Mature) in Kiss of Death

In the introduction to their survey of the bad men of Hollywood movies, The Heavies, Elizabeth and Ian Cameron suggest that 'the Heavy's suitability for his part is more a matter of appearance than it is of good acting'. This is a good general rule, but like most rules it has its exceptions. Probably the most obvious one is Robert Mitchum, whose forceful presence on the screen is so dominating that it is hard to credit any director with complete control over the actor's performance.

A more interesting exception, however, is Clifton Webb. In his first two sound films, Otto Preminger's Laura (1944) and Henry Hathaway's The Dark Corner (1946), Webb turned in magisterial performances as fragile but deeply treacherous aesthetes; he then took on the anodyne role of Mr Belvedere, a dreary bachelor baby-sitter in the comedy Sitting Pretty (1948) and never really got the chance to be nasty again. Webb was a talented actor, but what made his first two appearances so menacing was not so much the parts themselves as the grim romanticism of the sweet-smelling but foul world of darkness and vio-

lence that was film noir, which made the roles possible in the first place. The context of film noir gave an extra twist to the mannered severity of Webb's performances.

Film noir can be seen as a movement that for the first time allowed the traditional heavies to act as well as 'be'. Dealing as it did with claustrophobia, paranoia, fear and despair, and finding its natural home in B rather than A features, film noir required – even demanded – ambiguous heroes and villains rather than the clean-cut dramatics of 'good guys versus bad guys'. If, historically, the bad guy has always been the best role, in the tainted world of film noir there were no good guys anyway, only bad and ambiguous guys.

Such roles allowed a number of actors to shine: Dana Andrews, Richard Conte, Dan Duryea, Farley Granger, Alan Ladd, Charles McGraw, Fred MacMurray, Victor Mature, Robert Mitchum, and Richard Widmark – to name but a few. Take Fred MacMurray, for example. Prior to Billy Wilder's Double Indemnity (1944), his jocular easy-going nature (later re-established when he played the

'I killed Dietrichson – me, Walter Neff – insurance salesman – 35 years old, no visible scars – till a while ago, that is. I killed him for money – and for a woman. It all began last May . . .'
Fred MacMurray in Double Indemnity

---

understanding father in a number of Disney pictures of the Sixties) had cast him as a bland, second-string male lead. Double Indemnity revealed the possibility of emptiness behind that bluff good-humour. The insurance salesman he plays is rapidly and willingly corrupted by the pitiless woman (Barbara Stanwyck) who seduces him into murdering her husband. Caught between the puritan rigidity of Edward G. Robinson as the father-figure claims-investigator and Stanwyck's cold temptress, MacMurray was the perfect fall guy. If it was Billy Wilder who caught the exact desultory quality of urban Californian life (just as Michael Curtiz did with Mildred Pierce in 1945), it was MacMurray's performance that gave the film its tragically fatalistic trajectory.

Farley Granger, who, unlike MacMurray, had no screen persona to be twisted out of skew but simply looked fallible enough to play the terse nice guy in Hitchcock's Strangers on a Train (1951), is fooled by an insane offer from the mad Bruno (Robert Walker) to exchange

murders. Both performances were to haunt their creators, but outside the confines of film noir the deranged personalities they projected had little substance.

If MacMurray and Granger drifted quickly in and out of the shadows of film noir, Dan Duryea and Dana Andrews regularly walked down the mean streets of Hollywood in the Forties. Duryea, with his striped suits and fancy neck-ties, light sneering voice and petty sadism (which was to flower into true psychosis in Westerns like Anthony Mann's Winchester 73, 1955), was the small-time hustler pimping his way to the top of the heap. He perfected the role of the smiling corrupter in films like Mann's The Great Flamarion, Fritz Lang's Scarlet Street (both 1945) and Robert Siodmak's low-key Criss Cross (1949).

If Duryea was essentially working-class, Dana Andrews' chiselled, aristocratic features – he had disconcertingly cold, piercing eyes and a sense of disillusionment to match – suggested he came from the better side of town. Looking like a nice guy, more often than not he turned out to be false – and an evil influence. For Preminger, he was a confidence trickster in Fallen Angel (1945), a philanderer in Daisy Kenyon (1947) and a detective on the make in Where the Sidewalk Ends (1950) – all roles which had their origins in the neurotic detective of Laura.

The contrast between the working-class and

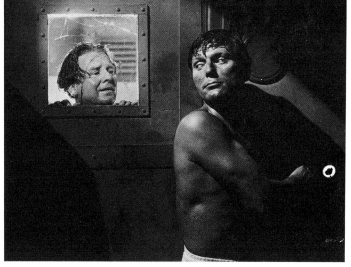

aristocratic backgrounds of such villains was paralleled by the different styles of the out-and-out hoods who also populated *film noir*. Thus Charles McGraw and Victor Mature brought a sweaty, hulking viciousness to their roles, while Richard Conte and Alan Ladd offered a more austere and disdainful violence. McGraw is best remembered as the heavy who takes great delight in turning up the steam in a Turkish bath on a trapped Wallace Ford (playing the fall-guy role usually reserved for Elisha Cook Jr) in Mann's *T-Men* (1947). McGraw later graduated to Western heavies, but Victor Mature's gross, strong-man presence proved surprisingly adaptable beyond the confines of *film noir*. Nevertheless, in films like Hathaway's *Kiss of Death* (1947) and Siodmak's *Cry of the City* (1948), he gave his venal gangster and sanctimonious policeman a particularly appealing doomed innocence.

Between 1945 and 1955, Richard Conte played the Hispanic or Italian hood so often that in 1972 Francis Ford Coppola used him in *The Godfather* to give an added touch of mythical 'realism' to the film's Mafia backdrop. A smart dresser, Conte brought a determined stylishness to the criminals he played in films like Hathaway's *Call Northside 777* (1948). He was even more successful as the wealthy psychiatrist in Preminger's *Whirlpool* (1949), proving his wife's innocence and thereby sending the hypnotist (José Ferrer) to the chair for murder. But it was primarily as an upper-crust gangster that Conte made his way suavely through the Forties.

If Conte's characters were always men who ran or worked for 'the Organization', Alan Ladd, from the moment of his first appearance as the fragile killer of Frank Tuttle's *This Gun for Hire* (1942), was always a man alone. Though George Stevens' Western *Shane* (1953) provided Ladd with his best-known role as a loner, his gangster films provided his best moments. Even better than his performance as the amoral private detective in Stuart Heisler's *The Glass Key* (1942) was his ex-serviceman suspected of murder in George Marshall's *The*

'I'm asking you . . . where's that squealing son of yours? You think a squealer can get away from me, huh? You know what I do to squealers? I let them have it in the belly. So they can roll around for a long time thinking it over'
    Richard Widmark in Kiss of Death

Blue Dahlia (1946). Veronica Lake was his co-star in both.

The two actors who best call to mind *film noir* of the Forties, yet survived as stars, are Richard Widmark and Robert Mitchum. Widmark's film debut, in *Kiss of Death*, was one of the most dramatic ever. As Tommy Udo, his skin stretched taut over his skull, he giggled maniacally as he vented his sadism on those around him. With a slight shift of character, he mixed gruesome sentimentality with gross sadism in his finest role as the three-time loser in Sam Fuller's *Pick Up on South Street* (1953). He has proved his versatility with differing roles in films by such diverse directors as Ford, Siegel and Minnelli – and even played the hypochondriac victim in the elaborate Agatha Christie period piece, Sidney Lumet's *Murder on the Orient Express* (1974).

If, in the Forties, Widmark was an actor who was all flashes and sparks, Robert Mitchum was the deepest of Hollywood's actors. Laconic in the extreme, he was the brooding man of action who suggested he had not only an inner self but intelligence as well. And Mitchum has survived more bad films than most actors. A one-time heavy in Hopalong Cassidy films, he graduated early in the decade to tough-guy roles in grander Westerns and war films and then, in 1947, turned in superb performances in two of the most stunning *films noirs*. The first was Raoul Walsh's *Pursued*, the blackest ever 'psychological Western' with its great, looming close-ups and doomed revenge structure; the second was Jacques Tourneur's *Out of the Past*. The latter had Mitchum as a man caught between the past – represented by a gangster (Kirk Douglas) and their former mistress (Jane Greer) – and a hopeless future with his girl (Rhonda Fleming). Forced to return to the past to save his future, he is doomed from the start.

With the arrival of the Fifties, Mitchum extended his range until by the late Sixties he had become a major star. Yet ironically, as the Seventies closed and remakes became popular in Hollywood, Mitchum was called in to be the tough guy again, playing detective Philip Marlowe brilliantly in Dick Richards' *Farewell, My Lovely* (1975) then disastrously in Michael Winner's *The Big Sleep* (1978).

Like Duryea, Ladd, Widmark and the others, like the directors, writers and lighting cameramen who together assembled *film noir* from a myriad of influences, Mitchum took the opportunity in the Forties to explore the dark side of life to the hilt. The results were some outstanding films and performances. PHIL HARDY

Above left: Charles McGraw turns the heat on Wallace Ford in T-Men.
Above: the gangster (Richard Conte) gets the drop on the cop (Victor Mature) who used to be his pal in Cry of the City. *Below: anxious moments for Guy (Farley Granger) in Hitchcock's* Strangers on a Train

On with the show

By the end of the Thirties musicals had lost their popularity. Band singers, skaters, even swimmers were recruited to bolster their appeal

When the Fred Astaire–Ginger Rogers team broke up in 1939 after *The Story of Vernon and Irene Castle*, it was the end of an era. Gone were the suave elegance and deco chic of the Thirties and gone was the musical based on the romantic tussles of a dancing team – for although people kept looking for a new partner for Fred Astaire, he never found one for more than two films together.

There had been another type of Thirties musical which was based on romantic teamwork – for instance, the well-upholstered operettas which had Jeanette MacDonald and Nelson Eddy trilling at each other in all kinds of fancy period rig-outs. But this couple's days were also numbered: the inseparables were increasingly separated and the end came when in 1942 they tried to go modern with an ill-fated version of the Rodgers and Hart stage show *I Married an Angel*.

Obviously tastes were making that noticeable, if not exactly definable, shift which seems to occur at the end of every decade. Musicals, apparently, were particularly vulnerable to this change. In the early Thirties they had hit an unexpected slump and had been labelled 'box-office poison' until in 1933 the genre was revitalized with the *Gold Diggers of 1933* and *42nd Street* – both of which had a new superspectacular formula, courtesy of Busby Berkeley. Now, once again, all the sure-fire formulas seemed to have worn out their efficacy: even Berkeley had left his old home at Warner Brothers to try his luck at MGM and elsewhere. No-one knew for sure what might be found to make musicals attractive to the public again – if, indeed, anything could be found.

In a spirit of try-anything-once, film-makers hit on two new gimmicks – youth and the popular classics. Of course, if the two could be combined in one package that would be even better. As luck would have it, just such a combination was waiting in the wings – Deanna Durbin. She was pretty, wholesome and hardly more than a child, but with a true adult coloratura soprano.

Her voice may not have been of operatic quality but it was more than good enough for the odd classical selection and songs like Tosti's 'Goodbye' and 'Ave Maria'. She had made her first appearance in an MGM young-talent short, *Every Sunday* (1936), alongside another singing hopeful, Judy Garland. According to a possibly apocryphal story, someone misunderstood Louis B. Mayer's instructions to 'fire the plump one' and let her go while putting Garland under contract. She was snapped up by Joe Pasternak at Universal and put into a cheery comedy with music – *Three Smart Girls* (1937) – a low-budget film which made millions and saved the company from bankruptcy.

From then on she received the full star treatment. Her next film, *One Hundred Men and a Girl* (1937), places her in the realms of highbrow music as she attempts to persuade Leopold Stokowski to conduct an orchestra of out-of-work musicians.

Later films like *Mad About Music* and *That Certain Age* (both 1938) kept closely to variations on the same winning recipe. Although the film-makers congratulated themselves loudly on their boldness in bringing 'great music' to a mass audience, it was not so much a desperate enterprise but rather seeing clearly which way the wind was blowing. The supposed battle between jazz and the classics had already been dramatized, rather cursorily, by Fred Astaire who was torn between ballet and tap in *Shall We Dance?* (1937), by the Romeo and Juliet ballet in *The Goldwyn Follies* (1938), and in *On Your Toes* (1939). There were also dozens of teenage musicals in which the swots wore bow ties and prated about Bach and Beethoven, only to be taken down a peg or two by their more enlightened hepcat fellows. As the Forties wore on, the schism was most frequently healed by embarrassing scenes in which Jose Iturbi played boogie-woogie, or Wagnerian singers showed that they were good guys at heart by, in the idiom of the day, 'cutting a rug'.

The high-school musical which provided a favourite location for 'jazzing the classics' flourished both at MGM, in the early days of Mickey Rooney and Judy Garland – *Babes in Arms* (1939) and its successors – and, in much humbler circumstances, at Universal. There Donald O'Connor and Peggy Ryan, who were hep, and Gloria Jean, who was not, appeared variously combined in any number of B films about co-eds, young army recruits and the like; all three were in *When Johnny Comes Marching Home*, *Mr Big* (both 1943) and *Follow the Boys* (1944). Meanwhile the other studios developed their own specialities. It was politic to have at least one musical star under contract, and so singers and dancers of all kinds (not to mention skaters, swimmers and various exotics) were under constant scrutiny in the hope that they might prove suitable film-star material.

Top left: Deanna Durbin played in One Hundred Men and a Girl *with Leopold Stokowski. The mixture of girlish charm and fine orchestration set a pattern for other musicals. Top:* Naughty Marietta (1935) *was the first film of the popular duo Jeanette MacDonald and Nelson Eddy. Above: Judy Garland and Deanna Durbin in an MGM test short* Every Sunday. *Joe Pasternak of Universal, after viewing the short, signed up Durbin for* Three Smart Girls

Below: Betty Hutton in Here Come the Waves tried a new image when she played twins, one of whom was quiet and refined. Centre: Eleanor Powell dubbed 'The World's Greatest Tap Dancer', in Rosalie. Bottom: the sisters in Tin Pan Alley (1940) were Alice Faye and Betty Grable. Bottom right: Astaire and Hayworth's first film together

Even MGM, which tended to be a law unto itself, had – as well as its fading singing duo, MacDonald and Eddy, and its teenage threats, Garland and Rooney – its own big dancing star, Eleanor Powell. She was an extraordinary, stainless-steel-clad lady who was no great shakes as an actress but, once she started on her machine-gun taps, was so magnetic that she could manage single-handed to hold the 'audiences' attention through such otherwise tiresome and patchy vehicles as the *Broadway Melodies* of 1936 and 1938 and *Rosalie* (1937). In *Broadway Melody* of 1940, for about the only time in her career, she was given a partner of equal standing, Fred Astaire, and some of the splendid Cole Porter numbers (particularly a long version of 'Begin the Beguine' which goes through many phases) represent a height of sheer style and technique rarely matched in the Hollywood musical. As things turned out, this proved to be the high point of her career: within three years she was reduced to playing second fiddle to Red Skelton, the company's new comic sensation, and she retired gracefully in 1944.

Other kinds of dancers were equally sought after. Vera Zorina, a ballet star, was introduced to the screen in *The Goldwyn Follies*. She went on to star in the film version of *On Your Toes*, which she had played on the stage in London, and then appeared sporadically in films like Paramount's spectacular *Star Spangled Rhythm* (1943) and *Follow the Boys* before retiring from dancing at the end of the war. On the masculine side there were attempts to build up Buddy Ebsen, a gangly junior later to know belated fame as the leading Beverly Hillbilly, and Ray Bolger, of the rubber face and legs that went on forever. Buddy Ebsen partnered ladies as various as Judy Garland, Eleanor Powell and Shirley Temple, but never really made it on his own; Ray Bolger remained one of the biggest stars on Broadway, but his unromantic appearance was against him as a leading man in films, and his finest screen moment was, heavily disguised, as the Scarecrow in *The Wizard of Oz* (1939).

These players tended to wander from studio to studio. The more fortunate stars were under contract to just one which took the trouble to care for them and build their careers, to select the right vehicles for their talents, to mix a little new material with the old in order to test the market and generally protect the studio's investment. The division of roles in a studio was carefully worked out. At Paramount, for instance, Bing Crosby was the reigning king of musicals, Bob Hope was the leading comedy star and sang a little, and there were four principal girls who divided most of the plum feminine roles at the studio between them. Paulette Goddard got the fiery dramatic roles, Dorothy Lamour was exotic in a sarong, Veronica Lake was the resident siren and Betty Hutton was

the hard-sell musical comedienne. Their areas were clearly defined and no-one stepped on anyone else's toes: they could all, from time to time, let their hair down (or put it up, according to the fashion of the moment) to play in comedy or even musical roles – though only Betty Hutton specialized in the genre with occasional assistance from the former band singer Dorothy Lamour.

Many aspirants to screen stardom during the Thirties and Forties originally sang with bands – including Bing Crosby. Paramount had snapped him up in 1932, after he had become an instant sensation with his own radio show, and kept him for 24 years (although he was occasionally loaned out to other companies). With his lazy charm and seemingly effortless crooning, he was the constant

The new musical attractions ranged from Carmen Miranda's exotic hats to Betty Hutton's biting humour

factor in Paramount musicals. He was never teamed with any particular leading lady for long, apart from the series of seven 'Road' films, starting with *Road to Singapore* (1940), in which he and Bob Hope were regularly rivals for the affections of Dorothy Lamour. Otherwise, Mary Martin was nearest to a romantic partner in *Rhythm on the River* (1940) and *The Birth of the Blues* (1941) when Paramount were trying to transform her from a Broadway to a Hollywood star – without success.

Curiously enough Crosby was only once teamed with Paramount's female musical star, Betty Hutton (or perhaps one should say twice, since in *Here Come the Waves*, 1944, she played twins – one was quiet and refined and the other her usual raucous self). Perhaps Paramount feared that Crosby's relaxed, easy style would not blend with the Hutton oversell, and indeed it was a lot easier and more satisfactory to team her with Eddie Bracken in *The Fleet's In* (1942), *Star Spangled Rhythm*, and *The Miracle of Morgan's Creek* (1943) or with Sonny Tufts in *Cross My Heart* (1945) since they offered no competition and did not have to be protected from her onslaughts.

In her frenzied, but rather pathetic, determination to shout down all opposition – not least from any of the mere men who attracted her attention – Betty Hutton was a specifically Forties kind of star who was born of the years when all the real male stars were likely to be off to war and women had to keep the home fires burning as well as the machines turning. The war and then the post-war situation created other new kinds of stars. The great government drive towards Pan-American friendship and the Good Neighbor policy encouraged producers to

look for a suitably Pan-American star to decorate films with titles like *Down Argentine Way* (1940), *That Night in Rio* and *Weekend in Havana* (both 1941). They found Carmen Miranda (who was in fact born in Portugal but nobody quibbled) – the Brazilian Bombshell. She belonged to another class of Forties star – those who could do only one thing but did that very well – the speciality star. As far as anyone could tell, all she was ever able to do was her characteristic hip-wagging, finger-twisting, pseudo-Latin number (usually written for her by old Hollywood stalwarts like Harry Warren) and wear her notorious tutti-frutti hats. The art of the film-maker consisted mainly of finding plausible ways to trundle her on and off screen between her big numbers.

Carmen Miranda was the most famous – or notorious – speciality star, but not the biggest. For that honour it was a close competition between skating Sonja Henie and swimming Esther Williams. Sonja Henie prettily skated her way to music through nearly a dozen films at 20th Century-Fox from *One in a Million* (1936) to *The Countess of Monte Cristo* (1948) and retired from the screen to make a fortune promoting ice shows. Esther Williams, MGM's home-grown mermaid, began in *Bathing Beauty* (1944) and was a regular in ever more exotic and elaborate watergoing romances until *Jupiter's Darling* (1955); she also retired with a fortune. Where Carmen Miranda was an incidental attraction, never called upon to provide more than semi-comic relief, Williams and Henie were undoubtedly stars, with whole big-budget films built around them. But then it was the era, above all, of the star musical.

After the eclipse of the Busby Berkeley-style spectacle (which was considered unpatriotic in wartime), everybody went instead for the fast, simple formula of picking a star and then selling him or her for all they were worth. Warners no longer had any tame musical stars, but then Warners did not make many musicals in the Forties. They produced only a handful of dramas with music which were quite frequently based on the life of a popular composer like George M. Cohan (*Yankee Doodle Dandy*, 1942), George Gershwin (*Rhapsody in Blue*, 1945) or Cole Porter (*Night and Day*, 1946). This continued until 1948 when they discovered yet another band singer called Doris Day and made her into a star with her first movie – *Romance on the High Seas*.

Columbia had Rita Hayworth and, since she was about all they had, they had to make her go a long way. Unfortunately she could not sing – or nobody could spare the time to coach her. But she could dance and, in between weightier assignments, she proved, in *You'll Never Get Rich* (1941) and *You Were Never Lovelier* (1942), to be one of the best partners Fred Astaire ever had and worked surprisingly well with Gene Kelly in *Cover Girl* (1944).

The best that RKO could come up with as a musical substitute for Astaire and Rogers was Anna Neagle, who was in Hollywood under contract at the beginning of the war in Europe and made such innocuous, undistinguished musicals as *Irene* (1940), *No, No, Nanette* and *Sunny* (both 1941).

Of the major independents, David Selznick had bigger things to do than bother his head with such frivolity, but Samuel Goldwyn discovered a musical comic in 1943 and unleashed Danny Kaye on the waiting world in *Up in Arms* (1944) and a succession of other tiresome, semi-musical vehicles.

But the big studio for musical stars and star musicals during the Forties was 20th Century-Fox. They had something for just about every taste. At the beginning of the decade there was still Shirley Temple, and there was Sonja Henie skating and very soon there was Carmen Miranda doing whatever she always did. Then when the studio went in for band singers the whole band would come along; two big Glenn Miller films – *Sun Valley Serenade* (1941) and *Orchestra Wives* (1942) – were made at that studio.

There were also the serious musical stars. Chief among them were Betty Grable and Alice Faye – both were blondes, both were Forces' sweethearts, but they were otherwise very different in style. Betty Grable had worked her way up from the chorus and did a bit of everything sufficiently, if nothing very well. She had bounce and good humour and rather short, pudgy legs which were regarded as the epitome of feminine allure. It was, perhaps, her very ordinariness that made her the great wartime pin-up – soldiers felt that, given the right breaks, the girl-next-door back home could probably do just as well, and they enjoyed Grable for being a trier. Alice Faye had been a band singer and, with her quivering bee-stung lips and throaty mezzo, was perfect for being soulful and singing songs like 'You'll Never Know' and 'No Love, No Nothing'.

Like goddesses of dissimilar races, they were usually kept apart, each in her own particular sphere, but it was a fair guess that one or other of them would be in any major 20th Century-Fox musical. The men who played opposite them – Don Ameche, John Payne, even Dan Dailey – were neither here nor there: they were merely moral support for the duration of the film. The films which surrounded them were brash and vulgar, conceived in the glaring tints of saturated Technicolor and made no grand claim to be works of art. They were, one might say, primitive Hollywood at its best, and as such they retain their vitality even today (so long as the stars retain theirs) when many more pretentious offerings have long since irretrievably faded.

Art, of course, is something else again. But for that one has to look elsewhere: to that special area of MGM where Arthur Freed and his team were up to something new and exciting and completely different.   JOHN RUSSELL TAYLOR

Top left: Sonja Henie, seen here in My Lucky Star *(1938), was the world figure-skating champion before turning to films. Top: Donald O'Connor, Peggy Ryan and Gloria Jean in the high-school musical* When Johnny Comes Marching Home. *Centre: Esther Williams in* Jupiter's Darling. *Above: England's Anna Neagle made* No, No, Nanette *in Hollywood*

155

From Stage to Screen

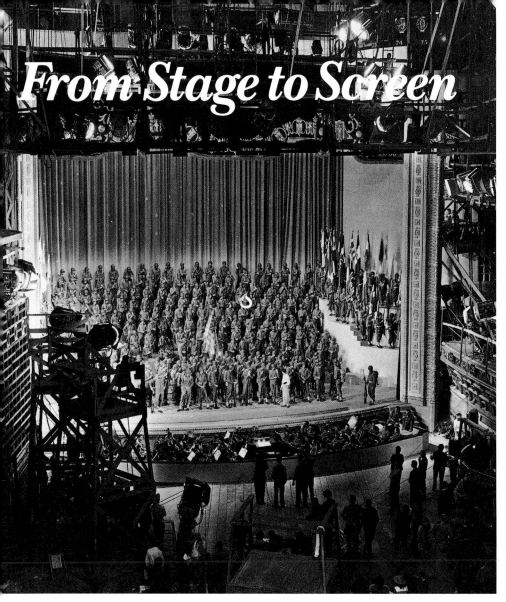

The great names of American popular music, such as Cole Porter, Irving Berlin, Jerome Kern and George Gershwin spelt big business for Hollywood. The studios bought their songs, shows and life stories and used their names as marketing devices. These composers helped shape the dance and drama of the screen but, despite their importance, often lost control of the films that celebrated their work

Porter, Berlin, Kern and Gershwin were all well-established on Broadway before they became associated with Hollywood during the theatre lull and cinema boom that followed the Depression. They were rapidly joined there by the songwriting team of Rodgers and Hart – responsible for such film musicals as *Hallelujah, I'm a Bum* (1933), *Babes in Arms* (1939) and *Pal Joey* (1957) – and the songwriter and actor George M. Cohan, whose 'life' (omitting his notorious activities as a strike-breaker against the struggling Actor's Equity) was the subject of *Yankee Doodle Dandy* (1942).

Rodgers and Hart, on whose lives *Words and Music* (1948) was loosely based, had to endure frequent censorship of their lyrics, which were thought too sophisticated for mass audiences even as late as *Pal Joey*. The four great names were at least spared that; Porter, Berlin, Kern and Gershwin all knew each other, helped each other and paid fulsome and public tribute to one another, especially when one of them was in trouble. All claimed to owe first allegi-

ance to the stimulation of the New York stage even when, from the early Thirties, they turned to the construction of musical numbers for the screen. Their Broadway backgrounds made them classy acquisitions for Hollywood. However, Hollywood was not always sure how to make best use of the class it had bought.

There's no biz like show biz

'It's easy to do a movie', proclaimed Irving Berlin, 'especially a package job like *Blue Skies* (1946) or *Easter Parade* (1948). But I can't always be sure of being able to write a score of [a show like] *Annie Get Your Gun*.'

Songs for most movies could be packaged, sorted and shuffled with little attention to the exigencies of plot and character. In these confections, songs worked like items in a revue. A number like Berlin's 'Easter Parade' first appeared on Broadway in *As Thousands Cheer* in 1933; it then did service in *Alexander's Ragtime Band* (1938) and finally had a movie named after it. *Holiday Inn* (1942) launched

'White Christmas' as a nostalgic wartime number (not at all what Berlin had intended) and helped establish the song as a classic; in 1954 it was shamelessly revived as the title number in Paramount's first exercise in the VistaVision process, complete with astounding deep-focus shots of obviously stage snow. Even theme tunes had a history; in 1953, Berlin wrote a romantic song called 'Sayonara, Sayonara' with no particular market in mind. Four years later, Marlon Brando starred in *Sayonara* and the song became its theme.

Born in 1888, Irving Berlin (real name Israel Baline) emigrated from his native Russia with his family and grew up in New York. Despite having no musical training, his natural talent

Above left: Irving Berlin's patriotic show This Is the Army *was directly transferred from stage to screen. Top and Above: Berlin's name was one of the main selling points of* Blue Skies *and* Alexander's Ragtime Band; *the latter was said to be based on his life*

was so great that he rose quickly to prominence as a songwriter. Joseph Schenck, the chairman of United Artists, first announced a version of Berlin's life story in 1928; it was to be called *Say It With Music*. It was formally publicized only as a story about a songwriter but the columnists took their cue from the news that Berlin would write the score. When *Alexander's Ragtime Band* was launched (the story of a bandleader and his girl singer), it was

again taken to be Berlin's life story since the music celebrated his work with 28 numbers, including the forgotten masterpiece 'I Can Always Find a Little Sunshine at the YMCA'. In the Sixties, an acknowledged film of Berlin's life fell foul of internal strife at MGM and financial problems; this lost MGM movie, like the Schenck project more than thirty years before, was to have been called *Say It With Music*. Through all those decades Berlin had declared to anyone who would listen that he did not want his life story told in any form – at least not until he was safely dead.

His name allowed him to dictate terms to Hollywood. Arthur Freed at MGM complained: 'It took longer to write one of Irving's contracts than a whole script.' Like Al Jolson – and, at the time, only like Al Jolson – he insisted on a share of a movie's profits as well as his flat fee. That was his rule in the Thirties and he maintained it fiercely. Years later, when 20th Century-Fox came to him with the idea of *Easter Parade* he turned them down and took the project to MGM because 20th Century-Fox would not offer a percentage of the gross.

Berlin also had written into his contracts an astonishing clause which forbade the studio to alter a single note of his score once filming had started. This intransigence went some way to ensure that he was spared the fate of his protégé George Gershwin, who found his scores for six violins inflated to forty and his melodies swamped by fine over-elaborate orchestration.

But Berlin did more than sell his music to the movies. His collaboration with Fred Astaire – resulting in *Top Hat* (1935), *Follow the Fleet* (1936) and *Carefree* (1938) – was close and meticulous. Astaire and Berlin went over each number in minute detail, checking that the music matched perfectly with the choreography. As Astaire insisted on the full-length photography of dance numbers without any cutting away, Berlin's contribution to the overall effect was central.

Under special circumstances Berlin performed himself. He was well known for having a quiet voice – 'You have to hug him to hear him', a friend once said – but he sang 'How I Hate to Get Up in the Morning' in the movie version of *This Is the Army* (1943), a stumpy, lonely figure standing before a backdrop of painted tents. The show was the product of Berlin's emotional patriotism for his adopted land (another was his song 'God Bless

Above left: Fred Astaire, Berlin and Peter Lawford talk over 'Easter Parade'. Above right: Betty Hutton and Howard Keel in Annie Get Your Gun. *Right: Cole Porter. Bottom: Astaire and Cyd Charisse in* Silk Stockings

America') and its cast was all soldiers – even the 'showgirls'. The movie faithfully followed the stage show (although with real women in the chorus) and was a flag-waving revue laced with rueful jokes at military routine. It was tested on stage, and presented on screen with the same tin helmets painted on the curtains and the same props.

Berlin certainly did his share of hack work for the studios, selling songs package by package. However he contributed far more than just his superb music to Hollywood; in his collaboration with Astaire, and through the rich material of stage shows like *Annie Get Your Gun* (filmed in 1950), he helped shape the conventions of the American movie musical.

Pure soap opera

Unlike Berlin, Cole Porter had a prosperous background. Born in 1891, he attended Yale and then invented a melodramatic war record before making it big on Broadway. Berlin first suggested the idea of a film about Porter to Jack Warner on patriotic grounds. In 1937, Porter had lost the use of his legs in a riding accident; Berlin felt that the story of how he had coped with his disability would act as an inspiration to returning World War II servicemen who had suffered similar injuries. Warner duly paid Porter $300,000 for what amounted to the screen rights to a fall. Porter was grateful for the cash as his career had temporarily run into trouble with the commercial failure of various stage ventures.

The film version of his life was called *Night and Day* (1946) but it started with the major problem that it could not possibly tell the truth. The life of a high-society wit who had a taste for sailors, truck drivers and black male prostitutes and who had contracted into an un-consummated marriage with a woman several years his senior was hardly suitable matter for family entertainment. Drastic action was required. Cary Grant was cast in the lead role; the Porter family's house in Peru, Indiana, became a mansion, mysteriously filled with black servants with Southern accents; Porter himself became a World War I hero, the tragic victim of an exploding bomb (ignoring the fact that he had never served a day in any of the USA's armed forces); and he emerged, inevitably, as a heterosexual. He said himself: 'None of it is true.'

Given Porter's notoriety in Hollywood, Warner's decision to purvey this fiction as his life story must seem curious; in fact, it made good commercial sense. Warner planned a series of star appearances from the likes of Fred Astaire, Mary Martin, Danny Kaye, Sophie Tucker, Jimmy Durante and Bert Lahr, all of whom, he hoped, would fiddle their contracts with other studios and work at cut fees out of loyalty to Porter. Warner gambled on producing an all-star revue with Porter tunes; all he eventually got was Mary Martin.

Night and Day attempted to pass off as fact myths about the creative process and about the heroism of the creator. In the film, songs are sparked off in Porter's mind by ridiculously literal stimuli; a clock ticking, rain falling or the sight of his screen lover's face produce memorable lines on just those topics. Creation is portrayed as a series of romantic flashes of inspiration; in a single shot the composer smites his brow, strikes the piano and conjures up a superb melody. Side by side with this fantastic view of the artist at work lies the quite separate myth of self-reliant heroism overcoming disability – an absurd weight for the film's otherwise trivial story to bear.

Like Berlin before him, Porter used to recycle songs to get the maximum mileage out of them. An uninspired effort called 'So Long, Samoa' (written in 1940) became, after doctoring, the theme song of *Adam's Rib* (1949), under the title 'Farewell, Amanda'. Porter's 'Don't Fence Me In', sung by Roy Rogers in *Hollywood Canteen* (1944), had actually been written under a Fox contract ten years earlier. 'The Laziest Girl in Town', sung by Marlene Dietrich in *Stage Fright* (1949) was a revival of a 1927 song, while 'From This Moment On', the hit of the screen version of *Kiss Me Kate* (1953), had originally been written for, and

dropped from, another stage musical.

Porter's film scores, which were made up of strings of songs, were subject to change by film-makers who wished to assemble the packages in a different way. *High Society* (1956), the musical remake of Cukor's *The Philadelphia Story* (1940), used numbers from other Porter shows and it remains a good example of how established songs could take on a new meaning by being placed in a new context.

It is doubtful whether the great studios remembered what composers had previously offered and sold to them; their lawyers certainly did not. When 'Well Did You Evah?' was put into *High Society*, MGM's lawyers checked the lyrics and asked solemnly if Porter had clearance from Miss Mimsie Starr (who, in the

Top: reporter Frank Sinatra takes advantage of finding heiress Grace Kelly alone to inform her in song that she's 'sensational' in High Society, *for which Porter wrote the music and lyrics. Above: the chorus girls take the stand in* Can Can, *which included some of Porter's best known songs, such as 'Let's Do It', 'I Love Paris' and 'Just One of Those Things'*

song, had been molested in the Astor Bar). The same question made lawyers look foolish when MGM were making *DuBarry Was a Lady* (1943), in which the song again occurred.

Porter also sold entire shows to Hollywood. His *Kiss Me Kate* was transferred to the screen with its score largely intact, its characters and action being defined by Porter's lyrics and

music – 'I am', he said, 'out to write hits'. Broadway was a problematic place to make a living in the Depression years and conditions worsened during the Thirties. In 1936 he took his talent West and 'manufactured' brilliantly for movies such as *Shall We Dance?* and *A Damsel in Distress* (both 1937). His notions of manufactured songs were 'Let's Call the Whole Thing Off', 'They Can't Take That Away From Me', 'A Foggy Day' and 'Nice Work if You Can Get It' (all with lyrics by Ira).

Yet his major contribution to Hollywood was made after his sudden death from an inoperable brain tumour in 1937 at the age of 39. His music gave class to *The Barkleys of Broadway* (1949) and animated *An American in Paris* (1951) and *Funny Face* (1957). His story was told in *Rhapsody in Blue* (1945), with the customary myth-making of the biopic. His work showed to best advantage on screen when used in ways that the composer never envisaged, such as in the ballet sequence of *An American in Paris*.

Top: Gene Kelly in Les Girls, *an original screen musical scored by Porter. Above: an autographed photo of the Gershwin brothers, George (left) and Ira, dedicated to another songwriter, Harry Warren. Above right: George Gershwin's music was used to great effect in the finale of* An American in Paris. *Right:* Porgy and Bess *was adapted from the Gershwins' 1935 folk opera*

melodies. Similarly, the film version of *Silk Stockings* (1957) had only two rather undistinguished additions ('Fated to Be Mated' and 'Ritz Rock'n'Roll') to Porter's original stage score. The Broadway hit *Can Can* suffered few changes when adapted for the screen in 1960, while *Les Girls* (1957) was directly conceived for the screen. In all these, Porter's contribution equals or parallels that of the screenwriter. Like a script, a musical score with numbers sets limits on timing, pointing and character. It is an important basis for the total effect of the film.

The melody lingers on

Porter knew he was a popular composer; George Gershwin had other ideas about his own status. His reputation as a serious musician so troubled his potential employers in Hollywood that his agent cabled: 'They are afraid you will only do highbrow songs so wire me on this score so I can reassure them.'

Gershwin's orchestral piece *An American in Paris*, before it inspired Gene Kelly and Stanley Donen, first appeared at the Carnegie Hall sandwiched between Franck and Wagner. In 1931 his *Of Thee I Sing* won a Pulitzer prize for the bite and substance of brother Ira's lyrics – a quite exceptional feat for a musical. And although he had once been a song-plugger, his later career inclined towards folk opera and symphonic jazz – finding perhaps its fullest expression in *Porgy and Bess* (filmed in 1959).

Gershwin's interest in Hollywood was purely financial; he never shared the enthusiasm of his brother Ira for the soothing climes of California. However, towards the end of his tragically brief career he became obsessed with winning real popularity for his

A man inspired

Jerome Kern, unlike Gershwin, turned his back on Broadway and embraced Hollywood. It was not exactly a love affair, but Kern was grateful for the money the studios paid for properties like *Show Boat*, having suffered severe losses in the Wall Street crash. He resented the producers' arbitrary power; he once worked for a month on the score of *Men of the Sky* (1931) for Warner Brothers and then saw the producer reject all his work, and put him on a blacklist of 'difficult' characters because he complained. He disliked Los Angeles, finding it dull and artificial. But after flirting for five years with movies, he decided in the mid-Thirties that economic pressures made the stage too risky and he became a full-time songwriter for the screen.

He was willing to adapt his style to the demands of cinema audiences, writing tunes with 'hotter' rhythms than the stately melodies for which he was famous. He struggled to produce the beat of the 'Bojangles of Harlem' number which Astaire danced to in *Swing Time* (1936). The number is largely a product of Astaire's tough, demanding attitude to all the material he performed. His precision helped to extend Kern's range.

In such films as *Roberta* (1935) and *Swing Time*, Kern mainly exercised that lyrical tenderness and wit which distinguished his stage work with songs like 'Smoke Gets in Your

Above: Jerome Kern (left) with Jean Harlow and the director Victor Fleming on the set of Reckless. *Above right and right: two contrasting images from different versions of Kern's* Show Boat. *The colour one tended to substitute glamour – here in the shapely form of Ava Gardner – for the resonant images of the 1936 version, reinforced by the voice and presence of Paul Robeson*

Eyes', 'The Way You Look Tonight' and 'Pick Yourself Up'. In his 1927 stage musical *Show Boat* he had tried for greater emotional depth, remaining faithful to the examination of racial issues in Edna Ferber's novel. The first movie version made in 1929 was perfunctory; but the second, directed by James Whale in 1936, was an extraordinary series of Expressionist images. This film also gave Paul Robeson the chance to do more than sing 'Ol' Man River' (his main contribution on stage). The third version (directed by George Sidney in 1951) lost the drama in a welter of Technicolor skittishness. Even with a fine cast (in particular Ava Gardner as the half-caste expelled from the boat when her racial origins are discovered), it was an undramatic movie – as though colour and process photography inevitably took the edge off the story. While Whale had created images of crushing, oppressive labour, Sidney dressed the screen and cut parts for blacks. Whale's film had made dramatic points; Sidney's scuttled gratefully to the next number. Kern's emotional stylization (his music, usually, is close to sentimentality but clear of it) needed an equivalent convention in

performance and shooting for it to have full effect. Whale gave it; Sidney did not.

Kern did not live to see that betrayal. By the time of his death in 1945 at the age of 60, he also missed, mercifully, his own biopic *Till the Clouds Roll By* (1946), in which he helped a friend find a lost daughter. This was, his partner Guy Bolton claimed, a true story. The film's musical climax was the delicate figure of

Frank Sinatra crooning 'Ol' Man River' from glossy staircase, with no suggestion of barg toting or bale-lifting or any other kind physical effort. At least Kern would not ha minded this distortion. 'You mustn't try to t my life story,' he once told Louis B. Mayer and not for reasons of determined privacy li Berlin, but because 'You'd find it far too dul

MICHAEL PY

Metro-Goldwyn-Musical

Arthur Freed's production unit at MGM created a new kind of musical where action, song and dance were carefully interwoven into a flowing story

'More stars than there are in the heavens' was the proud boast of MGM. When you consider the number of the very greatest stars, from Greta Garbo to Mickey Rooney, who were under contract to the company at the end of the Thirties, such an image does not seem too extravagant. But even if the stars were extraordinary, what the studio did with them was not necessarily quite so remarkable. The same patterns applied at MGM as elsewhere; the same cycles of popularity were observed; stars were built in the same way, and faded (or were broken) in the same way. There, as anywhere else, stars were sometimes brought into a film in order to enliven poor material. Even so, however wonderful stars may be on the screen, they cannot exist in a vacuum: they have to have the right (or at least reasonable) circumstances in which to display themselves.

MGM were seldom innovative in these respects. In musicals, as in other films, the studio tended to employ directors because they were good company men rather than because of their ability. It encased its stars in safe, well-upholstered vehicles which did not diminish them but which rarely spectacularly enhanced them and which often depended on the stars for vitality and appeal. It was entirely unexpected, therefore, that in the early Forties MGM should, in the one area of the musical, produce something very different from anything that had been seen on the screen since the early days of the sound film. There were, however, no signs of this change appearing at the end of the Thirties when MGM began to acquire the stars who were going to shine most brightly in their new kind of musical.

Mickey Rooney and Judy Garland were the first to appear. Rooney, who came from a show-business background, was in silent films (once as a midget), juvenile shorts and many features before arriving at MGM where, in 1937, he made the film that was to change his life. *A Family Affair* was the first of the seemingly unending series of small-town comedy-dramas featuring Andy Hardy and his family. Rooney was not specifically a musical star but he could do something of everything and his career continued to flourish as long as he could credibly play teenagers – which, since he was very small, was well into his twenties.

Judy Garland was virtually born in a trunk, like the heroine of one of her most famous numbers from *A Star Is Born* (1954); she had been performing almost as long as she could walk, originally as one of the singing Gumm Sisters and then by herself. She was not a pretty-pretty child, like Shirley Temple or Deanna Durbin, (allegedly Louis B. Mayer used to call her affectionately 'my little hunchback') but she had personality plus, a rich and vibrant singing voice which she knew how to use and, above all, youth. This made her perfect for the fashionable high-school musicals and, after her test with Deanna Durbin in a musical short, *Every Sunday* (1936), she eased her way into the movies by playing everybody's younger sister until the winning combination occurred when she was put

together with Mickey Rooney in *Thoroughbreds Don't Cry* (1937) and *Love Finds Andy Hardy* (1938). Even so, she had to make it on her own in *The Wizard of Oz* (1939) before she and Rooney became a major musical team in *Babes in Arms* (1939).

After this they made three more big musicals together – *Strike Up the Band* (1940), *Babes on Broadway* (1941) and *Girl Crazy* (1943). They also made a couple more Andy Hardy films which

Above: the spectacular 'Broadway Rhythm Ballet' was the climax of the film within the film Singin' in the Rain. *Arthur Freed, Stanley Donen and Gene Kelly collaborated on this musical about the early days of sound film. Below: Judy Garland and Mickey Rooney in* Strike Up the Band

Above: Judy Garland in the classic 'Born in a Trunk' routine from A Star Is Born. *The number was added after George Cukor had finished shooting and became a regular spot in Garland's later stage shows. Below: Ann Miller displays her dexterity and precision as a tap dancer in* Small Town Girl *(1953)*

one sequence to another.

The Wizard of Oz was a fantasy and therefore something of a special case in the musicals' tradition. There had been an unofficial 'rule' that the public would not accept performers in films bursting into song or dance without any rational justification. But it had been broken so often with impunity that, by the end of the Thirties, no-one really believed in it any more. Its legacy still persisted in the enormous number of putting-on-a-show musicals. These were felt to take the sting out of the exotic and irrational side of the musical by placing the major numbers in a rehearsal room or on a stage (however inconceivable this might be in theatrical terms). Even then, if the principals sometimes behaved a bit oddly by everyday standards well, show-people were like that. This meant that rather than being smoothly integrated into the story part of the film, the numbers were isolated interludes which had little functional relationship with the rest of the film and were quite often directed by someone else anyway. Those who made costume operettas (like the Jeanette MacDonald-

---

Gene Kelly, Fred Astaire and Judy Garland graced the screen with their song and dance routines to give the MGM musicals their unique flavour

---

Nelson Eddy films) or out-and-out fantasies had more freedom in this respect, but few film-makers had the special talents required to utilize it fully.

This was why Arthur Freed was so important. The first films he produced himself, *Babes in Arms* and *Strike Up the Band*, were traditional, youthful putting-on-a-show stories. However, he was plotting at the same time as he was planning. In 1940 he brought a very successful New York stage designer and director, Vincente Minnelli, to Hollywood just to have him hang around for a while observe the film-making process and help out directing odd sequences for films. This slow lead-in brought results when, in 1943, Minnelli directed his first film for Freed – a version of the successful black musical *Cabin in the Sky*. This film, like *The Wizard of Oz*, was a fantasy but Minnelli directed it with unique ease and fluidity, slipping comfortably between dramatic scenes and musical numbers. Each musical interlude took the plot forward and the numbers seemed to arise naturally out of what had gone before, as either a sort of crystallization of emotion or excitement, or a pause for reflection. For once, there was nothing arbitrary about the introduction of the musical element as it was incorporated into the very texture of the film.

There were still a few more films to come from Arthur Freed's unit (now virtually an independent company within MGM) which more or less followed the traditional line in musical films. These films unobtrusively introduced the elements which were to become important in the new kind of musical at MGM. Judy Garland was being developed into an adult performer from film to film; in 1942 she had been given her first really grown-up role and a new leading man, Gene Kelly, in *For Me and My Gal*. Kelly had been discovered in the original Broadway production of the brightly cynical 1940 Rodgers and Hart musical *Pal Joey*. Freed signed him up and although he was employed primarily as an actor dancer, he was also being prepared for other things. He was allowed, almost from the start, to stage and choreograph his own numbers in films, usually in collaboration with his colleague from *Pal Joey*, Stanley Donen.

usually featured the efforts of a group of talented youngsters to put on their own show ('Gee, there's that old big barn down the road . . .') and which ended in musical fireworks from the practised hand of Busby Berkeley who was briefly under contract to MGM at this period.

These musicals were very much the traditional kind, but the shape of things to come had already been hinted at in *The Wizard of Oz*. Although it is difficult to establish responsibility for the film – in the case of a famous victory everybody rushes in to claim that he alone achieved it – it seems certain that a very important part of its success was due to the work of its uncredited associate producer, Arthur Freed. Freed had been around MGM since 1929 when he had come to Hollywood to write the songs (with composer Nacio Herb Brown) for *The Broadway Melody* (1929). Their evergreen songs, including 'You Are My Lucky Star', 'Singin' in the Rain', 'You Were Meant for Me' and 'I've Got a Feeling You're Fooling' were featured in many MGM films of the decade. By 1939 Freed was being groomed as a producer. He bought the book of *The Wizard of Oz* for the studio and oversaw the whole musical side of it. He also pressed for the casting of Judy Garland when the studio wanted to borrow Shirley Temple. The resulting film closely corresponded to his ideal of a musical as a story told in speech, song and dance in natural progression from

Another star who was to prove hardly less important in the MGM constellation, Fred Astaire, had also been introduced into Freed's films. His first important film after leaving Ginger Rogers and RKO – *Broadway Melody of 1940* (1940) – had been made for MGM, but not for Freed. Very soon afterwards he was set to work on Freed's giant wartime spectacular *Ziegfeld Follies* (1946), creating two of the biggest numbers 'Limehouse Blues' and 'This Heart of Mine' for it with a new dancing partner Freed was grooming for stardom – Lucille Bremer.

Long before *Ziegfeld Follies* was finished, (it took two years to make) the film appeared which, more than any other, established the new kind of musical with the moviegoing audience: *Meet Me in St Louis* (1944). Directed by Vincente Minnelli, this was the prime example of cinematic, American nostalgia: it was a simple story of a year in the life of an ordinary mid-Western family – the year leading up to the St Louis International Exposition of 1904. It had that rarest of all qualities in films – genuine charm – and it starred Judy Garland who was soon to become Minnelli's wife. In it she sings one of her theme-

tunes, 'The Trolley Song', and demonstrates an unexpected maturity as an actress – a natural comic with the power to break your heart if she wanted to.

In the next five years the Freed unit turned out classic musicals in an almost unending stream. Judy Garland was kept busy in *The Harvey Girls* (1946), *The Pirate* and *Easter Parade* (both 1948), all of which are among her best films, as well as making memorable guest appearances in the composer-biographies of Jerome Kern – *Till the Clouds Roll By* (1946) – and Rodgers and Hart – *Words and Music* (1948). Gene Kelly in *The Pirate* was perfectly matched against Garland and had some of his most intricate and stylish routines to a superb original Cole Porter score. Then, in *Take Me Out to the Ball Game* (1949), he was allowed, in collaboration with Donen and supervised by Busby Berkeley, to try his hand at writing and directing his own vehicle.

Fred Astaire starred in an ambitious, if none too successful, musical fantasy *Yolanda and the Thief* (1945) – co-starring Lucille Bremer and directed by

Minnelli – then shortly afterwards announced his retirement. In 1948, however, he was lured out of it by Freed to replace the ailing Gene Kelly in *Easter Parade* opposite Judy Garland. This was such a success for both the stars that the formula was immediately repeated in *The Barkleys of Broadway* (1949). But this time Judy Garland was ill and Freed brought back Ginger Rogers to replace her – she was dancing with Fred Astaire again after a ten-year gap.

Freed encouraged people talented in other spheres to bring their skills to the cinema. He found new directors – like ex-dancer-choreographer Charles Walters who made *Good News* (1947) and *Easter Parade*, and ex-jazz musician George Sidney who made *The Harvey Girls* and *Annie Get Your Gun* (1950). He also brought back Rouben Mamoulian who had once been famous as the director of *Applause* (1929) and *Love Me Tonight* (1932) to make *Summer Holiday* (1947). This was a new musical adaptation of Eugene O'Neill's *Ah, Wilderness!* which failed to revive Mickey Rooney's flagging career.

But the really exceptional thing about the Freed unit was the high standard of its work in all departments: the musical arrangements were done by people like Conrad Salinger, Lennie Hatton and Adolph Deutsch; special numbers by Roger Edens and Kay Thompson; choreography by Robert Alton and Eugene Loring; design by Jack Martin Smith, Merrill Pye and Randall Duell; scripts by Betty Comden and Adolph Green, and so on.

It is worth noting that most of the musicals made between *Cabin in the Sky* and *Take Me Out to the Ball Game* were still either period pieces or biographical pictures with show-business backgrounds and putting-on-a-show stories, where the musical numbers could as a rule be rationalized if anybody thought to question them. The next stage in the evolution of the musical came when Kelly and Donen were given a free rein to create *On the Town* (1949) – a contemporary, urban musical which would closely integrate song, dance and story. It was adapted from a successful Broadway show about three sailors on shore leave in New York, but for the screen it was almost completely rewritten and featured extensive location shooting on the street where, if they thought about it, nobody could seriously suppose that it ever really happened. The film gave Kelly one of his definitive roles as the wise-guy hero and Frank Sinatra was perfectly cast as his blushing sidekick and Ann Miller, for long a regular in MGM musicals, as the man-eating anthro-

Top left: Vincente Minnelli and Gene Kelly were two of the people who contributed to the fame of the Forties MGM musicals. Top: Eddie 'Rochester' Anderson is accompanied by Lena Horne in Cabin in the Sky *– the first all-black musical and Minnelli's directorial debut. Above: The* Band Wagon, *a satire about life on Broadway, stars Fred Astaire as a musical-comedy dancer trying to make a comeback. Left, top: Gene Kelly and Frank Sinatra in* Take Me Out to the Ball Game. *Left, below: Fred Astaire in* The Barkleys of Broadway

Above: in Ziegfeld Follies *Lucille Ball tames her 'panthers' in the 'Bring on the Beautiful Girls' sequence. Above right: Barbra Streisand* On a Clear Day You Can See Forever, *one of Minnelli's later musicals*

pologist ready to tap anyone into submission. The large cast worked more as a team than as so many stars in their settings.

The film was enormously popular and sparked off many other musicals in modern surroundings including Kelly's next big success, *An American in Paris* (1951), which he choreographed while Minnelli directed. Although it can be accused of pretentiousness and trying to be too knowing about French Impressionism and modern ballet, it contains some of the most exciting and imaginative sequences in the history of the American musical – including the long and controversial ballet sequence at the end. It also introduced Leslie Caron to the screen. She came from the Roland Petit Ballet and was to become an important star as the heroine of *Gigi* (1958) – the film which next to *An American in Paris* earned Freed the largest number of Oscars and plaudits.

Kelly and Donen as a directing team had another hit with *Singin' in the Rain* (1952) which is a compendium of songs by Freed and Nacio Herb Brown attached to a story about the coming of sound to Hollywood. It has good claim to be the best musical ever made. It certainly allows Kelly his finest few minutes in his solo routine during a torrential downpour against the background music of the title number. The film also makes the most of Donald O'Connor – a dancer and comic who seldom got the right chances – and gave Debbie Reynolds her first substantial chance.

Almost simultaneously another musical, often regarded as the best ever, was in the works. Whereas the forte of the Kelly–Donen musicals

was brash energy, those involved in *The Band Wagon* (1953) – Minnelli, Astaire, Jack Buchanan and Cyd Charisse – favoured elegance and style. It was romantic, funny and nostalgic and was the putting-on-a-show musical to end all putting-on-a-show musicals. It told much of the uncomfortable truth about show-business as well as sending the audience out with the rousing reflection that 'That's Entertainment'.

This was pretty well the end of the great days of musicals at MGM. Kelly and Donen tried a strangely downbeat subject – the disenchantments of post-war life for the returning veteran – for their third directorial collaboration, *It's Always Fair Weather* (1955), before going their separate ways. Minnelli was less at home with the folksiness of *Brigadoon* (1954) and the broadness of *Kismet* (1955) and it is a matter of opinion whether he recovered his old form with *Gigi*. Mamoulian made one more musical, *Silk Stockings* (1957) with Fred Astaire and Cyd Char-

The heyday of the musical was over, but new stars like Barbra Streisand carried on the tradition and familiar faces made welcome comebacks

isse, but it was generally felt, a little unfairly perhaps, to fade in comparison with its non-musical original *Ninotchka* (1939). After Minnelli's charming but minor film *Bells Are Ringing* (1960), Arthur Freed retired from musicals production.

It was not exactly the end of musicals in Hollywood. There were still the super-productions based closely on Broadway hits, to be made at regular intervals. Minnelli directed one – *On a Clear Day You Can See Forever* (1970) – and Kelly directed another – *Hello, Dolly!* (1969) – both starring the new wonder of the age, Barbra Streisand. After he left MGM Stanley Donen directed one more wonderful musical *Funny Face* (1957) – which reunited most of the old MGM production team and brought together Fred Astaire and Audrey Hepburn with the music of George Gershwin.

When Gene Kelly and Fred Astaire were brought together as the singing-dancing compères of *That's Entertainment, Part 2* (1976), the second of MGM's musical anthologies which were tributes to its own past, Fred Astaire was already 77 and Gene Kelly 64, and there was no doubt that their point of view was entirely retrospective. But then, what marvellous wonders they had to remember.

JOHN RUSSELL TAYLOR

TEAMWORK

Left: Gene Kelly and Stanley Donen discuss the script of Singin' in the Rain. *Top: Jerry the mouse dances with Kelly in* Anchors Aweigh. *Above: Kelly in* Living in a Big Way

In the late Forties and early Fifties, Gene Kelly and Stanley Donen brought a welcome burst of vitality to the Hollywood musical. Their individual flair and eagerness to experiment has continued to sustain both artists in successful careers long after their partnership ended

The number of fruitful partnerships between two directors of equal standing is extremely small in Hollywood feature films. This is probably because of a commonly held belief that divided leadership is fatal when making a film. But, as always, there is an exception that proves the rule – the astonishing collaboration between Gene Kelly and Stanley Donen on three films from the heyday of the MGM musical, two of which – *On the Town* (1949) and *Singin' in the Rain* (1952) – still stand as all-time classics of the genre.

Kelly and Donen had a shared background in modern dance on the Broadway stage. Their association and friendship dates back to the 1940 Rodgers and Hart musical *Pal Joey*, in which Kelly had the starring role and Donen combined a small part in the chorus with the job of assistant choreographer.

Pals in Hollywood

Kelly (b.1912) had run a dance school in Pittsburgh with his brother Fred before he decided to try his luck on Broadway. *Pal Joey* was his big break; he was spotted by David O. Selznick and whisked off to Hollywood. Kelly's contract with Selznick was soon bought by MGM on the recommendation of the producer Arthur Freed.

Donen, 12 years younger, left for Hollywood a few months later. He first worked as assistant choreographer on MGM's *Best Foot Forward* (1943) and was then employed by Columbia on two minor musicals, *Hey, Rookie* and *Jam Session* (both 1944).

At this point Kelly was loaned out to Columbia to play opposite their biggest star, Rita Hayworth, in an original Jerome Kern musical, *Cover Girl* (1944); Donen was assigned to help

Kelly, who had been permitted complete control over the choreography of his solo numbers. The film gave both of them a great opportunity. Not that Kelly had been doing too badly at his 'home' studio, MGM. In 1942 he had starred in his first film *For Me and My Gal* opposite Judy Garland – a particularly happy matching of styles. He was then cast in four more films of which two – *DuBarry Was a Lady* and *Thousands Cheer* (both 1943) – were musicals. But apart from a little routine he had done with a mop for a partner in *Thousands Cheer*, he had not had much of a chance to demonstrate his talents. Kelly was thus delighted with the scope that *Cover Girl* gave him, and in the 'Alter Ego' dance he performs with himself by means of double exposure he was able to create (with Donen's assistance) his first classic routine on film.

Hello sailor

When Kelly returned to MGM he took Donen with him, and they worked together on the musical numbers of *Anchors Aweigh* (1945). This film brought Kelly and Frank Sinatra together for the first time, as sailors on shore leave, and established their screen personalities – Kelly a bit bumptious and know-all, Sinatra shy, retiring and constantly pursued by ravening women eager to mother him. In this respect the film provided a rough sketch for *On the Town* four years later. Also in *Anchors Aweigh* Kelly first experimented with combining a live-action dancer (himself) with cartoon characters and backgrounds – never a very satisfactory procedure, though he tried it again in *Invitation to the Dance* (1954) and in his TV film *Jack and the Beanstalk* (1967).

After *Anchors Aweigh* Donen choreographed some lesser musicals for MGM, and Kelly briefly appeared in *Ziegfeld Follies* (1946), performing the humorous Gershwin number, 'The Babbitt

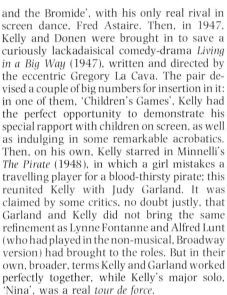

Left: Kelly displays his expertise on the tightrope in The Pirate. *Above: a theatre troupe, led by Kelly, put on a show in* Summer Stock, *directed and choreographed by Charles Walters. Right: silent-screen heart-throb Don Lockwood (Kelly) shows that he has what it takes to make it as a musical star in the new era of talking pictures in* Singin' in the Rain

and the Bromide', with his only real rival in screen dance, Fred Astaire. Then, in 1947, Kelly and Donen were brought in to save a curiously lackadaisical comedy-drama *Living in a Big Way* (1947), written and directed by the eccentric Gregory La Cava. The pair devised a couple of big numbers for insertion in it: in one of them, 'Children's Games', Kelly had the perfect opportunity to demonstrate his special rapport with children on screen, as well as indulging in some remarkable acrobatics. Then, on his own, Kelly starred in Minnelli's *The Pirate* (1948), in which a girl mistakes a travelling player for a blood-thirsty pirate; this reunited Kelly with Judy Garland. It was claimed by some critics, no doubt justly, that Garland and Kelly did not bring the same refinement as Lynne Fontanne and Alfred Lunt (who had played in the non-musical, Broadway version) had brought to the roles. But in their own, broader, terms Kelly and Garland worked perfectly together, while Kelly's major solo, 'Nina', was a real *tour de force*.

Their first home run

For some time Kelly and Donen had wanted to make a film that would knit the musical sequences and the dramatic parts of the story into a seamless whole. The MGM producer Arthur Freed, having watched them both carefully, decided to give them the chance to collaborate on *Take Me Out to the Ball Game* (1949) under the direction of Busby Berkeley. The film was scripted from an original story by Kelly and Donen about a young woman (Esther Williams, in one of her few non-swimming roles) who inherits a baseball team. The plot concerns the romantic entanglements of the three principal members of the team, played by Kelly, Sinatra and Jules Munshin. The film is very much a preliminary version of the pattern perfected in *On the Town* which came immediately afterwards. Both films have the same three male principals and the same close integration of numbers and plot. Though Berkeley was nominated the director of *Take Me Out to the Ball Game*, he seems to have

concerned himself mainly with the big clambake sequence. For the rest he just supervised his young choreographers while they tried out new techniques, such as segmenting the screen during dance numbers. The film anticipates *On the Town*, but also looks forward to *Damn Yankees* (1958) and Donen's other work after he had separated from Kelly. The success of *Take Me Out to the Ball Game* encouraged Freed to give Kelly and Donen the opportunity to direct *On the Town*, which revitalized screen musicals with its exuberance, virtuosity and its use of real locations.

However, the possibilities opened up by *On the Town* were not realized in Kelly's next musical, *Summer Stock* (1950), in which he appeared once more with Judy Garland. The film harked back to the old putting-on-a-show formula, though it included another classic Kelly solo, performed with an old newspaper and a creaky board. Then, in 1951, Kelly worked with Minnelli on one of the most famous and successful of all film musicals, *An American in Paris*. It gave Kelly the chance to create perhaps the most ambitious dance number ever conceived for a film, the climactic ballet to Gershwin's jazz symphony which gives the film its title and subject. In this there was perhaps some hint of a desire to impress, to be 'arty' rather than 'artistic', which has on and off been the bugbear of Kelly's career. But the combination of brilliant camerawork, dazzling design (inspired by a variety of Impressionist and Post-Impressionist painters) and intricate choreography was so impressive in this case that few critics were ready to argue.

Just singin' and dancin'

Donen, meanwhile, was directing his own, more modest films. In *Royal Wedding* (1951), he worked for the first time with Fred Astaire, a performer whose relaxed style seemed more readily matched with Donen's temperament than the brash, outgoing quality of Kelly. Yet at this point in their careers Kelly's raw energy and Donen's refinement balanced each other very well; the proof is in their next film

together, *Singin' in the Rain*.

This loving evocation of a half-forgotte Hollywood where silence was still golde contains one of Kelly's best performances. plays a star of silent films who realizes that hitherto unexploited musical abilities can the way to new success in the talkies. The tit number gave him the chance to create finest solo. The film also has one of the funnie scripts (by Comden and Green) a musical w ever blessed with, a charming female lead Debbie Reynolds, a perfect sidekick for the he in Donald O'Connor, with his big solo 'Mal 'Em Laugh', and a wonderful supporting pe formance from Jean Hagan as the awful Lir Lamont, whose face is her fortune and voi her ruin.

This was the high point of Kelly and Donen work together as co-directors. Their third fil in harness, *It's Always Fair Weather* (1955) was built on the same idea of using a team three as in *On the Town* and *Take Me Out to t Ball Game*, but this time the group (Kelly, Da Dailey and Michael Kidd) lacked the necessa sparkle. The basic plot of the film – a group wartime buddies meet again years later to fir they have nothing in common and that thin have not worked out quite right for any of the – had a curiously bitter quality which r

like Kelly, turned to other things. Donen looked back nostalgically only twice, first in *The Little Prince* (1974), a strange version by Lerner and Loewe of Antoine de Saint-Exupéry's fantasy about a child ruler of a small planet, and in the second half of *Movie Movie* (1978), in which rather half-hearted fun is made of all the Busby Berkeley, putting-on-a-show conventions of the early Thirties. But we have at least the astonishing productions of the Kelly–Donen partnership (and a handful of films by Donen alone) to remind us of what once was. These still seem as fresh and alive as the day they were made.

JOHN RUSSELL TAYLOR

: Leslie Caron partners Kelly in a vigorous ~tine from An American in Paris. *Top right: ~en Brides for Seven Brothers was one of ~nley Donen's most notable successes as a ~ctor in his own right. Above: Barbra ~eisand in* Hello, Dolly!, *a musical that Kelly ~cted when his dancing days were done*

~ount of whipped-up enthusiasm could quite ~e. But by that time Kelly and Donen both had ~jects of their own which clearly offered them ~re personal satisfaction than their collabor-~ons together. Kelly had starred in and ~reographed another Minnelli musical, ~gadoon (1954) – not one of the happier efforts ~ either – and had just finished his first solo ~ture as director, an ambitious (perhaps ~r-ambitious) three-part dance film called ~itation to the Dance. This allowed him to show ~ his gifts as a dancer and choreographer in ~ee styles – classical, jazz, and in the cartoon ~uence, experimental. The film was an ex-~sive failure at the box-office. He then ~eared in George Cukor's *Les Girls* (1957), the ~t major musical in which he starred. ~bsequently he did a memorable TV special, ~ncing: a Man's Game, which emphasized the ~her edgy over-insistence on virility which ~s always been part of his dancing style, and

directed, among a number of straight comedies and lightweight dramas, one elephantine musical, the multi-million-dollar *Hello, Dolly!* (1969) starring Barbra Streisand.

Raising the roof

Donen, on the other hand, went for a while from hit to hit. He directed one of the most delightful minor MGM musicals, *Give a Girl a Break* (1953), then scored a big success at the same studio with *Seven Brides for Seven Brothers* (1954), still remembered for the astounding acrobatic style of six of the seven brothers (the seventh was Howard Keel, who never did anything so flighty as to dance) in the big barn-raising ballet. After *It's Always Fair Weather*, Donen went to Paramount to make *Funny Face* (1957) with Fred Astaire and Audrey Hepburn, the best MGM musical MGM *never* made, with most of that studio's team transported bodily to Paramount because of Hepburn's contractual commitments. Then Donen moved to Warner Brothers as a producer-director, providing the cinematic know-how to match George Abbot's staging skills in two excellent musical collaborations, *The Pajama Game* (1957) and *Damn Yankees*.

The great days of the Hollywood musical were over by the end of the Fifties and Donen,

Gene Kelly: filmography
1942 For Me and My Gal (GB: For Me and My Girl). **'43** Pilot No 5; DuBarry Was a Lady; Thousands Cheer; The Cross of Lorraine. **'44** Cover Girl (+uncredited co-chor); Christmas Holiday. **'45** Anchors Aweigh (+co-chor). **'46** Ziegfeld Follies. **'47** Living in a Big Way (+chor). **'48** The Pirate (+co-chor); The Three Mus-keteers; Words and Music (+chor. of own number). **'49** Take Me Out to the Ball Game (+co-chor) (GB: Everybody's Cheering); On the Town (+co-dir;+co-chor). **'50** The Black Hand; Summer Stock (+uncredited chor. of own number) (GB: If You Feel Like Singing); It's a Big Country. **'51** An American in Paris (+chor). **'52** Singin' in the Rain (+co-dir;+co-chor); The Devil Makes Three. **'54** Brigadoon (+chor); Invitation to the Dance (+dir;+sc;+co-chor); Seagulls Over Sorrento (GB: Crest of the Wave); Deep in My Heart (guest). **'55** It's Always Fair Weather (+co-dir;+co-chor). **'57** The Happy Road (+prod;+dir); Les Girls (+uncredited co-chor). **'58** Marjorie Morningstar; The Tunnel of Love (dir. only). **'60** Inherit the Wind; Let's Make Love (guest). **'62** Gigot (dir. only). **'64** What a Way to Go!. **'67** Les Demoiselles de Rochefort (dubbed English version: The Young Girls of Rochefort); A Guide for the Married Man (dir. only). **'69** Hello, Dolly! (dir. only). **'70** The Cheyenne Social Club (prod;+dir. only). **'73** Forty Carats. **'74** That's Entertainment! (co-narr. only). **'76** That's Entertainment, Part 2 (dir;+co-narr. only). **'77** Viva Knievel!

Stanley Donen: filmography
1943 Best Foot Forward (ass. chor;+act. only). **'44** Hey, Rookie (ass. chor. only); Jam Session (ass. chor. only); Cover Girl (co-chor. only); Kansas City Kitty (co-chor. only). **'45** Anchors Aweigh (co-chor. only). **'46** Holiday in Mexico (co-chor. only); No Leave, No Love (co-chor. only). **'47** Living in a Big Way (ass. chor. only); This Time for Keeps (co-chor. only); Killer McCoy (ass. dir. only). **'48** Big City (ass. dir. only); A Date With Judy (ass. dir. only); The Kissing Bandit (ass. dir. only). **'49** Take Me Out to the Ball Game (co-chor. only) (GB: Everybody's Cheering); On the Town (co-dir;+co-chor. only). **'51** Royal Wedding (GB: Wedding Bells); Love Is Better Than Ever (GB: The Light Fantastic). **'52** Singin' in the Rain (co-dir;+co-chor. only); Fearless Fagan. **'53** Give a Girl a Break (+co-chor.). **'54** Seven Brides for Seven Brothers; Deep in My Heart (+co-chor). **'55** It's Always Fair Weather (co-dir;+co-chor. only); Kismet (some scenes only, uncredited). **'57** Funny Face; The Pajama Game (co-dir;+co-prod. only); Kiss Them for Me. **'58** Indiscreet (+prod.) (GB); Damn Yankees (co-dir;+co-prod. only) (GB: What Lola Wants). **'59** Once More, With Feeling! (+prod). **'60** Surprise Package (+prod) (GB); The Grass Is Greener (+prod) (GB). **'63** Charade (+prod). **'66** Arab-esque (+prod) (GB); Two for the Road (+prod) (GB). **'67** Bedazzled (+prod) (GB). **'69** Staircase (+prod). **'74** The Little Prince (+prod). **'75** Lucky Lady. **'78** Movie Movie. **'80** Saturn 3 (+prod).

I could go on singing

'I'm sick and tired of being called "poor Judy Garland". Maybe this will distress a lot of people but I've got an awfully nice life. I really have. I like to laugh. I like to have a bag of popcorn and go on a roller-coaster now and then. I wouldn't have been able to learn a song if I'd been as sick as they've printed me all the time'

Judy Garland

Judy Garland is one of the great legends of the movies; yet paradoxically, considerably less than half of her professional career – which occupied the best part of 44 of her 47 years of life – was spent in films. The intervening periods were taken up with her ever-growing and unkindly publicized personal problems. She was impatient with the view, constantly expressed by the popular press, that she was a show business tragedy. On one occasion she confided: 'People say and print and believe – the stupid ones, and that's the minority – that I'm either a drunk or a drug addict. It's a goddam wonder I'm not.'

She was born Frances Gumm in Grand Rapids, Minnesota, on June 10, 1922. Her parents, Frank and Ethel Gumm, had had a vaudeville act for a while before they settled in the movie business. Her father became a cinema proprietor and her mother – bent perhaps on fulfilling her own thwarted ambitions through her children – had formed the two older daughters into a sister act that performed in the vaudeville part of the cinema's shows. As legend has it, Baby Gumm (as the adored and spoiled youngest child was known) made her debut when she was around two and a half years old, bringing the house down with a rendering of 'Jingle Bells'; with great delight

she encored repeatedly until she was dragged off, struggling, by her father. She had tasted, for the first time, the adulation of audiences which was, it seemed, eventually to become a necessary drug like all the rest. Unsatisfied, she was later to confide: 'Being Judy Garland – sure I've been loved by the public. I can't take the public home with me . . .'

When they moved to California, the whole family had to work in vaudeville – the parents as Frank and Virginia Lee and the children as the Gumm Sisters – to eke out the meagre takings of the new cinema.

It soon became clear that Baby Gumm was the star, even though one unfeeling manager advised her: 'You may sing loud but you don't sing good'. At six she had a solo spot at Loews' State Theatre in Los Angeles, singing 'I Can't Give You Anything but Love', dressed as Cupid. With so precocious a repertoire and technique and so loud a voice, it was hardly surprising that audiences paid her the dubious compliment of suspecting she was a midget.

When she was 11 she changed her name. The Gumm girls had been rushed into a vaudeville bill in Chicago to replace a drop-out act – and arrived to find that they had been billed as 'The Glum Sisters'. The compere of the show was George Jessel, who persuaded them

Top left: Judy Garland waiting in the wings of the London Palladium. Top: 'Dear Mr Gable' convinced MGM of her gifts. Above: in the MGM canteen are, from left to right, Freddie Bartholomew, an unknown girl, Mickey Rooney, Deanna Durbin, Judy Garland and Jackie Cooper

that it was not a good stage name anyway an proposed Garland instead. A little later, France took the name 'Judy' from a current Hoag Carmichael hit song.

Mrs Gumm had battled, without success, t get her children into movies. Their only ap pearance had been with a troupe of othe infant performers, the Meglin Kiddies, in 1929 short – *The Old Lady and the Shoe*. In 1934 however, Judy Garland acquired an agent, A Rosen, and at least one admirer within MGM Joseph Mankiewicz. Between them they ma ged to arrange an audition. The story is a show business legend – how Judy was summoned at such short notice that she had not even time to change out of her play clothes or to her hair.

No doubt this impromptu and informal appearance enhanced the child's open and appealing personality. She made sufficient impression on Ida Koverman, Louis B. Mayer's influential secretary, and Jack Robbins, the company's talent chief, for them to bring in the studio rehearsal pianist, Roger Edens, and send for Mayer himself. Mayer, who was harassed by the current internecine struggles of the company, came reluctantly. He listened without a word and a few days later offered a contract – unprecedentedly without asking for a screen test.

The MGM days began inauspiciously with the sudden death of Frank Gumm, which can hardly have helped Judy Garland's emotional and psychological development. Despite this, she was later to say that the first days were 'a lot of laughs'. Labour laws required the studio to give its children adequate schooling and Garland found herself in a class-room with

Lana Turner, Jackie Cooper, Deanna Durbin, Freddie Bartholomew and other youthful actors. With Durbin she was teamed in a short, *Every Sunday* (1936), which was so unpromising that Durbin's option was dropped (she was triumphantly snatched up and made into a star by Universal) and Garland was loaned to 20th Century-Fox for *Pigskin Parade* (1936), a college musical in which she sang three songs, hated herself for looking like 'a fat little pig with pigtails' and won one or two favourable notices.

The studio still had no plans for her; it was Roger Edens who conceived the ruse that finally convinced MGM what a treasure they had on their hands. Clark Gable's thirty-sixth birthday was celebrated with a studio party on the set of *Parnell* (1937) and Edens devised a special treatment of 'You Made Me Love You' with Garland doing a monologue, 'Dear Mr Gable', in the character of a devoted admirer writing a fan letter. Gable was greatly touched and Garland was launched. MGM at once put her – and Edens' 'Dear Mr Gable' number – into *Broadway Melody of 1938* (1937).

She then co-starred with Mickey Rooney,

with whom she found an instant sympathy, in *Thoroughbreds Don't Cry* (1937) and with another school-fellow, Freddie Bartholomew, in *Listen, Darling* (1938) – in which the two youngsters kidnap the widowed Mary Astor and take her on a search for a suitable husband. In *Everybody Sing* (1938) she appeared alongside the great Broadway veteran, Fanny Brice.

In all of these films Garland sang, for the public had already succumbed to the extraordinary voice. It was thrillingly strident (as a child she had been disrespectfully dubbed 'Little Miss Leather Lungs') with a heart-rending catch, miraculously expressive and, even in those early days, so mature that she was able to give convincing interpretations of the great torch songs like Fanny Brice's 'My Man'. The musical staff at MGM, where the gifted Arthur Freed was already the dominant influence, wisely preferred to exploit the vivacity and humour of her gifts in songs like 'Swing, Mr Mendelssohn' and 'Zing Went the Strings of My Heart'.

Garland was teamed with MGM's most popular juvenile, Mickey Rooney, in the Andy

Right: Mickey Rooney and Judy Garland falling in love over ice-cream sodas in Love Finds Andy Hardy. *Bottom: MGM promoted their singing and dancing duo – Garland and Rooney – as 'the most popular young movie stars in the world'. Bottom right: Judy Garland as Dorothy with her dog Toto in the film that firmly established her in the hearts of the public* The Wizard of Oz

Above: Judy Garland was given a major adult part for the first time when she played a vaudeville performer caught up in World War I in For Me and My Gal. *Above right: on the set of* Meet Me in St Louis, *in which she plays the romantic Esther; it was directed by her future husband Vincente Minnelli. Right: with Robert Walker in the wartime romance* The Clock

Hardy series which acquired a new musical flavour. Garland acted and sang in three of the series – *Love Finds Andy Hardy* (1938), *Andy Hardy Meets Debutante* (1940) and *Life Begins for Andy Hardy* (1941) – although the studio saw fit to remove Garland's songs from the release print of the last of these.

This series was interrupted by the film which firmly and finally established Garland as a major star and gave her the theme tune which she sang and continually enriched until the end of her life – 'Over the Rainbow'. L. Frank Baum's series of Oz books for children had begun to appear in 1900 and had become best-sellers. A silent version of *The Wizard of Oz* had been made in 1925 with Larry Semon and Oliver Hardy. MGM were prepared to lavish colour and $2 million on a new version. They also intended to lavish Shirley Temple on it but, when she was not available, Garland was accepted as a second choice. There was difficulty and indecision over directors, but credit for *The Wizard of Oz* (1939) finally went to Victor Fleming as it did for *Gone With the Wind* (also 1939). The script was intelligent, the technical achievement high and the cast distinguished; but it was Judy Garland's picture.

Audiences adored Garland – as they were to go on doing – for her vitality, her gaiety, her openness, her intimacy and the generous, friendly, loving nature in her. But behind the scenes life was taking on a darker aspect. Her irrepressible *joie de vivre* included a hearty appetite; but the malted milks and Hershey bars to which she was addicted made her fat. Mayer himself laid down what she might eat (mostly chicken soup) and what she might not.

She discovered, among other evidence of the studio's parental care for her, that the lifelong friend with whom she had moved into a bachelor apartment, had become a company spy, paid to report on her every move. So, it transpired, was her own mother.

To help her fight off the pangs of hunger she was given the newly fashionable drug Benzedrine. To counteract its over-stimulant effects, she was given sleeping pills; to wake her up again, more stimulants and then other pills to calm her nerves. Despite all the later efforts of her friends and publicists to play down the inevitable effects of all this 'medication', the dependence was to become a nightmare and culminated in her death due to an accidental drug overdose.

The public could not have enough of her and the company worked her mercilessly. She was threatened with the fate that had afflicted Mary Pickford 20 years before: public and studio would not let her grow up. When she played the dual role of a girl and her mother in *Little Nellie Kelly* (1940), Mayer is said to have gone around wailing, 'We can't let that baby have a baby'. Mayer and the studio did no hide their displeasure when, in 1941, Garlan married orchestra leader David Rose and it certain that they did nothing to ward off th rapid break-up of the marriage.

In the next three years Garland appeared i a number of attractive musicals – *Ziegfel Girl* (1941), *For Me and My Gal* (1942), *Present ing Lily Mars* and *Thousands Cheer* (both 1943

In 1944 came *Meet Me in St Louis*, still th most cheering and charming of all the MGM musicals, in which Garland sings some of he most memorable songs. Her dramatic talent about which she continued to have doubts had become much more refined: her grea achievement in this film is to subsume hersel into the whole ensemble of finely cast actor portraying an ordinary family of 1904 and th excitements of the great St Louis Exposition.

The director of *Meet Me in St Louis* wa Vincente Minnelli, whom she married – thi time with the studio's delighted approval – i July 1945. In March of the following year thei daughter Liza was born. She was delivered b Caesarian section which added to the growing

Above left: Judy Garland with Fred Astaire in costume for their 'Couple of Swells' number from Easter Parade. Above: Vincente Minnelli adjusts his wife's collar before a comedy scene with Gene Kelly in The Pirate. Far left: as the rising singer in A Star Is Born. Left: in Judgement at Nuremberg as the German housewife who testifies about Nazi crimes

strains on Garland's health. Minnelli directed her in her first non-musical role, *The Clock* (1945), a short episode in the *Ziegfeld Follies* (1946) and in the wonderfully inventive *The Pirate* (1948) in which her co-star was the young Gene Kelly.

But the strain was taking its toll. The studio showed scant patience with her illnesses, her unpunctuality and absences and her growing nerviness. She was sick during the making of *The Pirate* and hospitalized after it. MGM planned a new Garland–Kelly musical but Kelly had an accident and was replaced by Fred Astaire in *Easter Parade* (1948), one of Garland's gayest films. A further Astaire–Garland vehicle was frustrated when she was replaced due to illness in *The Barkleys of Broadway* (1949). Without pause, however, she went into *Words and Music* (1948), a musical biography of Rogers and Hart, and *In the Good Old Summertime* (1949), a musical remake of *The Shop Around the Corner* (1940). Exhausted, she managed to record songs for *Annie Get Your Gun* (1950), but when filming began she was replaced as 'unreliable'.

Weak and sick she struggled through *Summer Stock* (1950), although on the screen she is as vital, as irresistibly cheerful as at any time in her career: the audience detects nothing of the intolerable exhaustion. After this she was, for once, herself called upon to replace another star: June Allyson was having a baby and could not do *Royal Wedding* (1951). Garland recorded the songs but then fell ill. MGM suspended her and her days with the company that, from her fourteenth year, had appointed itself her parent and family and keeper, were over.

The next four years saw her start a new career as a variety and concert performer. On April 9, 1951 she began a season at the London Palladium and in October of the same year she launched into a 19-week season at the Palace, New York, which is now regarded as vaudeville history. Again the strain proved too great for her and she missed several performances from illness.

Divorced from Minnelli, she married Sidney Luft, by whom she had two more children – Lorna and Joey – and with whom she formed a

production company, Transcona. For Warner Brothers, Transcona made *A Star Is Born* (1954), directed by George Cukor – who had style and taste and appreciation of both the talent and problems of an artist like Garland. The film was brutally manhandled by the studio who cut it extensively and then added new material (which, at least, included the memorable 'Born in a Trunk' number). This somewhat hoary sob story, about a Hollywood marriage between a rising star (the girl) and a falling meteor, had been filmed originally in 1936 by William Wellman with Fredric March and Janet Gaynor. In Cukor's hands it acquired new life and depth: at one level it poignantly echoed Garland's own real-life problems with Hollywood; at another, there was never any difficulty in believing in her as a star of supreme status.

Her role in *A Star Is Born* is perhaps her best and she certainly gave her most moving and dramatic performance. For all practical purposes it marked the end of her film career. She had a single impressive scene in Stanley Kramer's *Judgement at Nuremberg* (1961). *A Child Is Waiting* (1963), a low-pitched, appealing film about a home for sub-normal children, echoed, in Garland's touching scenes with the children, her hospital periods in which she had found relief in working and playing with child patients.

She had by this time developed a great liking for London, where she made *I Could Go on Singing* (dir. Ronald Neame, 1963). The film was an undistinguished melodrama with musical numbers but the theme – the struggle between a singing star and her husband (Dirk

Top: I Could Go on Singing, *the story of a famous singer who tries to reclaim her son from her ex-husband, had sad echoes of Garland's own life. Above: surrounded by retarded children in* A Child is Waiting

Bogarde) for possession of their children – was uncomfortably close to life. Garland was suing for divorce from Sidney Luft and their wrangles over the children added to the unattractive publicity Garland was to receive in her few remaining years.

The fans who crowded the concerts which were to be her work from this time on were more and more enthusiastic, more and more demanding. From her own account, she derived some sort of comfort from this public affection. Her private life became more difficult. After earning an estimated $8 million, mismanagement had left her with nothing but crippling debts. Her health progressively worsened. Non-appearances and tragically incapable performances, along with a short-lived marriage to Mark Herron, the struggles with Luft over the children, breach of contract suits and other major or minor misfortunes, invariably gathered publicity.

To the end, though, she could still suddenly snap back into form to excite her audiences as few other performers have done and then move them (and herself) to real tears as she sat on the edge of the stage, suddenly transported back in time, once again little Dorothy from *The Wizard of Oz,* singing – huskily and hopefully – 'Over the Rainbow'.

The end came unexpectedly. Garland had married actor Mickey Deane, and in the brief period that they were together seemed calm and happy, although by this time she was

terribly thin and her face showed, more than ever before, the strains of time. On the morning of June 22, 1969 her husband found her dead in their London apartment; her death, it seems, caused by an accidental overdose of sleeping pills.

'She was a lady', James Mason, her co-star in *A Star Is Born* said at her funeral, 'who gave so much and richly both to her vast audience whom she entertained and to the friends around her whom she loved that there was no currency in which to repay her. And she needed to be repaid, she needed devotion and love beyond the resources of any of us.'

DAVID ROBINSON

Filmography

1929 The Old Lady and the Shoe (short) **'35** La Fiesta de Santa Barbara (short). **'36** Every Sunday (short); Pigskin Parade (GB: The Harmony Parade). **'37** Broadway Melody of 1938; Thoroughbreds Don't Cry. **'38** Everybody Sing; Listen, Darling; Love Finds Andy Hardy. **'39** The Wizard of Oz; Babes in Arms. **'40** Andy Hardy Meets Debutante (GB: Andy Hardy Meets a Debutante); Strike Up the Band; Little Nellie Kelly. **'41** Ziegfeld Girl; Meet the People (short); Life Begins for Andy Hardy; Babes on Broadway. **'42** For Me and My Gal (GB: For Me and My Girl). **'43** Presenting Lily Mars; Girl Crazy; Thousands Cheer. **'44** Meet Me in St Louis. **'45** The Clock (GB: Under the Clock). **'46** The Harvey Girls; Ziegfeld Follies; Till the Clouds Roll By. **'48** The Pirate; Easter Parade; Words and Music. **'49** In the Good Old Summertime. **'50** Summer Stock (GB: If You Feel Like Singing). **'54** A Star Is Born. **'**Pepe (voice only). **'61** Judgement at Nuremberg. **'62** Gay Puree (voice only). **'63** A Child Is Waiting; I Could Go on Singing (GB).

Top: even under great strain Judy Garland could always look glamorous. Above: she relaxes while shooting A Star Is Born *with two of her children – Lorna Luft (in her arms) and Liza Minnelli, aged seven*

Back to the drawing board

During the Forties animated films reached a new maturity,
whether as comic cartoons, instructional aids, or painstaking masterpieces

For animation, that strangely peripheral art which existed within the comparatively new medium of cinema, the Forties represented the first decade of real expansion and self-discovery. In its infancy, animation had been little more than short silent cartoons accompanied by lively musical motifs knocked out on the cinema piano. Walt Disney, however, had turned this small-scale art into a viable industrial wing of movie entertainment and by 1940 he dominated the scene in Hollywood.

The recent success of his first feature-length picture – *Snow White and the Seven Dwarfs* (1937) – and his prolific output of cartoons meant that other potential animators, lacking the resources and business acumen which lay behind Walt Disney Enterprises, barely survived the high costs of production and could ill afford the specialized kind of marketing that animated films required if they were to be widely distributed.

Nevertheless, in spite of these problems, animators found new forms of expression through the demands of wartime propaganda. The post-war period saw the development of allied forms of animation, especially puppetry, and the many kinds of abstract, mobile designs pioneered by Norman McLaren in Canada.

The early Forties, however, belonged to Disney. For him it was a period of continued achievement in the particular style he had made his own. Moving on from the simple black-and-white, semi-silhouette stylization that had characterized the early cartoons, such as Felix the Cat and Disney's own *Steamboat Willie* (1928) or *Skeleton Dance* (1929), Disney's artists had been encouraged towards a degree of pictorial naturalism which was often at odds with the fantasy of his subjects. While Pluto, Goofy, Donald Duck and Mickey Mouse were all splendid creatures born of the comic imagination, Disney's more naturalistic humans – from Snow White onwards – were conceived with a kind

of childishly sentimental artistry. Their movements were given a spurious activity derived from the technique known as rotoscope, whereby the human figure was recorded in movement with a live-action camera and the resultant images were then traced in the form of graphics and used as models for the animation process.

As Disney gradually abandoned the production of shorts in favour of features, the conventional nature of his pictorial style and treatment became ever more atrophied. Even so, the sheer dramatic force of his early feature films was often admirable and was so strong, indeed, that *Snow White and the Seven Dwarfs* was restricted by the censorship authorities in Britain because it was felt the scenes with the witch would be frightening to children. Even *Pinocchio* (1940) had sequences that were reckoned to alarm the young.

But there was always a soft centre to the design of Disney's more humanized figures, including animals like Dumbo or Bambi. Elaborately modelled and curvaceously moulded, their movements tended to undulate with a kind of flatulent roll. The old sharpness of gesture and wild distortion of movement – so remarkable in the Thirties shorts

Top left: a typical Bugs Bunny situation as drawn by Chuck Jones with the initials 'BB' and the carrot-fetish pursued to surreal extremes. Above: an example of the propaganda value of cartoons. Above left: a characteristic scene from the Woody Woodpecker cartoons originated by Walter Lantz

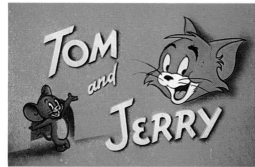

Above: the Jack-in-the-box and the dancing doll, animated toy figures from Paul Grimault's innovative short Le Petit Soldat. *Top right: Walt Disney, Mickey Mouse and a mountain of fan mail. Centre right: opening title from the Hanna/Barbera/Quimby cartoon* Tom and Jerry. *Right: John Halas and Joy Batchelor, the eminent British animators who began their work together in the Forties*

like *The Grasshopper and the Ants* (1934) or *Clock Cleaners* (1937) – gave way to softer, sweeter rhythms in the later, longer films.

However, by the Forties, the roster of Disney's feature-length successes grew and included *Pinocchio*, in which Jiminy Cricket appeared as one of Disney's more inspired comic characters, and the highly uneven *Fantasia* (1940), *The Reluctant Dragon*, the sentimental *Dumbo* (both 1941) and *Bambi* (1942). Groups of films were also released in packages and propaganda material like *Saludos Amigos* (1943) was also highly acclaimed. The latter was designed to promote the USA's image in South America during World War II and was financed with a grant from the US State Department. At the end of the decade *Ichabod and Mr Toad* (1949) was adapted from Washington Irving's folk tale *The Legend of Sleepy Hollow*.

The studios became small factories employing a large staff of highly talented designers and technicians to whom Disney permitted little artistic freedom. Among the major artists who worked for him were several who were later to become celebrated animators in their own right. It came as a grave shock to Disney when, during the summer of 1941, recurrent labour disputes came to a head and

Cartoonists often worked under trying conditions in the big studios but still made memorable films

closed the studios down for nine weeks. The staff grievances not only involved wages and hours of work but also the lack of recognition given to the senior artists.

The general popularity of short cartoons supporting the normal live-action feature films led the larger film corporations to found their own animation units. At Warner Brothers, for example, violence of action prevailed to the point of burlesque. In the Forties many new cartoon series rivalled the popularity of Disney's films – with work at once cruder and more anarchically vital than anything his studio could devise.

Walter Lantz became celebrated for his Woody Woodpecker character and Paul Terry for Terrytoons. Tex Avery and Chuck Jones developed the characters of Bugs Bunny for Warners and stayed at that studio from 1938 to 1952, working in the wooden animation building known as Termite

Terrace. Chuck Jones worked on many established cartoon characters including Bugs Bunny, Daffy Duck, Porky Pig, Sylvester and Tweety Pie. He even directed a propaganda film, *Hell Bent for Election* (1944), on behalf of Franklin D. Roosevelt's last election campaign. Jones also developed the fearful rivalries of Wile E. Coyote and Mimi the Road Runner: the road runner is the State bird of Arizona and Mimi emerged as an extraordinary, ostrich-like bird, totally indestructible, with the capacity to tear along highways in the desert at supersonic speeds – leaving a plume of smoke behind.

Friz Freleng revelled in the ceaseless pursuit of the diminutive bird Tweety Pie by the scraggy scavenger-cat Sylvester, who always gets the worst of Tweety Pie's destructive stratagems. At MGM, William Hanna, Joseph Barbera and Fred Quimby created the savagely fought cat-and-mouse wars of Tom and Jerry.

These films normally consisted of six minutes of mayhem in the form of cumulative gags lasting about one minute each, in which the pursuer aims to 'get' the pursued, only in turn to be foiled by the superior wits of his intended victim.

The characters, drawn with little or no solid moulding to suggest bodily vulnerability, are subected to every form of catastrophic destruction. They are crushed by massive, falling weights, pressed into the ground in incredible shapes or flattened against walls in hard-line, geometric patterns. For such highly schematic figures, no physical destruction is possible. The crudity of the gags flowed with insatiable, mischievous ingenuity from their tireless creators. The big factor in such animation was continuous movement; as Chuck Jones has put it: 'Movement is how animation *acts*. What makes a cartoon character significant is not how it looks, it's how it moves.'

Meanwhile, another powerful and very distinct form of dramatic imagery was being developed in France by Paul Grimault in collaboration with his long-term associate André Sarrut, most notably in the grim fairy-tale *Le Petit Soldat* (1947, The Little Soldier), a drama played out by animated toy figures – two lovers (a dancing doll and a toy soldier) and a huge grimacing Jack-in-the-box, who steals the mechanical key which activates the soldier's heart.

Grimault's heroic efforts to create a distinctive feature-length film, *La Bergère et le Ramoneur* (1952, The Shepherdess and the Chimney-sweep), involved him in years of struggle. The film was begun in the late Forties with a script derived from Hans Andersen by Jacques Prévert and was only completed in 1952. Grimault achieved a striking form of stylization; his figures were highly coloured and two-dimensional, with archetypal characterizations. Any trace of sentimentality in his more innocent characters was overridden by the menace

embodied in his villains. His films belong to the more melancholy branch of folklore and fairy-tale, their mood perhaps explained by the fact that his first successes were made during the Occupation and its aftermath: *L'Epouvantail* (1943, The Scarecrow), *Le Voleur de Paratonnerres* (1945, The Boy Who Stole Lightning Conductors) and *La Flûte Magique* (1946, The Magic Flute). Together these films represent a picturesque, even baroque branch of animation.

Another notable artist in France was the Hungarian Jean Image whose initial films, *Rhapsodie de Saturne* (1947, Saturn Rhapsody) and *Ballade Atomique* (1948, Atomic Ballad), were vigorous and original, though he was soon to settle for more commercial work. In the same period, the French animator Omer Boucquey made *Choupinet* (1946) and *Le Troubadour de la Joie* (1949, Troubadour of Joy). *Choupinet* was an elfin figure representing Good who struggles valiantly against the Devil. But Boucquey, like so many animators in Europe and the USA, had to use his medium for publicity and advertising in order to survive.

The particular pictorial style of cartooning represented by Disney and his rivals did not go unchallenged in the USA. European animators of

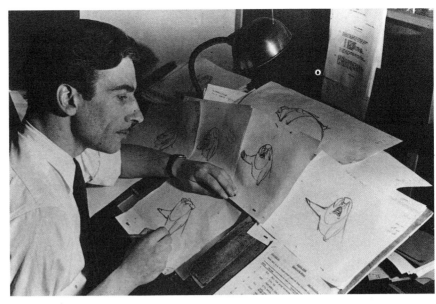

the Twenties and Thirties, such as Oskar Fischinger, Hans Richter, Viking Eggeling, Anthony Gross and Len Lye, had shown that animation could make effective use of many forms of art, however stylized and abstract. Indeed, the more stylized they were, the more the drawn characters appeared to belong naturally and organically to the art world of animation. The labour dispute at Walt Disney's studios in 1941 had had some effect. Gradually the artists who had led the protests left to work on their own. New styles of animation were already being evolved during the war years. John Hubley, Bill Hurtz and Bob Cannon all worked in the Air Force Motion Picture Unit during the war, experimenting with new ideas. Stephen Bosustow worked for Hughes Aircraft and made films on industrial safety, as well as a propaganda film, *Flat-Hatting* (1945), for the US navy. At the same time, the Disney studios made substantial contributions to wartime propaganda: they executed, among many other subjects, the mobile maps illustrating the progress of the war with huge probing arrows for the *Why We Fight* series. They also made the celebrated propaganda cartoon *Victory Through Air Power* (1943).

In Britain in 1940, a new animation unit was

Above: an artist working on the Halas and Batchelor animated feature Animal Farm *(1954), matching his drawings to the scenario. Left: Grimault's* La Flûte Magique. *Below: dancing puppets in Jiří Trnka's* The Czech Year, *a dramatization of legends about the first inhabitants of Bohemia*

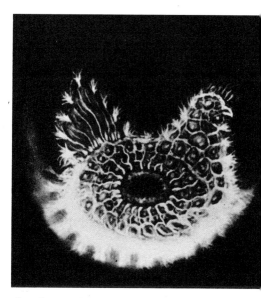

Above: Wile E. Coyote pauses between attempts to ensnare the Road Runner. Above right: La Poulette Grise (1947), one of several films made by Norman McLaren at the National Film Board of Canada on themes from popular folk songs. Below right: Fred, known as 'Tex' Avery was one of Hollywood's finest animators and his sense of humour established itself from the opening titles

established by another Hungarian artist, John Halas, who worked with his wife Joy Batchelor. During the war years, Halas and Batchelor began in the field of specialized technical instruction and propaganda; but their style of design, however simplified for speed of turnover, was of an entirely different nature from the art-work normally associated with the cartoon film.

Halas and Batchelor brought panache to such seemingly pedestrian subjects as cultivation of allotments in wartime and the virtues of saving and recycling waste. The climax of *Dustbin Parade* (1943), for example, was choreographed like a ballet with music by Matyas Seiber, who became one of the most distinguished composers for animated films.

The Home Office sponsored Halas and Batchelor to make *Water for Fire-Fighting* (1948). The twin techniques of graphic and model animation were used to give these films maximum clarity. Britain's post-war socialist government then commissioned the series of films about a character named Charley. These cartoons aimed to explain key points in the government's reformist legislation, such as the new Education Act, in terms of Charley's initial opposition and eventual conversion to the policies of the day. As a relief from five years of making propaganda films Halas and Batchelor, working with the artist Peter Foldes, made a symbolistic film about freedom of the spirit, *Magic Canvas* (1951), for which Seiber composed one of his finest scores.

In Canada, John Grierson, who headed the newly-founded National Film Board of Canada, invited the Scottish artist and film-maker Norman McLaren to join his staff. 'I can only afford one artist,' said Grierson characteristically. McLaren's technique was derived from his experiments in drawing, scratching and painting directly onto celluloid. The majority of McLaren's films were,

therefore, made without the use of the camera; his technical triumph was to synchronize the scratch marks on the celluloid with the beat of the music so that his lines moved precisely according to the rhythm of the soundtrack. Through films like *Stars and Stripes* (1939), *Hen Hop* (1942), *Fiddle-De-Dee* (1947) and *Begone Dull Care* (1949), McLaren developed many forms of experimental animation drawing on his distinctive wit and ingenuity.

McLaren was not the only animator to create a highly personal style for the National Film Board of Canada. George Dunning, who became most famous for his Beatles film *Yellow Submarine* (1968), began his career in the Forties along with Jean-Paul Ladouceur, René Jodoin and Grant Munro, all of whom collaborated on films such as *C'Est l'Aviron* (1944, It's the Oar) and *Là-Haut sur les Montagnes* (1945, Up There in the Mountains) adapted from a French folksong.

Alexandre Alexeieff of France and his American wife Claire Parker devised the infinitely laborious 'pin screen' technique whereby lateral lighting was cast over an area covered by closely set pins which could be raised and lowered to create an irregular surface with highlights and shadows. Very few

Eastern Europe took the lead in post-war animation and produced some of the finest ever cartoon films

films were made by this process but *En Passant* (1943), Alexeieff and Parker's contribution to the National Film Board of Canada's Chants Populaires series, was a remarkable achievement.

A group of American animators joined up with the Disney break-away Stephen Bosustow to form UPA (United Productions of America). They were determined to counteract the influence of Disney by exercising the fullest possible degree of artistic individuality. As a group they worked collectively, each serving the individual talent of the other.

In the early Fifties they set up shop in a series of bungalows in a Hollywood suburb – a marked contrast to Disney's large studio factory. Artists followed their own inclinations in the more abstract or stylized art forms, some of them basing their designs on Matisse's linear, graphic style. The UPA style, insofar as one style existed, was spare and economical; the artists employed the vaguest suggestion of background, furniture or properties necessary for the action. As in the classical Chinese

theatre, if a door or table were needed for momentary use, it would be sketched in for the duration of the action, disappearing the moment it was no longer needed. Otherwise, backgrounds were quite blank.

The UPA group stayed together for only a few years, but the collective experience of working together was a strong influence on each member's later, independent work. UPA was, indeed, an off-Hollywood springboard for these valiant independents. The more celebrated UPA films – Bob Cannon's *Gerald McBoing Boing* (1950) and *Madelene* (1952), John Hubley and Pete Burness's Mister Magoo films, Hubley's *Rooty-Toot-Toot* (1952) were all products of the Fifties, but their origins lay in the collaborative work of UPA in the late Forties. UPA was fortunate in securing distribution for their films through Columbia and thus the initial Mr Magoo films – *Ragtime Bear* and *Fuddy Duddy Buddy* (both 1949) – were released along with films like *Jolson Sings Again* (1949).

The broad distinction between the Disney style

and the UPA school of animation has been analysed by John Smith, an animator at Halas and Batchelor, in the following terms:

'In Disney's cartoon films, the rich, even sugary colouring and bulbous forms are matched by movements that resemble a bladder of water . . . The sentimentality of mood is matched with cute, coy, easy movement . . . excessive distortion and squashing. UPA artists favour simplicity of form and movement, the essence without the frills. Acid colours and sharp forms are matched by movement the way cane or wire would move – springy, whippy, staccato. The wit and cynicism of the cartoons is acted out in slapstick of a high but blasé kind.'

Important new schools of animation were also established in Europe after the war. Zagreb in Yugoslavia and Prague in Czechoslovakia were the centres of the animation industry for which Eastern Europe became famous. The Zagreb school of Dušan Vutokić, Nikola Kostelac and Vatroslav

Mimica belongs essentially to the Fifties and Sixties, but the groundwork for their careers was laid in the Forties. The Zagreb artists pursued the linear, schematic stylization – started by Anthony Gross in the Thirties and developed by UPA in the Forties – to its logical conclusion. Never have so few lines been needed to achieve such richness in character and action.

In Prague, one of the greatest of all talents in international animation was Jiří Trnka, a pre-war puppeteer who began working in films after the war. One of Trnka's earliest films was done in harsh black-and-white line drawings: *Pérák a SS* (1946, *The Springer and the SS*) told the story of a chimney-sweep who turns violent in his resistance to the Nazis. Trnka went on to make films with puppets using the stop-frame principle common to all animated films to effect movement in his puppet characters. His talent for endowing his vast range of puppet characters with uncanny life began in the Forties with such films as the spoof Western *Arie prérie* (1949, *The Song of the Prairie*) and his traditional Czech subject *Špalíček* (1947, *The Czech Year*). Other notable graphic animators whose careers began at the same time as Trnka's, were Jiří Brdečka, Zdenek Miler and Eduard Hofman. At the end of the Forties another Czech, Karel Zeman, created a new form of puppetry using animated figures made of glass in films like *Inspirace* (1949, *Inspiration*).

In both Europe and North America animation underwent widespread diversification during the Forties. The most advanced forms of design moved in the direction of a simplicity of line that recalled the experiments of early animators like Emile Cohl in France and Winsor McCay in the USA, re-establishing the essentials of the art. The finest animators of the Forties believed that animation should remain a highly stylized graphic form that delighted in its own wit of subject and artifice of line. They were also concerned to reduce the complexity of the image so that the labour costs which had made Disney's overheads so enormous could be substantially reduced. Indeed a new era had begun for animation. By the Fifties, it had become an internationally established part of creative cinema, matching every mood from comic caricature to political satire, from folklore to serious drama, from fantasy to the outer limits of mobile abstract art. Animation was soon to become the most technologically advanced form of film-making in existence. ROGER MANVELL

Far left, above: Sylvester and Tweety Pie – characters created by Friz Freleng. Far left, below: a designer's cel from the Mr Magoo cartoons. Above left: The Czech animator Karel Zeman, working with his animated glass figures

The Enchanted Realms of Walt Disney

For decades the release of each new, full-length animated film by Walt Disney has been an eagerly awaited event. Children have thrilled at seeing their favourite characters given the breath of life by his studio's artists, and adults rejoiced at being able to re-experience a child-like sense of wonder and delight

For over fifty years the name of Walt Disney has been synonymous with the production of animated feature films. Even when the Disney empire diversified into other, more lucrative, forms of entertainment, its continuing success was largely due to the consistent popularity of Mickey Mouse and the characters created in the animated features.

The secret of Disney's genius was his skill as a story editor, choosing tales that were ageless or had a period setting, and which could, therefore, be systematically reissued to each new generation of moviegoers. This formula

was established with the ambitious *Snow White and the Seven Dwarfs* (1937). Those critics who had dubbed the film 'Disney's folly' were finally forced to concede that his version of this well-loved story, told with music, humour, romance, pathos, suspense and no small amount of excitement and terror was a huge success – albeit, at a cost of $1,700,000, an expensive one.

The wooden hero
It was thus with confidence that in 1938 Disney launched his artists on several new

projects of which the first to see completion was *Pinocchio* (1940). *Snow White and the Seven Dwarfs* had been Disney's greatest personal achievement, but *Pinocchio* remains his greatest film.

Costing $2.5 million, the film is a masterpiece of animation, containing stunning set-pieces such as the opening multi-plane camera shot of Gepetto's village by starlight, the underwater sequences and the climactic whale chase, all of which proved that Disney's work could no longer be adequately described by the word 'cartoon'. *Pinocchio*'s pictorial richness, imaginative camera angles and fast-moving storyline were enhanced by such superb characterizations as Stromboli, the volcanic puppet-master, and the foxy Dickensian villain J. Worthington Foulfellow. The film also had an exceptional musical score, highlighted by the Oscar-winning song 'When You Wish Upon a Star' sung by Jiminy Cricket, whose moralistic role as Pinocchio's 'official' conscience' helps the film to avoid undue sentimentality. The song, with its promise of dreams coming true, became the touchstone of Disney's screen philosophy.

Brilliant and banal
The year 1940 also saw the premiere of *Fantasia*, a film made possible by the skills developed while working on *Snow White and the Seven Dwarfs* and *Pinocchio*, but which came to a public quite unprepared for any-

© Walt Disney Productions

...hing other than another fairy-tale.

Fantasia grew out of Disney's search for a starring vehicle for Mickey Mouse. Paul Dukas' 'The Sorcerer's Apprentice' was chosen as a musical pantomime for Mickey, and in 1938, Disney invited conductor Leopold Stokowski to record the music.

This collaboration developed into the notion of 'The Concert Feature', as *Fantasia* was first called, for which Disney's artists would animate an entire programme of classical music. The musicologist Deems Taylor was enlisted as an advisor and remained to provide the film's linking narration. Perhaps the selection of compositions was too diverse, perhaps the differing approaches of the various sequence directors is too perceptible – whatever the reason, the film is a patchwork of the brilliant and the banal.

Fantasia contains sequences of exquisite animation (the flowers, fairies' and dancing mushrooms of the 'Nutcracker Suite' and the terrors of the prehistoric pageant illustrating Stravinsky's 'The Rite of Spring'); and splendidly conceived passages of humour (Mickey's sorcery and the 'Dance of the Hours' ballet choreographed for ostriches, hippopotami and alligators). But *Fantasia* also contains items of pretentious trivia (the abstract accompaniment to Bach's Toccata and Fugue in D Minor); arch-sentimentality (the pseudo-religious 'Ave Maria', which serves as a gauche postscript to the fearful grotesqueries of Mussorgsky's 'Night on Bald Mountain'); and blatant tastelessness (the Hollywood kitsch with which Disney polluted Beethoven's pastoral landscape).

Fantasia remains a brave experiment, and a clear development of the use of music in the early Silly Symphonies, but Disney's uneasiness in the 'highbrow' atmosphere of the concert hall is reflected in the completed film.

Studio strike

Financial pressures caused Disney to abandon the sophisticated sound system (Fantasound) which he had developed for the film. Cut from 126 to 82 minutes, *Fantasia* went on general release in the USA with a Western. The press were divided over the picture and the public were confused by it. Plans to re-release the film with a varied repertoire never materialized, and it remained in its emasculated form until

1956, when most of the deleted footage was reinstated and, becoming a cult movie, it at last began to show a profit on the original investment of $2,280,000.

Fantasia was a financial failure at a time when Disney could least afford one. The war in Europe was curtailing overseas markets and had already affected the earning potential of *Pinocchio*. In addition, Disney's other major project, *Bambi* (1942) (in production since 1937), was costing vast sums of money.

Disney made economies and quickly put two less ambitious films into production. The first of these, *The Reluctant Dragon* (1941), combined live-action footage (featuring Robert Benchley on a tour of the studio) with three short cartoons. The second was the fully animated *Dumbo* (1941).

However, by this time financial uncertainties about the studio's future had led its huge work-force to become more discontented with labour relations in the studio. Disney refused to sign with either of the leading cartoonists' unions and a bitter strike ensued that was only finally resolved in his absence. Nelson Rockefeller, who was co-ordinator of Inter-American Affairs, asked Disney to make a goodwill tour of South America as part of the government's Good Neighbor policy. Disney agreed, on the understanding that he be allowed to gather film material while he was there, and that the movies that resulted would be underwritten by the government.

The tour was a success and a financial bonus to the studio. It also took Disney out of the centre of controversy so that others could settle the strike. However, the studio's unique creative atmosphere was irreparably damaged by the dispute.

Flights of fancy

By the time Disney returned from South America, *Dumbo* had been completed. In many ways, it is Disney's most satisfying feature. Running for just 64 minutes, the film tells a simple story dramatically and with great poignancy – and at a cost of only $700,000. The only extraneous sequence is that in which Dumbo has alcoholic hallucinations of pink elephants, and that is pardonable because of its sheer inventiveness.

There are many appealing qualities about *Dumbo*: the circus-poster colourings, the in-

Opposite page: the Prince finds his way to the castle blocked by a dragon in Sleeping Beauty. *Above left: Walt Disney. Above: Mlle Upanova and an alligator chorus in the 'Dance of the Hours' ballet from* Fantasia. *Below: The Three Caballeros was geared to the Latin American market. Bottom: as well as* Bambi, *the poster shows two of the film's most famous creations, Flower the skunk and Thumper the rabbit*

© Walt Disney Productions

Enchanting Entertainment for Everyone!

Walt Disney's
BAMBI
TECHNICOLOR

BUBBLING WITH *Laughter!* TINGLING WITH *Excitement!* SPARKLING WITH *Delight!*

© Walt Disney Productions

Above left: Lady and the Tramp's *urban setting made the film unusually realistic. Top left: Alice tries to reach the key to the door of Wonderland in* Alice in Wonderland. *Top right: Dick Van Dyke and Julie Andrews in an animated landscape in* Mary Poppins. *Above right: Kaa the snake eyes Mowglie in* The Jungle Book

genious score of funny songs and wistful ballads and the animation set-pieces, such as the raising of the big top by night in torrential rain and the circus train's journey across an animated map of the USA. The film's memorable cast includes Dumbo's champion, the spunky little Brooklyn tough-guy, Timothy Mouse, the negroid crow quintet who teach Dumbo to fly, the bitchy female elephants and the addled Mr Stork who is responsible for the baby Dumbo's delivery. At the centre of this group is the pathetic silent hero himself.

Released a year later, *Bambi* was a very different movie, being as naturalistic as *Dumbo* was stylized. *Dumbo* has the frenzied pace of the circus-ring, but *Bambi* has a hauntingly lyrical rhythm; and, whereas *Dumbo*'s triumph over adversity is lightly handled, the same moral in *Bambi* is heavily underlined.

Although the animals in *Bambi* were modelled on life studies, they were sufficiently 'Disneyfied' to make them appear uncomfortable

residents in the film's beautiful forest settings. The stock cartoon gags used from time to time are intrusive and the animal's childish voices only proved how right the studio had been to keep Dumbo dumb.

There are, nevertheless, moments of animation in *Bambi* which remain unsurpassed; in particular, the battle of the stags (impressively shot in dramatic browns and purples), and the terrifyingly vivid forest-fire sequence. However, American audiences of 1942, now fighting the war they had once hoped would pass them by, found little in the sequestered glades of Bambi's forest with which to identify.

Makeshift movies

The studio survived the war years by making propaganda and training films for the government, although Disney's standards of professionalism often led him to subsidize the official budgets. The most significant of these movies was *Victory Through Air Power* (1943), which had animated sequences of great potency, as when the American Eagle battles with a grotesque Japanese octopus to free the world from its tentacled grasp.

The material gathered on Disney's South American tour was made into two features: *Saludos Amigos* (1943) and *The Three Caballeros* (1945). The first of these films, running for just 43 minutes, scarcely merits feature status,

although it contains some remarkable sequences, particularly the concluding 'Acquarela de Brazil' ('Watercolour of Brazil'), in which an animated paint brush creates a lush jungle background against which a Brazilian parrot, José Carioca, teaches Donald Duck how to dance the samba. This episode heralded even wilder flights of surreal fancy in *The Three Caballeros* which combined real and animated characters. It was this technique which was later to be used in several other features including *Song of the South* (1946), *Mary Poppins* (1964), and *Pete's Dragon* (1978).

The compilation format used in the South American movies, was employed to construct a number of so-called features which contained anything from two to ten short subjects. These films, sometimes linked with live action, are a random rag-bag, in which even the best sequences are hardly masterpieces. Among the highlights are 'Peter and the Wolf' and 'The Whale Who Wanted to Sing at the Met', from *Make Mine Music* (1946); 'Mickey and the Beanstalk', from *Fun and Fancy Free* (1947) and 'Johnny Appleseed' and 'Little Toot', from *Melody Time* (1948).

A new era

This inconsistent, unstatisfying period concluded with the patchy *Ichabod and Mr Toad* (1949). *Cinderella* (1950) marked the beginning

Above left: Captain Hook and his henchman Smee prepare to place a bomb in Peter's underground home in Peter Pan. *Above: Pongo, Missus and their puppies watch TV in* 101 Dalmatians. *Left: alligators Brutus and Nero carry Penny and her teddy-bear off in* The Rescuers; *Bernard and Bianca the mice and their two friends look on helplessly*

and the Seven Dwarfs. But its neglect is undeserved; the wicked fairy Maleficent is the embodiment of evil, the ornate settings are full of gothic horror and the final battle between the Prince and the dragon is a *tour de force*.

The transition from traditional fables and established classics to contemporary stories like *101 Dalmatians* (also the first feature in which songs were of minimal importance) was the most surprising development in the studio's history. However the studio failed to follow up the success of this film with its next movie *The Sword and the Stone* (1963), having to wait until *The Jungle Book* (1967) for its next triumph which Disney, who died on December 15, 1966, was never to witness.

Jungle jive

Released 30 years after the premiere of *Snow White and the Seven Dwarfs*, *The Jungle Book* was the last animated film to be personally produced by Disney. He gave the stories by Rudyard Kipling a decidedly up-beat treatment, and his cast of finely delineated characters jive and swing through rich jungle landscapes. Much of the film's strength was derived from the use of the voice-actor's personalities as character models – particularly George Sanders' sneering Shere Khan, the tiger.

This proved so successful that it became adopted as a standard feature of the studio's post-Disney productions, *The Aristocats* (1970) and *Robin Hood* (1973), presumably in the hope of strengthening stories which show a singular lack of imagination and originality. *Robin Hood* also has the dubious distinction of being technically the worst animated film the studio has ever made, with much of its animation plundered wholesale from earlier films.

Not until *The Rescuers* (1977), did the Disney studio produce a movie which re-established its supremacy of line. Possessing a plot which balances drama with humour and sentiment, it is a film that is worthy of the name of the dream-merchant who 40 years before had laboured at building a folly that became a gateway to a realm of enchantment.

BRIAN SIBLEY

of a new era. This was the first animated feature since *Bambi*, and tried hard to re-create the brilliance of the studio's earlier films without quite capturing their graphic quality of line. *Cinderella* is a graceful film, but its heroine lacks the sympathetic qualities of Snow White, and much of the film's success is due to the mouse characters, Jac and Gus, and their cunning battle with Lucifer the cat.

Alice in Wonderland followed in 1951, and, despite the critics unanimous disapproval, is still the screen's most satisfying interpretation of Lewis Carroll's book. True, the crazy characters are constantly upstaging one another, and the pace is a shade too frenetic, but the comic invention never flags and there is much fine animation, especially in the 'March of the Cards' sequence and the Daliesque nightmare of the finale.

Increasingly in this period we find Disney making concessions to meet what he supposed were the narrow expectations and limitations of his audiences. In *Alice in Wonderland*, he failed to grasp the implicit seriousness of Lewis Carroll's humour and abandoned most of the disturbing elements in the story. Similarly, *Peter Pan* (1953) Disney shows no understanding of the story's sinister and emotional depths or the tragedy that is implicit in Peter's perennial youth. Disney's Peter has charm and bravado but lacks the self-sacrificing heroism

of the original, while the whimpering buffoonery of the film's Captain Hook has nothing of the genuine malevolence of J.M. Barrie's black-hearted Old Etonian.

Changing directions

The increased production of live-action movies and the studio's diversification into television and the amusement-park business contributed to a slowing up of Disney's output of animated films. His next feature, *Lady and the Tramp* (1955), was the first to use CinemaScope; Disney filled the wider screen with a picturesque conception of America at the turn of the century, with its opulent 'gingerbread' architecture and its seedy tenements. The canine characterizations are believable and endearing and the film has much adult appeal, not least because of Peggy Lee's 'bluesy' songs and her sophisticated vocal performance as Peg, the 'Dietrich' of the dog pound.

Sleeping Beauty in 1959 marked the end of another era at the Disney studios, being the last feature to have its characters inked onto the cels by hand – a costly process replaced, in *101 Dalmatians* (1961), by the freer, but less stylish, method of using Xeroxed drawings.

Sleeping Beauty cost an astronomical $6 million and was a financial disaster. It was poorly received by the critics, perhaps because the storyline seemed too close to *Snow White*

Norman McLaren
Scratching for a living

McLaren's career was devoted to extending the possibilities of film as a visual medium. By means of many unusual techniques, including the painting or scratching of designs directly onto celluloid, he created a uniquely personalized type of cinema

Norman McLaren has the unenviable responsibility of personifying experimental animation. At the first sign of an animated abstract squiggle on screen, movie buffs will be heard to mutter, 'Ah, Norman McLaren'. Such universal recognition (even if false) is rare in any branch of cinema, and is a measure of McLaren's astonishing ability to appeal to all nations and ideologies. McLaren's squiggles are still welcome where the 'capitalist lackey'

Donald Duck is *persona non grata*.

McLaren, who was born in 1914 in Stirling, Scotland, studied interior design at the Glasgow School of Art. He became interested in the possibilities of film at the very moment that the Film Society was introducing English audiences to the work of the avant-garde film-makers of the Twenties, such as Pudovkin, Eisenstein and the animators Fischinger and Alexeieff; McLaren quickly laid his hands on a camera

and began to make films. While still at Glasgow he submitted two films to the Scottish Amateur Film Festival and was rewarded by John Grierson, chairman of the Festival's judges, with not just a prize, but the promise of a job at the GPO film unit in London. Thus began an association with Grierson that was to last for a dozen years.

At the GPO McLaren was faced with the daunting task of promoting telephone directories and savings banks, but showed a determined inventiveness, making each film an essay in a different technique. His last film for the GPO, *Love on the Wing* (1938), should have been the first public demonstration of his drawing-on-film technique (he had done earlier experiments at Glasgow). This surreal tale of a love affair between two letters, however, contained the momentary metamorphosis of a pair of scissors into male genitalia, an image that was far too alarming for the Postmaster General of the day, who suppressed the film.

Moving to the USA at the outbreak of World War II, McLaren found little work, but heard

Above: Norman McLaren at work in his studio on Fiddle-De-Dee. *Below: An out-take from* Begone Dull Care, *in which McLaren ignored the filmstrip's frame divisions*

hat Baroness Rebay of the Guggenheim Museum of Non-Objective Art was interested in 'abstract' film (she had commissioned work from the German animator Oskar Fischinger, another recent immigrant); for her, McLaren made *Dots* and *Loops* (both 1940). For these films McLaren drew the soundtrack as well as the images directly onto the film, creating a wholly synthetic composition. At the time this radical procedure was ostensibly no more than an economy measure: 'I had no money for the sound-tape,' he later remarked. In the same year McLaren made *Boogie Doodle*, an improvisation of abstract Expressionist images to an existing musical track.

In 1941 McLaren was asked by Grierson to set up an animation unit at the National Film Board of Canada. Over the next decade McLaren continued to develop his camera-less technique, notably with *Fiddle-De-Dee* (1947), a linear composition drawn along the filmstrip, ignoring the frame line divisions, and the three-part *Begone Dull Care* (1949), a more controlled improvisation to music by Oscar Peterson. The popularity of these two films, which publicly established McLaren's style, derived from the wit and inventiveness with which he drew on film. The scratches and shapes often form recognizable images, a repertory of birds, trees, stars and crescents; and even the wholly abstract lines and fields of colour 'respond' to the music with a sense of life as convincing as that of any cartoon mouse.

During World War II, McLaren made several less abstract, camera-less short films in support of the war effort, but also began to look for a change of pace and method in his work. He discovered a new direction in a series of conventionally photographed films in which subtle changes were made to otherwise static images. In *A Little Phantasy* (1946), the Isle of the Dead (from Arnold Boecklin's painting) undergoes eerie transformations of light and substance by means of a series of overlapping dissolves between drawings. In *C'Est l'Aviron* (1944, It's the Oar), his camera relentlessly voyages into an apparently infinite space, created by adding a continuous zoom movement during the dissolves.

Blinkety Blank (1954), one of the wittiest of McLaren's works, began with the impulse to reverse his usual drawing-on-film procedure. He commented:

'I had made several films by drawing on a blank film. I wondered if I couldn't do the opposite: scratch on black.'

The images, mostly one frame in length, are spaced out along the film, creating brief visual explosions in which the eye, through the persistence of vision, sometimes perceives movement.

Left: Pas de Deux *was filmed in slow motion using multiple superimpositions to create images such as this. Above: two men battle with a chair in* A Chairy Tale *(1957). Right: a squiggle metamorphoses into a snail in* Love on the Wing

The simple logic underlying McLaren's inventiveness, and his willingness to apply it in extreme situations which no-one else would consider, is well demonstrated by the *tour de force* of *Neighbours* (1952) and the series of 'pixillated' shorts that followed. 'Pixillation', a word to which McLaren gave new meaning, involves filming people and objects one frame at a time. In *Neighbours* two men quarrel over the possession of a flower, their hostility escalating until all around them is laid waste and they kill each other. By means of pixillation, all movement in the film seems determined by the invisible force of their will to destroy. The men move without walking; in one shot one of them continually hovers above the ground while menacing his enemy. (The actor was asked to jump, and was then photographed in mid-air for each frame of film.) Made at the time of the Korean War, *Neighbours* is the closest that McLaren ever came to making an overt political statement. McLaren's pacifism had previously led him to work with UNESCO in China and later in India, where he taught simple animation techniques that could be used in health and educational instruction. These projects hint at a rarely acknowledged quality in McLaren's work, the *moral* imperative behind the search for a cinema that can be wholly controlled by the individual, a method of film-making which gives the artist total responsibility for the finished work.

An openly educational facet of McLaren's work can be seen in *Rhythmetic* (1956), in which cut-out paper numerals perform in (and

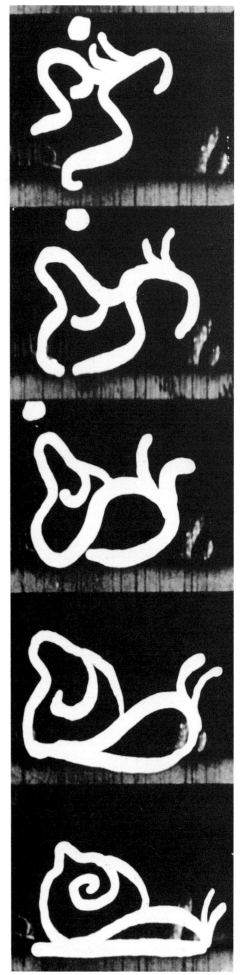

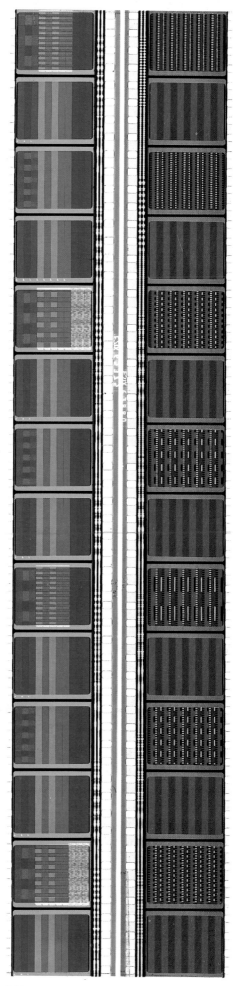

Far left: McLaren has been fascinated by methods of visually representing sound. In Synchromy, *he employed the same image for the soundtrack as for the film, although a conventional soundtrack has been added to thes sequences. Left: McLaren at work with his frequent collaborator Evelyn Lambart. Above: a paper cut-out for* Le Merle *(1958) is laid ou ready for shooting by the rostrum camera*

occasionally rebel against) simple mathematical equations, and *Canon* (1964), a demonstration of this classical musical form, undertaken by a procession of child's building blocks, humans, cats and even a butterfly. Possibly his most austere series of abstract films began with *Lines Vertical* (1960), made with his frequent collaborator Evelyn Lambart. What started life as an attempt to construct a composition from the simplest of means, 'a single vertical line moving in turn slowly then rapidly', grew to include the choreography of a whole company of vertical lines, spawning a second version, *Lines Horizontal* (1962) – the lines simply being re-orientated by means of a prism, but resulting in a very different visual 'mood' – and finally a version in which both vertical and horizontal lines were combined, *Mosaic* (1965), only the intersections of the lines being shown.

Synchromy (1971), equally formal and symmetrical, summarizes McLaren's many excursions into the relation of synthetic sound and image. Since the early Fifties he had used a set of cards, each with a different pattern of black and white stripes, to create the basic sounds on his synthetic soundtracks. Each card represented the wave pattern of a semitone in the musical scale. In *Synchromy* he used these cards for both sound and image, photographing as many as three cards simultaneously to create chords on the soundtrack and as many as 11 side by side to form the image. *Pas de Deux* (1965), often cited as the most elegant of McLaren's films, is, for him, a rare example of technical invention in the film laboratory after filming was completed. Two dancers execute simple ballet movements, their bodies side-lit to emphasize silhouette. By printing successive frames of film in multiple superimposition (up to ten frames at a time), the traces of the dancers' movements in *time* become complex, almost sculptural forms in *space*, the geometry

of choreography being visible as never before

As head of the animation unit at th National Film Board, McLaren encouraged th talents of successive generations of animator influencing many, but never imposing his ow style. Animators as individual as George Du ning, Ryan Larkin and Caroline Leaf develope under his wing, the example of his inventiv ness encouraging them to find styles of the own. Perhaps McLaren's most important con tribution to cinema remains his popularizatio of the notion that film can be a *tangib* medium, that cinema can be created simply b making marks on a strip of film.

DAVID CURTI

Filmography

1933 Hand Painted Abstractions (co-dir. only); Seven Till Five. **'35** Camera Makes Whoopee; Colour Cocktail. **'36** Hell Unlimited (+ co-prod); Defence of Madrid (photo. only). **'37** Book Bargain (animation only); News for the Navy; Mony a Pickle. **'38** Love on the Wing. **'39** The Obedient Flame; Allegro (USA); Rumba (USA); Stars and Stripes (USA). **'40** Dots (USA); Spook Sport (co-dir. only) (USA); Loops (USA); Boogie Doodle (USA). *All remaining films CAN unless specified:* **'41** Mail Early; V for Victory. **'42** Hen Hop; Five for Four. **'43** Dollar Dance. **'44** Alouette (co-dir. only); Keep Your Mouth Shut (co-dir. only); C'Est l'Aviron. **'45** Là-Haut sur Ces Montagnes. **'46** A Little Phantasy/A Little Phantasy on a Nineteenth Century Painting; Hoppity Pop. **'47** Fiddle-De-Dee; La Poulette Grise. **'49** Begone Dull Care (co-dir. only). **'50** Around Is Around (CAN-GB). **'51** Now Is the Time (CAN-GB); Pin Point Percussion. **'52** A Phantasy; Neighbours; Two Bagatelles. **'54** Blinkety Blank. **'56** Rhythmetic (co-dir. only). **'57** A Chairy Tale (co-dir. only). **'58** Le Merle. **'59** Serenal; Short and Suite (co-dir. only); Mail Early for Christmas. **'60** Lines Vertical; Discours de Bienvenue/Opening Speech. **'61** New York Lightboard (co-dir. only). **'62** New York Light Record; Lines Horizontal (co-dir. only). **'63** Christmas Cracker (assoc. dir. only). **'64** Canon (co-dir. only). **'65** Mosaic (co-dir. only); Pas de Deux. **'67** Korean Alphabet. **'69** Spheres. **'71** Synchromy (co-dir. only). **'72** Ballet Adagio. **'73** Pinscreen. **'74** Frame by Frame.

Home on the range

The great Western revival in the Forties reflected America's renewed interest in her history at a time when the war encouraged a spirit of national unity

The successful revival of the Western in 1939 may be ascribed to the mood of the times. War, for the Americans, was on the distant horizon. Europe was dominated by dictators, and alien doctrines were abroad. It was a time when men's minds turned to the nature of 'Americanism' and in particular to the nation's history and its values. It is significant that the Western, celebrating the heroic period of American expansion and highlighting its distinctive qualities of democracy, determination and self-reliance, now eclipsed the distinctly un-American swashbuckler. The latter genre, with its gentlemen heroes adventuring in the aristocratic and hierarchic world of Old Europe (a continent the Americans were currently inclined to mistrust), seemed suddenly anachronistic.

Warner Brothers, the home of swashbuckling films, put Errol Flynn, the erstwhile star of *Captain Blood* (1935) and *The Adventures of Robin Hood* (1938), into a series of expensive, lavish and vigorously staged Westerns in the wake of his success in *Dodge City* (1939). The following year Flynn was seen in *Virginia City* and *Santa Fe Trail* and went on to make other Westerns later in the decade – *They Died With Their Boots On* (1942) and *San Antonio* (1945).

In a hilarious piece of miscasting, Warners even put James Cagney and Humphrey Bogart into a Western romp called *The Oklahoma Kid* (1939). Cecil B. DeMille, the re-creator of the spectacle and grandeur of the Ancient World, had already contributed to the Western genre in the Thirties with *The Plainsman* (1936) and *Union Pacific* (1939). He followed these films with a tribute to the Canadian lawmen in *North West Mounted Police* (1940) and an epic celebration of America's own colonial past in *Unconquered* (1947).

During the war years, all the Hollywood studios contributed to the Western boom. 20th Century-Fox specialized in grand historical epics. They produced *Brigham Young* (1940), dealing with the Mormon trek to Utah in the 1840s, *Western Union* (1941), showing the creation of the telegraph system across the West, and *Buffalo Bill* (1944), a heavily fictionalized account of the career of the frontier scout, buffalo hunter and showman.

The creation by pioneers of the great new western states was celebrated in Columbia's *Arizona* (1940) and *Texas* (1941), MGM's *Wyoming* (1940), Republic's *In Old Oklahoma* (1943) and *Dakota* (1945) and Paramount's *California* (1946). The Texan leader Sam Houston and the frontier scout Kit Carson, two of the most famous heroes of the West, were the subjects of handsome and exciting epics from smaller studios: Republic's *Man of Conquest* (1939) and Monogram's *Kit Carson* (1940).

Other colourful characters of the West flooded into the screen. Many of them were glamorized outlaws committed to 'truth, justice and the American way' and were pitted against the villains of monopolistic corporations, railroad companies, banks and big business. Among the nineteenth-century bad men canonized on celluloid in the

twentieth century were Billy the Kid in *Billy the Kid* (1941) and *The Outlaw* (1943), Belle Starr in a 1941 film of the same name, the Daltons in *When the Daltons Rode* (1940), the Youngers in *Badmen of Missouri* (1941) and Quantrill's Raiders in *Dark Command* (1940).

The re-establishment of the Western as a cinema staple is demonstrated by the eagerness with which film comedians took the trail West to satirize the conventions of the genre. Among the comic cowboys were the Marx Brothers in *Go West* (1940) and Abbott and Costello in *Ride 'Em Cowboy* (1942). One of the best and most enduring of these films is *The Paleface* (1948), which teamed Bob Hope, in his familiar comic persona of the cowardly, lecherous braggart, and Jane Russell, guying the sultry, sexy, siren image she had created in *The Outlaw*.

During the Forties – and after the war in particular – certain trends began to be discerned, which were to flower in the Fifties when Westerns took on a new sharp edge and intensity. The themes of social significance, sexuality, violence and psychoanalysis testify to a process of maturing on the part of both the industry and the audiences. The move towards more demanding, more complex and more controversial Westerns was to find its full expression in the Fifties.

One of the earliest and most celebrated examples of the socially significant Western, however, was William Wellman's *The Ox-Bow Incident* (1943), a powerful and sombre indictment of lynch law. The obvious artificiality of the studio-shot landscapes emphasized the stark nature of the film's message, and a strong cast, headed by Henry Fonda, vividly portrayed the nature and effects of mob rule.

Equally controversial, but for a different reason, was Howard Hughes' production of *The Outlaw*. The film was designed to launch the career of his newest discovery, Jane Russell, and Hughes devoted much footage to advertising Miss Russell's breasts, which the judge who banned the film in Maryland described as hanging over the picture 'like a thunderstorm spread over a landscape'. After problems with the film censors and the Catholic Legion of Decency, Hughes withdrew the film following its premiere in 1943. He then shrewdly created a full-scale pub-

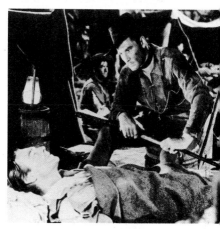

Top: in Texas *two Civil War veterans go into cattle farming. Centre: poster from Fritz Lang's* Western Union. *Above: Errol Flynn and Randolph Scott in* Virginia City

Top: in Go West, the Marx Brothers began the film in some semblance of Western costume but soon abandoned it for their more familiar garb. Above: Jack Benny and his manservant, Rochester, in the comedy Western Buck Benny Rides Again *(1939). Below: the controversial poster for the first openly sexy Western,* The Outlaw

licity campaign to exploit the situation and whip up popular interest in the film. Photographs of Jane Russell in a tight-fitting blouse made her a national sex-symbol long before the film went into release.

The Outlaw finally came out, slightly cut, in 1946 and grossed $3 million in the USA alone. In fact it is a poor film, clumsy, ponderous and slow-moving, the action centring on an all-male triangle, with Pat Garrett pursuing Billy the Kid because he is jealous of Billy's relationship with Doc Holliday. The three men are far more interested in each other and in the prize horse Little Red than in Rio (Jane Russell), the smouldering Mexican girl whose strictly peripheral role is mainly concerned with cooking meals and indulging in a couple of rather suggestive romps with Billy.

Nevertheless *The Outlaw*'s reputation ensured that sex had entered the Western for good. This was confirmed by the success of *Duel in the Sun* (1946), which dealt with the amatory adventures of the half-breed Pearl Chavez (Jennifer Jones), another hot-blooded figure in the tradition of Rio. The film was suffused with a sweaty eroticism and one critic irreverently dubbed it 'Lust in the Dust'.

David O. Selznick sought to repeat the scale and success of *Gone With the Wind* (1939) in *Duel in the Sun* which was directed in the main by King Vidor. Shot in bold Technicolor, this was a Texan *Gotterdämerung* ('Twilight of the Gods'), a veritably Wagnerian Western, full of lurid, blood-red sunsets, breakneck horseback chases, wild dances and intense love-making, punctuated by flashes of lightning and the pealing of bells. The screen constantly

erupted into large-scale action sequences, as wild horses were rounded up, cattlemen confronted the cavalry and a train was derailed. This torrent of activity counterpointed the violent love affair of Pearl Chavez, the spitting, scowling, sneering, tousled, tigerish, half-breed (Jennifer Jones) and Lewt McCanless (Gregory Peck), all-male, all bad, cigarette insolently drooping from the corner of his lips, hat perched jauntily on the back of his head, his whole being oozing an irresistible animal magnetism. Their relationship climaxes in true operatic style with a shoot-out at Squaw's Head Rock, which ends with both mortally wounded, crawling across the sun-baked rocks with bloodied hands to die in each other's arms.

Ritualized violence had always been a key ingredient in Westerns. In the main it was seen as exciting but essentially harmless fun. One of the best examples of this was the prolonged fist fight between hero and villain that was the highlight of the gold-rush Western *The Spoilers* (1942) with John Wayne and Randolph Scott as the protagonists. In the late Forties, however, critics began to voice their concern that violence was becoming much more realistic and brutal. Films like André de Toth's *Ramrod* (1947) were singled out for criticism on this count. The increasingly prevalent use of Technicolor for Westerns further highlighted blood and bruises, although the experience of war had conditioned audiences to accept a greater degree of screen violence.

During the war, public interest in psychology and psychoanalysis had grown and the cinema was quick to capitalize on the phenomenon. The theories of Freud came to the West in Raoul Walsh's

World War II may have conditioned audiences to more violence but the critics protested at the blood and gore in new Technicolor Westerns

moodily impressive *Pursued* (1947) with its hero (Robert Mitchum) dogged by a half-forgotten childhood trauma that is revealed in a complex series of flashbacks. After this, Western heroes could never again be simple, uncomplicated men in white hats riding white horses.

The early Forties saw two classic expositions of the traditional themes of the Western. William Wyler's *The Westerner* (1940) was a slow-moving but beautifully photographed tale that depicted the resistance of decent, hard-working homesteaders to the ruthlessly organized might of the cattlemen. The film offered powerful contrasts between the peaceful, communal celebrations of the settlers (a service of thanksgiving among the cornfields, a cheerful hoedown) and the eruptions of savage violence among the cowboys (trampling down the crops, carousing in the town and beating up their opponents). In the last resort it was a film of character rather than action, exploring the love-hate relationship between Cole Harden, personified by Gary Cooper as the soul of integrity, and Walter Brennan's cunning, hard-drinking old reprobate Judge Roy Bean, dispensing summary justice from a saloon and worshipping the beauty of the actress Lillie Langtry. The relationship ends inevitably but satisfyingly with a final shoot-out on the stage of a theatre where Lillie Langtry is due to appear.

The romance, excitement and glory of war was the subject of Raoul Walsh's sprawling and enthralling US cavalry movie *They Died With Their Boots On*. The film followed the flamboyant career of General Custer from West Point Academy through

JANE RUSSELL MEAN...MOODY...MAGNIFICENT!
IN
HOWARD HUGHES'
DARING PRODUCTION
THE OUTLAW
ACTION! THRILLS!! SENSATIONS!!!
PRIMITIVE LOVE!!!!
JACK BUETEL
THOMAS MITCHELL
WALTER HUSTON

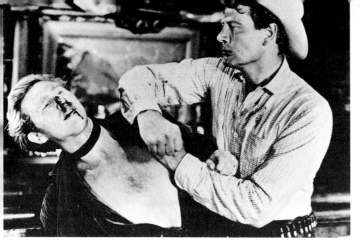

the Civil War to the Western Frontier and his death at the battle of Little Big Horn. In true Hollywood style, this final disaster was turned into an act of heroic self-sacrifice, with Custer knowingly and deliberately sacrificing himself and his troops to protect the main army column from massacre.

Errol Flynn was perfectly cast as the long-haired American general, a swashbuckling paladin of the plains, with a boyish enthusiasm for fighting, a hunger for glory, a delight in gaudy uniforms, a respect for his enemies and a chivalrous devotion to his wife Libby (Olivia de Havilland).

Howard Hawks' *Red River* (1948) provided a prototype hero for the next decade in John Wayne's tough, relentless, revenge-seeking cattle-rancher, Tom Dunson. This is a classic Hawksian film, with its emphasis on professionalism, male cameraderie and dangerous, exciting work on the fringes of civilized society. It re-creates the rigours of the cattle drive – complete with stampede, river crossing and Indian attacks. There are moments of sheer poetry, too, like the start of the drive: mist, dust, dawn, a 180° pan across the waiting herd, and then Dunson yells, 'Take 'em to Missouri, Matt' and Matt's wild yahoo is taken up by each of the drovers in turn in a rapid succession of close-ups as the great herd starts to move.

At the heart of the film is the relationship between Tom Dunson and his adopted son Matthew Garth (Montgomery Clift). When Tom's obsessive desire to get to Missouri leads to rebellion among the drovers, Matt takes over and Dunson pursues him, consumed with bitterness and seeking revenge. The final gunfight between them, however, is frustrated by the quintessential, self-possessed Hawksian heroine (Joanne Dru), who tells them that they really love each other and are not going to kill each other. They accept her logic and are reconciled at the last moment.

John Ford returned from wartime service to begin one of the most richly productive phases of his long career. In *My Darling Clementine* (1946), he took the historical facts of the confrontation between the Earps and the Clantons at the OK Corral and reworked them into a very personal and characteristically complex statement about the bringing of civilization to the West. The Clantons – brutal, lawless and anarchic, ruled with a bullwhip by a tyrannical old patriarch (Walter Brennan) – represent the unacceptable face of the Old West. They are destroyed by the Earps, whose family solidarity and mutual affection is placed at the service of the nascent community. The values of this community are demonstrated in the justly famous sequence in which the decent citizens of Tombstone hold a celebratory square dance in their half-built church, beneath the fluttering flags of the United States. The imagery represents a potent blending of religion, patriotism and community spirit, the cement of the society the Earps are helping to build. Shot, lit and

staged with an austere and strictly ritualized formality, the film undercuts its style with flurries of bustling action and comic interludes like that of the visit of a travelling theatrical troupe.

The same sense of community, allied to a powerful feeling for tradition and the unifying concept of service to the nation, provides the links in Ford's cavalry trilogy: *Fort Apache* (1948), *She Wore a Yellow Ribbon* (1949) and *Rio Grande* (1950). The values of the idealized society which Ford saw embodied in the US cavalry are succinctly encapsulated in the fluttering yellow ribbon, crossed sabres and lusty singing voices of the soldiers, seen and heard behind the credits of *She Wore a Yellow Ribbon*. They are affirmations of its continuity (the ribbon – a symbol of a cavalry sweetheart and hence of the family tradition of service), its role (crossed sabres – an emblem for the maintenance of peace and order), and its community spirit (male voices singing in unison 'The Girl I Left Behind'). It was these values that attracted Ford to the concept of the cavalry at a time when the USA had emerged from World War II to face new problems and rapid social change.

In *The Man Who Shot Liberty Valance* (1962) Ford uses the quotation 'When the legend becomes fact, print the legend'. But in *Fort Apache* Ford is at pains to show the truth behind the legend – in this case, Custer's last stand – at the same time as showing how the legend is born and endorsing the need for heroes and legends in the process of fortifying national memory. Ford lovingly re-creates the rituals of cavalry life – the parades and patrols, regimental balls and dinner parties – and thrillingly stages the battles, charges and Indian attacks as a background to the story of an embittered martinet, Colonel Thursday (Henry Fonda), a thinly disguised Custer figure whose ambition and stubbornness lead the regiment to disaster.

The virtues and strengths of the cavalry are fully embodied by Captain Nathan Brittles (John Wayne) the hero of *She Wore a Yellow Ribbon*. Tough, sentimental, dedicated and professional, he has grown old in the army and given his all to it. The film deals with his last mission – to avert an Indian uprising – before he retires. The mellow autumnal Technicolor in which the film is shot reflects this sense of a career's twilight. If we can see Shakespeare in Prospero breaking his wand and retiring to the country after *The Tempest*, then perhaps it is permissible to see John Ford in the character of Nathan Brittles, the hard-nosed, old professional whose life is his work and whose work is his life. Ford is so devoted to the character of Brittles that he sidesteps the clearly implied tragic ending to recall Brittles from his retirement and have him appointed chief of scouts for the army. *She Wore a Yellow Ribbon* is quintessential Ford and a mature middle-period masterwork that ranks with Hollywood's finest.

JEFFREY RICHARDS

Top left: the new violence of Forties Westerns, as meted out by Joel McCrea to Lloyd Bridges in Ramrod. *Top: the opening up of the West in* Brigham Young. *Above: John Wayne and Montgomery Clift in Howard Hawks'* Red River

'Wild Bill' Wellman

'William A. Wellman, 79, one of Hollywood's "immortals" among film directors, who directed a total of 82 films without once winning a director's Oscar but whose list of significant credits is unsurpassed, died December 9 of leukemia at his Brentwood, California home'
Variety, December 17, 1975

Whitney William's choice of words for his *Variety* obituary indicated the way the whole film industry viewed Wellman. Commercially, he was one of the most successful of all American directors, and his career spanned silents to CinemaScope and stereophonic sound. His pre-movie career, as a professional ice-hockey player and a World War I fighter pilot with the Lafayette Flying Corps, itself appears as unreal as a Hollywood movie.

After the war Wellman obtained a thorough grounding in film-making before he finally got a chance to direct; his first movie was a Western for Fox called *The Man Who Won* (1923), starring Dustin Farnum. This was followed by six films featuring the legendary cowboy star Buck Jones, although only one of these, *The Vagabond Trail* (1924), seems to have been a true Western – the doubt remains because the majority of Wellman's silent work is no longer in existence. Throughout his career Wellman returned to this genre. Although he never specialized in it, he may be regarded as the father of the modern Western.

During the Twenties, Wellman struggled to make his mark as a director. Then in 1927 he was assigned to direct *Wings*, a World War I flying epic. Wellman's boyhood fascination with flying and his experience of war invested the film with remarkable authenticity. None of his other films equal it for sheer scope, size, audacity or passion.

In the first half of the Thirties, Wellman further consolidated his standing in Hollywood, turning out 17 films for Warner Brothers in just three years. Although *The Public Enemy* (1931) is the most famous, the rest appear remarkably fresh and distinctly personal when seen today.

In the middle of his stint with Warners Wellman directed *The Conquerors* (1932) for RKO. This story of three generations of a banking family covers American history from the post-Civil War period to the Wall Street crash. For the first time since *The Vagabond Trail*, Wellman thus had Western elements to deal with. He made them extremely evocative – in particular a stark, sombre scene showing the mass hanging of a gang of raiders. In one shot, with no cutting, Wellman shows the audience a set of nooses slung over a tree, men walking with military precision to their horses, mounting up, fastening the ends of their ropes to their saddles and slowly riding away, to pull up from below the frame the now hanging bodies of a dozen men.

His best films are built around one-take sequences such as this – scenes that rely on the cumulative power of their visual information. The gradual presentation of this information allows an audience to come to its own understanding of the narrative situation as it builds into a full expression of a theme or idea, instead of being 'forced' into it by the selective process of editing.

The Public Enemy first used this style with total success, as did *Robin Hood of El Dorado*, Wellman's first true sound Western, made in 1936 for MGM. The film is based on the legend of the Mexican Joaquin Murrieta (played by Warner Baxter) who waged war with the Americans in pre-statehood California. Although much of the film's impact was

pacifist thesis, showing the racism underlying the goal of westward expansion. He refuses to take sides during the major battle sequence of War Bonnet Creek; it is shown, with dispassionate horror, as savage and chaotic. The film celebrates the virtues of 'natural' Man and bitterly denounces the materialism of the whites. Not until Delmer Daves' *Broken Arrow* (1950), made six years later, would a film take such an understanding view of the plight of the American Indian.

Wellman's next Western, *Yellow Sky* (1948) deals with a gang of bank robbers, led by Gregory Peck and Richard Widmark, who encounter an old man and his niece, the sole inhabitants of a ghost town. The film's complicated web of desire and intrigue centres around the old man's cache of gold; the outlaws' gold fever parallels the blood lust of the mob in *The Ox-Bow Incident*. Indeed, *Yellow Sky* reaches a similar nightmarish intensity, until Peck rediscovers his essential honesty.

Opposite page: Wings *made Wellman a big-name director. Far left: Barbara Stanwyck in* Lady of Burlesque. *Top left: Carole Lombard, Walter Connolly and Fredric March in* Nothing Sacred. *Left: Anne Baxter and Gregory Peck in* Yellow Sky. *Above: James Cagney and Mae Clarke in* The Public Enemy. *Below: Clark Gable in* Across the Wide Missouri

oftened by the studio, Wellman forcefully depicted the 'imperialist' injustice of the Americans towards the Mexicans. The sense of anger which Wellman invokes in his audience anticipates *The Ox-Bow Incident* (1943). Most typical of Wellman's style in *Robin Hood of El Dorado* is the final shoot-out; it is seen simply as mass slaughter, making the audience suddenly aware that human beings are paying the ultimate price for inhumanity and insanity.

Wellman next collaborated with the producer David O. Selznick on the famous duo, *A Star Is Born* and *Nothing Sacred* (both 1937). These films' success earned Wellman a producer-director contract at Paramount (where he had worked in the Twenties) and an enviable independence.

The Thirties ended for Wellman with three fascinating films written by Robert Carson. The first, *Men With Wings* (1938), is a loving homage to aviation with some breathtaking colour photography of aerial warfare; the second, *Beau Geste* (1939), is an examination of the notion of heroism with a French Foreign Legion setting; while the third, the mystical *The Light That Failed* (1939), contains a superlative performance from Ronald Colman as a painter who finds he is going blind.

For Wellman, as for most, the Forties were a time of great turbulence. His screen work shifted from snappy, cynical satires centring around hard-boiled dames such as Ginger Rogers in *Roxie Hart* (1942) and Barbara Stanwyck in *Lady of Burlesque* (1943) to the almost documentary immediacy of his celebrated war film *The Story of GI Joe* (1945). His work in the decade culminated with another war film *Battleground* (1949).

In this period Wellman made one of his most famous films, *The Ox-Bow Incident*, which changed the shape of Westerns as decisively as *Stagecoach*. Just as Ford had discovered nature, movement and 'fluidity' of camera, so Wellman invested the stereotyped characters of the genre with genuine emotional depth, and the film has the feeling of a waking nightmare.

Contemporary critics were confused when such an obviously 'important' film as *The Ox-Bow Incident* was followed by *Buffalo Bill* (1944), apparently a much more conventional Western. Yet here Wellman attempted to look at the whole myth of the Western through the legendary character of Buffalo Bill Cody. Cody is seen as a child of the plains, at one with nature and the Indians; around him are white Americans intent on 'civilizing' the West and exploiting its resources. As in *Robin Hood of El Dorado*, Wellman develops a tough anti-white,

man said that he wanted 'the audience to *feel* the intense sunlight, the desert heat and dust'. He also avoided false heriocs of any kind, and the film provides few traditional Western moments of 'slambang' action. Nevertheless, while the film may not be enjoyable as simplistic entertainment, its relentless execution of Wellman's brief, to 'put the audience through it', is astounding. When the women finally meet their new husbands, someone starts to play a tune on an accordian; a fiddle joins in, and we suddenly realize that there has not been a note of music in the film up to this point. Men and women come together as the music builds and the film exultantly ends.

Track of the Cat (1954), adapted from a novel

The climactic shoot-out between him and Widmark is not shown. To some observers this indicates that Wellman is 'divorced' from his material. But it is an example of exactly the same impulse which made him refuse to take sides in the battle scenes of earlier Westerns. As David Morse pointed out in *Brighton Film Review* of June 1970, to show the gunfight would have been:

'. . . to place the emphasis on a glamorized either/or moment of life or death and on the business of being quick on the draw, which Wellman [was] not greatly interested in. In place of false heroics Wellman always tries to present his heroes with real choices. The issue is never life or death, bravery or cowardice, but *survival with the fewest compromises.*'

Almost alone among American directors, Wellman was equally at home in the studio or out on location. For *Battleground*, his magnificent, jigsaw-structured war film, he brilliantly utilized the resources of the sound stage; *Across the Wide Missouri*, made just two years later in 1951, was almost exclusively shot on location in the Rockies.

Across the Wide Missouri was savagely cut by MGM after its completion, blurring the film's original conception. At heart the film is a celebration of the mountain man, and of his relationship with nature and the Indian. Set-piece sequences detail in almost documentary fashion the camaraderie of the mountain men's annual meeting, while the visualization of Indian life and culture have yet to be surpassed in any other film.

In contrast to the Technicolor glories of *Across the Wide Missouri*, Wellman's next Western, *Westward the Women* (1951), was austerely filmed in black and white. Robert Taylor plays a scout hired to transport a wagon train of mail-order brides on the 2000-mile trek to their husbands-to-be in California. Wellman and cameraman William C. Mellor eschewed any false pictorial glamour. Well-

Top left: Robert Mitchum as a hard-bitten backwoods farmer hunts a mountain lion in Track of the Cat. *Above: Tab Hunter as a World War I fighter pilot in* Lafayette Escadrille, *Wellman's last film. Top right: George Murphy in* Battleground, *the story of a group of soldiers during the Battle of the Bulge in World War II*

by Walter Van Tilberg Clark, author of *The Ox-Bow Incident*, contains Western elements, being set on a ranch near the snow-line. Its tortured protagonists are confronted by a mountain lion which marauds the countryside; the animal takes on a symbolic meaning for each of the characters. It is one of Wellman's most stylized films, for though shot in CinemaScope and colour, he had the film designed to appear to be black and white, with only a few props and costumes registering other colours. Typically for Wellman, the mountain lion itself is never shown to the audience.

Wellman now began to grow disenchanted with Hollywood. A new breed of grey-flannel corporation men was running the studios where he had been formerly used to fighting with feisty, picture-loving moguls. He was however, still a vastly successful director; his *The High and the Mighty* (1954) took $7 million in its first year alone. Wellman owned a third of the film and was thus financially set for life.

Of his remaining films as a director, only *Lafayette Escadrille* (1958), a look back at his own war experience as a fighter pilot, stands out as a personal statement. When Warner Brothers demanded various changes, including the removal of the original title, *C'est La Guerre*, Wellman did not have the energy to protest. Although he announced various other projects over the next few years, the aborted *Lafayette Escadrille* remains his final film.

Wellman was a resolute original; he worked from instinct, yet he made some of the most formal and cerebral American films. His heroes are usually 'imperfect', get slugged more often than they do the slugging and often lose more than they win. His heroines, though tough like Hawks', are natural, human and honest. For all his films' biting and sometimes callous humour, they are remarkably tender, communicating the nature of love with great understanding. Wellman's major achievements rank with the best of American cinema – and will always continue to do so.

CHRISTOPHER WICKING

Filmography

1919 Knickerbocker Glory (actor only); Evangeline (actor only). **'23** The Man Who Won; Second Hand Love; Big Dan; Cupid's Fireman. **'24** Not a Drum Was Heard; The Vagabond Trail; The Circus Cowboy. **'25** The Boob (GB: The Yokel); The Cat's Pajamas; You Never Know Women; When Husbands Flirt. **'27** Wings. **'28** Legion of the Condemned; Ladies of the Mob; Beggars of Life. **'29** Chinatown Nights; The Man I Love; Woman Trap. **'30** Dangerous Paradise; Young Eagles; Maybe It's Love. **'31** Other Men's Women; The Public Enemy (GB: Enemies of the Public); Night Nurse; Star Witness; Safe in Hell (GB: The Lost Lady). **'32** The Hatchet Man (GB: The Honourable Mr Wong); So Big; Love Is a Racket; The Purchase Price; The Conquerors; Frisco Jenny (GB: Common Ground). **'33** Central Airport; Lilly Turner; Heroes for Sale; Midnight Mary; Wild Boys of the Road (GB: Dangerous Age/Dangerous Days); College Coach (GB: Football Coach). **'34** Looking for Trouble; Stingaree; The President Vanishes (GB: The Strange Conspiracy). **'35** Call of the Wild. **'36** Tarzan Escapes (uncredited co-dir. only); Robin Hood of El Dorado (+co-sc. only); Small Town Girl (USA retitling for TV: One Horse Town). **'37** The Last Gangster (co-sc. only); A Star Is Born; Nothing Sacred. **'38** Men With Wings. **'39** Beau Geste (+prod); The Light That Failed (+prod). **'41** Reaching for the Sun (+prod). **'42** Roxie Hart; The Great Man's Lady (+prod); Thunderbirds. **'43** Lady of Burlesque (GB: Striptease Lady); The Ox-Bow Incident (GB: Strange Incident). **'44** Buffalo Bill. **'45** This Man's Navy; The Story of GI Joe (USA retitling for TV: War Correspondent). **'46** Gallant Journey (+prod; +co-sc). **'47** Magic Town **'48** The Iron Curtain (USA retitling for TV: Behind the Iron Curtain); Yellow Sky. **'49** Battleground. **'50** The Next Voice You Hear; The Happy Years; It's a Big Country (co-dir. only). **'51** Across the Wide Missouri; Westward the Woman. **'52** My Man and I. **'53** Island in the Sky. **'54** The High and the Mighty; Track of the Cat; Ring of Fear (uncredited co-dir. only). **'55** Blood Alley. **'56** Goodbye, My Lady. **'57** Darby's Rangers (GB: The Young Invaders). **'58** Lafayette Escadrille (GB: Hell Bent for Glory).

Never a dull moment

Crazy comedy and sophisticated wit existed side by side in the Forties,
but it was World War II that sparked off some of the funniest films of the decade

The Forties was a great age of film comedy. The previous decade had closed with one of the unlikeliest pieces of comic casting in Hollywood but one that had gone down well with audiences. 'Garbo Laughs' declared the publicity for *Ninotchka* (1939) in which the dramatic queen of the screen fell under the influence of champagne, Paris and Melvyn Douglas. After that, nothing was sacred.

The Boys From Syracuse (1940) was a racy comedy adapted from Shakespeare's *Comedy of Errors* with Joe Penner doubling up as identical twins. The humour derives from anachronisms such as a Ben-Hur style chariot-race climax. Equally improbable was the casting of the debonair William Powell in *Love Crazy* (1941), where he attempts to evade divorce by disguising himself as his own sister. In *I Love You Again* (1940) the suave star of the Thin Man films played an upright citizen who suffers from amnesia and becomes a con-man.

Some of the most memorable Forties comedies were imported Broadway hits. In *The Philadelphia Story* (1940) Katharine Hepburn returned to the role she had created on the stage as the rich socialite torn between James Stewart and Cary Grant. Another great stage comedy, *Arsenic and Old Lace* (1944), also exploited Cary Grant's comic talents, though in the film Raymond Massey took the role Boris Karloff had played on stage as the most monstrous of the family of poisoners. Broadway was also the source of *The Man Who Came to Dinner* (1941), a sophisticated comedy that satirized the vitriolic theatre critic Alexander Woolcott. In the same period, George Stevens and Howard Hawks, two major directors famous for their work in a variety of genres, made some of the classic comedies of the Forties. In *Talk of the Town* (1942), Cary Grant played a suspected arsonist and Jean Arthur tried to cover up for him. Stevens also made *The More the Merrier* (1943), a comedy in which Jean Arthur played a girl sharing her flat with two men. Hawks, who displayed a fine gift for comedy, made *His Girl Friday* (1940), a fresh and vigorous version of the stage comedy *The Front Page*, in which the reporter, Hildy Johnson, was cast as a woman (Rosalind Russell). Hawks' *Ball of Fire* (1941) exploited the comic panache of Barbara Stanwyck playing Sugarpuss O'Shea to Gary Cooper's mildmannered Professor Betram Potts. He was a philologist investigating 'hep-cat' slang and she was a nightclub singer. In the end both learned something from each other about the ways of the world.

At the end of the decade, comedy reached a kind of zenith with Hawks' *I Was a Male War Bride* (1949) in which Cary Grant played a Frenchman and, later in the film, tried to pass himself off as a US servicewoman. In the same year George Cukor made *Adam's Rib* in which Katharine Hepburn and Spencer Tracy were married lawyers who found themselves on opposite sides of the same case. For all the triumphs of sophisticated comedy, however, the genre still retained its essential touch of craziness as was exemplified in the extraordinarily zany *Hellzapoppin'* (1942).

The established film comedians of the Twenties and Thirties were mostly still working at the beginning of the Forties, but fashions in comedy were changing. The much-trumpeted new Laurel and Hardy comedy, *The Flying Deuces* (1939), was below their usual standard and showed the lack of Hal Roach's guidance. Stan and Ollie were in the Foreign Legion and the film contained enough farcical flying for it to pass as a topical comedy. Laurel and Hardy's rapid return to Hal Roach brought them better luck with *A Chump at Oxford* (1940). In this film Stan plays Lord Paddington, suffering from amnesia after a blow on the neck. *Saps at Sea* (1940) was also produced by Hal Roach and had Ollie suffering from 'hornophobia', seeking rest but finding none thanks to Stan's trombone.

Leaving Hal Roach once again – this time for 20th Century-Fox – Stan and Ollie began a six-picture contract that virtually ended their career. *Great Guns* (1941), despite expert direction by Monty Banks, tried to update Laurel and Hardy into another version of Abbott and Costello. The army plot was almost a carbon copy of the younger team's hit *Buck Privates* (1941). Speed had never been Stan and Ollie's style and their natural, slow pace was deemed old-fashioned by Forties standards. As more and more of their traditional foolery was cut from their films, their appeal grew less and less. Wisely the old gentlemen decided to retire after their last MGM picture, *Nothing But Trouble* (1944).

The downward path was crowded with comedians, as the great names of the Twenties and Thirties fell victims to the Forties mania for new faces. Harold Lloyd gave up acting and turned producer at RKO where he made *A Girl, a Guy and a Gob* (1941), with Lucille Ball, and *My Favourite Spy* (1942), with Kay Kyser. The latter film put Kyser into cliff-hanging situations typical of Harold Lloyd's own earlier films, but it was not funny. Persuaded to return to the screen by the writer-

Above: the enduring image of Forties comedy was provided by Bob Hope and Dorothy Lamour. In My Favourite Brunette, *Hope turned detective and rescued Dotty from mobsters*

Above: Cary Grant, Katharine Hepburn, James Stewart and Ruth Hussey in The Philadelphia Story, *one of the most sparkling Forties comedies – it was remade in 1956 as the musical* High Society. *Top right: Cary Grant in drag trying to get back to the USA disguised as a US servicewoman in* I Was a Male War Bride. *Right: the James Thurber story* The Secret Life of Walter Mitty *(1947) concerned a young man whose day-dreams became his reality and was an ideal vehicle for the comic talents of Danny Kaye*

director Preston Sturges. Lloyd was energetic but unfunny in *Mad Wednesday* (1946). The characteristic skyscraper stunts were there, this time with the added thrill of a live lion on a lead, but perhaps Lloyd was just over the edge for his age.

At least Lloyd fared better than Harry Langdon who, having survived a spell as a scriptwriter for Laurel and Hardy, was starred in a handful of minor movies at Monogram. In *Double Trouble* (1941) and *House of Errors* (1942), he was teamed with another ex-writer from the Roach two-reelers named Charley Rogers. In turn, Langdon's fate was probably better than Buster Keaton's. The Great Stone Face, having also put in some time behind the camera as a writer, would never achieve star billing again. Keaton did turn up, however, in occasional roles in B pictures like *Li'l Abner* (1940) where he played Al Capp's cartoon 'injun', Lonesome Polecat.

Of the older comedy stars, only Charles Chaplin remained at the top of the tree. *The Great Dictator* (1940) was his contribution to the war effort. The film was produced, quite bravely, before the USA entered the war. The similarity between Chaplin and Hitler – the famous toothbrush moustache – had often been noted; now Chaplin turned this chance likeness into brilliant satire. The British loved the film and Chaplin for it, and his long speech at the end was received with all the uplift of emotion intended.

The madness of the Marx Brothers, already somewhat watered down during their Thirties period at MGM, was further diluted in the Forties. *Go West* (1940) was saved by a magnificent train chase, engineered by Buster Keaton. *The Big Store* (1941) was more memorable for the dead-pan debut of Virginia O'Brien, the stony-faced songstress. The Marx Brothers nearly quit the business. Five years later, however, they returned in *A Night in Casablanca* (1946). This spy burlesque made allusions to *Casablanca* (1942) but the Marx Brothers did not provide a serious challenge to the Warner Brothers.

W. C. Fields stained his reputation by co-starring (and co-writing) with Mae West in *My Little Chickadee* (1940). It may have been a great idea on paper, but it was less successful on the screen. Fields followed it with *The Bank Dick* (1940), one of his finest and wildest pictures.

Fields' 1941 triumph, *Never Give a Sucker an Even Break*, proved to be the great man's last starring vehicle, although he would continue to appear in films and perform choice moments from his classic routines. Time has not mellowed Fields' films; they remain unique, idiosyncratic masterworks of non-conformism.

The Ritz Brothers, a popular comedy team of the Thirties, moved from 20th Century-Fox to Universal in 1940. Their first film under new management was *Argentine Nights* (1940) in which they burles-

qued their co-stars, the Andrews Sisters, singing 'Rhumboogie'. In *Behind the Eight Ball* (1942), the Ritzes were the Three Jolly Jesters who sang 'Atlas Did It but He Won't Admit It' and unmasked their clarinettist as a spy who blew messages in code. *Hi Ya Chum* (1943) starred the Ritz Brothers as the Merry Madcaps; this time they sang 'Cactus Pete for Sherriff' and squirted their audience with laughing gas. Their fourth film was *Never a Dull Moment* (1943) but, sadly, there were more than a few and it became their farewell to films. Universal cared little. The studio had discovered the key to a fortune in comedy with Abbott and Costello and were doing well at the box-office with another double act – Olsen and Johnson.

Among the newer funny men, first place must go to Bob Hope, a wisecracker from radio. His biggest hit came at the end of the Thirties with *The Cat and the Canary* (1939). A remake of the Twenties classic film this earned an 'H' (for Horrific) certificate from the British censor. Bob Hope's cheerful cowardice, gagging in the face of danger with lines like 'even my goose-pimples have goose-pimples', set his screen character for years ahead.

In 1940 Hope saved pretty Paulette Goddard (his co-star from *The Cat and the Canary*) from zombies in *The Ghost Breakers*. Life in the army was the theme of *Caught in the Draft* (1941) in which Hope was allowed to win the hand of his co-star from the 'Road' movies, Dorothy Lamour. This film also introduced Eddie Bracken, a former gag-writer for Bob Hope, as a shy, awkward, accident-prone goof. Bracken's best films were for Preston Sturges.

Bob Hope then began a second-string series with *My Favourite Blonde* (1942). She was the lovely Madeleine Carroll and Hope saved her from Nazi spies. The obvious follow-up, *My Favourite Brunette* (1947), turned out to be no surprise – the lady was Dorothy Lamour. *My Favourite Spy* (1951) wound

up the series and this time his co-star was the languorous Hedy Lamarr.

Hope's first flirtation with costume pictures touched a new nerve – comic anachronism. He brought his modern wit to *The Princess and the Pirate* (1944), his first film in Technicolor, and followed it with *Monsieur Beaucaire* (1946) in which he played a bumbling barber who impersonates a dandy at the court of Louis XV. Rudolph Valentino, who made a silent film of the same title in 1924, must have tango-ed in his tomb. At the end of the decade Hope was teamed with Jane Russell, who had gained some notoriety from her appearance in *The Outlaw* (1943), in *The Paleface* (1948) which was so successful that it spawned a sequel, *Son of Paleface* (1952), where Hope and Russell were joined by Roy Rogers.

MGM found a funny face in Richard 'Red' Skelton, an ex-clown who had made a dummy run at movies in a couple of 1939 shorts. Red's was the first new face of 1940. He played the comedy relief in two Dr Kildare films. His first starring role was as Wally the Fox, a radio detective in an updated version of the old comedy thriller, *Whistling in the Dark* (1941). The film was such a hit that two sequels were called for and MGM obligingly produced *Whistling in Dixie* (1942) and *Whistling in Brooklyn* (1943). Skelton was clearly MGM's answer to Paramount's Bob Hope. He even followed the Hope formula of building his costume comedy around a variety of anachronisms. *DuBarry Was a Lady* (1943) was a typical example in which he starred with another carrot-top – Lucille Ball. Red's next film, *I Dood It* (1943), was named after his catchphrase: 'If I dood it, I get a whippin' . . . I dood it'. The film marked his first contact with Buster Keaton who, as gag-writer, modelled it on his own comic masterpiece *Spite Marriage* (1929). Keaton continued to write gags for Skelton through to *A Southern Yankee* (1948), a remake of his 1926 classic *The General*. Despite starring in nearly thirty comedies, Skelton is best remembered today for a single routine – his 'Guzzler's Gin' spot in *Ziegfeld Follies* (1946).

Towering above all the new comics of the Forties is Danny Kaye. This frenetic entertainer, master of the half-closed eyelid and dean of double-talk, followed the same false start on a film career as Hope and Skelton. In the Thirties he made one or two shoddy two-reelers before his impressive debut. *Up in Arms* (1944) was Kaye's first feature film. Samuel Goldwyn produced, and it was one of the most expensively mounted, extravagant, Technicolored launches ever given to a film comic. The film cost a fortune and looked it. A GI ogles some nurses enjoying a sunbathe: 'The last war was never like this,' he says, 'Neither is this one,' says his glum buddy. Kaye plays a nervous hypo-

chondriac – a figure that was to become his screen persona – and performs several remarkable tongue-twisting numbers, including 'Melody in Four-F' a farrago of double-talk. His leading lady, Virginia Mayo, was promoted immediately and co-starred with him in *Wonder Man* (1945). In this Kaye was a meek professor 'inhabited' by his murdered twin, a nightclub comedian. *The Kid From Brooklyn* (1946) was a remake of Harold Lloyd's *The Milky Way* (1936), with Kaye as the mild-mannered milkman who becomes a swell-headed boxer. In *A Song Is Born* (1948), a reworking of Hawks' *Ball of Fire* (1941), Kaye played the shy student of jazz.

Kaye's films, wondrous entertainment in their day, have not worn well but were genuine escapism run wild. Like so many funny men of the Forties, Kaye was a comedian for his time.

The first British comedian to take up arms on the screen in World War II was Arthur Lucan, better known as Old Mother Riley. With his partner Kitty McShane, he was half of a double act that was popular throughout the Thirties. Lucan and McShane took up the wartime challenge with *Old Mother Riley Joins Up* (1939). This first comedy film of World War II was trade-shown just six weeks after war broke out. 'Machine Gun Mirth and Quick Fire Fun in the Big Bertha of Merriment' promised the topical catch-lines, as Mother Riley, district nurse, rode her boneshaker headlong into an Air Raid Precautions parade, an elderly arms manufacturer, and a gang of Nazi spies. Daughter Kitty joined the Auxiliary Territorial Service as a medical officer, and fell for Lieutenant Bruce Seaton. Meanwhile Old Mother Riley rounded up the plane-snatchers, in a chase involving the army, the fire brigade and the boy scouts.

Northern comedians were top of the cinema bill during the first year of the war. Sandy Powell, whose catchphrase was 'Can you 'ear me Mother?', joined the navy – by accident, of course, in *All at Sea* (1939), and saved a secret explosive from the enemy.

Another comic, Albert Burdon, starred in *Jail Birds* (1939), a Butcher's version of Fred Karno's old stage sketch. A wartime touch was added when Burdon donned a toothbrush moustache and imitated Hitler.

Gracie Fields, the Lancashire Lass, sang her way through *Shipyard Sally* (1939). Her theme song, 'Wish Me Luck as You Wave Me Goodbye', became

Far left: a typically zany scene from the Red Skelton slapstick comedy I Dood It *in which Red plays a tailor and presser who falls in love with a movie star (Eleanor Powell); Thurston Hall looks on from above. Centre left: in* A Chump at Oxford Laurel *and* Hardy *were treated to a university education*

Top: with the decline of music hall, radio had become the home of British comedy and films in the Forties were happy to turn ready-made comedy shows like Band Waggon into popular pictures. Above: The Crazy Gang (Flanagan and Allen, Nervo and Knox, Naughton and Gold) floated off to Germany in Gasbags but escaped back to England in an enemy submarine. Right: trade ad for Somewhere in England which made an unexpected star of Frank Randle

the first great hit song of the war as the troops sailed for France. It became Gracie's farewell, too. When the authorities interned all Italians as enemy aliens, she and her Italian-born director, who was also her husband, waved goodbye to Britain for the duration. They both continued their careers in Hollywood but not with the success they had known in England.

Gracie Fields' brother-in-law, Duggie Wakefield, played in *Spy for a Day* (1940). Based on a short story by Stacy Aumonier, with a screenplay by Emeric Pressburger and Anatole de Grunwald, the film was dressed up with Northern dialogue by Tommy Thompson. But Mario Zampi's direction failed to make a star of Wakefield and he never appeared in another film.

Most extraordinary of all the Northern variety comedians who made the transition to films was Frank Randle, a peerless eccentric from Wigan. Second-billed in his first film, *Somewhere in England* (1940), he quickly rose above his co-star, the veteran Harry Korris, despite Korris' popularity on radio. What plot there was served only to link the comedian's set-pieces: the 'awkward squad' drill routine and the inevitable camp concert finale.

The comedian's popularity grew through all nine succeeding Randle films, several of which were in the 'Somewhere' series (*Somewhere in Camp*, 1942, *Somewhere on Leave*, 1942, *Somewhere in Civvies*, 1943). The last of this series of films was *It's a Grand Life* (1953) – a virtual remake of the first.

Randle, flat of foot, baggy of pants and gaping of gob, like some startled chicken, was no more a film star than his pictures were films. They were simply recordings, via the camera, of his inspired, spontaneous, erratic, eccentric portrayals of the familiar Randle character.

Of all the Northern comedians the most successful was still George Formby. He grinned gormlessly and sang strummingly through a string of cheerful comedies – three for Ealing and the rest for Columbia British – where his pay improved but his pictures did not. *Let George Do It* (1940) has our hero sent to Norway after a mix-up in the blackout. Once there, he discovers that the band-leader Garry Marsh is sending code messages in the dance music. *Spare a Copper* (1940) has a similar situation at home: George, a wartime reserve policeman, unmasks a wall-of-death rider as a shipyard saboteur. His next few films were all escapist entertainment, but in 1943 George was back in action: first as a village Home Guard in *Get Cracking* and then as a saucy sailor in *Bell Bottom George*. Formby finished the war, and his film career, with *George in Civvy Street* (1946), as a demobbed soldier running a pub.

Northern comics did not have it all their own way. London favourites were also big box-office draws in the cinemas. The cockney Tommy Trinder had made a false start in films when Elstree cast him in a 1938 remake of their earlier success *Almost a Honeymoon* (1930). The obligatory top hat was no replacement for Trinder's rakish trilby, but a tin hat was and in *Laugh It Off* (1940), he played himself as a called-up comedian putting on any army show. Trinder joined the navy in *Sailors Three* (1940). Along with his shipmates, Claude Hulbert and Michael Wilding, he captured a German pocket battleship whilst on a drunken spree. Trinder's natural acting style first emerged in *The Foreman Went to France* (1942) scripted by J.B. Priestley.

Trinder played the cockney soldier who cracked the classic joke 'England expects – that's why they call her the mother country!' He continued his role of the wisecracking cockney in *The Bells Go Down* (1943), Ealing's tribute to the London Fire Brigade, in *Champagne Charlie* (1944), a musical about the music halls, and in *Fiddlers Three* (1944), as a jolly

Jack Tar who goes back in time to Nero's Rome.

The Crazy Gang, a popular trio of double acts, made but one wartime film, *Gasbags* (1940). In this film the six comedians were blown to Germany in their barrage balloon, incarcerated in a concentration camp with Moore Marriott, and returned home via Hitler's secret weapon (an underground submarine). Of the Crazy Gang, only Flanagan and Allen continued a screen career. In *We'll Smile Again* (1942), *Theatre Royal* (1943), *Dreaming* (1944) and *Here Comes the Sun* (1945), they broke up their crazy, cross-talk sequences with cheerful, though occasionally tearful, songs of hope for a brighter tomorrow.

Will Hay joined Michael Balcon at Ealing and *The Ghost of St Michael's* (1941) found him back in his familiar schoolmaster's mortar-board but evacuated to a Scottish island. The spooks turned out to be fifth columnists, of course. *The Black Sheep of Whitehall* (1941) cast Hay as principal of a one-pupil correspondence school who is mistaken for an economics expert and kidnapped by saboteurs. The

villains are caught, but only after a misguided return to the kind of chase comedies that Gainsborough specialized in. Mistaken identity again motivates *The Goose Steps Out* (1942), in which Hay plays a seedy teacher sent to Germany to pose as his double, a Nazi spy.

Radio was a great source of many film comedies in the Forties. The leading pre-war comedy show *Band Waggon* arrived as a major Gainsborough film early in 1940. Starring its original radio team – 'Big-Hearted' Arthur Askey and Richard 'Stinker' Murdoch, boosted by Pat Kirkwood and Jack Hylton's band – the film included all the favourite gags of the series. Askey was an instant hit and followed up his success with an updated farce, *Charley's Big-Hearted Aunt* (1940) and a version of *The Ghost Train* (1941) in which saboteurs replaced Thirties-style crooks. In *Back Room Boy* (1942) he was the guardian of the BBC's 'six pips' time signal and caught some spies in a lonely lighthouse, while *King Arthur Was a Gentleman* (1942) found him as a timid Tommy in Africa, gaining bravery through the use of the legendary sword of Excalibur.

Other radio-based films included *What Would You Do, Chums?* (1939), with Syd Walker, the BBC junkman and *It's That Man Again* (1943). The latter film, adapted from Tommy Handley's brilliant radio series, was a brave try but it failed to flesh out the extraordinary array of characters who lived only in the imagination of listeners.   DENIS GIFFORD

Preston Sturges:

A pretty girl is better than a plain one
A leg is better than an arm
A bedroom is better than a living room
An arrival is better than a departure
A birth is better than a death
A chase is better than a chat
A dog is better than a landscape
A kitten is better than a dog
A baby is better than a kitten
A kiss is better than a baby
A pratfall is better than anything

Preston Sturges' Golden Rules for Successful Comedy

Comedy with a kick

make no claim to any artistic ambition, I am erely a story-teller . . . and success is judged ly by how many persons see your pictures.' Preston Sturges, one of the giants of screen medy, was 'different'. He was the screenriter who dispensed with collaborators and en with directors, pioneering the idea that e scribes could sometimes successfully direct eir own work. For five hectic years, Sturges d the satisfaction of delighting audiences d critics with a succession of films he wrote d directed himself, including *The Great cGinty* (1940), *The Lady Eve, The Palm Beach ory* (both 1941) and *Hail the Conquering Hero* 944).

After this frantic display of creative energy ring the early Forties, Sturges seemed to ve burnt himself out; although he kept on orking, further success largely eluded him. evertheless, Sturges' achievements were as markable as those of Woody Allen today; like llen, and despite his hankering for popular ccess, Sturges expressed an intensely pernal vision of life.

Born in 1898, Sturges came from an unnventional background, shunted – at six-

monthly intervals – between a mother in Paris and a stepfather in Chicago. The mother claimed to have dosed the infant with champagne to cure a bronchial ailment that threatened his life. Being the closest friend of Isadora Duncan, she also dosed him with excessive helpings of art and music. By contrast, his stepfather taught him to ride a bicycle and showed him the business world.

Sturges went to work as manager of one of his mother's beauty salons, created a kissproof lipstick and then set out to be a freelance inventor without much financial success. While in hospital in 1927, recovering from appendicitis, he turned his thoughts towards playwriting. *Strictly Dishonorable* was a runaway success on Broadway in 1929; Hollywood snapped up this romantic comedy for filming in 1931 and Sturges was hired to write dialogue for the early sound pictures being shot in New York.

Meanwhile, he continued writing in his own time and sold one of his screenplays to an enthusiastic Jesse Lasky in Hollywood. It was filmed at Fox and called *The Power and the Glory* (1933). It displayed the typical Sturges preoccupation with success in its story of a

railroad magnate's phenomenal career rising from humble beginnings to despairing suicide and was daringly constructed in non-chronological flashbacks.

Then came the screenplays of such comedies as *Easy Living* (1937), in which a discarded mink coat sets off a train of events that causes Wall Street to crash – then rise again for the happy ending – and *Remember the Night* (1940), both directed by Mitchell Leisen.

However, Sturges felt that he could do a better job of shooting his scripts and persuaded Paramount to let him direct *The Great McGinty* on a small budget, if he sold the studio his screenplay for a mere ten dollars. The comedy – a cynical study of American political chicanery in which a corrupt governor, played by Brian Donlevy, attempts to reform under the influence of a good woman and has to flee the country – was a big hit and won Sturges an Oscar in 1941. Like *The Great McGinty, The Lady Eve* was the story of a man, this time played by Henry Fonda, who is putty in the hands of a determined woman.

In *Sullivan's Travels* (1941), Sturges made an extraordinary justification for screen comedy in telling the story of a young and successful

ght: Henry Fonda, Barbara Stanwyck and reston Sturges pose for a production shot ring the filming of The Lady Eve, *the mantic farce which helped to launch Sturges a writer and director*

JOEL McCREA ★ VERONICA LAKE

SULLIVAN'S TRAVELS

ROBERT WARWICK WILLIAM DEMAREST
MARGARET HAYES PORTER HALL
FRANKLIN PANGBORN ERIC BLORE

Top left: Jimmy Conlin, Brian Donlevy and Dewey Robinson in The Great McGinty. *Top right: Ellen Drew and Dick Powell in* Christmas in July *(1948). Above: Joel McCrea as Sullivan researches the hobo life for his film in* Sullivan's Travels *and (above right) in more familiar surroundings. Far right: Joel McCrea as Morton tests his anaesthetic in* The Great Moment. *Below:* Mad Wednesday *with Harold Lloyd and Jimmy Conlin*

Hollywood director, much like Sturges himself, who is tempted to make a serious picture about poverty, goes off to do some research as a hobo and discovers that the people need his gift for humour: 'Laughter is all some people have.'

Two uncomfortably hard-hitting satires won Sturges Oscar nominations for best screenplays. *The Miracle of Morgan's Creek* (1943) and *Hail the Conquering Hero*. Both starred Eddie Bracken as a nervous small-town figure, mistakenly acclaimed as the father of quintuplets in one and as a war hero in the

other. The former film had a delayed release owing to censorship problems; a pregnant heroine is about to bear illegitimate offspring as a result of an in-haste marriage that is not properly recorded. The latter film managed to make Bracken's Woodrow Truesmith a sympathetic character even though he masqueraded as a war hero. Unfit for military service, owing to hayfever, Truesmith is unable to emulate his father's heroic effort in World War I. He is concerned at disappointing his mother and so agrees to the masquerade suggested by real marine heroes – and duly squirms with embarrassment at the consequences.

The Great Moment was also released in 1944, and is the biography of the nineteenth-century dentist W.T.G. Morton, who may have discovered anaesthetics. Sturges relieved a rather grim and downbeat story with 'injections' of slapstick comedy and arranged it to end on an uplifting note when the dentist (Joel McCrea) reveals his discovery to end someone's immediate pain instead of patenting it for personal benefit. As in *The Great McGinty*, the noble gesture ends in personal ruin. Filmed in 1943, then shelved for a year, *The Great Moment* was the one commercial flop of Sturges' golden years from 1940 to 1944.

All his films during this period were an extraordinary blend of sophistication and slapstick, of verbal and visual humour. The subsidiary roles were taken by a gallant band of largely unsung supporting actors, who made richly idiosyncratic contributions to the proceedings. William Demarest had substantial roles in all of them, and portly Robert Greig, prissy Franklin Pangborn, jittery, sparrow-like

Jimmy Conlin, burly Dewey Robinson, ostric[h] necked Torben Meyer, monotoned Har[ry] Hayden, and blowzy Esther Howard we[re] among the ageing players who made up th[e] unofficial Preston Sturges stock compan[y]. Many of them appeared together in *The Pal[m] Beach Story* as the Ale and Quail Club, [a] sporting bunch of millionaires who adopt th[e] film's heroine as a mascot and shoot up the[ir] carriage on a train in a bout of drunke[n] revelry.

Preston Sturges parodied the American su[c]cess story. He celebrated the unpredictability [of] fate and the sudden reversals of fortune th[at] mocked the ethic of hard work rewarded. H[is] leading men were usually innocents, i[ll] equipped to deal with life but sticking the[ir] necks out, inviting the confusion and cha[os] that descends upon them. Sturges' hero[es] succeed when they least expect or deserve [it]. Norval Jones (Eddie Bracken) has 'greatne[ss] thrust upon him' in *The Miracle of Morgan[...*

Filmography
1930 The Big Pond (co-dial only); Fast and Loo[se] (dial only). '33 The Power and the Glory (G[B: The] Power and Glory) (sc only). '34 Thirty Da[y] Princess (co-sc); We Live Again (co-sc); Imitati[on] of Life (adapt uncredited). '35 The Good Fai[ry] (sc); Diamond Jim (co-sc); The Gay Decepti[on] (song lyrics only). '36 Next Time We Love (G[B: Next Time We Live) (adapt uncredited); O[ne] Rainy Afternoon (song lyrics only). '37 Ho[t] Haywire (sc); Easy Living (sc). '38 Port of Sev[en] Seas (sc); If I Were King (sc). '39 Never Say D[ie] (co-sc). '40 Remember the Night (sc); The Gre[at] McGinty (GB: Down Went McGinty) (+sc); Christmas in July (+sc). '41 The Lady Eve (+s[c...

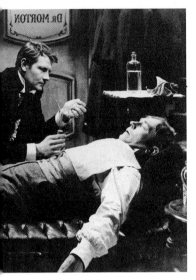

Creek when he receives the credit for fathering the quintuplets.

Unfortunately, Sturges' own career was to take as big a dip as that of any of his heroes. He left Paramount in 1944 to join up with Howard Hughes, expecting more artistic freedom and a bigger income from a share in the profits. However, their first production, *The Sin of Harold Diddlebock* (1946), was stalled by the post-war shortage of film stock and then by the whim of Hughes, who withdrew it for re-editing and finally re-released it as *Mad Wednesday* in 1950.

A come-back picture for Harold Lloyd, *Mad Wednesday* re-introduced the 'cliff-hanger thrill comedy' for which Lloyd was famous, showing the exhilarating result of a meek clerk's spending spree after he is fired from his job of 20 years. In one memorable moment, a veteran bartender accepts the challenge of providing the teetotal Diddlebock with his first drink. 'Sir, you arouse the artist in me,' he declares – yet another example of how people are stimulated by the activity that Sturges' plots generate.

However, the partnership with Hughes did not live up to Sturges' expectations and they broke up. In 1948 Sturges was hired at a phenomenal salary by 20th Century-Fox. Unfortunately he failed to earn his keep. *Unfaithfully Yours* (1948) was a dazzlingly imaginative, complex comedy about an irascible musician who devises various solutions to the apparent infidelity of his young wife as he conducts a concert. When he tries to put them into effect, he finds that what seems simple in the mind's eye is fraught with difficulties in practice. It was a box-office failure.

Sturges finished his Hollywood career with another flop. *The Beautiful Blonde From Bashful Bend* (1949) starred one of 20th Century-Fox's hottest stars, Betty Grable, and was a very expensive Western satire that came out as a crude hillbilly farce. The old skill with actors remained, but suddenly in this one film Sturges' sense of style and timing, his visual and verbal ingenuity, mysteriously collapsed.

He returned to the theatre and later went to live in France where he shot his last film – an efficiently-made but impersonal bilingual – *The Diary of Major Thompson/Les Carnets du Major Thompson* (1955). Back in New York, he negotiated a huge advance to write his memoirs, piquantly entitled *The Events Leading Up to My Death*; the last chapter came ahead of schedule when Sturges died in mid-manuscript – he was only 60.

Preston Sturges was more than just a writer: his films were technically adventurous – as illustrated by the long takes in many of them –

Top left: Claudette Colbert as the mascot of the Ale and Quail Club in The Palm Beach Story. *Top right: Porter Hall, Betty Hutton and Eddie Bracken in* The Miracle of Morgan's Creek. *Above left: Bracken again as a nervous, reluctant hero. Above: Betty Grable as* The Beautiful Blonde From Bashful Bend. *Below: Les Carnets du Major Thompson starred Jack Buchanan and Noel-Noel but had none of Sturges' old flair*

and he knew and loved the medium, frequently paying homage to other great directors. The projection-room scene of *Sullivan's Travels* draws on *Citizen Kane* (1940) just as Welles' film drew on the earlier *The Power and the Glory*.

William Wyler wrote this of him in 1975:

'I never could make a good film without a good writer – but neither could Preston Sturges. Only he had one with him all the time. He was a true *auteur*, the compleat creator of his own films.'

ALLEN EYLES

Sullivan's Travels (+sc); The Palm Beach Story (+sc). '42 Star Spangled Rhythm (as himself). '43 The Miracle of Morgan's Creek (+sc). '44 The Great Moment (+sc); Hail the Conquering Hero (+sc). '46 The Sin of Harold Diddlebock (re-issued as Mad Wednesday, 1950) (+sc). '47 I'll Be Yours (sc. basis). '48 Unfaithfully Yours (+prod; +sc). '49 The Beautiful Blonde From Bashful Bend (+prod; +sc). '51 Vendetta (add dir; +sc). '55 Les Carnets du Major Thompson (USA: The French, They Are a Funny Race; GB: The Diary of Major Thompson) (FR) (+sc). '56 The Birds and the Bees (sc. basis). '58 Paris Holiday (act only); Rock-a-bye Baby (sc. basis).

What Katharine Did

More than any other Hollywood heroine, Katharine Hepburn embodied dynamism, courage and idealism. Although compromised by many of her roles, she opened up visions of a fuller life to generations of women

After her bright entry into the firmament of Hollywood in the early Thirties, including an Oscar for Best Actress in *Morning Glory* (1933), Katharine Hepburn's career took a dramatic plunge. Commercial failures such as *Sylvia Scarlett, Mary of Scotland, A Woman Rebels* (all 1936) and *Quality Street* (1937), left her and RKO producer Pandro S. Berman despondent. Despite the overwhelming popularity of *Stage Door* (1937) and the critical acclaim the delightful comedy *Bringing Up Baby* (1938) received, Harry Brandt, President of the Independent Theatre Owners of America, pronounced her 'box-office poison'. Hepburn decided that her career needed a new direction, so she bought herself out of her contract at RKO.

The Forties, despite a 'flat' period in the middle of the decade, were to re-establish her position as a top-rank performer, defining the two major qualities which may be seen as informing both her films and her status as a star – her image as an 'independent' lady and her commitment to left-of-centre politics.

A mind of her own

Her independent image dates back to 1933 and her second film, *Christopher Strong*; the compromises which her roles in this and subsequent films demanded were often wholly subverted by her strong, vivacious personality. *Bringing Up Baby*, however, was the first of her films to show that her headstrong independence could be a major asset in comedy; she and Grant went on to make *Holiday* (1938) and *The Philadelphia Story* (1940), which confirmed her comic talent.

Her next film, *Woman of the Year* (1942), turned out to be crucial both for her career and her private life. It marked the beginning of her long relationship with the picture's co-star, Spencer Tracy, and was a forerunner of the pair's later and better known comedies on the question of the equality of the sexes, *Adam's Rib* (1949) and *Pat and Mike* (1952).

The meaning of love

These two films, together with *The African Queen* (1951) in which Hepburn starred with Humphrey Bogart, are her most interesting explorations of women's place in society. Not only do they directly confront the issue of the potentialities and role of women as the equals of men and the possibilities for heterosexual relationships under those circumstances, but they do so without unduly compromising their heroines' struggles for self-fulfilment with lame 'male-chauvinist' endings. In addition, *Pat and Mike* and *The African Queen* cast Hepburn as a woman who does not have any advantages of wealth, education or social position – elements which had coloured her earlier roles as an independent woman in films like *Christopher Strong* (1933), *Bringing Up Baby* and *The Philadelphia Story* with a fantastic quality. In *Pat and Mike* Hepburn plays a sportswoman whose confidence is completely destroyed by her fiancé. A small-time sports promoter (Tracy) treats her as an individual and builds up her belief in herself; eventually they fall in love. In *The African Queen*, a rough, alcoholic, Canadian steamer captain (Bogart) finds himself fleeing the Germans with a virgin spinster (Hepburn). Their growing love and respect are intelligently and movingly represented. The film avoids any suggestion that her sexual awakening is a 'gift' bestowed on her by Bogart, but represents each of the protagonists as giving and learning in equal measure.

Hepburn's nine films with Tracy seem to form a central and separate part of her career, to the point where her other work appears peripheral. After *Woman of the Year* they made *Keeper of the Flame* (1942), in which Hepburn played her first directly political role. As Christine Forrest, the widow of a national figure, she tries to protect her former husband's good name from the investigations of a journalist (Tracy) who correctly suspects him of having been a fascist. The film was aimed at alerting the USA to fascism at home, but sadly it is melodramatic and liberal in the worst sense. Frank Capra's *State of the Union* (1948) was another political film, in which Hepburn help

Above: Hepburn out walking during the making of The Lion in Winter. *Below: Spencer Tracy looks po-faced as Hepburn turns on the waterworks in* Adam's Rib

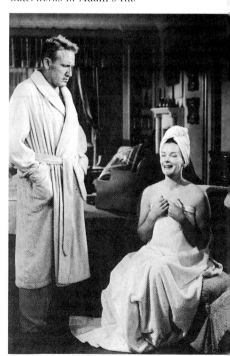

beliefs), many of her roles in the Thirties as an 'independent' heroine were of women from the same moneyed and privileged class. Later on, her roles in *Summer Madness* and *The Rainmaker* could only be seen as conforming to inveterate male attitudes towards female virginity. Her political films suffered not so much from a lack of genuine commitment as from the soft-centredness which liberalism, by definition, produces. On the other hand, given these observations, can she really be criticized for the faults which her films can now be seen to contain? In this regard it is apt to compare her with Jane Fonda, who has had all the advantages of access to contemporary political theory and practice. Today, Fonda's political naivety is both inexcusable and irrelevant, but Hepburn's ingenuousness was not in itself harmful to the positive image she offered – indeed it was part of it. To see Hepburn as she was in the Thirties and Forties is to glimpse not only someone ahead of her time but someone, as David Thomson says in his biographical dictionary, whose 'beauty grew out of her own belief in herself and from the viewer's sense that she was living dangerously, exposing her own nerves and vulnerability along with her intelligence and sensibility.'

That is her triumph, which outweighs all else.   SHEILA WHITAKER

---

her husband, a presidential candidate (Tracy), recognize that he is being manipulated by crooked politicians.

Rude awakenings

After *Pat and Mike*, Hepburn's career was largely a matter of fine performances in mediocre films. In *Summer Madness* (1955), she plays a repressed spinster who finds love with Rossano Brazzi in Venice; in *The Rainmaker* (1956) she plays Lizzie, another unhappy, small-town spinster who meets Starbuck (Burt Lancaster). In his biography of Hepburn, *Kate*, Charles Higham wrote that Starbuck's:

'. . . physical assurance and powerfully masculine charm break through her protective shell. Starbuck promises to bring rain to the parched soil of the southwestern state, and his promise is metaphorically fulfilled when he enriches Lizzie's sterile and sexless existence.'

Following the disastrous *The Iron Petticoat* (1956), (virtually a remake of Lubitsch's *Ninotchka*, 1939), and the likeable but unremarkable *Desk Set* (1957), which was another permutation on male-female relationships with Tracy, Hepburn was cast in an adaptation of Tennessee Williams' outrageous *Suddenly, Last Summer* (1959). She plays a wealthy widow who tries to hush up the circumstances of her homosexual son's murder by having a pre-frontal lobotomy performed on the only witness, her niece (Elizabeth Taylor). The film is remarkable only for its repressed sense of homosexuality and its representation of a demonic and destructive mother besotted with her dead son, although the film did seem to prompt the confrontation of taboo subjects in later films.

Having given a good performance as the drug-addicted mother in *Long Day's Journey Into Night* (1962), Hepburn made no films for five years in order to nurse an ailing Tracy. Then, in 1967 they made together *Guess Who's Coming to Dinner?*. This was an excruciating, albeit genuinely motivated, liberal 'message' film about the horrors of racial intolerance:

Above: a confrontation between the two redoubtable protagonists of The African Queen. *Hepburn and Humphrey Bogart. Right: George Cukor, who has directed Hepburn in many of her finest performances, the actress herself and Laurence Olivier during the filming of* Love Among the Ruins

Hepburn, however won her second Oscar.

Although she won her third Oscar for her performance in *The Lion in Winter* (1968), her major acting achievement in the Sixties was not on film but on the stage, in the 1960 musical *Coco*, based on the life of Coco Chanel.

In 1975 she played opposite Laurence Olivier in *Love Among the Ruins*, a delightful comedy of lovers meeting again after many years. Directed by George Cukor for American TV, it is a gentle reprise of the theme of male-female relationships explored by her earlier films, and particularly delightful for its portrayal of elderly people rediscovering the excitement of love. Hepburn's next film, *The Corn Is Green* (1978) was also made for TV and directed by Cukor. Sadly, its story of a schoolteacher who helps a young boy miner win a scholarship to Oxford was simplistic and poorly realized.

A free spirit

Apart from her three Oscars, Hepburn was nominated another eight times; she has rightly always been regarded as a vital force in American cinema, although surprisingly little has been written about her. Her extraordinary personality and unconventional private life (not least her wearing of men's clothes) combined with her passionate desire for privacy, particularly during her long affair with Tracy, gave her an aura of freedom. Many of her more successful films capitalized on this image, and for generations of women she offered a vision of life's potential, although with hindsight her career can be seen as entrenched in the ethos of the Hollywood dream factory. Born (in 1909) into a wealthy and privileged upper-middle-class family (although of sound socialist

Filmography
1932 A Bill of Divorcement. '33 Christopher Strong; Morning Glory; Little Women. '34 Spitfire; The Little Minister. '35 Break of Hearts; Alice Adams. '36 Sylvia Scarlett; Mary of Scotland; A Woman Rebels. '37 Quality Street; Stage Door. '38 Bringing Up Baby; Holiday (GB: Free to Live/Unconventional Linda). '40 The Philadelphia Story. '41 Women in Defense (narr. only) (short). '42 Woman of the Year; Keeper of the Flame. '43 Stage Door Canteen. '44 Dragon Seed. '45 Without Love. '46 The Sea of Grass; Undercurrent; The American Creed (guest) (short) (GB: American Brotherhood Week). '47 Song of Love. '48 State of the Union (GB: The World and His Wife). '49 Adam's Rib. '51 The African Queen. '52 Pat and Mike. '55 Summer Madness (USA: Summertime)(USA/GB). '56 The Rainmaker; The Iron Petticoat (GB). '57 Desk Set (GB: His Other Woman). '59 Suddenly, Last Summer. '62 Long Day's Journey Into Night. '67 Guess Who's Coming to Dinner? '68 The Lion in Winter (GB). '69 The Madwoman of Chaillot. '71 The Trojan Women. '73 The Glass Menagerie.* '74 A Delicate Balance.* '75 Rooster Cogburn; Love Among the Ruins.* '78 The Corn Is Green.*
* shot as TV film but shown in cinemas

On the Road

A producer's intuition and a fair slice of luck brought together the Forties' most famous comedy team, Bob Hope, Bing Crosby and Dorothy Lamour. Hope and Crosby's wisecracking charm and musical abilities plus Lamour's exotic glamour proved an unbeatable combination in a hugely popular series – the Road films

'After *The Cat and the Canary* (1939), Paramount told me to hit the road,' jokes Bob Hope in his book, *The Road to Hollywood*. The seven films in the Road series were strictly Forties-style fun pictures, even if the last two, *Road to Bali* (1952) and *The Road to Hong Kong* (1962), were made in later decades. To Road addicts, it is the first five that count: the rest are usually seen as sentimental journeys or slightly desperate cash-ins.

The story of the Road films began on the golf course – a popular area of sparetime activity for many of the show-biz fraternity. Bob Hope, comedian, and Bing Crosby, crooner, were good golfing buddies, and had been such since they met on a vaudeville bill at the Capitol on Broadway in 1932. Seven years later they met professionally again on the Paramount lot, both under contract to the studio – Hope for comedies and Crosby for musicals. The fateful day came when the boys made up a foursome on the links with the producer Harlan Thompson and the director Victor Schertzinger. They had so much fun that Schertzinger said to Thompson, 'What a team those boys would make in pictures'. Thompson agreed enthusiastically; once the non-golfing Dorothy (Dotty) Lamour, sarong girl from a string of South Sea Island epics, was added, a perfect team had been created.

Paramount handed the trio *Road to Singapore* (1940), an old script by Harry Hervey that had already been doctored twice – once for George Burns and Gracie Allen, and once for Jack Oakie and Fred MacMurray. Whether or not Hervey ever recognized the Hope-Crosby-Lamour version, the trio lifted a medium-budget picture into the $1.5 million profit class. This led the studio to call for sequel after sequel, until a classic comedy series

had been developed – the most successful of its kind in cinema history.

The affectionate rivalry between Hope and Crosby, which had already begun on their respective radio programmes, carried over into the films. They cracked gags about their contrasting ages, their waistlines, their hairlines and their vocal abilities; Hope joked about Crosby's outstanding ears, Crosby about Hope's 'ski-snoot' nose; Hope called Crosby 'Dad', and Crosby called Bob 'Junior'. Their screen rivalry expressed itself most fully for Lamour's sultry charms. Their radio personas also played an important part in the pictures, as Paramount's publicity proves – 'The Dean of the Kraft Music Hall meets the Top Man of the Pepsodent Show!' The wisecracking gag and insult formulas pioneered on the airwaves came fresh to the moviegoing millions, especially to the British, for whom the snappiest radio comedian was Tommy Handley.

Hope actually brought his radio writers to work on *Road to Singapore* without telling the director, Schertzinger. He and Crosby would stroll onto the set to start a scene and reel off a stream of freshly-minted gags, much to the director's surprise. Although first takes were invariably ruined by the technicians' laughter, Schertzinger was smart enough to realize that in *Road to Singapore* he was capturing on film all the spontaneity of a live performance.

'When Bing and Bob meet – those Torrid Tropics sure Get Hot!' quipped the ads, continuing 'They put the Sing in Singapore!'; the team certainly did, with five songs (two of which were by Schertzinger). Crosby's 'Too Romantic' made the hit parade; Hope had fun with 'Captain Custard', an off-beat ditty about a cinema commissionaire; and Lamour crooned 'Kaigoon'. However, the best song,

Left: in Road to Rio *Hope and Crosby play a couple of musicians who try to save the beautiful Lucia De Andrade (Lamour) from the hypnotic influence of her evil aunt. Above:* Road to Zanzibar *found the team on safari in darkest Africa and allowed them to make fun of every Hollywood jungle epic ever made*

'Sweet Potato Piper', featured all three in a jazzy novelty number that set audiences' toes tapping.

Two other ingredients of *Road to Singapore* that became perennial favourites were the 'Patty-cake, patty-cake, baker's man' routine with which the boys confused antagonists before socking their way out of tight corners, and the brief appearance of 'Professor' Jerry Colonna, a pop-eyed, walrus-whiskered refugee from Hope's radio show.

Road to Zanzibar (1941) was next season's follow-up, and funnier by far. It was originally named *Find Colonel Fawcett*, but the studio decided that the success of the first film was too good to miss and quickly changed the title. Hope plays Fearless Frazier the Living Bullet, while Crosby plays Chuck, his con man manager. Dorothy Lamour was cast as Donna Latour, saved from the slave trade after the boys 'patty-cake' the baddies. But not before more songs have been sung and Hope has wrestled a gorilla.

Road to Morocco (1942) was promoted as 'The Greatest Road Show of 'Em All!' – and for once the fans agreed with the publicity. Crosby ('He's a Pasha with the accent on the Pash') and Hope ('He's a Wolf in Sheik's Clothing') meet Lamour ('The Queen of Araby') in 'A Harem-Scarem Riot of Song and Laughter!'. Yet even this high-pressured oversell failed to describe adequately the wild and wacky goings-on once Crosby and Hope, 'like Webster's dictionary, were Morocco-bound'. As Mabel the Talking Camel aptly remarked courtesy of Paramount's 'Speaking of Animals' shorts): 'This is the screwiest picture I ever was in!'

There were more animals sharing the screen in *Road to Utopia* (1944), a period piece set during the Alaskan gold-rush. Hope cuddles up to a grizzly bear, believing it to be Lamour: 'Dear, you've been working too hard', he says, patting a paw. The boys, playing washed-up vaudevillians, sing 'Put It There, Pal', one of their best double-act ditties, while the urbane humourist Robert Benchley wanders in and out of the proceedings, trying to make sense of the story. One of Hope's best-remembered gags occurs in this film: 'Gimme a lemonade', he snarls at the barman, 'In a dirty glass!'

Road to Rio (1947), the fifth and last of the Forties Road films, saw a return to a strong plot-line and a consequent lessening of spontaneity. As Scat Sweeney and Hot-lips Barton the boys perform another splendid number, 'Apalachicola, Florida'. 'America's most Glee-some Threesome', as the publicity called them, played opposite two other trios, the Andrews Sisters, who sang 'You Don't Have to Know the Language', and the Three Weire Brothers, fiddle-playing zanies from the cabaret circuit. These acrobatic eccentrics, usually confined to straight filmings of their regular routine, were here worked into the plot with hilarious results.

The Fifties were well under way before Paramount broke the news that Hope, Crosby and Lamour were 'paving a New Love-happy Road for you – Rocked with Laughter, Bumpy with Songs, Curved with Girls and Splashed with Colour!'. As the ads proudly revealed, *Road to Bali* (1952) was the first Road film to be made in Technicolor. Hope and Crosby (whom Hope called 'a collapsible Como') were hoofing the boards once more, this time as Harold Gridley and Gene Cochran, singing 'Hoot-Mon' in Hollywood Scottish, Lamour played Princess Lalah MacTavish and the animal opposition took the form of a giant squid, evidently left over from Cecil B. DeMille's

Reap the Wild Wind (1942). For once, Hope nearly got the girl, even if she was not Lamour but Jane Russell in an unbilled guest spot. Humphrey Bogart also made a brief, uncredited appearance, looking for his boat, *The African Queen*.

In the late Fifties, at the height of the sci-fi boom, Paramount announced *The Road to the Moon*. It was never made, but some of the script was used in *The Road to Hong Kong* (1962). This final outing was filmed in England and featured an ageing trio trying desperately to recapture their youthful spirits. At first Lamour was not going to be cast, but in the end sentiment, and sense, prevailed – although her part was reduced to rather long-range walk-ons; the younger Joan Collins took over her third-line billing. Even the addition of a string of guest stars (Peter Sellers, doing his famous Indian doctor impression, plus Frank Sinatra, Dean Martin, David Niven, Zsa Zsa Gabor, Dave King and the ever-popular Jerry Colonna) failed to lure back the fans. Perhaps, feeling as old as the 'Roadsters' now looked, they preferred to stay home, watching re-runs of the other Road films on TV. For, in their prime, there was never such good company as Paramount's 'Road' company – Bing, Bob and Dotty.

DENIS GIFFORD

Above left: Road to Bali *was the only Road film made in colour. Above: Hope and Lamour in the Alaskan wilderness of* Road to Utopia. *Below left: the boys try to escape the cruel Mullay Kasim (Anthony Quinn) in* Road to Morocco. *Below: Joan Collins provided the love interest in* The Road to Hong Kong

Peak years at Paramount

After the financially disastrous Thirties, Paramount Pictures founded a new fortune on comedies, musicals, war films and melodramas in the Forties

In the mid-Thirties, after bankruptcy proceedings, the 'dream factory' of Paramount studios was becoming a nightmare for the stockholders. In 1935, as a result of the crisis, the investors agreed to shuffle executive responsibilities, reducing Adolph Zukor – the president and founding father of Paramount – to chairman of the board and chief West Coast executive officer. Barney Balaban, whose Balaban and Katz chain of 130 Paramount theatres had been the only branch of the empire to show a consistent profit during the Depression, seemed the right man to restore the company to solvency and was elevated to president. He surrounded himself with an experienced staff: Henry Ginsberg, who had worked for such disparate producers as Hal Roach and David O. Selznick, was in charge of West Coast operations; Leonard H. Goldenson supervised the running of the theatre chain; Russell Holman searched for literary and theatrical properties; and from February 1941 Y. Frank Freeman was studio boss (executive in charge of film production) – a post held in former years by Jesse Lasky, Zukor, Buddy De Sylva and Ernst Lubitsch. The Astoria Studio, which had been built in New York in 1919 for East Coast production and had been a fount of activity during the silent and early sound eras, was closed down and all films were thereafter to be produced in Hollywood.

The lot of laughs

The anxiety produced by World War II forced audiences to seek escapist entertainment and at Paramount comedy was emphasized. Preston Sturges, increasingly disgruntled as his screenplays were assigned to routine directors, offered the studio his script for *The Great McGinty* (1940) for a low fee if he were permitted to direct. Sensing a bargain, Paramount agreed and, following the success of this political satire, Sturges was afforded *carte blanche* on studio personnel for his subsequent comedies, which included *The Lady Eve* (1941) and *The Miracle of Morgan's Creek* (1943). Unfortunately, by the close of the decade, his Voltairean vision of society dimmed and his films away from Paramount revealed only a modicum of his original comedic lustre.

In 1940 Bing Crosby and Bob Hope, two of the studio's foremost light romantic comedy leads, were teamed with Dorothy Lamour in a comedy with music, *Road to Singapore*, which proved so popular that this zany trio were starred in four more Road films in the Forties. Crosby was also in *Going My Way* (1944), a comedy drama with songs, portraying a young priest at odds with the elderly pastor (Barry Fitzgerald) of a poor parish. Both stars won Oscars, two of seven awarded to the film.

The girl from Broadway

As well as comedy, musicals proved to be perfect escapist fare for the war-troubled world. In December 1939 Paramount released a period-musical, *The Great Victor Herbert*, loosely based on the last years of the Irish composer, which introduced Broadway star Mary Martin in a cast that also included the tenor Allan Jones with Walter Connolly in the title role. Miss Martin sang with a lovely soprano voice and also proved capable of handling dramatic material, but, although she co-starred in later films with Bing Crosby, Fred MacMurray, Dick Powell and Jack Benny, she never conquered the public as had, say, Dorothy Lamour. A few days after the release of *True to Life* (1943) – her last film for Paramount – she triumphed on Broadway in *One Touch of Venus*; she subsequently became the toast of the New York and London theatre and left Hollywood cameras far behind.

Betty Hutton, an ex-band vocalist, whose

Above left: Paramount's gateway to stardom and success. Above: Sam Goldwyn, Adolph Zukor and Jesse L. Lasky at the time of the merger that created Famous Players-Lasky (later Paramount) in 1916. Goldwyn was bought out soon afterwards and Lasky went in 1932, but Zukor retained his seat on the board until his death at the age of 103 in 1976. Below: musical stars Mary Martin and Allan Jones in The Great Victor Herbert. *Below right: the making of* Lady in the Dark, *with Ginger Rogers. Above right: Veronica Lake and Alan Ladd, the tough, blond duo who appeared together in several Paramount crime thrillers of the Forties*

xuberant Broadway performances in *Two for the Show* and *Panama Hattie* excited studio interest. began her film career as Lamour's room-mate in a musical remake of *The Fleet's In* (1942) with William Holden, Eddie Bracken and Jimmy Dorsey's orchestra. Hutton's dynamic comedy performance, as well as her rowdy rendition of 'Arthur Murray Taught Me Dancin' in a Hurry', made her one of Paramount's most valuable properties. She eventually walked out on the studio in the early Fifties when it turned down her request that her dance-director husband Charles O'Curran direct her next film.

Irving Berlin's musical hit *Louisiana Purchase* was brought to the screen by Paramount in 1941 with Victor Moore repeating his performance as a crusading senator framed by swindlers. Co-stars Vera Zorina and Irene Bordini were joined by Bob Hope (who replaced Broadway's William Gaxton), most of the score was retained, and Technicolor glorified Raoul Pene DuBois' costumes. In 1943 Zorina swirled across a studio landscape (choreographed by husband George Balanchine) to 'That Old Black Magic' in the *Star Spangled Rhythm*.

Moss Hart's play with music *Lady in the Dark* (1944) was directed by Mitchell Leisen in a splendid production which eliminated all but one of the songs, utilizing the score as background music. Ginger Rogers, visually too young as the psychotic fashion-magazine editor of the title, conveyed mental anguish with furrowed brows. *Lady in the Dark* was a smash and the mink-lined sequin gown created by Leisen for Ginger's 'Jenny' number (the one song retained) is a landmark in Hollywood couture.

These Wilder Years
Billy Wilder, like Sturges, was finally granted a director's chair for one of his screenplays. His comedy *The Major and the Minor* (1942) had Ginger Rogers masquerading as an adolescent in order to travel half-fare on a train and Ray Milland as the major sharing the compartment. The film's success enabled Wilder to make *Five Graves to Cairo* (1943) with Erich von Stroheim as the Nazi desert fox, Rommel. Wilder continued in a melodramatic vein

when he made *Double Indemnity* (1944), with Barbara Stanwyck and Fred MacMurray cast against type as the lovers conspiring to murder her husband. Wilder's next venture, *The Lost Weekend*, based on Charles Jackson's harrowing portrait of a dipsomaniac's three-day bout with the bottle and starring Ray Milland, swept the Academy Awards in 1945 with four triumphs. Two Teutonic views followed: *The Emperor Waltz* (1948), set at the court of turn-of-the-century Austria and brightened by Bing Crosby songs and Joan Fontaine; and *A Foreign Affair* (1948), set in post-war Berlin with Marlene Dietrich as a Nazi sympathizer operating on the black market.

Paramount enters the fray
World War II was not totally ignored by the studio. John Farrow (Mia's father) was nominated for an Oscar for his direction of *Wake Island* (1942), which paid homage to the heroic struggle of the Marine Corps to hold that South Pacific Island. *I Wanted Wings* (1941), an airforce drama, was one of many recruiting pictures released at that time. It also served as a springboard to stardom for Veronica Lake, a slender reed of a blonde with her tresses sexily draped over one eye. Her coiffure proved hazardous to the war effort as girls employed in munitions factories affected her style and found that their hair could become entangled with the machinery. Miss Lake graciously swept back her peek-a-boo bang for the duration of the war, bringing a sigh of relief from the government. Alan Ladd, who had been one of the reporters in *Citizen Kane* (1940), was cast as a paid gunman opposite Lake in *This Gun for Hire* (1942) and became a star overnight. His career, guided by his ex-actress wife Sue Carol, continued, mostly at Paramount but also at other studios, until his untimely death after completing work on *The Carpetbaggers* (1964).

Veronica Lake also starred in Mark Sandrich's *So Proudly We Hail* (1943), a tribute to women in the service, with other Paramount box-office stars Claudette Colbert and Paulette Goddard. In 1943 Gary Cooper played an American involved in the Spanish Civil War in Sam Wood's adaptation of Ernest Hemingway's novel *For Whom the Bell Tolls*,

with Ingrid Bergman as Maria and Katina Paxinou winning an Oscar for her screen debut as Pilar. Cooper was also the doctor who fights to evacuate wounded seamen from a cruiser in Cecil B. DeMille's *The Story of Dr Wassell* (1944).

Top of the mountain
Balaban's position at Paramount was cemented when the financial status of the company became known after the war. The net income for 1946 was $44 million, higher than that of every other Hollywood studio; 20th Century-Fox announced $22 million for the same fiscal period, establishing that studio as second in

Above: Betty Hutton and ace Paramount director Mitchell Leisen confer during the shooting of Dream Girl. *Top: Jean Arthur and Marlene Dietrich in the Berlin nightclub setting of Wilder's* A Foreign Affair. *Above right: poster for one of the finest Paramount melodramas of any decade*

the running. Six years earlier, in 1940, Paramount had netted $8 million, placing the ledgers in the black after the monetary decline of the Thirties.

Paramount's post-war roster of producers included the veteran DeMille, Charles Brackett and Hal Wallis, who joined Paramount as an independent producer after many years at Warner Brothers. The ranks of directors were headed by Sturges, Wilder, Farrow, Sandrich, Leisen, Fritz Lang, Lewis Milestone, William Dieterle, George Marshall and William Wyler. Composing the songs were Johnny Burke and Jimmy Van Heusen, Frank Loesser, Victor Young and Irving Berlin. Costume design was in the hands of Edith Head, who came to Paramount as assistant to the master of glamour, Travis Banton.

After the wartime success of *Holiday Inn* (1942), the story of a road-house celebrating each holiday with songs written by Irving Berlin and sung by Fred Astaire and Bing Crosby, the songsmith and the stars were all

signed for *Blue Skies* (1946). Berlin went to his song bag for a couple of golden oldies and submitted some new songs for this backstage saga of friendly rival song-and-dance men. Among the many numbers is a classic routine with Astaire tapping before a chorus of Fred Astaire clones to 'Puttin' on the Ritz'.

Despite studio objection, Mitchell Leisen chose Marlene Dietrich for the lead in *Golden Earrings* (1947) as a gypsy rescuing a British officer (Ray Milland) from the Nazis. Dietrich dispelled the executives' doubts that she would appear in the unglamorous role of a greasy peasant, stained brown from head to toe and sucking on fish heads. It was also Leisen who guided Olivia de Havilland to her first Oscar as an unmarried mother in *To Each His Own* (1946), and Betty Hutton in her first dramatic role in *Dream Girl* (1948).

Hal Wallis' first production, *You Came Along* (1945), served to introduce Lizabeth Scott, who next supported Barbara Stanwyck in *The Strange Love of Martha Ivers* (1946), a film which marked the debut of Kirk Douglas. Wallis also produced the film version of Lucille Fletcher's melodramatic radio monologue, *Sorry, Wrong Number* (1948), with Stanwyck and Burt Lancaster.

The last year of the decade found Bing Crosby in a musical remake of *A Connecticut Yankee in King Arthur's Court* and Bob Hope

and Lucille Ball in *Sorrowful Jones*. Olivia de Havilland won her second Oscar in Wyler's *The Heiress*, with Montgomery Clift as the fortune hunter who desperately knocks on her closed door. Hal Wallis signed a nightclub team, Dean Martin and Jerry Lewis, to support Marie Wilson in a film of the radio series *My Friend Irma*; the critics detested the film but were impressed by the freakish clowning of Lewis, and by Martin's crooning. DeMille wrought another biblical spectacle, *Samson and Delilah*, with Victor Mature and Hedy Lamarr.

The shooting of one of the scenes for *Samson and Delilah* served as background for the visit of Norma Desmond (Gloria Swanson) to DeMille in Wilder's *Sunset Boulevard* (1950). During the making of this film Zukor greeted Swanson while she was relaxing on the set and mentioned that he had heard she was working in television. When she teased him with, 'Mr Zukor, you have just said a naughty word!' he replied, 'Gloria, there is where the future of our industry lies.' Zukor, who had based his career – which began in 1903 as a penny arcade operator – on the maxim 'The public is never wrong', was making an astute prediction. Within the next ten years the Paramount studio was facing another financial crisis. Its future was in jeopardy because the movie-going public was sitting at home in front of the telly.

WILLIAM S. KENLY

204

All in the mind

Films featuring angels and devils, ghosts and other supernatural beings said as much about the state of mind of post-war cinema as movies that made conscious reference to psychology

During the Forties a considerable number of widely differing films, both American and European, seemed preoccupied with the themes of death, life after death, heaven and hell. What appears to unify this selection of films is the way in which they express doubts about the nature of reality. Most of them are horror movies, although some only by virtue of an isolated scene or sequence.

The attitudes articulated in these films are undoubtedly linked to the war but this common experience is not the whole story. The post-war cinema scene in the USA, Britain and France was not uniform and the war had interrupted the cross-fertilization of cinematic styles that had been developing in the Thirties. The reasons for the thematic links between the following films may go deeper, testifying to an unconscious response in the face of world conflict.

Accordingly, the major preoccupation of post-war cinema, as has been demonstrated in the *film noir* chapter, is the uncertainty of external reality. Two considerations which are fundamental to our perception of reality are time and death; significantly, both are 'denied' by cinema. For example, cinematic time is not linear as it is in life; the flashback device, so beloved of Forties cinema, enables us to know the results of a plot before it happens. The journalist hero of René Clair's *It Happened Tomorrow* (1944) knows the most important events in the action 24 hours before they occur. Time can also be cyclical: the heroes of the Jean Cocteau/Jean Delannoy film *L'Eternel Retour* (1943, *Love Eternal*) relive in the present day the ancient myth of Tristan and Isolde. These examples are taken from French cinema but similar distortions or repetitions of time-scales can be found in post-war Hollywood movies notably in the complex structure of the *film noir*.

Death in the movies also ceases to be the definitive end and insurmountable barrier it is in reality. It can be personified, as indeed it has been throughout popular mythology, and may even be rendered powerless. In *On Borrowed Time* (1939), for example. Death is depicted as having taken refuge in a tree from which it can only descend when invited. An old man (played by Frank O'Neill) refuses to die until he is ready. When he finally calls Death down, he is returning to the natural order.

Death can also be suspended or postponed in favour of a second chance of life, as in Alexander Hall's *Here Comes Mr Jordan* (1941). The story is the frequently imitated tale of a man who dies prematurely and is allowed to return to Earth only to find that his body has already been cremated.

In several movies of the period, Death is seen to co-exist with the living. Following the success of *Topper* (dir. Norman McLeod, 1937), in which Cary Grant and Constance Bennett are 'phantom lovers', the ghost character became very popular. In terms of their physical appearance and moral values, these spirits were quite human. They even help solve murder mysteries as in the sequels *Topper Takes a Trip* (1938) and *Topper Returns* (1941).

Occasionally, Death is portrayed as the incarnation of an ideal which does not exist in the world of the living. A French film and a Hollywood movie provide fine examples of this notion. In William Dieterle's *Portrait of Jennie* (1948), the phantom (Jennifer Jones) becomes the object of adoration and inspiration for a penniless artist (Joseph Cotten). In *Sylvie et le Fantôme* (dir. Claude Autant-Lara, 1945) the situation is reversed and a girl of sixteen falls in love with a castle ghost. Soon a horde of suitors arrive at the castle, impersonating the ghost to the dismay of the real phantom. Noel Coward's play *Blithe Spirit*, filmed by David Lean in 1945, argues that the state of being a ghost is the only one that permits a complete and durable love. The same idea brings about the happy ending to Joseph L. Mankiewicz's *The Ghost and Mrs Muir* (1947); here the lovers were Rex Harrison and Gene Tierney.

Significantly, none of these films is a tragedy. Each takes place in a fantasy world which is dream-like and wonderful and where the harsh reality of death is obliterated. Most are comedies and some are even farces that depend primarily on trick photography to reproduce the effects of 'invisibility' and chance appearances.

Ghosts are not the only supernatural creatures to populate the movies of the Forties. Angels are usually portrayed as beneficent figures with a matter-of-fact, 'down-to-earth' attitude of which the best example is Claude Rains' archangel whose job is to send souls to their destinations in *Here Comes Mr Jordan*.

Supernatural monsters, with odd exceptions like Robert Siodmak's *Son of Dracula* (1943), were no longer the frightening creatures they had been in the Thirties. In order to win back audiences, scriptwriters packed the horror movies of the Forties with a whole collection of monsters. After *Frankenstein Meets the Wolf Man* (1943) the two monsters seemed to have been frozen in eternity but they were thawed out the following year to provide

Top: the body of Tristan is borne away, followed by his faithful Isolde, in L'Eternel Retour; *Jean Marais and Madeleine Sologne star in this dreamlike, modern-dress version of the folk myth, scripted by Jean Cocteau. Above: the no-man's-land between dream and reality was the setting for another French adaptation from German mythology – this time of the Faust legend – in René Clair's* La Beauté du Diable. *Michel Simon played the Devil with characteristic humour and guile*

Top: Sylvie et le Fantôme *created fantasy through the love of a young girl for a kindly ghost. Top right: Hollywood's fantasies of life and death took the form of tricksy ghost films like* Topper Returns, *in which the stuffy old man (Roland Young) is haunted by a girl ghost (Joan Blondell) or* The Horn Blows at Midnight *(1945), which made a neat comic subject of the Day of Judgment. Above: the figure of Death watches over his 'clients' from a tree in* On Borrowed Time

Universal with a couple more hits in *House of Dracula* and *House of Frankenstein* (both 1944).

Unfortunately the humanization of the movie monsters rendered them so ordinary and unfrightening that they became objects of ridicule as in *Abbott and Costello Meet Frankenstein* (1948).

In the darkest days of the war, the most evil of all supernatural beasts, the Devil, made some significant appearances and underwent a revealing metamorphosis in a variety of European and Hollywood films. In Marcel Carné's *Les Visiteurs du Soir* (1942, *The Devil's Own Envoy*) the Devil was a character from France's medieval past, and in René Clair's *La Beauté du Diable* (1949, *Beauty and the Beast*), Satan is portrayed as a commonplace individual – grumbling, greedy, a figure of farce – in a superb performance by Michel Simon.

The Danish director Carl Dreyer made his own unique comment on diabolism in *Vredens Dag* (1943, *Day of Wrath*), a spellbinding melodrama that revolves around the curse placed on a village pastor by an old woman he has condemned for witchcraft. As the film progresses, the intolerance of men seems much more terrifying than either the Devil or his supposed servants.

Similar preoccupations with the Devil were evident in the notable Hollywood film *All That Money Can Buy* (1941, also known as *The Devil and Daniel Webster*). This variation on the Faust legend, in which a farmer (Walter Huston) sells his soul to the Devil but is rescued from hell by a cunning lawyer, proves that humans can sometimes trick the superhumans.

Most of the films featuring angels, monsters or the Devil can be related to uncertainties about man's moral values. Human nature may be present in each of these forms but the world which they inhabit is more ideal than 'realistic'. If ghosts are rendered innocuous and made to look ordinary, they cease to inspire fear; instead man becomes afraid of the spectres within his soul.

Man's internal reality is, therefore, the frequent subject of post-war horror and thriller films. The introduction of psychoanalysis, the high incidence of dream sequences and the popularity of the 'doppelganger' or 'double' theme all reflect the new interest in the subconscious.

Charles Vidor's thriller *Blind Alley* (1939) is the first film to make psychoanalysis a feature of the narrative. The plot deals with an escaped killer who takes refuge in the home of a psychiatrist. Under analysis the killer goes back into his past and reveals the two sides of his personality: the brutal bandit persona conceals an unhappy child.

Of all the films that use psychoanalysis either as a plot device or as a fashionable allusion, Alfred Hitchcock's *Spellbound* (1945) and Raoul Walsh's *Pursued* (1947) are the most crucial examples. *Spellbound* is set in a mental institution and shows how psychoanalysis can be used to reveal the

innocence of a suspected killer (Gregory Peck). Th psychological 'landscape' of the film was mem orable for Salvador Dali's surrealist designs. *Pur sued*, on the other hand, places its protagonis (Robert Mitchum) in a Western setting and traces through a violent tale of vengeance the exorcism of childhood trauma.

Fritz Lang's *Secret Beyond the Door* (1948) i another intriguing example of the way in whic Hollywood cinema assimilated contemporary psy chology into the format of movie melodrama. A impressionable young woman (Joan Bennett) mar ries a man (Michael Redgrave) who is suspected being a psychotic murderer: 'I married a stranger. man I did not know at all', says the Bennet character, but gradually discovers that she does nc know herself either. Lang's direction emphasize the insecurity of the relationship, breaking up th symmetry of the sets and filling the visual spac with shadows to suggest that all surfaces, actua and metaphorical, are deceptive. Eventually, th Redgrave character, who has been presente throughout as an ambiguous figure – both in nocent and guilty – undergoes instant psychoanaly sis and liberates himself from any suspicion c having killed his first wife.

Dreams can be used to unearth the truth; the reveal innocence under guilt and vice versa. In Fri Lang's *The Woman in the Window* (1944) we ar shown the monster that lurks beneath the ver moral exterior of the college professor played b Edward G. Robinson. Giving way, in a wea moment, to an erotic fantasy, he seduces a woma and commits a crime of passion, thus exposing th repressed personality. Dreams are used in th English horror film *Dead of Night* (1945) to under mine accepted notions of reality, and in *Dar Passage* (1947) the role of the subconscious revealed through subjective camerawork.

Another popular approach to the problem c shifting identities can be seen in the use of 'double *The Picture of Dorian Gray* (1945) is an elegant an

intelligent adaptation of the Oscar Wilde novel and a notable example of how the Freudian alter ego, can be demonstrated cinematically. The story revolves around a libertine who keeps a secret picture of himself in his attic that reveals his progressive depravity while he remains eternally young. When the true nature of Dorian Gray is disclosed the original portrait is shown in colour, even though this is a black-and-white film.

Victor Fleming's 1941 version of *Dr Jekyll and Mr Hyde* stars Spencer Tracy in the dual role and is remarkable for its Freudian dream sequences and for the transmutation of Dr Jekyll into Mr Hyde.

Compassion for monsters was not confined to Hollywood. In Jean Cocteau's *La Belle et la Bête*

(1945, *Beauty and the Beast*) the beast's monstrosity provides no obstacle to love; beneath the ugly exterior there is beauty for those who care to look.

Finally, the cycle of films produced by Val Lewton at RKO between 1942 and 1946 marks the point of intersection between interest in the supernatural and preoccupations with psychoanalysis. Both *Cat People* (1942) and *Curse of the Cat People* (1944) are premised on the notion that the central character, Irena, (Simone Simon) may be descended from a race of cat-women and that the violence she demonstrates towards people in *Cat People* and the influence she exerts over the little girl in *Curse of the Cat People* can be traced back to an obscure legend. At the same time, however, both films suggest that Irena is the victim of her own subconscious. Jacques Tourneur's *The Leopard Man* (1943) is based on the reverse of this idea: the crimes supposedly committed by a mysterious panther are in fact perpetrated by a man. In both this film and *Cat People* the uncertainty and ambivalence are implicit in Tourneur's direction. When the heroine of *Cat People* goes for a solitary swim in the town pool, the camera 'stalks' her, photographing the sinister reflections of the water and the empty, shadowy staircases, while the soundtrack is made to suggest menace through the use of strange, echoing noises.

In the last analysis, all the foregoing films, whether comedies or tragic horror movies, employ the devices unique to cinema to present changes and distortions of reality. In the case of the ghost films, trick photography is used to great effect; slow-motion photography creates a feeling of time slowing down in *La Belle et la Bête*; in one short sequence in *Dead of Night*, rapid intercutting of images from earlier sections of the film represents the nightmare of the central character; and the use of negative shots for the nightmares in *Blind Alley* is a remarkably courageous technique for a mainstream Hollywood film. There is, indeed, no more appropriate medium than cinema for representing alternative visions of reality. ALAIN GARSAULT

Above: original design by Salvador Dali for Hitchcock's Spellbound. *Above left: Carl Dreyer's* Day of Wrath *used a story of witchcraft to explore the torments of the human mind. Left: overtly Freudian imagery from Fritz Lang's thriller* Secret Beyond the Door

Raoul Walsh: action speaks loudest

Although Raoul Walsh is chiefly thought of as a director of action movies, his heroes and heroines are seldom straightforward figures with simple motives but people troubled and pursued by shadows of the past. And, though Walsh himself might be amused at the thought, his films were among the first to be quoted and studied when psychoanalysis found its way into film criticism

Raoul Walsh was born in New York in 1892, the son of a prosperous tailor and garment manufacturer. He ran away to sea and then later went on the stage, like his brother George (one of the many stars of the silent screen whose light was dimmed by the coming of sound). After drifting into the cinema, he became one of D. W. Griffith's many protégés. For Griffith, Walsh directed the battle scenes of *The Life of General Villa* (1914), with Pancho Villa playing himself (a 'camera louse' was Walsh's verdict on the Mexican liberator). Walsh then played John Wilkes Booth, Lincoln's assassin, in Griffith's *Birth of a Nation* (1915), on which he also worked as an assistant director. His work with Griffith attracted the attention of Winfield Sheehan, agent for the newly formed Fox Film Company which Walsh joined in 1915. He was now firmly set on his career in the cinema and was to direct over a hundred films, in virtually every genre, before ill-health forced him into unofficial retirement in the Sixties.

Before examining that career, it is worth

stepping back and looking at the man himself, not because the man is the key to the work but because – uniquely among Hollywood film-makers – his character has obscured the qualities of his work as a director. Like many of Hollywood's old-timers, Walsh is a wry raconteur, a teller of tales about the movie capital and its crazy inhabitants – but never a serious commentator on his own films. Indeed, in his vividly written autobiography, *Each Man in His Time*, the films are scarcely mentioned unless as settings for the most bizarre anecdotes. Certainly Walsh delighted in his image as a primitive man of action who lived and slept in cowboy boots. He has been known to pass a thread through his pierced nose – acquired when filming *Lost and Found on a South Sea*

Above: the slave-girl (Anna May Wong) poisons the princess (Julanne Johnson) in The Thief of Bagdad. *Top left: Walsh with Ida Lupino, Humphrey Bogart and the script of* High Sierra. *Top: Robert Mitchum in* Pursued

Island in Tahiti in 1923 – for the amusement of interviewers while bending their ears with tales of hard drinking with the likes of Errol Flynn and John Barrymore, or of how he lost his right eye when a jack-rabbit crashed through the windscreen of a jeep he was driving in 1929. He will offer succinct descriptions of fellow denizens of Hollywood, like Mae West – 'We spoke the same language' – with whom he made *Klondike Annie* (1936), before reciting passages of Shakespeare from memory

and then, in case anyone should get the wrong impression, repeating studio jokes about himself, such as Jack Warner's often-quoted remark, 'I'll tell you what constitutes a tender love scene for Raoul Walsh: a scene where he gets to burn down a whorehouse.' Faced with such a wild-man-on-the-loose image, it is not surprising that writers on his work have written Walsh's personality into the making of the films and overstressed his genuine commitment to action rather than reflection.

Accordingly J.P. Coursodon's wrote of him in *Trente Ans de Cinéma Américain*:
'Clearly he is only happy when he is working. Walsh would accept any kind of an assignment just to get on the set. He will efficiently direct rather dull scenarios, even though he is more inspired by other subjects. But he needs to be directing, calling "Action!"'
And Andrew Sarris, writing in *The American Cinema*, has observed:
'If the heroes of Ford are sustained by tradition and the heroes of Hawks by professionalism, the heroes of Walsh are sustained by nothing more than a feeling for adventure.'
In Coursodon's view, Walsh himself becomes the adventurer; in Sarris' view, the films are subsumed into the concept of adventure, an elastic concept if ever there was one. Yet, quite clearly, both remarks hold some truth, for Walsh had a biding affinity for action pictures. By his own testament, he forsook 'Art for Main Street' after making *Evangeline* (1919). Adapted from Longfellow's poem, this film is Walsh's one prestigious 'art' movie but, although rapturously received by the critics, it was a box-office failure. However, to seek the sum total of Walsh's identity within the context of the robust, lusty humour that floods through much of his work is to mistake the man for his films. Moreover, some explanation is required to account for the trajectory of his work and its uneven quality. For if *Objective, Burma!* (1945) is a marvellous example of pictorial storytelling, *Every Night at Eight* (1935) – a musical romance with Alice Faye – is just plain awful.

Ironically enough, the most persuasive pointer to Walsh's films is not any theme that runs through them but the circumstances in which they were made, the development of Hollywood and the studio system. In the silent era, working at Fox, Walsh scripted and acted in his films, but after the arrival of sound, facing a very different Hollywood from the loosely organized studio system with which he was familiar, he had little control over the films he turned out. He neither produced nor scripted his films. Indeed it was only when he joined Warners in 1939 – where he was to stay until 1951 – that he again worked closely with a fairly regular group of actors (Flynn, Bogart, Alan Hale) and cameramen (James Wong Howe, Sid Hickox) as he had done in the silent era. And even then he was working for a studio that had a clear identity and was firmly committed to the 'man-in-the-street' philosophy of the New Deal.

This nonetheless resulted in an ambience in which Walsh could work successfully, most notably in the Warners' staple crime melodramas with a degree of social comment. And it is only necessary to compare the studio's predominantly socially conscious *I Am a Fugitive From a Chain Gang* (dir. Mervyn LeRoy, 1932) with *The Roaring Twenties* (1939),

Above: poster for Walsh's 1942 biopic of the world heavyweight boxing champion, James J. Corbett

Walsh's first film for Warners, to see how Walsh was attempting to concentrate on dynamic action. In *The Roaring Twenties* he brusquely pushed aside the social explanation for Eddie Bartlett (James Cagney) taking to a life of crime. He concentrates on depicting him as a demented bundle of energy on the loose, aspiring to the heights and unconcerned how he gets to there – a type Cagney would later amplify for Walsh when he played Cody Jarrett in *White Heat* (1949). But if the atmosphere at Warners was conducive to the type of films Walsh wanted to make – and generally his best films were made during his stay at that studio – he was still unable to develop personal projects as he had done in the Twenties. This may be partly explained by the fact that, in addition to having a very heavy regular work load, Walsh

was also Warner's 'tank man' (on call for any aquatic scenes that had to be shot) and general 'film doctor'. Only at the end of his career did he secure a degree of control over personal projects, most notably *Marines, Let's Go!* (1961) which, like his earlier and equally unfashionable *A Private's Affair* (1959), can be regarded as a bitter parody of even earlier war films made by Walsh, such as *What Price Glory?* (1926).

If Walsh was restricted from realizing his full potential in the Thirties, Forties and Fifties, there is no doubt that he had shown what he was capable of before the coming of sound. It is sad that for comment on Walsh's silent pictures we have, in the main, to rely on contemporary reviews. The few films that remain, however, clearly demonstrate that Walsh was a major director of the silent period. Four silent films in particular are central to any understanding of Walsh. *The Thief of Bagdad* (1924) is generally remembered for Douglas Fairbanks' performance as the thief and for Walsh's spectacular orchestration of the special effects, but equally important is the director's characterization of the princess' sexually tormented slave (Anna May Wong). *The Wanderer* (1926), a biblical epic based on the story of the Prodigal Son, with its superb tinted sequences, reveals Walsh's flair for the exotic. *What Price Glory?* saw Walsh transforming Maxwell Anderson's pacifist play into knockabout farce in which Victor McLaglen and Edmund Lowe made their first of several appearances as Flagg and Quirt, two sergeants entwined around the scheming fingers of Charmaine (Dolores Del Rio). With its profanity – if you can lip-read – and explicit sexuality, *What Price Glory?* won Walsh the description 'virile director' in *Photoplay*. But the equally explicit *Sadie Thompson* (1928), starring Gloria Swanson in the title role, is far more impressive, centring as it does on the notion of repression which in later Walsh films was to become a regular theme – in *White Heat*, for example, Cody Jarrett's idea of 'fun and games' is to carry his wife (Virginia Mayo) around on his shoulders. *Sadie Thompson* was also Walsh's last film as an actor: he played Tim O'Hara, the Marine sergeant who falls for Sadie.

Turning from Walsh's silent films to his sound films, the unevenness of his career is best explained by the fact that he worked on such a wide range of films. Despite their patchiness, however, Walsh's seemingly disparate films clearly hang together: for example, *The Man I Love* (1946) and *The Revolt of Mamie Stover* (1956), both of which feature women in the central roles. *The Man I Love*, one of Walsh's greatest films, stars Ida Lupino as Petey Brown, a professional songstress who sorts out the domestic problems of her married sister and rescues her from the murderous clutches of a mobster nightclub owner. *The Revolt of Mamie Stover* stars Jane Russell as a dance-hall girl who makes good in Honolulu when the Americans arrive soon after Pearl Harbor, and tries to buy the respectability denied her in the past because of her origins. The heroines of both films are active women, women who are more independent than Howard Hawks' heroines and undomesticated, unlike the mothers and brides-to-be in Ford's films. Petey Brown and Mamie Stover – and the heroines of *The Yellow Ticket* (1931), *They Drive By Night* (1940), *The Tall Men* (1955), *The King and Four Queens* (1956) and *Band of Angels* (1957) – use

their charms to further their own ends: not to trap men into domesticity but to attain their own identities. Surprisingly for so 'masculine' a director, Walsh consistently portrays women as active forces rather than merely as sex objects to be schemed after.

Petey in *The Man I Love* is ambitious and self-contained; Mamie in *The Revolt of Mamie Stover* is close to being obsessed with her self-given task. Walsh's heroes, too, tend to become obsessive once they set out on their journeys of self-discovery. *They Died With Their Boots On* (1942) stars Errol Flynn, in the first of seven films he was to make with Walsh, as George Armstrong Custer, a man caught between a hopelessly romanticized notion of heroism, the practical problems of domesticity and the difficulties of serving the War Department. His death at the hands of the Sioux is the perfect solution to all his problems: he achieves heroism, avoids domesticity and directs the War Department's attention to gun-trading with the Indians. Cody Jarrett in *White Heat* is literally mad by the end of the film when he dies amidst a conflagration of his own making, standing on top of a burning oil refinery and defiantly shouting, 'Made it Ma, top of the world!' *Pursued* (1947), with Jeb Rand (Robert Mitchum) desperately trying to find out why he is being pursued so insistently, is more than

simply the first psychological Western. The dynamic of the film underlines the Walsh hero's need to know his own identity and his past history before he can act meaningfully. Thus for the most part of *Pursued*, Jeb can only react; it is only at the end of the film when he relives the death of his father – which has haunted his memory – and achieves self-discovery that he can act for himself.

If *Pursued* shows the need for restraint in the Walsh hero, *Blackbeard the Pirate* (1952) is perhaps Walsh's most delirious film. Starring Robert Newton, one of Hollywood's most excessive actors, in the title role, the film presents Blackbeard as demonic in his energetic search for hidden gold as he gleefully savours every insult and lashing he can give – and yet bizarrely impotent in his endless circling around himself. Like Cody Jarrett, Blackbeard lives only in the present, a present that lies heavy in the shadows of the past. In *The Tall Men*, Ben Allison (Clark Gable) is similarly weighed down by the past. He is a Confederate soldier, turned thief after the Civil War, who lives for the future, but it is a future that echoes his past – he wants to return to his birthplace. The movement of the film, as it follows a cattle drive from Texas to Montana, is away from the conflicts of the past and towards a future shared with his girl (Jane Russell).

Above left: Robert Newton in a typical part as the villainous, eye-rolling Blackbeard the Pirate, with Linda Darnell. Above: the melodrama Manpower *(1940) starred Edward G. Robinson and George Raft as power-line men and Marlene Dietrich as the night-club hostess who comes between them*

The tension that runs through the best of Walsh's films is created by the director's celebration of the individualism of his heroes and a fatalistic sense that they have little control over their lives. If in his later films Walsh transformed that tension into an equilibrium by scaling down his heroes until they could achieve and control their desires, it is the earlier – mostly Warners – films that remain the most satisfactory with their demented heroes and forceful heroines who can only reach an understanding, if at all, of the whys and wherefores of their proudly and swiftly trodden paths through life at death's door. *Pursued*, *White Heat* and another film – *Colorado Territory* (1949), a remake of *High Sierra* (1941), with Joel McCrea as an outlaw on the run – are first-class examples of the flexibility of that basic scenario and lasting testaments to the erratic genius of Raoul Walsh.

PHIL HARDY

Filmography
1914 The Life of General Villa (some scenes only); For His Master (actor only); The Death Dice; The Great Leap (actor only); The Dishonored Medal (actor only); The Double Knot (+act); Lest We Forget (actor only); The Mystery of the Hindu Image (+act); The Gunman; Sierra Jim's Reformation (+act); The Final Verdict (+act); Sands of Fate (actor only); The Availing Prayer (actor only). **'15** Birth of a Nation (act; +ass. dir); The Fatal Black Bean; His Return (+act); The Greaser (+act); The Fencing Master; A Man for All That (+act); The Smuggler (actor only); The Celestial Code; Eleven-Thirty; The Buried Hand; A Bad Man and Others; The Regeneration (+prod; +co-sc); Carmen (+prod; +sc). **'16** The Serpent (+prod; +co-sc); Blue Blood and Red (+prod; +sc); Intolerance (ass. dir. only); Pillars of Society. **'17** Betrayed (+prod; +sc); The Conqueror; The Honor System; The Silent Lie; This Is the Life (+co-sc); The Innocent Sinner (+sc); The Pride of New York (+sc). **'18** The Woman and the Law (+sc); The Prussian Cur (+sc); On the Jump (+sc); Every Mother's Son (+sc); I'll Say So. **'19** Evangeline (+prod; +sc); Should a Husband Forgive? (+sc). **'20** The Strongest (+sc); The Deep Purple; From Now On (+sc). **'21** The Oath (+prod; +sc); Serenade. **'22** Kindred of the Dust. **'23** Lost and Found on a South Sea Island (GB: Lost and Found). **'24** The Thief of Bagdad. **'25** East of Suez (+prod); The Spaniard (GB: Spanish Lore). **'26** The Wanderer (+prod); The Lucky Lady (+prod); The Lady of the Harem; What Price Glory? **'27** The Monkey Talks (+prod); Loves of Carmen. **'28** Sadie Thompson (+sc; +act); The Red Dance (+prod) (GB: The Red Dancer of Moscow); Me, Gangster (+sc); In Old Arizona (co-dir). **'29** The Cock-Eyed World (+sc) (both sound and silent versions); Hot for Paris (+co-sc). **'30** The Big Trail (sup. only on German version: Die Grosse Fahrt, 1931). **'31** The Man Who Came Back; Women of All Nations; The Yellow Ticket (+prod) (GB: The Yellow Passport). **'32** Wild Girl (GB: Salomy Jane); Me and My Gal (GB: Pier 13). **'33** Hello Sister (add. dir. uncredited); Sailor's Luck; The Bowery; Going Hollywood. **'35** Under Pressure; Baby-Face Harrington; Every Night at Eight. **'36** Klondike Annie; Big Brown Eyes (+co-sc); Spendthrift (+co-sc). **'37** OHMS (GB) (USA: You're in the Army Now); Jump for Glory (GB) (USA: When Thief Meets Thief); Artists and Models; Hitting a New High. **'38** College Swing (GB: Swing, Teacher, Swing). **'39** St Louis Blues; The Roaring Twenties. **'40** Dark Command; They Drive By Night (GB: Road to Frisco); Manpower. **'41** High Sierra; The Strawberry Blonde. **'42** They Died With Their Boots On; Desperate Journey; Gentleman Jim. **'43** Background to Danger; Northern Pursuit. **'44** Uncertain Glory. **'45** Objective, Burma!; Salty O'Rourke; The Horn Blows at Midnight; San Antonio (add. dir. uncredited). **'46** The Man I Love. **'47** Pursued; Stallion Road (add. dir. uncredited); Cheyenne (retitling for TV: The Wyoming Kid). **'48** Silver River; Fighter Squadron; One Sunday Afternoon. **'49** Colorado Territory; It's a Great Feeling (guest appearance as himself only); White Heat; Montana (add. dir. uncredited). **'51** Along the Great Divide; Captain Horatio Hornblower; Distant Drums; The Enforcer (Murder Inc.) (some scenes only, uncredited). **'52** Glory Alley; The World in His Arms; The Lawless Breed; Blackbeard the Pirate. **'53** Sea Devils (GB); A Lion Is in the Streets; Gun Fury. **'54** Saskatchewan (GB: O'Rourke of the Royal Mounted). **'55** Battle Cry; The Tall Men; Helen of Troy (2nd unit dir. only). **'56** The Revolt of Mamie Stover; The King and Four Queens. **'57** Band of Angels. **'58** The Naked and the Dead; The Sheriff of Fractured Jaw (GB). **'59** A Private's Affair. **'60** Esther and the King (+prod; +co-sc). **'61** Marines, Let's Go!; Come September (co-prod, uncredited). **'64** A Distant Trumpet.

Walsh worked on the scripts of many of the 1914–15 films he made and acted in other early silents but there are no reliable listings.

Top left: The FBO studios at 780 Gower St in Hollywood in 1926. Above: the same building three years later when the studio had been taken over and renamed RKO. Below: Dore Schary, production chief during 1947–48. Bottom: Merian C. Cooper, production chief at RKO during 1933–36, pictured here 'pipe dreaming' his great hit King Kong

the big ones keep coming from RKO RADIO PICTURES

By a curious accident of history, RKO Radio Pictures had British origins. A company named Robertson-Cole, which sold automobiles in the USA, opened a small film studio in Hollywood in 1920. Among the silent stars contracted to Robertson-Cole in the early years were Sessue Hayakawa, Mae Marsh and ZaSu Pitts, but the studio's top star was Pauline Frederick.

In 1922 Robertson-Cole was reorganized and the studio's corporate name changed to Film Booking Office of America. As FBO, the company had a modest record in production and was distinguished by having the financier and politician Joseph P. Kennedy as president from 1926 to 1929. Moves to purchase FBO began in 1928 and in early 1929, the Radio Corporation of America (RCA) acquired a majority; by the end of the same year the new management had merged with the Keith-

Albee-Orpheum cinema chain to become Radio-Keith-Orpheum or RKO. The first all-talking picture released under the name RKO was *Street Girl* (1929), shot on the original Robertson-Cole lot in Hollywood.

The early product may not have suggested it, but RKO was a major studio right from the start. The premises may have been small and intimate by comparison with, say, MGM's Culver City, but RKO ranked alongside MGM, Warners, Paramount, Universal and Fox in the Thirties and Forties. A first-rate list of contract stars was developed in the early years and included Betty Compson, Bebe Daniels, Dolores Del Rio, Richard Dix, Irene Dunne, Constance Bennett, Ann Harding and Joel McCrea.

Throughout 1930 musicals and gangster films predominated: *Hit the Deck* (with songs by Leo Robin) and *Dixiana* starring Bebe Daniels, signalled the growing success of the studio.

Above: Betty Compson and John Harron in Street Girl, *RKO's first all-talking film. Above right: Victor McLaglen and Margot Grahame in John Ford's* The Informer. *Right: Katharine Hepburn won an Oscar for her role as an aspiring actress in* Morning Glory (1933)

Mary Astor appeared as a gangsters' moll in *The Runaway Bride* and Richard Dix played a hood in *Shooting Straight*. Lowell Sherman went one better and directed himself as a gang leader in *The Pay-Off*

Westerns and weepies
Status was assured when in 1931 RKO won their first Best Picture Oscar for *Cimarron*, an epic Western with a budget to match ($1.7 million), but the studio's staple product was the women's weepies that saw Ann Harding, Irene Dunne and, most often of all, Constance Bennett slogging their way through domestic tragedy and suffering at every turn in films like *Devotion*, *Born to Love*, and *The Common Law* (all 1931).

For one valuable year, 1931–32, RKO enjoyed the services of David O. Selznick as head of production. Given a brief to improve the quality of the studio's films, Selznick hired George Cukor, whose *What Price Hollywood?* (1932) starring Constance Bennett and Lowell Sherman was an early and highly successful version of *A Star Is Born*. The same year Cukor made *A Bill of Divorcement* and introduced Katharine Hepburn as a new star.

RKO was well into its stride, and the following year's ape epic, *King Kong* (1933), was not only a great money-spinner but a triumph of technique on the part of the studio's designers artists and special-effects men. For the time being, however, musicals were the most consistent guarantee of success. After *Flying Down to Rio* (1933), in which Fred Astaire and Ginger Rogers played supporting roles, a whole series of song-and-dance vehicles was designed for them: *The Gay Divorcee* (1934), *Roberta*, *Top Hat* (both 1935), *Follow the Fleet*, *Swing Time* (both 1936), *Shall We Dance?* (1937), *Carefree* (1938) and *The Story of Vernon and Irene Castle* (1939). Astaire and Rogers dominated the decade and put RKO Radio Pictures on the map artistically and financially.

First into colour
Merian C. Cooper replaced Selznick as head of production in 1933. Under Cooper's guidance they became the first studio to make and release a feature film – *Becky Sharp* (1935) – in the new three-colour Technicolor process. The

film that carried off 1935's top awards, however, was *The Informer*. One of John Ford's Irish tales, the film had a highly literate script by Dudley Nichols.

The following year, Katharine Hepburn gave an impressive performance as another independent-minded woman in *Sylvia Scarlett*, in which her co-star was Cary Grant. Once again Cukor was Hepburn's director and he counted the film as his favourite. Unfortunately, it flopped at the box-office, possibly – Cukor mused in an interview – because of the 'unusual relationships' and 'because Kate was masquerading as a boy most of the time.'

The next incumbent in RKO's head of production office was Pandro S. Berman, who produced Ford's *Mary of Scotland* and encouraged him to tackle another Irish subject *The Plough and the Stars* (both 1936). Fred and Ginger danced on, and Gregory La Cava made *Stage Door* (1937), co-starring Katharine Hepburn and Ginger Rogers as young hopefuls in a theatrical boarding-house. Berman also produced *Winterset* (1936), a version of Maxwell Anderson's Pulitzer Prize play about a man who is executed for a crime he has not committed.

In addition to an impressive list of productions, RKO also earned money and prestige

from the films they released, through their distribution arm, for independent producers like Samuel Goldwyn and Walt Disney. Furthermore, David O. Selznick retained his affection for the old studio, lending RKO some of his own players and directors such as Joan Fontaine and Alfred Hitchcock for *Suspicion* (1941), and Dorothy McGuire, who appeared in *The Spiral Staircase* (1945).

Hollywood's *annus mirabilis* of 1939 was a fairly routine year for RKO, though two historical pieces – George Stevens' *Gunga Din* and William Dieterle's *The Hunchback of Notre Dame* – were impressive.

House directors maintained their consistently high standards: Gregory La Cava's comedy *The Primrose Path* (1940) saw Ginger Rogers in a non-musical role; John Cromwell made a biopic *Abe Lincoln in Illinois* (1940), and Dorothy Arzner, a lone woman director in a male-dominated industry, reworked the familiar backstage story of feuding actresses into *Dance, Girl, Dance* (1940), a musical that threw the spotlight on women for a change. In 1940 Orson Welles, together with his Mercury Productions company, was hired by the studio's new president George Schaefer and proceeded to make two outstanding films, *Citizen Kane* (1940) and *The Magnificent Ambersons* (1942)

Despite their critical reception, neither of these films made money for RKO and the board used every legitimate force to get Welles out of the studio. When he finally quit, Welles left a lavish South American film half-finished, to gather dust in the RKO vaults.

Koerner's shop
In 1941 Charles Koerner was appointed general manager of the studio. He was an experienced showman, and on arrival at RKO he instituted an audience-research programme. As a result of his findings, Koerner began to develop a new production plan that included low-budget, exploitation films. Main features continued to attract critical acclaim but at the box-office it was *Cat People* and *Hitler's Children* (both 1942) that scored the most remarkable

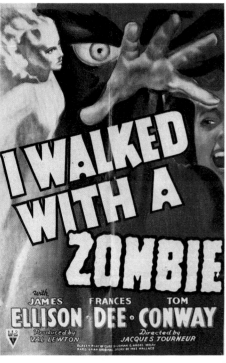

and unexpected successes.

Koerner also brought Liberty Productions – an outfit comprising Frank Capra and George Stevens – under the aegis of RKO and assigned Val Lewton the task of overseeing the B-feature unit. This move provided consistent revenue and, retrospectively, a measure of critical acclaim for the studio.

Among RKO's top contract players of the Forties were George Sanders and Tom Conway (brothers in real life) and the dependable Kent Smith. Conway took over the part of the Falcon from brother George in *The Falcon Strikes Back* (1943), a fine example of an above-average thriller series.

By the mid-Forties, the *film noir* had well and truly arrived. Edward Dmytryk's *Murder, My Sweet* (1944) was one of the first of many *noir* thrillers from RKO. The style was also evident in the horror films produced by Lewton: *I Walked With a Zombie, The Seventh Victim* (both 1943), *The Curse of the Cat People* (1944) and *The Body Snatcher* (1945).

Finest hour
Mainstream movie-making continued to work magic at the box-office. *The Bells of St Mary's* (1945), starring Bing Crosby and Ingrid Bergman, earned more money than any other RKO film to that date. John Wayne refought the Japanese to great public acclaim in *Back to Bataan* (1945). Early in 1946 Koerner died suddenly of leukemia and Dore Schary was brought in to head the studio's production department. From this point, until Howard Hughes bought out the studio in 1948, RKO enjoyed a remarkably fertile period: Siodmak's *The Spiral Staircase*, Capra's *It's a Wonderful Life*, Brahm's *The Locket* (both 1946), Dmytryk's *Crossfire* and Tourneur's *Out of the Past* (both

Left: for all its lurid advertising, I Walked With a Zombie *was high-class horror. Below: Boris Karloff and Victor McLaglen in Ford's* The Lost Patrol *(1934). Right: Laraine Day as the femme fatale and Robert Mitchum in* The Locket, *a typical RKO film noir*

1947) all rolled off the production line before Schary, too, was dismissed in 1948.

The roster of talented directors working in major and B-feature production is impressive: Jacques Tourneur, Nicholas Ray, Anthony Mann, Don Siegel, Robert Wise and Edward Dmytryk; and among their star players, RKO could number Robert Mitchum, Robert Ryan, Cary Grant, Fred Astaire, Henry Fonda, Joan Fontaine, Maureen O'Hara, Loretta Young and Rosalind Russell.

Unfortunately, by 1950 the studio's product became less consistent, despite occasional gems like Robert Wise's *The Set-Up* (1949), Christian Nyby and Howard Hawks' *The Thing* (1951), Fritz Lang's *Rancho Notorious* and Richard Fleischer's *The Narrow Margin* (both 1952).

The decline set in when Howard Hughes began to supervise the new product and indiscriminately reissue the old. Gradually, most people under contract found that their contracts were not being renewed. Those who were kept on had little to do or were given minor assignments. Hughes himself spent money wildly on a couple of John Wayne films – *Jet Pilot* (1951) and *The Conqueror* (1956) – that were among the worst the star ever made. Eventually Hughes wearied of the studio as if it were a toy for which he no longer cared. He sold it, lock, stock and barrel, in 1957.

There is some ironic justice in the fact that Lucille Ball, who had been one of RKO's brightest stars, wound up as the co-owner of the premises in 1957 when the studio was sold to Desilu (the TV company run by Lucy and her husband Desi Arnaz), although the work that occupied the great stages was no longer the noble art of film-making.

DeWITT BODEEN

INDEX

217